Accounting, Finance, Sustainability, Governance & Fraud: Theory and Application

Series editor

Kiymet Tunca Caliyurt, Iktisadi ve Idari Bilimler Fakültesi, Trakya University Balkan Yerleşkesi, Edirne, Turkey

This series acts as a forum for book publications on current research arising from debates about key topics that have emerged from global economic crises during the past several years. The importance of governance and the will to deal with corruption, fraud, and bad practice, are themes featured in volumes published in the series. These topics are not only of concern to businesses and their investors, but also to governments and supranational organizations, such as the United Nations and the European Union. *Accounting, Finance, Sustainability, Governance & Fraud: Theory and Application* takes on a distinctive perspective to explore crucial issues that currently have little or no coverage. Thus the series integrates both theoretical developments and practical experiences to feature themes that are topical, or are deemed to become topical within a short time. The series welcomes interdisciplinary research covering the topics of accounting, auditing, governance, and fraud.

More information about this series at http://www.springer.com/series/13615

Kıymet Tunca Çalıyurt · Roshima Said
Editors

Sustainability and Social Responsibility of Accountability Reporting Systems

A Global Approach

IGonGFESR
INTERNATIONAL GROUP ON GOVERNANCE FRAUD
ETHICS AND SOCIAL RESPONSIBILITY

Springer

Editors
Kıymet Tunca Çalıyurt
Trakya University
Edirne
Turkey

Roshima Said
Universiti Teknologi MARA
Kedah
Malaysia

ISSN 2509-7873 ISSN 2509-7881 (electronic)
Accounting, Finance, Sustainability, Governance & Fraud: Theory and Application
ISBN 978-981-10-3210-3 ISBN 978-981-10-3212-7 (eBook)
https://doi.org/10.1007/978-981-10-3212-7

Library of Congress Control Number: 2017962047

Printed on acid-free paper

This Springer imprint is published by Springer Nature
The registered company is Springer Nature Singapore Pte Ltd.
The registered company address is: 152 Beach Road, #21-01/04 Gateway East, Singapore 189721, Singapore

Acknowledgements

First, as editors of this book, we would like to thank each one of the authors for their contributions. Our sincere gratitude goes to the chapter's authors who contributed their time and expertise to this book.

We would like to express our sincere gratitude to our member of International Group on Governance Fraud Ethics and CSR. This group performed eight successful conferences in Turkey, Malaysia, and Canada.

Of course, we have big thanks to our Book Series Editor William Achauer Business/Economics Editor in Springer/Singapore and his group from editing to publishing.

We would also like to express the profound gratitude to our beloved husbands, *Rashdan and Okan*, and our kids, *Syahida, Syahmi, Syahira, Syaqilla and Batu*, for their endless love, prayers, and continuous support.

We would also like to express our sincere thanks to all our friends for their kindness and moral support.

As a result, we would like to share our motto with readers for more a sustainable world:

> Sustainability should be a lifestyle for human being in business and private life which begins with consumption decreasing

Kıymet Tunca Çalıyurt
Roshima Said

Contents

Editors and Contributors

About the Editors

Prof. Dr. Kıymet Tunca Çalıyurt, CPA, CFE graduated from the Faculty of Business Administration at Marmara University, Istanbul, Turkey. Her master's and Ph.D. degrees are in Accounting and Finance Program from the Social Graduate School, Marmara University. She has worked as auditor in Horwath Auditing Company, manager in McDonalds, and finance staff in Singapore Airlines. After vast experience in private sector, she has started to work in academia. She is holding CFE and CPE titles. Her research interests are in accounting, auditing, fraud, social responsibility, corporate governance, finance and business ethics, with a special interest in aviation management, women rights in business. She is the Founder of the International Group on Governance, Fraud, Ethics and Social Responsibility (IGonGFE&SR) and the President of the National-International-Students' Conference Series on Governance, Fraud, Ethics and Social Responsibility (IConGFE&SR). In 2009, she also founded the International Women and Business Group, which organizes a global, annual conference. she has published papers, chapters, and books both nationally and internationally on fraud, social responsibility, ethics in accounting/finance/aviation disciplines and NGOs in Springer and Taylor Francis Routledge; some titles are Emerging Fraud (with Sam Idowu), Corporate Governance: An International Perspective (with Sam Idowu), Women and Sustainability in Business: A Global Perspective, Sustainability and Management: An International Perspective (with Ulku Yuksel), Globalization and Social Responsibility (with David Crowther). She is regular speaker at International Economic Crime Symposium in Jesus College, Cambridge University. She is Member in Editorial Board of Social Responsibility Journal, Journal of Financial Crime, International Journal of Law and Management.

Associate Professor Roshima Said, Ph.D. is working in Universiti Teknologi MARA, Malaysia. Her research interests are in the area of Corporate Governance, Corporate Social Responsibility, Ethics and Financial Criminology. She has conducted a number of researches that were presented at international and national seminars and conferences and published in proceedings and journals. She also has published books and chapters both nationally and internationally. She acts as an Editorial Advisory Board for Social Responsibility Journal published by Emerald Group Publishing Limited. She also acts as Members of Board in Issues in Social and Environmental Accounting (Issues in SEA), Advisory Board of Emerald Book Series on Developments in Corporate Governance and Responsibility, and Editorial Board Member of Journal of Corporate Responsibility and Governance. She also has been awarded "Outstanding Author Contribution Award Winner" by Emerald Literati Network Awards for Excellence 2012. In the year 2016, she has been awarded "Diamond Award" for the idea and product innovation by the 3rd International

Innovation, Design and Articulation (i-idea 2016). She is Member of International Group on Governance Fraud Ethics and CSR and representative of the group in Malaysia.

Contributors

Ipek Altinbasak-Farina Faculty of Economics, Administrative and Social Sciences, Bahcesehir University, Istanbul, Turkey

Nevin Altug Department of Business Administration, Management and Marketing, Faculty of Economics and Administrative Sciences, Trakya University, Edirne, Turkey

Azlan Amran Graduate School of Business, Universiti Sains Malaysia, Gelugor, Penang, Malaysia

Ioan Batrancea Faculty of Economics and Business Administration, Babes-Bolyai University, Cluj-Napoca, Romania

Larissa Batrancea Faculty of Business, Babes-Bolyai University, Cluj-Napoca, Romania

Bilge Bicer Graduate School of Social Sciences, Bahcesehir University, Istanbul, Turkey

Ana Maria Roux Valentini Coelho Cesar Graduate School of Accounting, Applied Social Sciences Center, Mackenzie Presbyterian University, São Paulo, Brazil

Fatma Cesur Faculty of Economics Administrative Science, Trakya University, Edirne, Turkey

Faizah Darus Accounting Research Institute & Faculty of Accountancy, Universiti Teknologi MARA, Shah Alam, Selangor, Malaysia

Alessandra De Chiara Department of Human and Social Sciences, University of Naples "L'Orientale", Naples, Italy

Emel Esen Faculty of Business Administration, Yildiz Technical University, Istanbul, Turkey

Denis Forte Ph.D. Program, Strategic Finance Department, Mackenzie Presbyterian University, São Paulo, Brazil

Graham Gal Isenberg School of Management, University of Massachusetts, Amherst, MA, USA

Lina M. Gomez Universidad del Este, Puerto Rico, USA

Mehmet Ali Hatikler Ministry of Justice, Ankara, Turkey

Serol Karalar Trakya University, Edirne, Turkey

Iffet Kesimli Kırklareli University, Kırklareli, Turkey

Onur Kiziltas Trakya University, Edirne, Turkey; Migros, Edirne, Turkey

Elbé Kloppers North-West University (Potchefstroom Campus), Potchefstroom, South Africa

Henk Kloppers North-West University (Potchefstroom Campus), Potchefstroom, South Africa

Mohamed Knouch Trakya University, Edirne, Turkey

Yasemin Koldere Akin Department of Econometric, Faculty of Economics and Administrative Sciences, Trakya University, Edirne, Turkey

Maria Lai-Ling Lam Research Department, AJ-Great Limited, Hong Kong, China

Mehran Nejati School of Business and Law, Edith Cowan University, Joondalup, Australia

Anca Nichita Faculty of Business, Babes-Bolyai University, Cluj-Napoca, Romania

Say Keat Ooi Graduate School of Business, Universiti Sains Malaysia, Gelugor, Penang, Malaysia

Seniz Ozhan Department of Business Management, Çorlu Vocational School, Namik Kemal University, Tekirdag, Turkey

Arzu Ozsozgun Caliskan Faculty of Business Administration, Yildiz Technical University, Istanbul, Turkey

Ayşe Pamukçu Marmara University, Istanbul, Turkey

Tiziana Russo Spena Department of Economics, Management Institutions, University of Naples Federico II, Naples, Italy

Danijela Sarcevic Institute of Meat Hygiene and Technology, Belgrade, Republic of Serbia

Duygu Talih Akkaya Department of Marketing, Yalova Vocational School, Yalova University, Yalova, Turkey

Özgür Tasdemir Trakya University, Edirne, Turkey

Shahin Vassigh Associate Dean for the College of Communication, Architecture and the Arts, Florida International University, Miami, USA

Kıymet Tunca Çalıyurt Faculty of Business Administration and Economics, Trakya University, Edirne, Turkey

Okan Çalıyurt Medicine School, Trakya University, Edirne, Turkey

Onur Çetin Trakya University, Edirne, Turkey

Ayça Akarçay Öğüz Marmara University, Istanbul, Turkey

List of Figures

List of Tables

Introduction

In the past few years, due to instability of world economies have driven organization to reconsider the way they define, evaluate and measure corporate performance. Currently, executives and board members are frequently seeking ways in order to improve the tools or mechanism that bonds its business strategy to performance (Adams 2008). In modernization era, information is easily spread, especially through the Internet and social media network that causes higher demand for an organization to provide more information regarding their activities and future strategies to stakeholders and investors where this information must be transparently disclosed (Abeysekera 2013).

Traditional reporting no longer assures reporting needs to reflect corporate long-term development because activities which cannot be measured must be excluded from the reports. Companies should now extend the existing traditional reporting practices that coupled with the social and environmental impact that was generated by companies itself. Companies should rethink and recognize their way of doing business that benefited the shareholders and specifically other stakeholders. It may not be adequate for stakeholders and investors to measure the economic value that an organization had created or its potential value creating if they only rely on information provided in financial statements (Adams 2008; Hussainey and Al-Najjar 2011). Furthermore, the information provided in financial statements alone may mitigate the investors and stakeholders' ability to predict the sustainability of cash flows and current performance (Hussainey and Al-Najjar 2011; Van Zyl 2013). Therefore, to enhance the transparency and relevance information that disclosed by an organization, it must consistently provide quantitative and qualitative or narrative reports as a supplement and compliment for financial statements.

The issues of the sustainability and corporate social responsibility (CSR) have been of much research attention from academia and put into practice by practitioners for several decades (Deegan 2002; Gherghina et al. 2015; Gray et al. 1995; Gray et al. 2001; Gray 2002; Hackston and Milne 1996; Haniffa and Cooke 2005; Haron et al. 2006; Kanwal et al. 2013; Mohammad Zain and Janggu 2006; Said et al. 2009; Said et al. 2011; Said et al. 2013) . Past studies showed that engaging in corporate social responsibility leads to better financial performance, access capital, reduced operating costs, enhanced brand image and reputation, increased sales and customer loyalty, and increased productivity and quality. This eventually contributes to the market value of the company and business sustainability (Cochran and Wood 1984; Lin et al. 2009; Orlitzsky et al. 2003; Tsoutsoura 2004; Waddock and Graves 1997).

Corporate Social Responsibility

There are many available definitions of CSR, and they are consistently referring to five dimensions, namely environmental, social, economic, stakeholders, and voluntariness dimensions. Even though there are different phrases, the definitions are mainly congruent, making the lack of one universally accepted definition less problematic than it might seem at first glance (Dahlsrud 2008). Matten and Moon (2008) define CSR as implicit and explicit CSR. Explicit CSR refers to corporate policies to assume responsibility for the interests of the society. Explicit CSR consists of voluntary, self-interest-driven policies, programs, and strategies of corporations addressing issues perceived as being part of their social responsibility by the company and/or its stakeholders. While implicit CSR normally consists of values, norms, and rules which result in (mostly mandatory, but also customary) requirements for corporations to address issues, stakeholders consider a proper obligation upon corporate actors.

Corporate social responsibility (CSR) essentially covers three key areas, namely environmental performance, economic performance, and social performance. Environmental issues include the impact of production processes, products and services for air, land, biodiversity, and human health. Economic performance covers wages and benefits, productivity, job creation, outsourcing expenditures, research and development investments, and investments in training and other forms of human capital. Social performance includes traditional topics such as health and safety, employee satisfaction, and corporate philanthropy, as well as more external topics such as labor and human rights, diversity of the workforce, and supplier relations. CSR therefore focuses beyond financial (economic performance) as the bottom-line figure. It also looks at how the company has performed in terms of its environmental and social performance. Hence, CSR essentially constitutes triple bottom line. The core idea of the CSR concept is that the business sector should play a deeper (noneconomic) role in society than only producing goods and making profits. This includes society and environmentally driven actions, meaning that the business sector is supposed to go beyond its profit-oriented commercial activities and increase the well-being of the community, thereby making the world a better place (Robins 2005). Ness (1992) defines corporate social responsibility (CSR) as a strategic decision undertaken by organization as an obligation to society such as commitment to local communities, providing sponsorship, and giving attention to environmental issues as well as responsible advertising. Holme and Watts (1999) define corporate social responsibility (CSR) as a duty of each corporate body to protect the society's interests at large where initiatives should be taken by corporations for the welfare of the society as well as perform its activities within the environmental framework although its main motive is to earn profit.

Corporate social responsibility (CSR) reporting is an approach for companies to disclose or published their corporate social responsibility activities. By reporting the activities of a company together with additional disclosure, it may reduce the gaps between the company and its key stakeholders (Said et al. 2009). Globally, several countries and stock exchanges have required listed companies to disclose non-financial information. Some require it to be mandatory and some require it voluntarily. According to ACCA (2011), a country like France, USA, Denmark, Sweden, and European Commission played a vigorous role in implementing requirements for companies to disclose non-financial matters. France established a framework for sustainability disclosure, including matters like environmental management, social and community impacts, workplace practices, and corporate governance where the framework is part of Nouvelles Regulations Economiques. In the USA, new corporate governance disclosure requirements, code of conduct, and environmental information were introduced under the Sarbanes-Oxley Act 2002. In Denmark, Danish Financial Statements Act has been expanded to include sustainability reporting. In Sweden, there are guidelines issued for sustainability reports.

For the European Commission, European Alliance for corporate social responsibility (CSR) has been created in 2006 by the European Commission and European business community to promote corporate social responsibility (CSR) and social and environmental integration. ACCA (2011) further added those four international stock exchanges, including TMX Group; NYSE Euronext; BM & FBOVESPA; and Bourse de Luxembourg that have developed sustainability indices. Johannesburg Stock Exchange claims that disclosure of non-financial information is mandatory by listed companies. Bursa Malaysia also demands for similar requirements together with a description of companies corporate social responsibility (CSR) activities, whereas Singapore Stock Exchange promotes voluntary disclosure for sustainability reporting. Shanghai Stock Exchange claims that companies affecting the environment are mandatory to provide environmental reporting.

The Bursa Malaysia CSR Framework (2006) defined corporate social responsibility as open and transparent business practices that are based on ethical values and respect for the community, employees, the environment, shareholders, and other stakeholders. This CSR framework was designed to deliver sustainable value to society at large. CSR supports triple bottom line reporting which emphasizes the economic, social, and environmental bottom-line wellness. Chambers, Moon, and Sullivan (2003) investigated corporate social responsibility (CSR) reporting in seven countries through Web site analysis of the top 50 companies in Asia. Their study investigated the penetration of CSR reporting within countries and the extent of CSR reporting within companies and the waves of CSR engaged in. The findings in Chambers, Moon, and Sullivan (2003) showed that there were fewer CSR companies in the seven selected Asian countries as compared to UK and Japan companies. The mean for the seven countries studied show a score of 41%, which is below half the score for the UK (98%) and Japan companies (96%).

Organizational Sustainability

Generally, the conception of sustainability has been connected mainly with the dimension of economic performance or synonym known as "bottom line," such as financial or economic strength and good products or services. Steurer et al. (2005) defined financial performance, long-term competitiveness, and organizational economic or financial impact on stakeholders as the key economic issues of economic sustainability. Choi and Ng (2011) claim that economic sustainability is concerned with economic well-being and standard of living. Coblentz (2002) defines organizational sustainability as an ongoing process rather than a state of perfection. He asserts that sustainability means continuation. To keep an organization sustainable requires a constant effort and unity of purpose focused on one overarching mission.

A sustainable organization needs to be strong institutionally, financially, and morally. A sustainable organization has a mission. A mission statement provides a concise definition of why the organization exists and what it hopes to accomplish. Based on that mission, a sustainable organization has a process in place to develop strategic plans that define how the organization will carry out its mission over a set period of time. Financial sustainability is the ability to project resource needs and to account for resources in a proper way. A sustainable organization needs to know what financial resources it is able to generate through its own income, what it has on hand at any given time, what it needs over the long-, medium-, and short term to carry out its activities, how it will gather the resources it needs from other sources of funding, and what those other sources could be. Simply stated, an organization is ethically sustainable when:

1. The organization's leader has a clear vision of and commitment to the mission and communicates it effectively to all staff.
2. Staff come together around the leader and become committed to it as well.
3. Staffs feel that their commitment to the mission is rewarded by career development opportunities, adequate compensation, and a dynamic work environment that allows each to use his or her capabilities for a greater good.
4. Morale is high as a result. The general feeling is that problems are challenges that staff will overcome with unity of purpose and strength of commitment.
5. Leadership, management, and staff not only act ethically, but are also perceived as doing so.

Corporate Social Responsibility (CSR) and Organization's Sustainability

Past studies show that corporate social responsibility has a relationship between the financial sustainability (long- and short-run corporate financial performance). Many studies have been conducted to measure the statistical association between corporate social responsibility (CSR) and corporate financial performance (CFP), to assist the understanding of the relationship between CSR and CFP.

Previous studies show that corporate social performance has a positive correlation with corporate financial performance (Cochran and Wood 1984; Orlitzsky et al. 2003; Tsoutsoura 2004; Waddock and Graves' 1997). For example, Orlittzsky et al. (2003) carried out a meta-analysis of 52 studies and the study found out that there was a positive relationship between corporate social performance and corporate financial performance. Stanwick and Stanwick (1998) examined the relationship between the corporate social performance of an organization and the size of the organization, the financial performance, and environmental performance. The study measured corporate social performance by empirically testing data from 1987 to 1992 using Fortune's Corporate Reputation Index. The results of their study showed that firm's corporate social performance is indeed impacted by the size of the firm, the level of profitability of the firm, and the amount of pollution emissions released by the firm. McWilliams et al. (2006) state that CSR activities have been posited to include incorporating social characteristics or features into products and manufacturing processes, adopting progressive human resource management practices, achieving higher levels of environmental performance through recycling and pollution abatement, and advancing thc goals of community organizations. Tsoutsoura (2004) also addressed a question whether corporate social performance has an effect on financial performance. Using empirical methods, he tested the sign of the relationship between corporate social responsibility and financial performance. His study used extensive data covering a five-year data, 1996–2000. The dataset included most of the S&P 500 firms, and the results revealed that the sign of the relationship is positive. The findings showed that CSR is positively related to better financial performance and the relationship is statistically significant, supporting the view that, therefore, socially responsible corporate performance can be correlated with a series of bottom-line benefits.

Lin et al. (2009) examined Taiwanese firms which include R&D expenditures as one of their business strategies for sustainable development and also charitable expenditures as contributions to CSR. Based on theoretical assertions and empirical evidence in the literature, they found a positive relationship between CSR and financial performance. When the model is properly specified, they found that CSR does not have much positive impact on short-term financial performance, but it does give a significant long-term fiscal advantage. Du et al. (2010) stated that by engaging in corporate social responsibility (CSR) activities, companies not only be able to generate favorable stakeholder attitudes and better support behaviors but also produce the long run, build corporate image, reinforce the stakeholder–

company relationships, and improve stakeholders' advocacy behaviors. This is consistent with the study by one of UK's leading CSR consultancies, where they found that engaging in corporate social responsibility leads to better financial performance, access capital, reduced operating costs, enhanced brand image and reputation, increased sales and customer loyalty, and increased productivity and quality. This eventually contributes to the market value of the company. Effective and accountable management systems help companies shape cultures that support and reward CSR performance at all levels. As part of this effort, many companies are working to increase accountability for CSR performance at the board level. This can lead to changes in who serves on the board, how directors handle social and environmental issues, and how the board manages themselves and fulfills its responsibilities to investors and other stakeholders.

Mishra and Suar (2010) examine whether corporate social responsibility (CSR) toward primary stakeholders influences the financial and the non-financial performance (NFP) of Indian firms. The study used perceptual data on CSR and NFP that were collected from 150 senior-level Indian managers including CEOs through a questionnaire survey. The findings of the study show that stock-listed firms demonstrate more responsible business practices and better financial performance (FP) as compared to the non-stock-listed firms. The study also showed that the controlling confounding effects of stock-listing, ownership, and firm size, a favorable perception of managers toward CSR is found to be associated with an increase in firm's financial performance (FP) and non-financial performance (NFP). The findings of the study suggest that responsible business practices can be profitable and beneficial to the Indian firms.

Arendt and Brettel (2010) investigate the effects of corporate social responsibility (CSR) on corporate identity, image, and firm performance in a multi-industry setting. The study used the preexisting CSR scales, and it is tested using data collected from a sample of 389 European companies. The hypotheses are based on the examination of the moderating effects of CSR using a group comparison method. The study found that contingency models demonstrate that CSR triggers the corporate-image-building process and that its relationship to company success varies significantly based on company size, industry, and marketing budget. They also state that CSR proves to be as much or even more important for smaller companies, not as a mean of cause-related marketing, but as a way of generating a competitive advantage in the market. Nelling and Webb (2009) examined the causal relation between corporate social responsibility (CSR) and financial performance. Consistent with past studies, they found that the two variables appear to be related. Though using a time series fixed effects approach, they found that the relation between CSR and financial performance is much weaker than previously thought. They also discovered little evidence of causality between financial performance and narrower measures of social performance that focus on stakeholder management. The results of their study proposed that strong stock market performance leads to greater firm investment in aspects of CSR devoted to employee relations, but that CSR activities do not affect financial performance.

Table 1 shows that many past studies have proved that engaging in corporate social responsibility activities directly and indirectly leads to financial sustainability (long- and short-run corporate financial performance).

Table 1 Past studies on the relationship between corporate social responsibility activities and financial sustainability (long- and short-run corporate financial performance)

Authors	Findings of the study
Kanwal et al. (2013)	The study result shows that there is a considerable positive relationship between the CSR and financial performance of the firm, and firms spending on CSR not only benefits from continuous long-term sustainable development but also enjoy enhanced FP
Gherghina et al. (2015)	The empirical evidence is consistent with the instrumental stakeholder theory view, since the companies involved in corporate social responsibility undertakings use in a more effective way their resources in order to better satisfy stakeholders' needs. CSR activities can add value to the firm if they are wisely managed and implemented, as well as sufficiently disclosed and reported
McGuire et al. (1988)	Results show that a firm's prior performance, assessed by both stock market returns and accounting-based measures, is more closely related to corporate social responsibility than its subsequent performance. Results also show that measures of risk are more closely associated with social responsibility than previous studies have suggested
Cochran and Wood (1984)	The findings of the study show that average age of corporate assets is found to be highly correlated with social responsibility ranking. After controlling for this factor, there still is some correlation between corporate social responsibility and financial performance
Rajput et al. (2012)	The preliminary results revealed statistically significant relationship between corporate social responsibility (CSR) and corporate financial performance (CFP) as measured by sales revenue and profits of five hundred Indian companies; i.e., it concluded that there is a marked financial benefit for companies that are innovative to invest in CSR
Tsoutsoura (2004)	The results indicate that the sign of the relationship is positive and statistically significant, supporting the view that socially responsible corporate performance can be associated with a series of bottom-line benefits
Hull and Rothenberg (2008)	The results support both innovation and the level of differentiation in the industry as moderators for a positive relationship between corporate social performance and financial performance: Corporate social performance most strongly affects performance in low-innovation firms and in industries with little differentiation
Karagiorgos (2010)	The findings show that there is a positive correlation among stock returns and CSR performance in Greek companies. In operational level, these results aim at persuading managers to implement CSR actions in a greater extent in order to enhance firm market efficiency
Wibowo (2012)	The findings of the study show a positive impact of the social performance to the profitability of the firms, and also, there is positive impact of the profitability of the company to the social performance of the firms. The result of this study indicates that there is a positive interaction between corporate social responsibility disclosure and profitability of firms

Conclusion

CSR supports triple bottom line reporting, GRI (Global Reporting Initiatives), which emphasizes the economic, social, and environmental bottom-line wellness. CSR helps improve financial performance, enhance brand image, and increase the ability to attract and retain the best workplace, contributing to the market value of the company. Effective and accountable management systems help companies shape cultures that support and reward CSR performance at all levels. As part of this effort, many companies are working to increase accountability for CSR performance at the board level. This can lead to changes in who serves on the board, how directors handle social and environmental issues, and how the board manages themselves and fulfills its responsibilities to investors and other stakeholders.

CSR and organizational sustainability signify the way how companies achieve enhanced ethical standards and a balance of economic, environmental, and social imperatives addressing the concerns and expectations of their stakeholders. Undoubtedly, the sustainability of any organization depends on the economic and social conditions in the communities in which it operates. Corporate social responsibility and sustainability as a business management approaches that should provide in the short and long run, better value for shareholders as well as for other stakeholders. Corporate sustainability in practice is about contribution of an organization toward global partnership for sustainable development. It is about contributing toward wide societal value, including support for environmental concerns, health and human rights improvements, and fair globalization. It is also about companies that make long-term performance steadiness as a top precedence in organizational strategy. Eccles et al. (2014) proved that high sustainability companies are more likely to have established processes for stakeholder engagement, to be more long-term oriented, and to exhibit higher measurement and disclosure of non-financial information and significantly outperform their counterparts over the long term, in terms of both the stock market and accounting performance. Sustainability management is essential for long-term corporate development and performance. Research showed that companies embracing sustainable practices reported lower operation costs, improved corporate reputation, developed more green products, and performed much better at risk. Sustainable business entities contribute significantly to a nation's environment, economy, and social well-being at the micro- and macrolevel management.

References

Abeysekera I (2013) A template for integrated reporting. J Intellect Capital 14(2):227–245

ACCA (2011) Adoption of integrated reporting by the ASX 50—A joint report from ACCA and the Net Balance Foundation

Adams CA, Frost GR (2008) Integrating sustainability reporting into management practices. In Acc Forum, vol 32. Elsevier, pp 288–302

Arendt S, Brettel M (2010) Understanding the influence of corporate social responsibility on corporate identity, image, and firm performance. Manage Decis 48(10):1469–1492
Bursa Malaysia's CSR Framework (2006) CSR Framework for Malaysian PLCs. Retrieved from http://www.bursamalaysia.com
Chambers E et al (2003) A seven country study of CSR website reporting
Choi S, Ng A (2011) Environmental and economic dimensions of sustainability and price effects on consumer responses. J bus ethics 104(2):269–282
Coblentz JB (2002) Organizational Sustainability: The three aspects that matter. Washington, Acad Educ Devel
Cochran PL, Wood RA (1984) Corporate social responsibility and financial performance. Acad manage J 27(1):42–56
Dahlsrud A (2008) How corporate social responsibility is defined: an analysis of 37 definitions. Corp Soc Responsib Environ Manag 15(1):1–13
Deegan C (2002) Introduction: the legitimising effect of social and environmental disclosures-a theoretical foundation. Account Audit Accoun J 15(3):282–311
Du S et al (2010) Maximizing business returns to corporate social responsibility (CSR): The role of CSR communication. Int J Manage Rev 12(1):8–19
Eccles RG et al (2014) The impact of corporate sustainability on organizational processes and performance. Manage Sci 60(11):2835–2857
Gherghina SC et al (2015) An empirical research on the relationship between corporate social responsibility ratings and us listed companies' value. J Econ Stud Res 2015, 1
Gray R (2002) The social accounting project and Accounting Organizations and Society Privileging engagement, imaginings, new accountings and pragmatism over critique?. Account Organ and soci 27(7):687–670
Gray R et al (2001) Social and environmental disclosure and corporate characteristics: a research note and extension. J Bus Account 28(3) & (4)
Gray R et al (1995) Corporate social and environmental reporting: a review of the literature and a longitudinal study of UK disclosure. Account Audit Accoun J 8(2):47–77
Hackston D, Milne M (1996) Some determinants of social and environmental disclosures in New zealand companies. Account Audit Accoun J 9:7–108
Haniffa RM, Cooke TE (2005) The impact of culture and corporate governance on corporate social reporting. J Account Public Policy 24:91–430
Haron H et al (2006) Governance, ethics and corporate social responsibility of listed companies in Malaysia. Unpublished Research. Universiti Sains Malaysia.
Holme R, Watts P (1999) Corporate social responsibility. Geneva: World Business Council for Sustainable Development
Hull CE, Rothenberg S (2008) Firm performance: The interactions of corporate social performance with innovation and industry differentiation. Strateg Manage J 29(7):781–789
Hussainey K, Al-Najjar B (2011) Future-oriented narrative reporting: Determinates and use. J Appl Account Res 12(2).123–138
Kanwal M et al (2013) Impact of corporate social responsibility on the firm's financial performance. J Bus Manage 14(5):67–74
Karagiorgos T (2010) Corporate social responsibility and financial performance: An empirical analysis on Greek companies. European Res Stud 13(4):85
Lin CH et al (2009) The impact of corporate social responsibility on financial performance: Evidence from business in Taiwan. Technol Soc 31(1):56–63
Matten D, Moon J (2008) "Implicit" and "explicit" CSR: a conceptual framework for a comparative understanding of corporate social responsibility. Acad Manage Rev 33(2):404–424
McGuire JB et al (1988) Corporate social responsibility and firm financial performance. Acad Manage J 31(4):854–872
McWilliams A et al (2006) Corporate social responsibility: Strategic implications. J Manage stud 43(1):1–18

Mishra S, Suar D (2010) Does corporate social responsibility influence firm performance of Indian companies?. J of Bus Ethics 95(4):571–601

Nelling E, Webb E (2009) Corporate social responsibility and financial performance: the "virtuous circle" revisited. Rev Quant Financ Acc 32(2):197–209

Ness MR (1992) Corporate social responsibility. British Food J 94(7):38–44

Orlitzky M et al (2003) Corporate social performance: A Meta Analysis. Organ Stud 24(3):403–441

Pérez A, Del Bosque IR (2012) The role of CSR in the corporate identity of banking service providers. J Bus Ethics 108(2):145–166

Rajput N et al (2012) Linking CSR and financial performance: an empirical validation. Probl Perspect Manage 10(2):42–49

Robins F (2005) The future of corporate social responsibility. Asian Bus Manage 4(2):95–115

Said R et al (2011) Chapter 9 The Extent of Disclosure of Corporate Social Responsibility in Malaysia. Governance in the Business Environment (Developments in Corporate Governance and Responsibility, Vol 2) Emerald Group Publishing Limited, 2:177–194

Said R et al (2009) The relationship between corporate social responsibility disclosure and corporate governance characteristics in Malaysian public listed companies. Soc Responsib J 5 (2):212–226

Said R et al (2013) Empirical investigations on boards, business characteristics, human capital and environmental reporting. Soc Responsib J 9(4):534–553

Stanwick PA, Stanwick SD (1998) The relationship between corporate social performance, and organizational size, financial performance, and environmental performance: An empirical examination. J Bus ethics 17(2):195–204

Steurer R et al (2005) Corporations, stakeholders and sustainable development I: a theoretical exploration of business–society relations. J Bus Ethics 61(3):263–281

Tsoutsoura M (2004) Corporate social responsibility and financial performance. Center for responsible business

Van Zyl AS (2013) Sustainability and integrated reporting in the South African corporate sector. The Int Bus Econ Res J (Online) 12(8):903

Waddock SA, Graves SB (1997) The corporate social performance-financial performance link. Strateg Manage J 18 (4):303–319

Wibowo AJ (2012) Interaction between corporate social responsibility disclosure and profitability of Indonesia firms. In UMT 11th International Annual Symposium on Sustainability Science and Management (pp 373–380)

Part I
Sustainability

Chapter 1
Cultural Issues and Supply Chain Sustainability of Multinational Companies

Tiziana Russo Spena and Alessandra De Chiara

1.1 Introduction

Since its foundation, the debate regarding corporate social responsibility (CSR) has been dominated by large companies (Carroll 1999) and strongly associated with MNCs' global strategy and their international development (Carroll and Shabana 2010; Collier and Wanderley 2005).

More recently, the literature has addressed the strategic role of suppliers in the achievement and development of MNCs' goals and their responsibility mandate (Reuter et al. 2010). Hence, the importance of suppliers in the MNCs' CSR policy planning and its key role in the supply chain (Andersen and Skjoett-Larsen 2009; Carter and Jennings 2004; Carter and Rogers 2005; Murphy and Poist 2002). Carter and Rogers (2008) have clearly demonstrated the triple bottom line of economic, environmental and social goals that lead supply relationships and the importance of suppliers in improving the long-term success of companies and their partners. Different authors (Krueger 2008; Preuss 2009; Wittstruck and Teuteberg 2012) have stressed ethical sourcing as a social feature of companies' sustainability and suggested a definition of supply chain management sustainability (SSCM) that emphasizes this aspect in the supply chain; others (Leire and Mont 2010; Park-Poaps and Rees 2010) have focused on the strategic dimension of collaboration with supply partners by emphasizing the importance of integrating internal and external relationships for a more effective sustainability strategy.

T. Russo Spena (✉)
Department of Economics, Management Institutions, University of Naples Federico II, Via Cintia Monte S. Angelo, 80126 Naples, Italy
e-mail: russospe@unina.it

A. De Chiara
Department of Human and Social Sciences, University of Naples "L'Orientale", Largo S. Giovanni Maggiore, 30, 80134 Naples, Italy
e-mail: adechiara@unior.it

K. T. Çalıyurt and R. Said (eds.), *Sustainability and Social Responsibility of Accountability Reporting Systems*, Accounting, Finance, Sustainability, Governance & Fraud: Theory and Application, https://doi.org/10.1007/978-981-10-3212-7_1

Some researchers (Pagell et al. 2010) have shifted their focus to the requirement for efficiency in managing sustainable flows, stating that this aspect is essential throughout the lifecycle of firms' products or services. These studies have flourished mainly within the environmental literature considering that firms have control over environmental performance at each production stage, including the performance of their main suppliers (Pagell et al. 2010).

Other researchers (Trent and Monczka 2003) have started to debate the effectiveness of the conventional command-and-control approach of MNCs to sustainable supply chain strategy. Studies from different authors have shown that major suppliers' compliance could not be achieved by strengthening MNCs' monitoring activities, which, on the contrary have often proven to be prejudicial to the so-called buyer–supplier relationship over time. Moreover, suppliers' involvement and engagement have always been seen as crucial factors for successful MNC cooperation (Russo-Spena and De Chiara 2012; Wiemer and Plugge 2007), since they provide suppliers with the opportunity to demonstrate their contribution to and increase their commitment towards the sustainability goals of multinational companies (Fliess et al. 2007). Thus, MNCs best practice has generally focused on the development of CSR strategies in consultation with salient suppliers and other stakeholders.

On the other hand, many other MNCs noncompliant behaviours (e.g. the Mattel case[1]) have resulted in poor CSR strategic planning due to underestimation of their partners' cultural differences (Roloff and Aßländer 2010). MNCs operate through complex networks and globally dispersed units. This implies the need to find a balance between diverse stakeholders' environments and to increase the ability to manage the diversity of values and social practices across countries (Husted and Allen 2008).

At present, research has only marginally addressed the sociocultural issues involving MNCs' business relations with host countries (Logsdon and Wood 2002; De Chiara and Russo Spena 2013). These studies focus on cultural conflicts,

[1]In August 2007 Mattel was forced to recall 19 million Chinese-made toys worldwide because the toys contained too high a level of lead. The recall was the latest in a series of such actions that in the same year involving Chinese-made goods, including contaminated pet food ingredients, children's jewellery, defective tires and tainted toothpaste. In July, one of Mattel's European retail partners noticed lead paint on some of its toys, and Mattel began an extensive investigation of the toys in its distribution chain and of the contract manufacturers that make half of its toys. The scandal fought because contract and subcontract Chinese manufactures deliberately violated their production agreements with Mattel. According to Roloff and Aßländer (2010), some potential causes for the violation were identified. First of all, the delegation of control and then the lack of commitment of the foreign partners were seen as crucial factors for Mattel. As the authors reported, in one case, the CEO of the partner company deliberately ignored the agreement with Mattel when he bought the paint from a friend. In addition, many Chinese manufacturers found it difficult to produce at low cost while meeting the requests of Western customers which demanded both low prices and higher social and environmental standards. Thus, they were forced to bend some of the rules and hide the violations to stay in business with. Also, differences in national cultures contributed to the supplier's non-compliance as well as the high expectations of consumers and society regarding ethical production standards contributed to aggravate the problem.

supporting the idea of MNCs using their power to improve the ethical standards of the host country that provides the market in which they operate (DeGeorge 1993; Parker 1996). If MNCs have the power to influence standards in the host country for the better, then they have an obligation to do so (Hamilton and Knouse 2001).

A well-known branch of business research emphasizes how norms and cultural values can affect and determine partners' behavioural patterns, their grouping attitudes and preferences (Hofstede 1980, 2001).

More recently, studies on cross-cultural dynamics, especially the sociocultural factors in the supply chain management have been considered significantly important to understanding the nature and the extent of business relations (Cannon et al. 2010; Zhao et al. 2011).

However, the nature of relationships between MNCs and different sociocultural business contexts still stand somewhere on the fringe in the contemporary discussion on CSR, although CSR itself seems to be a consequence of how this relationship is understood. The responsibility debate cannot be separate from questions of cultural meaning; thus, there is a need to provide a starting point for an in-depth analysis of business relationships in dispersed and differentiated contexts.

To fill this gap, this chapter aims at deepening the role of cultural factors in the sustainability management of MNCs' supply chain. In more depth, the study aims at identifying whether and to what extent the dimensions of culture are relevant in shaping MNCs' supply sustainability practices. The analysis underlines the sustainability approach adopted by MNCs during their interaction with suppliers and provides an initial insight into sociocultural issues indicated in the literature, as being crucial for supply chain sustainable management.

The rest of the chapter is organized as follows: The first part analyses the concept of culture in relation to the supply chain and the study of CSR; the second part mainly focuses on empirical research, reports findings, conclusions and discussions.

1.2 Supplier Business Relationships and the Role of Culture in International Studies

Much is known about the role that culture plays in creating and maintaining long-term relationships between business and value chain partners (Cannon et al. 2010; Zhao et al. 2011).

Some authors have stressed the importance of cultural differences to determining both the soundness and evolving nature of the buyer–supplier relationship (Kouvelis et al. 2006; Gereffi and Lee 2016; Giuliani and Macchi 2014; Pagell et al. 2005; Stringfellow et al. 2008; Trent and Monczka 2003).

The literature identifies in culture the major influencing factor over trust, which has become an increasingly relevant issue among production and operation management scholars. Trust is, in fact, a key element for the creation and development of relationships whose impact is apparent in different models (Hill et al. 2009;

Giuliani 2016; Ireland and Webb 2007; Johnston et al. 2004; Monczka et al. 1998; Palmatier et al. 2006; Williams et al. 1998).

In international studies, a large part of the research has started to examine the differences in buyer–supplier relationships in specific cultural contexts (Dong-Jin et al. 2001; Scheer et al. 2003, Liu et al. 2008). More specifically, some researches have examined the impact of the cultural factor on the buyer–seller relationship in China and Korea as opposed to Western countries (Krueger 2008; Zhao et al. 2006). Furthermore, Scheer et al. (2003) have underlined dissimilarities in terms of cultural differences perception in Dutch firms and USA.

Other preliminary studies have also been conducted to explore the role of trustworthy relationships in the management of cross-cultural differences. Döring and Feix (2004) have emphasized how a high level of trust and cultural differences are critical to building a successful and trustworthy relationship between the negotiating parties; they have identified cultural differences as one of the main barriers to international negotiations. Many other authors have stressed out the importance of showing tolerance and understanding for their counterparts' different cultural backgrounds in order to carry out successful business negotiations internationally (Giannakis 2007; Khan and Lund-Thomsen 2011; Köllen 2016, Lund-Thomsen et al. 2016; Prahinski and Benton 2004).

In this respect, Kouvelis et al. (2006) have pointed out that on a global business level the hardest part is to manage all those interfirm relationships that go well beyond their functional, national and corporate boundaries. Cross-cultural differences may raise difficulties and challenges concerning how to communicate, interact and manage in interfirm relationships because of the different interpretive approaches of partners from different nationalities. Cultural asymmetry could engender an unbalanced aptitude for decoding and interpreting formal and informal signs, information and contexts (Hofstede 1980; Schwartz 1994). Therefore, it is vital to know how cultures hinder different relational norms, going beyond simple transactional or business mechanisms in buyer–supplier relationships (Liu et al. 2008; Zhao et al. 2011). In order to maintain and develop successful and long-lasting buyer–supplier relationships, it is then necessary to thoroughly understand the role of trust and the impact of cultural factors on behaviour (Ang and Inkpen 2008; Muller 2006).

To understand diversity in business relationships, some authors have considered the dimensions proposed by Hofstede (1980), along which cultures differences (Ketkar et al. 2014; Guang and Yang 2015). In this respect, individualism/collectivism is indicated as being one of the prime dimensions enabling cultural differentiation among members (Hofstede 1980; Schwartz 1994), while several studies highlight its impact in terms of values, norms and self-orientation in global firms-suppliers relationship.

Individualist and collectivist cultures play a critical role in determining distinctive normative orientation towards building long-lasting relationships. Furthermore, in highly collectivist cultures managers are more likely to adopt face-to-face communication, which appears to have a positive rebound effect on suppliers' engagement and trust (Ketkar et al. 2014). Similar results have been demonstrated by a previous study of Hewett and Bearden (2001), who concluded that trust is crucial to boost behavioural patterns especially in collectivist cultures.

An interesting perspective in some studies (Lim and Phillips 2008; Gonzalez-Padron et al. 2008) is the analysis of the relationships between corporate values and the performance of the supply chain: generally, the headquarters imposes its responsible value system on the rest of the chain, but undoubtedly mutual understanding between partners is considered a key factor to overcome the inevitable obstacles and conflicts (Carter and Jennings 2004). In addition, the distribution of benefits among supply chain partners is seen as a major factor in developing long-lasting and successful relationships (Drake and Schlacter 2008).

Many of the barriers to effective supply chain management are demonstrated to be down to the corporate culture of MNCs in dealing with leadership and control, as well as to the specificity of each business. The main theoretical argument puts forward the need for the development of a new global supplier relationship approach that will take into account the cultural elements of different countries (Krueger 2008).

1.3 Cultural Matters in the CSR Literature

As is well known, CSR include all those responsibilities in economic, social and environmental terms that businesses voluntary take up to meet their stakeholders' expectations (Carroll 1979, 1999).

While the strategic role of CSR has become a well-established topic in the literature by promoting an integrated socio-economic logic at the basis of a firm's business success (Luo and Bhattacharya 2006; Porter and Kramer 2006), less is known about the variables that influence CSR practices when firms move from decisions to the real context of policy implementation.

However, it has been argued that little emphasis has been placed on the driving factors influencing the effective behaviour of firms (Aguilera et al. 2007; Campbell 2007), the implementation of CSR best practices and the impact of cultural implications.

Defined as the collection of beliefs, values, work styles and assumptions held by an organization (Schein 1984) culture has been identified as shaping the extent to which business is conducted responsibly or irresponsibly. Taking as a reference Prahalad's and Bettis's (1986) conceptualization of dominant logic, Husted and Allen (2007, 2008, 2011) have shown that the bond between cultural variables and social responsibility is highly remarkable and that the overall business' system of values affects the decision-making process on an organizational level and more precisely, corporate goals, objectives and beliefs.

Other researchers claimed that cross-cultural comparison would enable businesses to effectively influence behavioural patterns (Christie et al. 2003; Clements et al. 2009), enhance product/service quality with a responsible view and ensure fair management of employees, customers and suppliers (Blodgett et al. 2001).

In so doing, culture may be determining either a positive and negative influence over CSR. On the other hand, Galbreath (2010) has also shown that by comparing humanistic and competitive cultures, the cultural variable exerts a powerful influence over CSR effectiveness. This study points out that corporate sustainability activities and strategies have to be embedded in a supportive organizational culture in order to be successful.

Hofstede's dimensions[2] have been taken as reference points to extensively examine the impact of ethical behaviour and culture not only to confirm the effective relationships with businesses' CSR practices, but also to assess its moral implications (Scholtens and Dam 2007; Sims and Gegez 2004; Smith and Hume 2005). In this respect, the analysis conducted by Chan and Cheung (2012) over 271 businesses in 12 countries has shown that Hofstede's cultural dimensions are the interpretation key to understand the differences in corporate governance (CG) practices as well as the impact of culture on ethical awareness leading to specific CG policy in different regions.

The nine culture dimensions provided by the GLOBE study[3] (Global Leadership and Organizational Behaviour Effectiveness), based on differences in leadership,

---

[2]Hofstede (1980) considered values "broad tendency[-ies] to prefer certain states of affairs over others" (p. 19). The scholar studied national culture differences through the analysis of some 116,000 survey questionnaires administered to employees of the IBM Corporation and identified five main dimensions of the national culture. They are: (1) Power Distance, i.e. the degree to which the less powerful members of a society accept or expect that power is distributed unequally; (2) Individualism versus Collectivism (IDV) that explores the degree to which people in a society are or not integrated into group; (3) Masculinity versus Femininity that represents a preference in society for achievement, heroism, assertiveness and material rewards for success in opposition to femininity that stands for a preference for cooperation, modesty, caring for the weak and quality of life; (4) Uncertainty Avoidance dimension expresses the degree to which the members of a society feel uncomfortable with uncertainty and ambiguity; and (5) Long-term orientation versus Short-term orientation that associates the connection of the past with the current and future actions/challenges.

[3]The "Global Leadership and Organizational Behaviour Effectiveness" (GLOBE) Research Program conceived in 1991 by Robert J. House of the Wharton School of Business empirically established nine cultural dimensions that make it possible to capture the similarities and/or differences in norms, values, beliefs—and practices—among societies. They build on findings by Hofstede (1980), Schwartz (1994), Smith and Hume 2005, and others. Power Distance: the degree to which members of a collective expect power to be distributed equally. Uncertainty Avoidance: the extent to which a society, organization or group relies on social norms, rules and procedures to alleviate unpredictability of future events. Humane Orientation: the degree to which a collective encourages and rewards individuals for being fair, altruistic, generous, caring and kind to others. Collectivism I: (Institutional) the degree to which organizational and societal institutional practices encourage and reward collective distribution of resources and collective action. Collectivism II: (In-Group) the degree to which individuals expresses pride, loyalty and cohesiveness in their organizations or families. Assertiveness: the degree to which individuals are assertive, confrontational and aggressive in their relationships with others. Gender Egalitarianism: the degree to which a collective minimizes gender inequality. Future Orientation: the extent to which individuals engage in future-oriented behaviours such as delaying gratification, planning and investing in the future. Performance Orientation: the degree to which a collective encourages and rewards group members for performance improvement ad excellence. (for more details see Chhokar et al. (2007).

have caught the interest of authors who have examined the influence of national culture on various facets of a country's sustainability indicators. For example, within research on social entrepreneurship, Stephan and Uhlaner (2010) have identified the performance-based culture and the socially supportive culture as the main cultural practices of a country's sustainability; furthermore, Roy et al. (2014) have identified a third factor, gender egalitarianism, and examined the effects of all three factors of culture on the triple bottom line in different countries.

Other researches (Adnan et al. 2011; Chambers et al. 2003) while focusing on CSR disclosure practices and their bonds with culture have shown in their cross-country analyses that the quality of CSR disclosure highly relies on the specific national culture of the examined regions and their level of commitment to CSR when relating to Western corporations. It is important to note that the application of any of the cultural aspects debated above comes with important implications for CSR. However, while cultural frameworks are certainly considered useful in comparing one culture with another, they only represent general issues at the level of national orientation, rather than a description of specific social and environmental behaviours of firms within different national contexts.

1.4 Research Process

1.4.1 Aim and Objectives

The brief literature review presented above has shown that cultural issues are part of a fragmented debate involving both buyers–suppliers and the social responsibility literature, with no linkage between these perspectives.

As supply chains expand overseas, cultural differences become increasingly important, since they can provide both the theoretical and the practical underpinnings of international firms' sustainability practices.

Conversely, what the supply chain sustainability literature seems to stress is more the standalone perspective of the corporate culture and or culture of the firms' leaders. Indeed, the impact of MNC leaders has been analysed in terms of internal CSR practices, with a focus on leaders' capacity and motivation to behave ethically (Galbreath 2010). Little is still known about the strategic impact of national cultures, their distinctive influencing factors on MNCs and how CSR practices are regularly implemented on a global sourcing level. The area of questioning is based on the notion that CSR involves a set of management practices and principles that have to be considered within the context of cultural boundaries, as culture produces values and norms that could hinder the transferability and applicability of those practices (Lim and Phillips 2008).

Despite the appealing cultural variable, more in-depth researches should indeed expand and focus on examining internal and external MNC relationships to better substantiate these casual links. Moving from this reasoning, our work has gone in-depth into the analysis of the role of culture in the CSR practices followed by MNCs in their interactions with their suppliers. Three main objectives have guided the analysis:

- The investigation of MNCs' orientation to supply chain sustainability
- The role of culture and its underlying factors in the CSR strategy of MNCs
- The cultural dimensions and practices shaping MNCs' supply chain relationships.

1.4.2 Research Context

In line with the intended goals of this study, our choice focused on analysis within a single industry.

The automotive industry has been chosen as it complies with different criteria. Firstly, this industry enjoys a special business recognition due to its well-established cooperative supplier relations on a global scale (Schlie and Yip 2000; Underwood 2012). Furthermore, social and environmental issues along with the power of larger corporations and their influence in less developed countries have increasingly become source of attention and concern (McKinsey and Company 2013) and, at a highly concentrated rate, allows for a thorough examination of the phenomenon at issue. Finally, despite the international resonance in the global economy, the automotive industry has been marginally examined in CSR terms, and therefore further investigation is needed to assess whether and how the cultural dimension plays an important relational role internationally.

The official database, the World Motor Vehicle Production 2011, also available on line, has been used for the selection of the relevant holdings (OICA Report 2011). Our analysis included a sample of businesses with a quantitative annual production (2011) of more than 300,000 units counting with 26 firms overall (see Appendix). All the investigated businesses are characterized by a high geographical dispersion of production activities with the exception of firms operating in business niches (such as the case of Porsche) and even smaller ones (such as the case of company Dongfeng) (see Appendix). In this respect, all the MNCs have built value chain relationships with partners in emerging countries characterized by cultural and geographical differences with the aim of exploiting the potential of their markets.

In such a context, geographical and cultural distances are expected to influence the CSR practices of the investigated companies, and particularly those present in a larger number of geographical areas that develop highly spread supply relationships.

1.4.3 Data Collection and Analysis

In order to understand CSR strategic approach, a qualitative data analysis of firms' formal documents in line with the content analysis method has been conducted (Weber 1990).

As Weber pointed out (1990), 'content analysis classifies textual material, reducing it to more relevant, manageable bits of data', which turns out to be all the more useful if the investigation relies on the interconnection of different elements (Tesch 1990).

The data collection has been carried out by exploring the firms' corporate Websites and retrieving all relevant files including CSR and sustainability reports, Web pages. The analysis has been conducted over a sample of 26 firms although four of them were excluded due to their CSR policy restrictions. Moreover, some of the firms have not yet reported on their sustainability activities in 2014, which is why we had to rely on the evidence from 2013 as the year of investigation. Finally, 35 documents from the Websites of 22 automotive MNCs were collected overall (Table 1.1).

The data were analysed in two steps.

The first step consisted in defining the categories. Our coding strategy followed an inductive and deductive approach (Silver and Lewins 2014), providing greater flexibility to the research, especially when phenomena 'cannot be viewed in isolation' (Layder 1998).

In particular, the keywords used stemmed from three main recurrent themes in the literature, namely supplier, sustainability and culture. Each element as considered by including the main term and the different headwords or synonyms under which it could be coded. For example, regarding the word 'supplier' we considered terms such as suppliers, supply, supply chain, value chain. Additional terms were added when the key element could be associated with different alternative themes, such as the case of the term 'culture'. Here, we selected established synonyms for culture, such as traditions, beliefs, values, customs and habits, and we also extended this set by including other terms, such as diversity, trust, respect, consciousness, tolerance/permissiveness, norm/rule. These additional terms were chosen on the basis of the links posed with the subject of culture by the supplier management literature (Ang and Inkpen 2008; Williams et al. 1998) and more recent studies in the CSR literature (Campbell 2007; Khan and Lund-Thomsen 2011;

Table 1.1 Documents dataset (year 2013)

Kind of documents	No.
CSR/sustainability report (including report in Website form)	17
CSR supplier report/supplier CSR guidelines	9
Green procurement guidelines/green purchasing guidelines	7
Others documents on ethical/business policy	2
Total	35

Lund-Thomsen et al. 2016; Smith and Hume 2005). Moreover, we were careful to remove terms not used in a sense linked to the cultural aspect of the supplier management situation. In addition, we carried out an interpretive analysis in order to identify the major themes associated with the keywords.

The second step of the analysis was developed according to the first sample results. In order to determine and classify the presence of cultural elements, the selected area of investigation was restricted to specific sets of data. The database included qualitative data from CSR reports, especially firms' policy relating to the supply chain and sustainability guidelines. The tools used for the investigation included the index of reports and selected paragraphs and subparagraphs relevant to suppliers. This second dataset consisted of more than 300 sentences and 4000 words.

Both steps have been conducted through the identification and quantification of words as they appeared, not in an isolated context but with their respective connections by comparing the key terms frequency of occurrence. In line with Gray et al.'s (1995) assumptions, the volume of disclosed information should be treated as a predictor of the significance granted to the theme under investigation. The aim was to understand the contextual use of the words or content related to all three topics.

Text analysis quantification meant to explore usage and not the pure meaning, as suggested by Hsieh and Shannon (2005). However, the analysis was not only limited to measuring the frequency of specific words or content (i.e. manifest content), it also included a summative approach and used quotes to illustrate issues of the investigated phenomenon. The summative approach included latent content analysis; that is, the process of interpretation of latent content where the focus is on discovering underlying meanings of the words or the content' (Hsieh and Shannon 2005).

The research finally aimed at improving the identification and description of sustainability practices in supplier management as well as the inherent cultural factors affecting the supply chain sustainability of MNCs through the examination of the relationships of the identified words.

1.5 Findings

The results have been disclosed under three main headings:

1. an overview of the main issues shaping the supply chain sustainability of MNCs;
2. the analysis of cultural issues regarding the general aspects of MNCs' sustainability strategy; and
3. crossing cultures with regard to the issue of supply sustainability.

1.5.1 Suppliers and MNCs' Sustainability Strategy

All the examined documents seemed to direct MNCs towards a holistic vision of corporate social responsibility. This was apparent in their effort to ensure the management of sustainability throughout every stage of products' lifecycle in every business sites (Badurdeen et al. 2009).

However, in some cases (5 firms) the analysis of documents did not allow express identification of suppliers' position in the text. Particularly, the reports examined at BYD Auto, Brilliance Auto, Geely were intended for all stakeholders: investors, employees, suppliers, consumers, nongovernmental organizations (NGOs) and communities; in other cases (e.g. Dongfeng, Porsche), the focus was on business general policies with regard to the social and environmental initiatives promoted.

The totality of firms' documents expressly including the word 'supplier' and other words related such as supply, suppliers counted more than 1890 occurrences. However, all those firms specifically reporting the word 'supplier' in their CSR documents (17) seemed to emphasize the role of suppliers as well as the priority given to related themes represented in different ways (Table 1.2). A great number of firms' documents (14 firms) reporting on the value chain or supply sustainability policy covered information about each relevant statement in the CSR debate (human rights, labour practices, community and society development, environment and so on). Also in some cases, in-depth detail of supplier management practices is codified and presented in the documents. Instead, a few reports (3 firms) combined the discussion on supplier sustainability issues to narrow sustainability topics namely green procurement (e.g. Hyundai/Kia) and environmental strategy (e.g. Mitsubishi and Suzuki; Table 1.2).

The word 'supplier' also emerged in connection with a wider set of topics within the index organization of CSR documents (Table 1.2). The main topics included those related to the presentation of the firm's environmental strategy (14 occurrences), corporate and strategic management (5 + 5 occurrences), employee policy (3 occurrences), as well as people (3 occurrences) and community commitment (Table 1.3).

With reference to suppliers' sustainability orientation, all firms handled their relationships with suppliers differently. The analysis of a selective concordance with the word supplier/s showed the presence of strong active actions of firms in the management of their supplier relationships, e.g. 123 relations between the word 'manage' and the word 'supplier'. These actions aimed at guaranteeing firms' sustainability goals within the supply chain.

An enlightened strategy of collaboration with an inclusion of suppliers was also derived by evidence related to the concordance of the word 'supplier' with the word 'develop*' (103 occurrences). Other words such as support*, train*, provide* showed a frequency of more than 50; this also confirmed the orientation towards a collaborative supplier management approach in a significant number of the investigated firms.

Table 1.2 Positioning of the word 'supplier' in firms' CSR reports

Firm	Chapter title including supplier	Subchapter title including supplier	Firm	Chapter title including supplier	Subchapter title including supplier
BMW Group	Supply chain management		Mazda	Management	Implementing CSR in the value chain
Daimler AG	The suppliers		Mitsubishi	Sustainability	Creating sustainable corporate value
Fiat/ Chrysler	Social dimension	Suppliers	Nissan	Value chain	
Ford	Supply chain		Renault	Stakeholders	Supplier relation
Fuji	Procurement		Suzuki	Efforts for the environment	Promoting green procurement
General Motors	Supply chain		Tata	Supply chain management	
Group PSA	Excellence in supplier relations		Toyota	Mutual beneficial relationships with dealer, distribution and suppliers	Collaboration with suppliers
Honda	Suppliers		Volkswagen	Sustainability in supplier relations	
Hyundai/ Kia	Energy and climate change	Green partnership			

Table 1.3 Word 'supplier' and its connection to CSR topics

Mission/vision	Frequency	Operative function	Frequency
Strategy	1	**Product responsibility**	2
Corporate governance	5	Operation/quality	2
Management	5	Procurement	1
Firm's stakeholders		**Aim/results**	
Employees	3	Economic	2
Customers	1	Environmental	14
Stakeholders	1	**Results/data**	
Other stakeholders		Social	1
People	3	Financial	2
Community	3		

Table 1.4 Selective concordance with the word 'supplier'

Words	Frequency	Words	Frequency
Manage*	123	Implement*	36
Develop*	103	Select*	33
Support*	59	Engag*	33
Train*	58	Conduct*	32
Provid*	56	Improv*	27
Risk	55	Communicat*	27
Meet*	47	Enhance	26
Expect*	45	Report*	26
Complyance*	44	Collaborat*	26
Promot*	43	Build*	22
Assess*	41	Evaluat*	21
Inform*	41	Reducing*	20
Share*	41	Commitment	19
Cooperat*	39	Requirement*	19
Encourag*	38		

The sign '*' means that the single word investigated also includes all its different headwords

At the same time, the risk business implication in the supplier strategy was also taken into consideration (55 occurrences of the word 'risk'). Conversely, this aspect drew attention on those firms' compliance policy, characterized by the high focus of CSR reports on such words as 'expect*', 'comply*', 'assess*' and 'selection*'. The disclosure of firms' strong control and evaluation activities in implementing their supplier partnerships for sustainability also represented a typical approach of the firms included in the investigated dataset (Table 1.4).

1.5.2 Cultural Issues in MNCs' Sustainability Strategy

The focus on cultural issues allowed for a thorough examination of the supplier relationships and the sustainability approach adopted by the MNCs herein investigated.

On the first level, the analysis of reports including all aspects of firms' CSR strategy showed a marginal interest in some culture-related topics, as only some themes emerged from the keyword analysis.

The first level of analysis showed that not all keywords culture related stood out in the companies' reports with only a few terms showing a higher frequency.

For example, only a few words such as 'respect', 'trust', 'integrity' and 'diversity' had frequencies equal to or more than 20. Only in a few cases, the term 'values' was mentioned while the term 'culture' had a marginal position (13 occurrences).

Table 1.5 Frequency of culture-related keywords

Words	Single presence in the file (frequency)	Concordance with word 'supply' (frequency)
Culture/s/ural	13	4
Diversity	20	12
Integrity	25	7
Respect (also ing form)	49	18
Rule	9	2
Tolerance	1	1
Trust	23	6
Values	15	4
Total no. of words in the documents	18,242	

By restricting the analysis of cultural words to their specific context of use, it emerged that for some of the occurred words, such as 'respect' and 'diversity', the relation with the term supplier was well represented (Table 1.5).

The sign '*' means that the single word investigated also includes all its different headwords.

1.5.3 *Cultural Dimensions in Supply Chain Sustainability*

In order to better investigate the cultural topics, a further step in the analysis was conducted by considering the specific parts of CSR reports dedicated to supply chain policy and other additional documents reporting sustainability guidelines for suppliers, where they were available. This analysis contributed to better qualifying the concrete position of cultural matters in CSR strategy and documented the concrete actions triggered by enterprises to the management of cultural aspects in supply chain sustainability.

As a result, the approach to firms' global supply chain identified the issues of 'respect' (23 occurrences), 'trust' (13 occurrences) and 'diversity' (9 occurrences) as the main points regarding cultural issues in supply chain sustainability (see Table 1.6).

Regarding the word 'respect', all the companies investigated claimed to integrate in their purchasing policies the principle of respect for others, as defined in international codes of conduct, such as the Global Compact or that of the International Labour Organization (ILO).

Compliance with a supplier code of conduct was an integral part of firms' contractual agreements with their suppliers. Some examples shown in Box 1 show companies' efforts to build and support their image as globally responsible companies. Many reports asserted the economic and ethical importance of rules for fair

Table 1.6 Frequency of keywords related to culture in the selected dataset

Word	Frequency
Culture/s/ural	3
Diversity	9
Integrity	5
Respect	23
Rule/s	4
Tolerance	1
Trust	13
Values	8
Total no. of words in the documents	4061

working conditions and recognized the importance of improving the conditions of all employees who directly or indirectly are involved in companies' businesses.

Box 1

General Motors adopts a policy of 'zero tolerance', which essentially relates to the protection of human rights, and maintains a training programme (Supply Chain Responsibility training) to make clear to suppliers this policy, but also business ethics and environmental standards. Mazda declares, in its purchasing policies and supplier CSR guidelines, that it does not discriminate and respects individuals, listing several tools used for this purpose: training, reports, intranet, site visits, awards.

Ford adopts a code of human rights for suppliers, including a commitment to protect minorities.

Honda has published supplier CSR guidelines, articulating considerations such as human rights and labour practices, asking suppliers to actively conduct CSR activities based on the same awareness as Honda.

Mitsubishi declares that it spreads the concept of respect for human rights among its suppliers, which, among other things, are to avoid discrimination and to respect the races, customs and languages of different countries. It formalizes this issue, among others, in the Mitsubishi Corporation Sustainable Policy for Supply Chain Management and also conducts investigations and visits to suppliers.

Toyota declares that it does not ignore cultural issues (the concept of openness). In its suppliers CSR guidelines there is a reference to respect, dignity and harassment.

Fuji has created the SUBARU CSR guidelines for suppliers by incorporating a CSR policy for the business partners of SUBARU Automotive Business. It says that it aims to continuously promote harmony between people, society and the environment, while contributing to the prosperity of society, and respecting the rights and characteristics of individuals. An internal audit check sheet is prepared for use by suppliers to conduct self-diagnosis and improvements in CSR activities.

Daimler spreads its integrity code. It publishes Ethical Business—Our Shared Responsibility to disseminate the principles of integrity and sustainability standards, organizes training and forums to strengthen dialogue on the subject of respect, creates a working group on human rights and the implementation of sustainability standards, creates a risk management structure for suspected violations of human rights, and launched the Daimler Supplier Portal as a platform for dialogue with its partners.

Source Authors' elaboration

Regarding the word trust, firms stressed the importance of establishing mutually beneficial relationships with business partners, in order to trust each other and improve their business relationships. Some companies (e.g. Ford, Fiat Chrysler, Nissan, PSA) often choose to use a range of activities to encourage confidence in the reliability and integrity of their other partners and to allow suppliers to meet their performance requirements. These activities were reported as an 'improvement in relationship conditions' that the firms developed with key suppliers (distinguishing their performance), based on transferring key knowledge and support of reciprocal monitoring and learning. Trust was seen as an important condition to ensure adequate sustainability and awareness of good governance among suppliers. Various initiatives included the online course on responsible working conditions at Fiat Chrysler that was provided to 460 Chrysler Group buyers and suppliers, and the training that Ford provided as needed to its suppliers to ensure understanding of its code of conduct. In addition, some firms reported a focus on diversity by explaining the tools they have in place both to successfully manage it and to enhance diversity with a view to improving the performance of the relationship.

For example, Nissan, Ford, Daimler Group and PSA have a clear focus on diversity: they respect the diversity of suppliers, and they do not admit any discrimination (item 6 of the Code of Conduct). These companies implemented several initiatives, including internal reports, to collect opinions and improve the working environment. Nissan explicitly stated that it made cultural diversity a strength of the company and to this end the firm organized e-learning programmes to train people in the management of cultural differences; in addition, it created a company intranet and specific committees and offices were structured to manage the various initiatives. The PSA Group has created a policy of 'regional integration' in which reference is made to the principles of mutuality, diversity and transparency. For this purpose, it implements four policies: (1) locating purchasing teams close to host communities; (2) strengthening supplier relationship management; (3) supporting supplier development; and (4) incorporating sustainability development criteria into its supplier relations policy. In Daimler Group's report two instruments emerged in order to manage diversity: the High Focus Programme, which assists suppliers (Tier 1) in developing strategies for diversity (the company spent $493 million on this in 2013); and the W/MBE Mentoring Programme, the result of a partnership between Fiat/Chrysler and General Motors, to help smaller companies identify areas for improvement, appointing an assistant to help them in solving their problems.

It is noteworthy that within each group the companies had different origins, with the consequence that the culture of origin could be seen as a variable with no influence on the cultural approach of companies to supply chain sustainability.

1.5.4 Cross-Cultural and Sustainability Issues in Supply Chain Management

The results of this study provided a first attempt at the analysis of cultural issues connected to MNCs' supply chain sustainability. However, once the preliminary results had been obtained, the inferences data analysis was considered to provide a categorization that described the MNCs' different approaches to cultural and sustainability issues in supply chain management. The fundamental question arose about how cultural issues could be linked to MNCs' supply management, and what should be the level of influence of cultural dimensions on MNCs' sustainability strategy.

In particular, two dimensions were identified through a cross-analysis of the data: the dimension—namely a reference to the suppliers axis—showed the extent to which suppliers are explicitly or not explicitly cited in MNCs' sustainability reports. The second dimension—the orientation to suppliers axis—concerned a focus on firms' orientation to suppliers and the way they have been taken into account in the development of MNCs' sustainability strategy. Regarding this dimension, the label 'third party' was used to emphasize smoothing activities and relationships, while the term 'partner' stressed collaboration and a culture-driven approach to supplier relationships. Both these dimensions emerged through the thematization of the words 'culture' and 'suppliers' in the sustainability report.

We suggest that this additional analysis contributed more to the understanding of the investigated phenomenon, since it allowed firms to be represented by a profile in two-dimensional space rather than a single point. Indeed, it provided categorizations of firms' orientations into three main types, as shown in Fig. 1.1. In particular, this figure provided evidence of how firms are grouped and positioned in the matrix in accordance with their approach to culture and sustainability in their supply chain relationships.

The first group—positioned in the lower left corner of the matrix (see Fig. 1.1)—included firms that only incidentally reported about suppliers in their document and see the supplier as a third party to which simple disclosure information about sustainability activities and related performance applies.

The second group—positioned in the lower right corner of the matrix—included firms with a less marginal and more explicit role recognized for suppliers in the sustainability report. This group, however, often limited their supplier relationships to a third party approach. The focus was more on evaluation of suppliers in

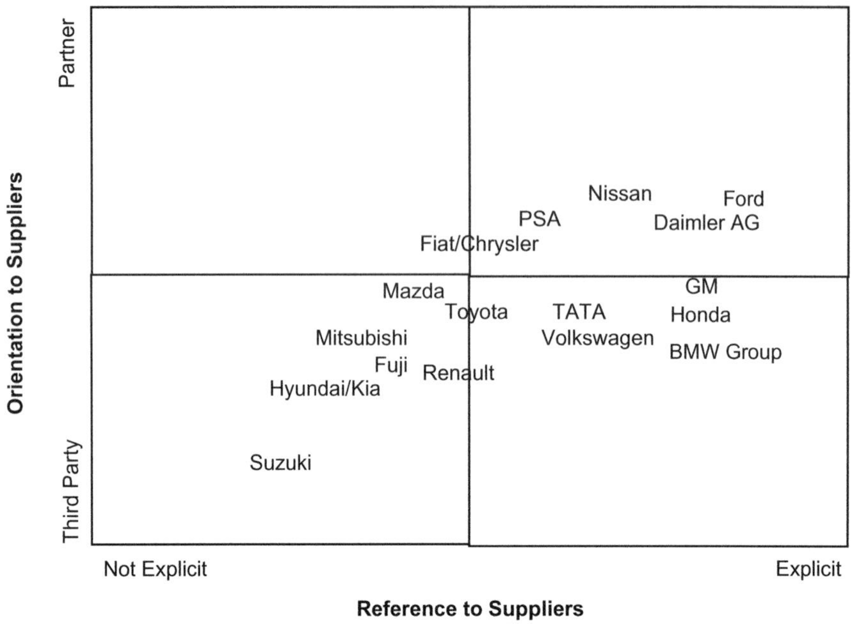

Fig. 1.1 MNCs' approach to cultural and sustainability issues in the supply chain

compliance with laws, regulations and standards and their alignment with MNCs' business philosophy. Formal and normative statements were established as monitoring and selection criteria for suppliers, which provide guidelines on how to behave and decide, for example, in a situation with conflicts of interest. Apart from relying on formal guidelines to reflect their culture, formalization further referred to incentivizing corporate value-oriented decision-making as well as a punishment mode in case of noncompliant decision-making.

The third group—positioned in the upper right corner of the matrix—included the bigger and leading firms in CSR strategy. These companies embraced a broad vision by extending the MNC CSR path to the entire supply chain. All the main supply management processes were identified not only by the presence of specific supplier evaluation and selection processes, but also by strong supplier engagement and well-established supplier development and enactment programmes. This approach recognized the importance that firms placed in cultural issues in sustainability, a theme in which suppliers were seen as active partners and respect, diversity and trust were considered as useful tools in leading suppliers' actions to be in line with firms' sustainability programmes and aims.

The suppliers' relationships were established not simply on an auditing philosophy and the methodology relied on standards and documents to monitor the condition of the supplier. The strategy of these firms was to have suppliers working together with firms to obtain opinions, feedback, ideas and input for improvement and alignment towards the same goals; instead of compliance being the goal, supplier empowerment and strengthening were in focus. These practices are presented as stemming from the necessity to disseminate a culture of sustainability along the wider value chain, as well as contributing to promoting standardization and implementation of best practices throughout the supply chain. This vision is supported by a culture over business approach to supply sustainability and finds its roots in the building of trust, transparency and competences.

These MNCs strove to promote the development of cultural glue in supply chains by giving evidence of their awareness of the importance of sharing values, information and goals with suppliers. To support this level of visibility, they have to enable suppliers' commitment to sustainability.

1.6 Conclusion

The topic of supply chain management sustainability (SSCM) is gaining increasing interest among researchers and practitioners, and the literature focuses on the necessity and importance of defining the meaning and scope of SSCM in wider terms. Approaches are suggested to explore this topic further (Carter and Rogers 2008; Fliess et al. 2007; Roloff and Aßländer 2010).

The focus on cultural issues in supply chain sustainability contributes to opening up new questions about the effectiveness of MNCs' CSR strategy.

As the analysis in this chapter shows, the results are in line with previous research (Chan and Cheung 2012; Husted and Allen 2008, 2011) and confirm the marginal role of cultural issues in the supply chain sustainability approach of MNCs, even if some differences in the MNCs' orientation can be noticed.

In particular, three main orientations seem to emerge when the crossovers between cultural and sustainability issues in the supply chain were analysed. These three different approaches can be named as follows:

1. an incidental focus, which characterizes those firms for which suppliers have no role and for which being engaged with them is not a concern;
2. a compliance approach, limited to the evaluation of suppliers in compliance with norms and standards;
3. a value seeking approach, which characterizes the group of MNCs that demonstrated interest in culture over business issues in the management of their supplier relationships. For these firms, values and information sharing, knowledge transfer and thus trust and transparency in the supply chain were central aspects of their sustainability supply chain strategy.

It is interesting to note that the behaviour of companies in each of these three groups is not conditioned by the culture of their country of origin; instead, it is evident that there is a significant role for MNCs' dominant culture in supply chain sustainability. In line with previous research (Fliess et al. 2007), a major part of MNCs' interest is in buffering their CSR operations from suppliers' influences in order to assure the effectiveness of their CSR strategy. The suppliers are typically recognized or modelled as an external constraint, requiring effort to encourage them to work within prescribed limits. Also, when the complexity of suppliers' CSR issues is put into focus, suppliers' greater contributions are considered by MNCs in order to align suppliers' environmental and social activities strictly within MNCs' CSR vision.

A value seeking strategy in supplier relationships does not hide the main dominance of MNCs' corporate culture (Webley and Werner 2008; Galbreath 2010). Even in cases where CSR strategy takes into account the cultural aspect within supplier relationships, these only marginally considered the different cultures of suppliers. Few initiatives directly address the management of the cultural context of their suppliers. MNCs founded their CSR strategy on supplier relationships, but less emphasis was dedicated to the consideration of specific suppliers' values, norms and other cultural dimensions.

This is perhaps related to the cultural supremacy of multinational enterprises: if they are strongly oriented to CSR, they do not feel the need to deal with the cultural differences of their suppliers. Great attention is dedicated to the more general dimensions of respect, diversity and trust in connection with suppliers, a theme in which the CSR supply chain approach continues to be more focused on the main operative contribution to the supply chain, instead of taking care of the human and individual aspects of the people involved.

It seems that a growing interest is emerging in taking more account of cultural factors in supply chain sustainability. However, the real strategic scope of culture and its multifaceted nature are not well understood as the diversity of business and geographical contexts comes into evidence.

If it is true that companies are driven by their corporate values and culture in order to address sustainability issues, there are multiple drivers to be considered in addressing supply chain sustainability practices. Many guidelines on effective supply chain sustainability programmes carried out by international organizations (e.g. UN Global Compact 2015) address the need to take into account different aspects such as specificity of industrial sector, firm's supply chain footprint, stakeholder expectations, business strategy and organizational culture. In addition, we find that an important role has to be played by the understanding of the cultural diversity of partners and the inclusion of this diversity in firms' sustainability practices.

An approach to the management of culture as a strategic factor for sustainability should bring MNCs to an understanding of the key cultural values of the specific context that they share. To reach a gradual integration of these values with CSR practices, the pursued goals are to find a new balance or, as suggested by anthropologists Trompenaars and Hampden-Turner (1998), to seek a 'cultural synergy', which can lead to considering the 'best' of several worlds.

We find that decisions about MNCs' sustainability strategy have to be analysed by considering how the cultural differences influence relationships within the supply chain. A sustainability strategy has to be operationally integrated with the cultures of global suppliers to realize MNCs' CSR strategy.

So further research efforts are needed to support the evaluation of supply chain sustainability practices. More in-depth analysis could include interviews of actors in order to verify the consistency between company documents and actors' behaviours, as well as involving suppliers' viewpoints in data collection.

Appendix: List of Companies

Companies	International value chain and supply chain	Companies	International value chain and supply chain
BMW Group (Germany)	Plants: 12 in Europe, 2 in USA, 1 in Africa, 3 in Asia	Hyundai Motor Group (South Korea)	Plants: 5 Asia, 2 in USA, 3 in Europe. 14 assembly plants: 2 in Africa, 1 in USA, 5 in Asia; R&D centres in Europe, Asia, North America and the Pacific
Brilliance Auto (China)	Plants: 1 in Europe, 4 in Asia, 9 in Middle East, 5 in Africa, 4 in South America	Mazda Motor Corporation (Japan)	Plants: 7 in Asia, 4 in USA 2 in Africa; R&D: 3 in Asia, 1 in USA, 1 in Europe
BYD Auto (China)	10 Industrial parks across China; Other offices in the USA, Europe, Japan, South Korea, India, Taiwan, Hong Kong and other regions; 2 Assembly plants: 1 in Russia, 1 in Ethiopia; R&D: 4 in Asia	Nissan (Japan)	Plants: 36 in Asia, 6 in USA, 3 in Europe, 3 in Africa, 1 in Australia; R&D: 11 in Asia, 1 in USA, 1 in Europe
Daimler AG (Germany)	Plants: 31 in Europe, 26 in USA, 8 in Asia, 3 in Africa	Porsche (Germany)	Plants: 4 in Germany
Dongfeng (China)	Plants: 4 in Asia	PSA Group (France)	Plants: 5 in Europe, 2 in South America; R&D: 4 in France, 1 in Brazil
Fiat Spa—Chrysler group (Italy)	Plants: 46 in Italy, 31 in Europe, 47 in North America, 19 in South America, 12 in Asia-Oceania; R&D: 38 in Italy, 13 in Europe, 16 in North America, 5 in South America, 5 in Asia-Oceania	Renault (France)	38 industrial sites in 17 countries; commercial subsidiaries: 21 in Europe, 7 in Africa, 6 in Eurasia, 8 in USA, 12 in Asia; R&D: 4 in USA, 7 in Europe, 1 in Africa, 1 in Asia

(continued)

(continued)

Companies	International value chain and supply chain	Companies	International value chain and supply chain
Ford (USA)	100 factories in 25 countries (Canada, Mexico, Germany, UK, Spain, Turkey, Brazil, Argentina, Australia, China, South Africa); Commercial sites: 1 in Turkey, 2 in Far East R&D: 2 in USA, 2 in Asia, 2 in Europe	SAIC (China)	Plants: 7 in China, 1 in UK; R&D: 1 in UK
Fuji Heavy Industries Ltd. (Japan)	Plants: 5 in Asia; Commercial sites: 5 in Asia, 2 in USA, 1 in Europe R&D: 2 in Japan, 1 in USA	Tata Motors	Plants: 5 in India. Subsidiaries and associate companies in the UK, South Korea, Thailand, Spain, South Africa and Indonesia; R&D: 5 in Asia, 2 in Europe
Geely	Plants: 15 in China; Assembly and production lines in Russia and Indonesia; 400 Overseas sales outlets in over 50 countries and regions such as Russia, Ukraine, Cuba, Turkey, Syria and Egypt; R&D: 4 in China	Toyota (Japan)	Plants: 7 in South America, 1 in Australia, 7 in Europe, 8 in North America, 1 in South Africa, 21 in Asia; 540 subsidiaries and 226 affiliates
General Motors (USA)	Plants: 19 in North America, 6 in Central America, 7 in South America, 29 in Europe, 8 in Africa, 30 in Asia, 4 in Australia; Branches: 4 in USA, 1 in South Korea, 1 in Australia, 2 in Europe	Volkswagen (Germany)	Plants: 8 in Europe, 2 in Asia, 1 in Brazil, 1 in Russia, 1 in South Africa; Commercial sites: 2 in Europe, 2 in China, 1 in Mexico;. R&D: 6 in Europe
Honda Motor Company, Ltd. (Japan)	25 production subsidiaries, 2 affiliates, 42 commercial subsidiaries, 2 commercial affiliates, 6 commercial branches, 7 R&D subsidiaries, 1 R&D affiliate	Mitsubishi (Japan)	Plants: 11 in Asia, 1 in Europe, 1 in USA; 75 subsidiaries and affiliates

References

Adnan SM, van Staden C, Hay D (2011) Does the interaction of national culture with governance structure influence quality and quantity of CSR disclosure? In: NZ sustainability accounting research symposium, University of Auckland Business School, Aug 2011

Aguilera R, Rupp C, Williams A, Ganapathi J (2007) Putting the S back in corporate social responsibility: a multi-level theory of social change in organizations. Acad Manage Rev 32:836–863
Andersen M, Skjoett-Larsen T (2009) Corporate social responsibility in global supply chains. Supply Chain Manage Int J 14(2):75–86
Ang S, Inkpen AC (2008) Cultural intelligence and offshore outsourcing success: a framework of firm-level intercultural capability. Decis Sci 39(3):337–358
Badurdeen F, Iyengar D, Goldsby T, Metta H, Gupta S, Jawahir IS (2009) Extending total life-cycle thinking to sustainable supply chain design. Int J Prod Lifecycle Manage 4(1):49–67
Blodgett JG, Lu LC, Rose GM, Vitell SJ (2001) Ethical sensitivity to stakeholder interests: a cross-cultural comparison. J Acad Market Sci 29(2):190–202
Campbell JL (2007) Why would corporations behave in socially responsible ways? An institutional theory of corporate social responsibility. Acad Manage Rev 32:946–967
Cannon JP, Doney PM, Mullen MR, Kenneth J, Petersen KJ (2010) Building long-term orientation in buyer–supplier relationships: the moderating role of culture. J Oper Manage 28:506–521
Carroll A, Shabana K (2010) The business case for corporate social responsibility: a review of concepts, research and practice. Int J Manage Rev 12(1):85–105
Carroll AB (1979) A three-dimensional conceptual model of corporate social performance. Acad Manage Rev 4:497–505
Carroll AB (1999) Corporate social responsibility-evolution of a definitional construct. Bus Soc 38:268–295
Carter C, Rogers DS (2008) A framework of sustainable supply chain management: moving toward new theory. Int J Phys Distrib Logistics Manage 38(5):360–387
Carter CR, Jennings M (2004) The role of purchasing in the socially responsible management of the supply chain: a structural equation analysis. J Bus Logistics 25(1):145–186
Carter CR, Rogers D (2005) A framework of sustainable supply chain management: moving toward new theory. Int J Phys Distrib Logistics Manage 38(5):360–387
Chambers E, Chapple W, Moon J, Sullivan M (2003) CSR in Asia: a seven country study of CSR website reporting. Research Paper Series International Centre for Corporate Social Responsibility, Nottingham University Business School
Chan AW, Cheung HY (2012) Cultural dimensions, ethical sensitivity, and corporate governance. J Bus Ethics 110(1):45–59
Chhokar J, Brodbeck F, House R (2007) Culture and leadership across the world: the GLOBE book of in-depth studies of 25 societies. Lawrence Erlbaum Associates, Mahwah
Christie PM, Kwon IG, Stoeberl PA, Baumhart R (2003) A cross-cultural comparison of ethical attitudes of business managers. India, Korea and the United States. J Bus Ethics 46(3):263–287
Clements CE, Neill JD, Stovall OS (2009) The impact of cultural differences on the convergence of international accounting codes of ethics. J Bus Ethics 90(3):383–391
Collier J, Wanderley L (2005) Thinking for the future: global corporate responsibility in the twenty-first century. Futures 37(2/3):169–182
De Chiara A, Russo Spena T (2013) Cultural issues in sustainable supply chain management. In: Proceedings of 2013 Naples Forum on Service. Giannini Publisher, Ischia, Naples, 18–21 June
DeGeorge R (1993) Competing with integrity in international business. Oxford University Press, New York
Dong-Jin L, Jae HP, Wong YH (2001) A model of close business relationships in China (Guanxi). Eur J Mark 35(1–2):51–69
Döring P, Feix M (2004) The impact of culturally determined differences on the supply chain management of French and German companies. INP Grenoble ENSGI
Drake MJ, Schlacter JT (2008) A virtue-ethics analysis of supply chain collaboration. J Bus Ethics 82:851–864
Fliess B, Lee HJ, Dubreuil OL, Agatiello O (2007) CSR and trade: informing consumers about social and environmental. OECD Trade Policy Paper, vol 47, Part 1, pp 31–39
Galbreath J (2010) Drivers of corporate social responsibility: the role of formal strategic planning and firm culture. Br J Manag 21:511–525

Gereffi G, Lee J (2016) Economic and social upgrading in global value chains and industrial clusters: why governance matters. J Bus Ethics 133(1):25–38
Giannakis M (2007) Performance measurement of supplier relationships. Supply Chain Manage Int J 12(6):400–411
Giuliani E (2016) Human rights and corporate social responsibility in developing countries' industrial clusters. J Bus Ethics 133(1):39–54
Giuliani E, Macchi C (2014) Multinational corporations' economic and human rights impacts on developing countries: a review and research agenda. Camb J Econ 38(2):479–517
Gonzalez-Padron T, Hult TG, Calantone R (2008) Exploiting innovative opportunities in global purchasing: an assessment of ethical climate and relationship performance. Ind Mark Manage 37:69–82
Gray R, Kouhy R, Lavers S (1995) Corporate social and environmental reporting: a review of the literature and a longitudinal study of UK disclosure. Account Auditing Accountability 8(2): 47–77
Guang WQ, Yang Z (2015) The effect of uncertainty avoidance and social trust on supply chain collaboration. J Bus Res 68:911–918
Hamilton JB, Knouse SB (2001) Multinational enterprise decision principles for dealing with cross cultural ethical conflicts. J Bus Ethics 31:77–94
Hewett K, Bearden WO (2001) Dependence, trust, and relational behavior on the part of foreign subsidiary marketing operations: implications for managing global marketing operations. J Market 65(4):51–66
Hill JA, Eckerd S, Wilson D, Greer B (2009) The effect of unethical behavior on trust in a buyer–supplier relationship: the mediating role of psychological contract violation. J Oper Manage 27(4):281–293
Hofstede GH (1980) Culture's consequences: international differences in workrelated values. Sage Publications, Beverly Hills
Hofstede GH (2001) Culture's consequences: comparing values, behaviors, institutions, and organizations across nations. Sage Publication, Beverly Hills
Hsieh HF, Shannon SE (2005) Three approaches to qualitative content analysis. Qual Health Res 15(9):1277–1288
Husted B, Allen D (2007) Corporate social strategy in multinational enterprises: antecedents and value creation. J Bus Ethics 74(4):345–361
Husted B, Allen D (2008) Toward a model of cross-cultural business ethics: the impact of individualism and collectivism on the ethical decision-making process. J Bus Ethics 82:293–305
Husted B, Allen D (2011) Corporate social strategy: stakeholder engagement and competitive advantage. Cambridge University Press, Cambridge
Ireland RD, Webb JW (2007) A multi-theoretic perspective on trust and power in strategic supply chains. J Oper Manage 25(2):482–497
Johnston DA, McCutcheon DM, Stuart FI, Kerwood H (2004) Effects of supplier trust on performance of cooperative supplier relationships. J Oper Manage 22(1):23–38
Ketkar S, Kock N, Parente R, Verville J (2014) The impact of individualism on buyer–supplier relationship norms, trust and market performance: An analysis of data from Brazil and the U.S. A. Int Bus Rev 21:782–793
Khan F, Lund-Thomsen P (2011) CSR as imperialism. Towards a phenomenological approach to CSR in the developing world. J Change Manage 11(1):73–90
Köllen T (2016) Acting out of compassion, Egoism, and Malice: a Schopenhauerian view on the moral worth of CSR and diversity management practices. J Bus Ethics 138(2):215–229
Kouvelis P, Chambers C, Wang H (2006) Supply chain management research and production and operations management: review, trends, and opportunities. Prod Oper Manage 15(3):449–469
Krueger DA (2008) The ethics of global supply chains in China—convergences of East and West. J Bus Ethics 79(1–2):113–120
Layder D (1998) Sociological practice: linking theory and sociological research. Sage, London

Leire C, Mont O (2010) The implementation of socially responsible purchasing. Corp Soc Responsib Environ Manag 17(1):27–39
Lim SJ, Phillips J (2008) Embedding CSR values: the global footwear industry's evolving governance structure. J Bus Ethics 81:143–156
Liu Y, Luo Y, Liu T (2008) Governing buyer–supplier relationships through transactional and relational mechanisms: evidence from China. J Oper Manage 27:294–309
Logsdon JM, Wood DJ (2002) Business citizenship: from domestic to global level of analysis. Bus Ethics Q 12(2):155–187
Lund-Thomsen P, Lindgreen A, Vanhamme J (2016) Industrial clusters and corporate social responsibility in developing countries: what we know, what we do not know, and what we need to know. J Bus Ethics 133(1):9–24
Luo X, Bhattacharya CB (2006) Corporate social responsibility, customer satisfaction, and market value. J Market 70(4):1–18
McKinsey & Company Inc. (2013) The road to 2020 and beyond: what's driving the global automotive industry? Accessed through www.mckinsey.com. Accessed: 25 Oct 2014
Monczka RM, Petersen KJ, Handfield RB, Ragatz GL (1998) Success factors in strategic supplier alliances: the buying company perspective. Decis Sci 29(3):553–577
Muller A (2006) Global versus local CSR strategies. Eur J Manage 24(2/3):189–198
Murphy PE, Poist RF (2002) Social responsible logistics: an exploratory study. Transport J 41 (4):23–35
OICA 2011 Production statistics, downloaded 15 June 2011. http://www.oica.net/category/production-statistics/2011-statistics/
Pagell M, Katz JP, Sheu C (2005) The importance of national culture in operations management research. Int J Oper Prod Manage 25(4):371–394
Pagell M, Wu Z, Wasserman ME (2010) Thinking differently about purchasing portfolios: an assessment of sustainable sourcing. J Supply Chain Manage 46(1):57–73
Palmatier RW, Dant RP, Grewal D, Evans KR (2006) Factors influencing the effectiveness of relationship marketing: a meta-analysis. J Market 70(4):136–153
Parker B (1996) Evolution and revolution: from international business to globalization. In: Gregg SR, Hardy C, Nord WR (eds) Handbook of organizational studies. Sage, Thousand Oaks, pp 484–506
Park-Poaps H, Rees K (2010) Stakeholder forces of socially responsible supply chain management orientation. J Bus Ethics 92(2):305–322
Porter ME, Kramer MR (2006) Strategy and society. The link between competitive advantage and corporate social responsibility. Harvard Bus Rev 1–15
Prahalad CK, Bettis RA (1986) The dominant logic: a new linkage between diversity and performance. Strateg Manage J 7(6):485–501
Prahinski C, Benton WC (2004) Supplier evaluations: communication strategies to improve supplier performance. J Oper Manage 22:39–62
Preuss L (2009) Ethical sourcing codes of large UK based corporations: prevalence, content, limitations. J Bus Ethics 88(4):735–747
Reuter C, Foerstl K, Hartmann E, Blome C (2010) Sustainable global supplier management—the role of dynamic capabilities in achieving competitive advantage. J Supply Chain Manage 46 (2):45–63
Roloff J, Aßländer MS (2010) Corporate autonomy and buyer-supplier relationships: the case of unsafe Mattel toys. J. Bus. Ethics 97(4):517–534
Roy A, Brumagimb A, Goll I (2014) Predictors of social entrepreneurship success: a cross-national analysis of antecedent factors. J Social Entrepreneurship 5(1):42–59
Russo-Spena T, De Chiara A (2012) CSR, innovation strategy and supply chain management: toward an integrated perspective. Int J Technol Manage 58(1/2):83–108
Scheer LK, Kumar N, Steenkamp J (2003) Reactions to perceived inequity in U.S. and Dutch interorganizational relationships. Acad Manage J 46(3):303–316
Schein EH (1984) Coming to a new awareness of organizational culture. Sloan Manage Rev 25(2):3–16

Schlie E, Yip G (2000) Regional follows global: strategy mixes in the world automotive industry. Eur Manage J 18(4):343–354
Scholtens B, Dam L (2007) Cultural values and international differences in business ethics. J Bus Ethics 75(3):273–284
Schwartz S (ed) (1994) Beyond individualism/collectivism: new cultural dimensions of value. In: Kim U, Triandis HC, Kagitcibasi C, Choi S-C, Yoon G (eds) Individualism and collectivism: theory, method, and application. Sage, Newbury Park, pp 81–119
Silver C, Lewins A (2014) Using software in qualitative research: a step-by-step guide, 2nd edn. Sage, London
Sims R, Gegez A (2004) Attitudes towards business ethics: a five nation comparative study. J Bus Ethics 50(3):253–265
Smith A, Hume EC (2005) Linking culture and ethics: A comparison of accountants' ethical belief systems in the individualism/collectivism and power distance contexts. J Bus Ethics 62:209–220
Stephan U, Uhlaner L (2010) Performance-based vs. socially-supportive culture: a cross-national study of descriptive norms and entrepreneurship. J Int Bus Stud 41:1347–1364
Stringfellow A, Teagarden MB, Nie W (2008) Invisible costs in offshoring services work. J Oper Manage 26(2):164–179
Tesch R (1990) Qualitative research: analysis types and software tools. Psychology Press, New York
Trent RJ, Monczka RM (2003) International purchasing and global sourcing—what are the differences? J Supply Chain Manage Global Rev Purchasing Supply 39(4):26–37
Trompenaars F, Hampden-Turner C (1998) Riding the Waves of culture: understanding cultural diversity in global business. Nicholas Brealey Publishing, London
UN Global compact guide to corporate sustainability (2015) Available at http://issuu.com/anadomingues0/docs/un_global_compact_guide_to_corporat. Accessed 2 May 2015
Underwood RL (2012) Automotive foreign direct investment in the United States: economic and market consequences of globalization. Bus Horiz 55(5):463–474
Weber RP (1990) Basic content analysis (No. 49). Sage, London
Webley S, Werner A (2008) Corporate codes of ethics: necessary but not sufficient. Bus Ethics Eur Rev 17(4):405–415
Wiemer J, Plugge L (2007) Transparency in the supply chain. Briefing Paper, GRI report. Accessed 23 July 2007
Williams JD, Sang-Lin Han JD, Qualls WJ (1998) A conceptual model and study of cross-cultural business relationships. J Bus Res 42(2):135–143
Wittstruck D, Teuteberg F (2012) Understanding the success factors of sustainable supply chain management: empirical evidence from the electrics and electronics industry. Corp Soc Responsib Environ Manage 19(3):141–158
Zhao X, Flynn BB, Roth AV (2006) Decision sciences research in China: a critical review and research agenda. Found Overview Decis Sci 37(44):451–496
Zhao X, Huo B, Selen W, Yeung JHY (2011) The impact of internal integration and relationship commitment on external integration. J Oper Manage 29(1–2):17–32

Author Biographies

Tiziana Russo Spena is Assistant professor of International Management at the Department of Economics, Management and Institutions, University of Naples Federico II. She obtained her Ph.D. in management and economics in 2002. Her main areas of interest are innovation and internationalization strategy. She has written articles and papers and published in Italian and International Journals, including Industrial Marketing Management, Managing Service quality, the Journal of Service Management, British Food Journal, International Journal of Technology

Management, International Journal of Retail & Distribution Management, International Journal of Innovation Management, International Journal of Quality Service Sciences.

Alessandra De Chiara is Associate Professor of Business Management at the University of Naples "L'Orientale", Italy. She is Professor of Ethics and Market and International Management. Her scientific activity is dedicated to study the themes of corporate social responsibility; international management; stakeholder engagement, knowledge management and social mechanism; SMEs innovation and learning. She has written several articles in Italian and international journals, including Journal of Small Business Management, Journal of Global Responsibility, International Journal of Technology Management, Journal of Business Market Management, Journal of Science and Technology Policy in China. She has participated in many Italian and International Conferences.

Chapter 2
Effects of Psychiatric Disorders on Women in Sustainable Business

Okan Çalıyurt

2.1 Introduction

There are many different cultural and social roles and behaviours developed between men and women. Beyond those differences, individual's health was also affected by sex. There are certain biological differences between men and women. Those biological, hormonal and genetic factors have great impact on gender-specific health issues. Finally, many diseases and health problems occur with different rates by gender in the population. On the other hand, some other factors like occupational health risks generated with division of labour by gender and social norms that preventing women access to health care are also very important factors that negatively affect women's health.

Many factors negatively affect women's health. Exposure to health risk factors and accessing the appropriate prevention or treatment systems can be different between men and women. Women are more likely to have part-time employment compared to men. Women are also exposed to different social risk factors and social roles that affect mental health negatively. Foreign-born women showed to have higher rates of mental disorders than natives (Lytsy et al. 2015). Beyond those negative factors, women on average have lower cash incomes than men. In most countries, women earn significantly less money than men for similar work. Interestingly, even though same educational background is provided for women, men have better health (Dahlberg et al. 2007).

World Health Organization's definition for health is "Health is a state of complete physical, mental and social well-being and not merely the absence of disease or infirmity" (World Health Organization 1946). That definition of health underlines that mental health is the integral part of health. Similarly to the biological conditions, some psychiatric disorders are more common in women than men.

O. Çalıyurt (✉)
Medicine School, Trakya University, Edirne, Turkey
e-mail: caliyurt@hotmail.com

K. T. Çalıyurt and R. Said (eds.), *Sustainability and Social Responsibility of Accountability Reporting Systems*, Accounting, Finance, Sustainability, Governance & Fraud: Theory and Application, https://doi.org/10.1007/978-981-10-3212-7_2

Psychiatric disorders can affect women at any age, status and occupational position. Finally, effects of psychiatric disorders on women in business raise an important problem for women. Understanding and learning the psychiatric disorders which are more common in women, and how they express themselves with their symptomatology and whom more susceptible to those disorders are important factors to help women in business.

In this review, epidemiology of psychiatric disorders in women, their symptoms, risk factors for psychiatric disorders in working women and finally effects of psychiatric disorders on women in business have been highlighted.

2.2 Psychiatric Disorders and Woman

There are certain sex differences in the prevalence of some psychiatric disorders. Common mental disorders affecting women are mood disorders, eating disorders, anxiety disorders and postpartum psychiatric disorders; on the other hand, men are more likely to have alcohol and substance use disorders and antisocial personality disorder. In a large epidemiologic population, both lifetime and 12-month prevalence of psychiatric disorders are studied. In this study, affective disorders and anxiety disorders are found more common in women. Results showed that lifetime prevalence of major depressive disorder was found to be 12.7% in men compared to 21.3% in women, dysthymia 4.8% in men compared to 8.0% in women, panic disorder 2.0% in men compared to 5.0 in women, agoraphobia 3.5% in men compared to 7.0 in women, social phobia 11.1% in men compared to 15.5% in women, simple phobia 6.7% in men compared to 15.7 in women, generalized anxiety disorder 3.6% in men compared to 6.6 in women and any anxiety disorder 19.2% in men compared to 30.5 in women (Kessler et al. 1994).

Depression or its clinical synonym major depressive disorder is one of the most common psychiatric disorders. Women are nearly twice as likely as men to have depression. Beyond its high prevalence rates, depression is the one of the most leading causes of disability. Diagnostic criteria for depression include depressed mood, markedly diminished interest or pleasure in all or almost all, activities, weight loss or gain, insomnia or hypersomnia, psychomotor agitation or retardation, fatigue or loss of energy, feeling of worthlessness or guilt, diminished ability to think or concentrate or indecisiveness, and recurrent thoughts of death, recurrent suicidal ideation or suicide attempt. Those symptoms cause clinically significant distress or impairment in social, occupational or other important areas of functioning (American Psychiatric Association 2013). Depression is the most prevalent mental disorder to cause absenteeism from work. Depression may also cause job loss or changing job in severe cases.

Eating disorders are rare psychiatric disorders. Women are much more likely than men to develop an eating disorder. There are two important eating disorders listed in Diagnostic and Statistical Manual of Mental Disorders; anorexia nervosa and bulimia nervosa (American Psychiatric Association 2013). The 12-month prevalence of anorexia nervosa is about 0.4% and bulimia nervosa 1–1.5%. Male-to-female ratio of eating disorders is about 1:10. Anorexia nervosa is characterized by body image problems. Despite patients with anorexia nervosa show low body weight, they struggle to lose more. They reduce their food intake and engage binge eating. The eating disorders tend to start in adolescence or early adulthood. Beyond its social and occupational functional limitations, all eating disorders show increased mortality risk (Smink et al. 2012). Vocational and social factors are important aetiological factors in anorexia nervosa. For example, it is showed that women who join ballet school, risk for anorexia nervosa increases significantly.

Prevalence rates of anxiety disorders are higher in women. These higher rates explained with the some personality traits that women have. It is showed that women tend to internalize their emotions more than men. Internalization of the emotions leads depression and anxiety symptoms (Eaton et al. 2012). Anxiety disorders are panic disorder, agoraphobia, specific phobia, social anxiety disorder or phobia and generalized anxiety disorder. Prevalence rates of panic disorder in women are 3–4 times higher than men. Increased rates of stressful life events and history of childhood sexual abuse in women have been shown in the aetiology. Specific phobia is the most common mental disorder in women, and prevalence rates are about twofold compared to men. Similarly, social phobia is more prevalent in women compared to men. Finally, prevalence rate for generalized anxiety disorder is about two times higher in women (Benjamin and Pedro Ruiz 2015).

Childhood maltreatment is another important factor that affects women, and its consequences are related with psychiatric disorders. Some cultural and ethnic groups found more vulnerable for childhood maltreatment. Cultural aspects and female gender role in those groups may be underlying factors for increased childhood maltreatment. Physical or sexual abuse may be associated with depressive disorders, anxiety disorders and post-traumatic stress disorder (Warner et al. 2012).

Sexual violence is a common problem in our society. Some of the sexual violence occurs in workplace. As an example, female film performers showed to have significantly worse mental health that that 37% of them had forced sex (Grudzen et al. 2011). Unfortunately, more than 90% of sexual assault victims are women, and it is estimated that half of the cases remain unreported. Sexual violence can be very traumatizing. Women who experience sexual assault are more likely to use mental health services. The literature and statistics are showing higher psychiatric correlation between childhood sexual assault and increased mental health service utilization and severity of psychiatric disorder. Lifetime prevalence of rape found to be about 15% in national samples of women. Similarly, post-traumatic stress disorder, major depressive disorder and alcohol use disorder are associated with rape (Zinzow et al. 2012). Sexual disorders may also be triggered by rape in women. As a conclusion, being women in workplace increases the risk for sexual assault and increases the risk and severity of psychiatric disorders (McLindon and Harms 2011).

2.3 Women's Mental Health and Pregnancy

Because of the some biological, psychological and hormonal changes occur during peripartum period, women are vulnerable for psychiatric disorders and also vulnerable for the exacerbation of the psychiatric symptoms. Some other factors like disruption of treatments and sleep problems during peripartum period are important for psychiatric disorders. A postpartum prevalence study revealed higher rates of depression and anxiety in postpartum women (Bener et al. 2012). Those results are contrary to the belief that pregnancy protects women from psychiatric disorder. Furthermore, women who have history of psychiatric disorder or stop taking their medication during pregnancy have higher risk for psychiatric disorders (Coble et al. 1994). On the other hand, because of the many of the psychotropic medications are not safe during pregnancy, especially at first trimester, many women tend to discontinue their psychiatric treatment.

Postpartum period is very important for women. Many women in postpartum period experience affective symptoms that associated with rapid hormonal changes. Those symptoms may last several days. Postpartum blues is not a clinical syndrome and not require treatment. But only small percentage of women in postpartum period experience depression and psychosis. Both depression and psychosis are severe psychiatric disorders and require appropriate treatment.

Contrary to the effects of pregnancy on mental health, psychiatric disorders also affect probability of marriage and pregnancy. Studies demonstrated that fertility of patients with psychotic disorders like schizophrenia or severe mood disorders is reduced (Stevens 1969).

Prevalence of women working with pregnancy is increasing. Most of the pregnancies occur between 15 and 35 years of age, and today, most of the women work while pregnant. Interestingly, pregnant working women tend to stay in their jobs into their last one or two months. In most cases, it affects working life of women and conversely some occupations adversely affect pregnancy. Prolonged standing, hard physical work, heavy lifting and shift work may be underlying risk factors for occupational adverse effects (NHS Plus Royal College of Physicians 2009). Most women can return their jobs in one or two months after delivery.

2.4 Effects of Psychiatric Disorder on Women in Business

Mental health problems have negative effect on quality of life, social and occupational functioning. Previous studies have shown that women with mental health problems have higher rates of unemployment than healthy women (Bursalioglu et al. 2013). Psychiatric disorders like major depressive disorder and anxiety disorder are the important cause of disability in women. Disability and subsequent sick leave negatively impact work life for women. During this period, interpersonal relations and business career may be affected and finally losing a job may occur for severe cases. The loss may not be limited to job but women can lose social roles at home and at work (Nielsen et al. 2013). Many studies have shown the effects of mental health problems on involuntary job loss. Mostly, the depressive symptoms were found associated with job loss compared to anxiety symptoms (Dew et al. 1992). Contrary to the higher incidence of mood disorders, anxiety disorders and emotional problems seen in women, they showed to underutilize mental health services and overutilize physical health services to deal with their psychiatric problems (Jimenez et al. 1997). This underutilizing of psychiatry can partly explain increased vulnerability to mental health problems and disability in women. Obviously, only women who have correct diagnosis and receiving appropriate treatment may recover form psychiatric disorders.

Work-related factors can also cause stress in working women. High workload, problems with colleagues and poor working conditions may play role on increased stress in workplace. On the other hand, women have different roles except career. Responsibilities in home, family and children are also associated with increased stress in women. If women experience stress over a prolonged time, it may affect health. Finally, perceived poor physical and mental health is one of the most important factors for poor working ability. Reduced working ability is associated with mental distress.

According to the workplace gender segregation, women work generally in different occupations than men. Women working in sedentary positions may show low level of physical activity. Studies showed protective effect of physical activity for mental health in women. Gender segregation may have influence on women's mental health in workplace. Decreasing workplace gender segregation may help to increase physical activity in women. Increased physical activity positively affects mental health. Increasing physical activity is also beneficial for menopausal symptoms (Griffiths et al. 2014).

Pregnancy is not considered an illness. But on the other hand, significant physical, hormonal, psychological changes occur during pregnancy. Pregnant women showed to have increased rates of sickness absence compared to the normal women population, and also duration of the sickness absence is significantly longer in pregnant women (Sydsjo et al. 2001). High level of stress during pregnancy may also affect psychological well-being. Psychiatric disorders are common in pregnancy. But without direct relationship with psychiatric disorders, sick leave rates are shown to be increased during last decades. This increase cannot be explained with actual physical or psychological illness (Sydsjo et al. 1998). But on the other hand, high prevalence rates of psychiatric disorders on peripartum period negatively affect occupational performance of women. Moreover, occupational factors may negatively affect pregnant women like miscarriage, premature birth, low birthweight or birth anomalies.

Premenstrual dysphoric disorder is some kind of depressive disorder. During the premenstrual period, women experience mood lability, irritability, dysphoria and anxiety symptoms. Premenstrual dysphoric disorder occurs up to 10% of menstruating women. Generally, premenstrual dysphoric disorder symptoms are seen during the week before menstruation. According to the severity of the symptoms, social and occupational impairments may occur (American Psychiatric Association 2013). Women who experience moderate-to-severe premenstrual difficulties are demonstrated to have increased lifetime prevalence of mood disorders and drug abuse (Mackenzie et al. 1986). In particular, patients diagnosed with bipolar disorder report higher rates of menstrual dysfunction prior to the onset of psychiatric disorder (Joffe et al. 2006).

Diagnosing premenstrual dysphoric disorder requires that symptoms should be associated with clinically significant distress or interference with work, school, usual social activities or relationships with others. Emotional and behavioural symptoms related to the premenstrual dysphoric disorder may lead long-term difficulties in interpersonal relationships and occupational roles. Evidently, women with premenstrual dysphoric disorder experience long-term difficulties in work life.

In some patients, mental problems or stress can cause physical symptoms that is known as somatization or somatic symptom disorder. Atypical physical symptoms, chronic conditions in the workplace or long-term sickness absence should be evaluated in detail for possible somatization (Olaya-Contreras et al. 2010). Since the symptoms are physical, medical care utilization is very high in somatic symptom disorder. But because the aetiology is related with psychological origins, most patients with somatic symptom disorder do not benefit from medical treatments. Like many other psychiatric disorders, prevalence of somatic symptom disorder is higher in women and women tend to report more somatic symptoms. Somatic symptom disorder is associated with impairment in social and occupational life.

Job loss and its effects on women is another important topic, and there are bidirectional interaction between job loss and psychiatric symptoms and stress. Impact of psychiatric disorders on occupational life and job loss is underlined before. On the other hand, job loss is a stressful life event, and this traumatic experience can negatively affect individual's mental health. Job loss is associated with psychiatric symptoms and depression. Job loss is recognized as less stressful for women because women have alternative roles other than career. Studies demonstrated that most women do not perceive job loss as a stressful life event. Most of them perceive job loss as a challenge and threat. But single woman tends to report more psychiatric symptoms after job loss compared to married women. Consequently, because unmarried women lack social support, they are more vulnerable to job loss (Nuttman-Shwartz et al. 2009). Additionally, job insecurity showed to affect men and women differently; job insecurity is positively associated with major depressive disorders in men, but there is no association in women (Wang et al. 2008).

Psychiatric disorders are associated with disability and decreased quality of life. Consequently, those disabling mental disorders can cause long-term sick leave. There are also many medical conditions like musculoskeletal pain that may cause disability during long-term sick leave but comorbid depression with those medical conditions showed to increase disability and decrease quality of life of women (Jansen et al. 2011). Workplace-related psychological factors may affect men and women differently. On the other hand, work-related stress is showed to an important factor for predicting future sick leave risk in women (Holmgren et al. 2013). Women with psychiatric disorders showed to have higher rates of sick leave. Combination with psychiatric disorders and physical disorders is associated with even higher rates of sick leave (Hensing et al. 1997).

Alcohol dependence and alcohol abuse prevalence are increasing in women. Similar to the men, alcohol use disorders negatively affect social and occupational life. Studies showed strong association between alcohol use disorders and sick leave in women (Spak et al. 1998).

Longer, shorter or no sick leave demonstrated to affect psychiatric patients differently in various mental disorders. Patients with anxiety disorders with long-term sick leave showed deterioration in symptoms compared to short-term sick leave, and patients with depressive disorder with long-term sick leave showed to have higher improvement compared to short-term or no sick leave. Those results indicate that sick leave in different psychiatric disorders should be evaluated separately (Tritt et al. 2005).

Psychiatric disorders may lead disability for whom permanently or temporarily unable to work due to psychiatric morbidity. Granting disability pension is investigated in outpatient psychiatric patients diagnosed with major depressive disorder. Including other factors such as age, educational level or living alone, being female found to be associated with granting disability pension (Mittendorfer-Rutz et al. 2014). Those results are interesting, that among other factors being female increase the disability support pension.

Finally, subjective evaluation of patients' self-health is very important to predict disability pension, sick leave or hospital admission. High inverse correlation between self-rated health and sick leave and disability pension is demonstrated in both men and women (Halford et al. 2012).

There are many factors affecting returning to work after long-term sick leave for women. Studies demonstrated that unemployed women are exposed to more risk factors compared to men or employed men and women. Individual, occupational or environmental factors are important ones. A study showed that some emotions like desire, longing and vanity play an important role for women when return to work (Ahrberg et al. 2010).

2.5 Conclusion

As a conclusion, women report more occupational problems and sick leave than men. Similarly, increased early retirement pensions are higher in women. During the last few decades, prevalence of psychiatric disorders is also increased in women. Primarily major depressive disorder, anxiety disorders and stress-related problems are increased. Therefore, work-related stress is also increased and negative impacts of stress in work is demonstrated to impair mental health in women (Holmgren et al. 2009).

Women live longer than men, but medical and psychiatric health risks are not low. There are certain biological differences between men and women. Additionally, women experience other risk factors like marriage, pregnancy or lactation. Sexual violence, income inequalities and social roles also influence women's mental health. Prevalence of many psychiatric disorders is higher in women than men. In conclusion, all those factors and psychiatric disorders with their psychological, social and occupational impact negatively affect women in workplace. Finally, there is need for separate approach to women's mental health in business world.

References

Ahrberg Y, Landstad BJ, Bergroth A, Ekholm J (2010) Desire, longing and vanity: emotions behind successful return to work for women on long-term sick leave. Work 37:167–177

American Psychiatric Association (2013) Diagnostic and statistical manual of mental disorders fifth edition DSM-5. American Psychiatric Association, Arlington

Bener A, Gerber LM, Sheikh J (2012) Prevalence of psychiatric disorders and associated risk factors in women during their postpartum period: a major public health problem and global comparison. Int J Womens Health 4:191–200

Benjamin JS, Pedro Ruiz VAS (2015) Kaplan and Sadock's synopsis of psychiatry. Lippincott Williams & Wilkins, Philadelphia

Bursalioglu FS, Aydin N, Yazici E, Yazici AB (2013) The correlation between psychiatric disorders and women's lives. J Clin Diagn Res 7:695–699

Coble PA, Reynolds CF, Kupfer DJ, Houck PR, Day NL, Giles DE (1994) Childbearing in women with and without a history of affective-disorder. 1. Psychiatric symptomatology. Compr Psychiatry 35:205–214

Dahlberg R, Bildt C, Vingard E, Karlqvist L (2007) Educational background: different processes and consequences on health and physical and mental exposures among women and men. Work 28:57–66

Dew MA, Bromet EJ, Penkower L (1992) Mental health effects of job loss in women. Psychol Med 22:751–764

Eaton NR, Keyes KM, Krueger RF, Balsis S, Skodol AE, Markon KE, Grant BF, Hasin DS (2012) An invariant dimensional liability model of gender differences in mental disorder prevalence: evidence from a national sample. J Abnorm Psychol 121:282–288

Griffiths A, Kouvonen A, Pentti J, Oksanen T, Virtanen M, Salo P, Vaananen A, Kivimaki M, Vahtera J (2014) Association of physical activity with future mental health in older, mid-life and younger women. Eur J Public Health 24:813–818

Grudzen CR, Meeker D, Torres JM, Du Q, Morrison RS, Andersen RM, Gelberg L (2011) Comparison of the mental health of female adult film performers and other young women in California. Psychiatr Serv 62:639–645

Halford C, Wallman T, Welin L, Rosengren A, Bardel A, Johansson S, Eriksson H, Palmer E, Wilhelmsen L, Svardsudd K (2012) Effects of self-rated health on sick leave, disability pension, hospital admissions and mortality. A population-based longitudinal study of nearly 15,000 observations among Swedish women and men. BMC Public Health 12:1103

Hensing G, Spak F, Alexanderson K, Allebeck P (1997) Sick-leave among women and the role of psychiatric disorder. Scand J Soc Med 25:185–192

Holmgren K, Dahlin-Ivanoff S, Bjorkelund C, Hensing G (2009) The prevalence of work-related stress, and its association with self-perceived health and sick-leave, in a population of employed Swedish women. BMC Public Health 9:73

Holmgren K, Fjallstrom-Lundgren M, Hensing G (2013) Early identification of work-related stress predicted sickness absence in employed women with musculoskeletal or mental disorders: a prospective, longitudinal study in a primary health care setting. Disabil Rehabil 35:418–426
Jansen GB, Linder J, Ekholm KS, Ekholm J (2011) Differences in symptoms, functioning, and quality of life between women on long-term sick-leave with musculoskeletal pain with and without concomitant depression. J Multidiscip Healthc 4:281–292
Jimenez AL, Alegria M, Pena M, Vera M (1997) Mental health utilization in women with symptoms of depression. Women Health 25:1–21
Joffe H, Kim DR, Foris JM, Baldassano CF, Gyulai L, Hwang CH, Mclaughlin WL, Sachs GS, Thase ME, Harlow BL, Cohen LS (2006) Menstrual dysfunction prior to onset of psychiatric illness is reported more commonly by women with bipolar disorder than by women with unipolar depression and healthy controls. J Clin Psychiatry 67:297–304
Kessler RC, Mcgonagle KA, Zhao S, Nelson CB, Hughes M, Eshleman S, Wittchen HU, Kendler KS (1994) Lifetime and 12-month prevalence of DSM-III-R psychiatric disorders in the United States. Results from the national comorbidity survey. Arch Gen Psychiatry 51:8–19
Lytsy P, Larsson K, Anderzen I (2015) Health in women on long-term sick leave because of pain or mental illness. Int J Rehabil Res 38:27–33
Mackenzie TB, Wilcox K, Baron H (1986) Lifetime prevalence of psychiatric disorders in women with perimenstrual difficulties. J Affect Disord 10:15–19
Mclindon E, Harms L (2011) Listening to mental health workers' experiences: factors influencing their work with women who disclose sexual assault. Int J Ment Health Nurs 20:2–11
Mittendorfer-Rutz E, Harkanen T, Tiihonen J, Haukka J (2014) Association of socio-demographic factors, sick-leave and health care patterns with the risk of being granted a disability pension among psychiatric outpatients with depression. PLoS ONE 9:e99869
NHS Plus, R. C. O. P., Faculty Of Occupational Medicine (2009) Physical and shift work in pregnancy: occupational aspects of management. A national guideline. RCP, London
Nielsen MB, Rugulies R, Hjortkjaer C, Bultmann U, Christensen U (2013) Healing a vulnerable self: exploring return to work for women with mental health problems. Qual Health Res 23:302–312
Nuttman-Shwartz O, Gadot L, Kacen L (2009) Recurrent job loss and mental health among women. Women Health 49:294–309
Olaya-Contreras P, Persson T, Styf J (2010) Comparison between the beck depression Inventory and psychiatric evaluation of distress in patients on long-term sick leave due to chronic musculoskeletal pain. J Multidiscip Health 3:161–167
Smink FR, Van Hoeken D, Hoek HW (2012) Epidemiology of eating disorders: incidence, prevalence and mortality rates. Curr Psychiatry Rep 14:406–414
Spak F, Hensing G, Allebeck P (1998) Sick-leave in women with alcohol dependence or abuse: effects of additional psychiatric disorders. Soc Psychiatry Psychiatr Epidemiol 33:613–619
Stevens B (1969) Impact of community-orientated psychiatry on marriage and fertility of psychotic women. Br Med J 4:22–24
Sydsjo A, Sydsjo G, Alexanderson K (2001) Influence of pregnancy-related diagnoses on sick-leave data in women aged 16–44. J Womens Health Gend Med 10:707–714
Sydsjo A, Sydsjo G, Wijma B, Kjessler B (1998) Changes in sick leave rates and the use of pregnancy-associated social benefits among pregnant Swedish women: an outcomes study. J Womens Health 7:249–260
Tritt K, Schneider H, Bidmon RK, Nickel M, Leiberich P, Joraschky P, Loew TH (2005) Do patients with different psychiatric diagnoses require different strategies for certifying sick leave? First indications from a prospective study. Croat Med J 46:308–314
Wang JL, Lesage A, Schmitz N, Drapeau A (2008) The relationship between work stress and mental disorders in men and women: findings from a population-based study. J Epidemiol Commun Health 62:42–47
Warner LA, Alegria M, Canino G (2012) Childhood maltreatment among hispanic women in the united states: an examination of subgroup differences and impact on psychiatric disorder. Child Maltreatment 17:119–131

World Health Organization (1946) Preamble to the constitution of the World Health Organization. In: International health conference, New York

Zinzow HM, Resnick HS, Mccauley JL, Amstadter AB, Ruggiero KJ, Kilpatrick DG (2012) Prevalence and risk of psychiatric disorders as a function of variant rape histories: results from a national survey of women. Soc Psychiatry Psychiatr Epidemiol 47:893–902

Author Biography

Okan Çalıyurt is working as an academician at the Trakya University School of Medicine Psychiatry Department in Edirne—Turkey. He is the current director of the psychiatry department. He was born in Istanbul, Turkey, in 1967. He graduated from the Trakya University School of Medicine in 1990 and completed the psychiatry residency training 1998. He worked as a postdoctoral fellow in Douglas Hospital Research Centre at Montreal—Canada, in 2001. He is working as an adult psychiatrist in Trakya University Hospital and also as a lecturer in the same university as professor of psychiatry. His main interest areas are circadian rhythms in psychiatry, sleep deprivation therapies in mood disorders and bright light therapy in psychiatry.

Chapter 3
Reputation Indicators of Participating Companies to United Nations Global Compact

Arzu Ozsozgun Caliskan and Emel Esen

3.1 Introduction

Companies are vital components of economic system, and their mission is to meet the needs and expectations of other human groups. Since the firms and the human groups together form the society, there is an interrelationship among corporations, community, and environment; the role of corporations in sustainability attached greater importance. The role has become more complex when it is considered that the largest companies in the world control 25% of global financial value (Gardiner et al. 2003; Jones 2010). In the circumstances, firms' competitiveness is related to their adaptation capacity to new social, environmental, and economic factors (Porter and Kramer 2003). Companies that incorporate and translate society's social values into concrete corporate management practices, and disclose the adopted values in their annual reports and also Web site are seen to have good corporate values intangible assets that could be positively translated in many ways (Esen 2013) such as having competitive advantage in industry, expressing corporate culture, and improving long-term profitability and corporate reputation (Chaudhry and Krishnan 2007; Wagner et al. 2009; Keeler 2002). The stakeholders' expectancy for all information and responsibilities from organizations related to the outputs of their operations while evaluating the organizations' reputation. For this purpose, a corporation that aims to have favorable reputation needs to meet its stakeholders' demands. The increasing demand of all parties expects companies to meet their stakeholders' nonfinancial expectation.

A. Ozsozgun Caliskan (✉) · E. Esen
Faculty of Business Administration, Yildiz Technical University, Istanbul, Turkey
e-mail: ozsozgun@yildiz.edu.tr

E. Esen
e-mail: emeloz@yildiz.edu.tr

K. T. Çalıyurt and R. Said (eds.), *Sustainability and Social Responsibility of Accountability Reporting Systems*, Accounting, Finance, Sustainability, Governance & Fraud: Theory and Application, https://doi.org/10.1007/978-981-10-3212-7_3

Many business organizations commit to CSR, corporate citizenship, and corporate reputation initiatives from the globalization perspective by being an active member of social and environmental initiatives—UNGC. UNGC initiative is a universally accepted set of principles that presented for businesses. The aim behind the principles is encouraging businesses to array their activities and policies with committed values in the areas of human rights, labor, environment, and anti-corruption. The initiatives can encourage organizations to have a solution about global governance concerns by understanding and practicing corporate social responsibility (Baumann-Pauly and Scherer 2013).

The aim of this chapter is to shed light on corporate reputation components of companies in Turkey that are the members of Global Compact initiative. For this purpose, the UNGC, corporate reputation, and component of corporate reputation were defined and examined, and a content analysis will be conducted to determine reputation practices by investigating companies.

3.2 Global Compact Platform

The UN Global Compact initiative is leadership platform that aimed at encouraging business for the establishment, performing, and publishing of responsible and sustainable corporate procedures and implementations (UNGC 2014b). The Global Compact is *a public and private, global and local, as well as voluntary initiative* (Rasche et al. 2013), and aimed to encourage business to work with United Nations. Not only companies, but also NGOs, governments, academic institutions, and other stakeholder groups are the participants of the international voluntary initiative (Runhaar and Lafferty 2009). More than 10,000 participants spread across 145 countries are involved in the Global Compact (UNGC 2014a).

Global Compact seeks to promote companies to be member of this voluntary organization by 10 principles (Whitehouse 2003, 300). The principles are classified into four cornerstones: human rights, labor, environment, and anti-corruption. The Universal Declaration of Human Rights (1948); the Rio Declaration on Environment and Development (1992); the International Labor Organization's Fundamental Principles and Rights at Work (1998); and the UN Convention Against Corruption (2003)[1] are the source of where the principles come from (Williams 2007; Ruggie 2001; Kell and Ruggie 1999).

As a voluntary initiative, the Global Compact relies on public accountability, transparency, and the enlightened self-interest of companies, labor, and civil society in order to pursue its principles (Enquist et al. 2006). Participants of the Global Compact, such as corporations, governments, civil society advocates, and labor organizations join a voluntary coalition to work individually and collectively for

[1]http://www.un.org/en/udhrbook/pdf/udhr_booklet_en_web.pdf.

Table 3.1 UN Global Compact principles

Human rights	
Principle 1	Businesses should support and respect the protection of internationally proclaimed human rights and
Principle 2	make sure that they are not complicit in human rights abuses
Labor	
Principle 3	Businesses should uphold the freedom of association and the effective recognition of the right to collective bargaining
Principle 4	the elimination of all forms of forced and compulsory labor
Principle 5	the effective abolition of child labor; and
Principle 6	the elimination of discrimination in respect of employment and occupation
Environment	
Principle 7	Businesses should support a precautionary approach to environmental challenges
Principle 8	undertake initiatives to promote greater environmental responsibility; and
Principle 9	encourage the development and diffusion of environmentally friendly technologies
Anti-corruption	
Principle 10	Businesses should work against corruption in all its forms, including extortion and bribery

Reference: http://www.unglobalcompact.org/AboutTheGC/TheTenPrinciples/index.html, accessed: July 11th, 2014

international cooperation (Nason and Robert 2008). Therefore, this initiative encourages private sector to participate in United Nations.

The Global Compact is related to human rights, labor, the environment, and anti-corruption, but also it forms platforms for corporations and NGOs to consider subjects related to CSR progress and execution, and through interaction and cooperation (Runhaar and Lafferty 2009). On January 31, 1999, Kofi Annan who is United Nations Secretary invited the private sector to "*initiate a global compact of shared values and principles, which will give a human face to the global market*" (Fritsch 2008). Table 3.1 represents the global compact principles.

United Nations system, businesses (at the heart of the Global Compact), government (set up regulations to facilitate ten principles), and civil society organizations are the core actors of the Global Compact platform (Rasche 2009). The aim behind the principles is encouraging businesses to align their operations and strategies with committed values. The values that involved in the United Nations Global Compact create a mechanism for organizations about corporate social responsibility and sustainable development (Perez-Batres et al. 2011).

3.3 Corporate Reputation and Components of Corporate Reputation

In today's competitive work environment, companies are trying to build favorable relations and meet expectations with all stakeholder groups of them. Corporate reputation reflects the stakeholders' standpoint about the overall awareness regarding both internal and external facets about a corporation.

Providing a single definition for corporate reputation is a major problem in the literature, and corporate reputation usually described in the academic literature as organizational standing, goodwill, esteem, organizational identity, organizational image, brand and prestige (Wartick 2002). Corporate reputation is an emotional capital that reflects the various shareholders' perceptions about organization's past and future actions and intangible asset (Esen 2013).

There are numerous methods and tools to measure corporate reputation; however, there is no consensus about it. Some scholars as Siltaoja (2006) supports that there is no right set of criteria because different evaluators use different concepts. Several scholars have used some methods to measure corporate reputation as we discussed below.

Reputation quotient (RQ) which was devised by Haris Interactive[2] is most common measurement method for corporate reputation (Fombrun and Foss 2001). Emotional appeal, products and services, vision and leadership, workplace environment, financial performance, and social responsibility are drivers of this reputation model. Quality of management, capability to attract and develop talented people, responsive to the community and environment, innovativeness, soundness of financial position, quality of product and service, wise use of corporate assets, global competitive and value as a long-term investment are also other indicators that are used in Fortune's in its annual survey of America's Most Admired Companies[3] (Fryxell and Wang 1994; Caruana and Michael 2010). In this study, among these different measurements both in Turkey and in the World, we will use RQ to compare reputation tool between organizations.

Research Questions

This study was undertaken to shed light on the following research questions: The main research question is about to determine reputation indicators in organizations of the automobile industry in Turkey that are the members of Global Compact platform.

1. Which reputation indicators will appear in these sectors?
2. Which reputation indicators are mostly important when it was compared with other reputation indicators.

---

[2]http://www.theharrispoll.com/reputation-quotient.

[3]http://fortune.com/worlds-most-admired-companies/.

3.4 Method

The aim of this study is to examine the indicators of corporate reputation in companies participating UNGC. For this purpose, this study focuses on organization members of Global Compact in automobile industry. The reputation indicators are analyzed by content analysis and discussed with the reference of RQ (Fombrun and Foss 2001). *Emotional appeal, products and services, vision and leadership, workplace environment, financial performance, and social responsibility* are drivers. RQ, which was created by Fombrun, Gardberg, and Sever (2000), is a valid, reliable measure of corporate reputation.

As it was shown in Table 3.2, there are nine organizations in the sample of our study. Five of them are companies, and four of them are small- and medium-sized organizations in automobile sector in Turkey.

The automotive industry has a crucial role in the manufacturing sector of Turkey. Turkey has a strong production and engineering hub for global automotive value chain. This sector is gaining importance not only in Turkey, but also in global markets. Therefore, the Turkish society has big expectations from this sector. Specifically, sustainable growth and reputation practices are critical mechanisms for all stakeholders. If the leaders of this sector want to protect sustainability and continuity of market demand, they should make changes and new challenges in being sustainable and reputable. But, it is difficult to say that the automotive sector is reputable between 2012 and 2015.

According to the study about corporate reputation of RepMan in 2013, automotive sector has the lowest reputation score when it was compared with the other sectors as banking, retailer, and construction.[4] In RepMan Study, there are seven components of corporate reputation. These are Management Quality, Product and Service Quality, Employee Brand, Financial Soundness, Emotional Commitment, Corporate Social Responsibility and Recognition. If the company has reputation score between 65 and 70, this score is beginning for corporate reputation. If the organization wants to have strong reputation, the score should be at least 70. In a 2011 survey, the score of automotive industry was 59, and in 2012 and in 2013, it was 62. (In the scope of the automotive sector in this study, 20 companies were investigated and analyzed.)[5]

Table 3.2 shows the comparison of organizations about corporate reputation components. The comparison is among organizations in automotive sector from the perspective of measurement on reputation quotient. Reputation indicators are checked according to the information gathered from Web sites of the companies.

---

[4] http://www.repman.com.tr/tr/category/arastirmalar/repman-arastirmalari/.

[5] http://www.repman.com.tr/tr/turkiyenin-2013-itibar-sonuclari/repman-forum-2014_200314/.

Table 3.2 Companies in the automotive sector that have signed UNCG in Turkey

Name	Type	Sector	Participant since
Doğuş Automotive Service and Trade Incorporation	Company	Automotive	2010/03/16
Otokoç Automotive	Company	Automotive	2010/05/11
Mesa Casting Machines Incorporation	SME	Automotive	2010/06/03
Rollmech Automotive	Company	Automotive	2012/01/04
Katmerciler Vehicle Equipment Industry and Trade Incorporation	SME	Automotive	2012/03/12
Martur Sponge and Armchair Facilities Trade Incorporation	Company	Automotive	2012/10/11
Motus Automotive Machinery and Metallurgy Industry and Trade Incorporation	SME	Automotive	2013/03/05
Brisa Bridgestone Sabanci Rubber Industry and Trade Incorporation	Company	Automotive	2013/07/17
Imortas Auto Spare Parts Manufacturing Organization and Trade Incorporation	SME	Automotive	2014/02/05

3.5 Findings

Dogus Automotive is using corporate identity and reputation measurement to provide a basis about corporate communication strategies. This organization prepares corporate social responsibility reports annually since 2009. Also, they have stakeholder map to provide products and services for different stakeholders. They use ethical codes to determine how their employees behave in a right way. About products and services, they have responsibilities in some areas as product safety, occupational health and safety, informing customers, environmental responsibility by brands, customer satisfaction. Fundamental vision of these organizations is to provide innovation service beyond expectations. As it was shown in Table 3.3, all corporate reputation dimensions were carried out by Dogus Automotive.

Otokoç is the first automotive industry of Koç Holding. As other companies in Koç Holding, Otokoç is trying to pursuit all group strategies. They are committed to trust and esteem for all stakeholders as they mention in their vision and values.

Brisa is one of the automotive companies in Turkey that established by the Sabanci Group. The main mission of the company is to provide sustainable growth to the society. For this purpose, they are trying to focus on basic business processes related to corporate reputation: obtaining customer satisfaction through effective and efficient approaches, making innovative practices, maintaining clean and standard-complaint work environments, and lastly becoming an admirable and trustable workplace.

Mesa Machine that was founded in 1979 is one of the producers in providing machined casting, as it was examined in their company Web site, being a member of UNCG, this company seeks to maximize its market recognition not only in Turkey, but also in the global context. Their values are teamwork, being innovative,

Table 3.3 Comparison of organizations about corporate reputation components (Information about companies was gathered from the Web sites of the organizations.)

Organization/ reputation components	Emotional appeal	Products and services	Vision and leadership	Workplace environment	Financial performance	Social responsibility
Doğuş	X	X	X	X	X	X
Otokoç	X	X	X	X	X	X
Mesa		X				X
Rollmech				X		X
Katmerciler		X				X
Martur		X	X		X	X
Motus		X				
Brisa Bridgestone Sabanci	X	X		X	X	X
Imortas		X				X

working efficiently and effectively, achieving customer satisfaction, and being aware of environment and society.

Rollmech was established in 1999 to provide service as co-designer. Their values to being innovative, creating value, supporting safety and social responsibility projects, designing a peaceful and enjoyable workplace environment, creating solutions.

Katmerciler has a vision about to grow with its stakeholders and become a world brand. Their principles are giving importance to customer satisfaction, protecting consumer rights, pursuing technological developments. Their fundamental values are integrity, self-confidence, reliability, transparency, perfect in quality, and coordination.

Martur is the member of group companies supplying components to the automotive industry. They have also fundamental values as transparency, independency, leadership, reliability, sustainability, customer-focused solutions, environmental management, and innovation.

Motus Crankshaft is active in automotive sector since 2013. In the Web site of the company, mission and vision were not stated, but in the definition of about us, company is mentioned as becoming a rule-based company with broad product range and production capacity.

Imortas Incorporation tries to becoming continuously innovative about their products and services; also they have sensitivity to the environment and their stakeholders' expectations. They have also separate environmental policies to protect natural resources.

3.6 Discussion and Results

There is a strong interest from both academicians and business world in reputation, but it is not clearly defined so far. Organizational standing, goodwill, esteem, organizational identity, organizational image, brand, and prestige are the some of the notions that used in the literature to refer reputation. Although there is no consensus about its definition, it is generally accepted that corporate reputation reflects the stakeholders' standpoint about the overall awareness regarding both internal and external facets about a corporation. Corporate reputation is an intangible asset of an organization, and it is expected that all the assets of an organization should create value for its stakeholders. A company that creates more benefit over the long term obtains competitive advantage. In today's business world, if a firm incorporates and translates society's social values into concrete corporate management practices, this consideration create positive effect on corporate reputation.

The aim of this chapter is to shed light on the indicators of corporate reputation in companies participating UNGC. The Global Compact seeks to promote organizations to be member of this voluntary organization by 10 principles that are classified into four cornerstones: human rights, labor, environment, and anti-corruption. The Global Compact is not only a set of 10 norms for CSR (corporate social responsibility) related to human rights, labor, the environment, and anti-corruption, but also it forms platforms for corporations and NGOs to consider subjects related to CSR progress and execution, and through interaction and cooperation (Runhaar and Lafferty 2009). In line with the purpose of this study, the reputation indicators of the members of Global Compact in automobile industry are analyzed by content analysis and discussed with the reference of reputation quotient (RQ). Reputation indicators are checked according to the information gathered from Web sites of the companies (Table 3.3).

There are nine organizations in the sample of our study. Five of them are companies, and four of them are small and medium-sized organizations from automobile sector in Turkey. The results show that there are only two firms in which all corporate reputation dimensions were carried out. Among the drivers of corporate reputation, product and services, and social responsibility are the most accomplished measures of the RQ in automobile sector in Turkey. Workplace environment and financial performance is in the secondary most carried out, and emotional appeal and vision and leadership is in the third most considered dimensions.

Sustainable growth and reputation practices are critical mechanism for all stakeholders. If the leaders of this sector want to protect sustainability and continuity of market demand, they should make changes and new challenges in being sustainable and reputable. But, it is difficult to say that the automotive sector is reputable in last three years. To endeavor to align corporate social responsibility practices with all directions of companies' practices and channelize gradually concentration and resources to social dilemma could result in making profit and increment in corporate reputation. From the point of view, accomplishing social responsibility dimension of corporate reputation could be interpreted as eliminating the negative effects of automobile sector on sustainability. And firms could earn profit by selling their products and services. Although consideration of impact of firms' social and environmental results is important, making profit is still vital for companies since making profit could satisfy current stakeholders needs while sustainability involves future one.

References

Baumann-Pauly D, Scherer AG (2013) The organizational implementation of corporate citizenship: an assessment tool and its application at UNGC participants. J Bus Ethics 117 (1):1–17

Caruana A, Michael TE (2010) How corporate reputation, quality, and value influence online loyalty. J Bus Res 63:1103–1110

Chaudhry K, Krishnan VR (2007) Impact of corporate social responsibility and transformational leadership on brand community an experimental study. Glob Bus Rev 8(2):205–220

Enquist B, Johnson M, Skålén P (2006) Adoption of corporate social responsibility—incorporating a stakeholder perspective. Qual Res Account Manag 3(3):188–207

Esen E (2013) The influence of corporate social responsibility (CSR) activities on building corporate reputation. Adv Sustain Environ Justice 11:133–150

Fombrun C, Foss C (2001) The gauge: Fombrun and Foss on measuring corporate reputation. Gauge Delahaye Medialink's Newsl Worldw Commun Res 14:3

Fombrun CJ, Gardberg N, Sever J (2000) The reputation quotient: a multi-stakeholder measure of corporate reputation. J Brand Manag 7(4):241–255

Fritsch S (2008) The UN Global Compact and the global governance of corporate social responsibility: complex multilateralism for a more human globalisation? Glob Soc 22(1):1–26

Fryxell G, Wang J (1994) The fortune corporate 'reputation' index: reputation for what. J Manag 20(1):1–14

Gardiner L, Rubbens C, Bonfiglioli E (2003) Research: big business big responsibilities. Corp Gov 3(3):67–77

Jones MJ (2010) Accounting for the environment: towards a theoretical perspective for environmental accounting and reporting. Account Forum 34(2):123–138

Keeler D (2002) Spread the love. Glob Finance 16(5):20–25

Kell G, Ruggie JG (1999) Global markets and social legitimacy: the case of the 'global compact'. Transnatl Corporations 8(3):101–120

Nason RW (2008) Structuring the global impact, the impact of the United Nations Global Compact, 418–425

Perez-Batres LA, Miller VV, Pisani MJ (2011) Institutionalizing sustainability: an empirical study of corporate registration and commitment to the United Nations Global Compact guidelines. J Clean Prod 19:843–851

Porter ME, Kramer MR (2003) Corporate philanthropy: taking the high ground. Found Strategy Gr 13

Rasche A (2009) A necessary supplement—what the United Nations Global Compact is and is not. http://dx.doi.org/10.1177/0007650309332378

Rasche A, Waddock S, Mcintosh M (2013) The United Nations Global Compact retrospect and prospect. Bus Soc 52(1):6–30

Repman İtibar Araştırmaları. http://www.repman.com.tr/tr/category/arastirmalar/repman-arastirmalari/, 30 Aug 2015

Reputation Quotient Ratings. http://www.theharrispoll.com/reputation-quotient, 30 Aug 2015

Ruggie JG (2001) Global-governance. net: the global compact as learning network. Glob Gov 7:371–378
Runhaar H, Lafferty H (2009) Governing corporate social responsibility: an assessment of the contribution of the UN Global Compact to CSR strategies in the telecommunications industry. J Bus Eth 84(4):479–495
Siltaoja ME (2006) Value priorities as combining core factors between CSR and reputation—a qualitative study. J Bus Eth 68(1):91–111
Türkiye'deki Sektörlerin ve Şirketlerin İtibar Yönetimi Değerlendirmesi. http://www.repman.com.tr/tr/turkiyenin-2013-itibar-sonuclari/repman-forum-2014_200314/, 13 Aug 2014
UNGC (2014a) United Nations Global Compact, UN Global Compact. http://www.unglobalcompact.org/Docs/News_Events/8.1/GC_Brochure_FINAL.Pdf, 21 July 2014
UNGC (2014b) How to Participate UN Global Compact. http://www.unglobalcompact.org/Howtoparticipate/Index.Html, 21 July 2014
Universal Decleration of Human Rights. http://www.un.org/en/udhrbook/pdf/udhr_booklet_en_web.pdf, 30 Aug 2015
Wagner T, Lutz RJ, Weitz BA (2009) Corporate hypocrisy: overcoming the threat of inconsistent corporate social responsibility perceptions. J Mark 73(6):77–91
Wartick SL (2002) Measuring corporate reputation: definition and data. Bus Soc 41(4):371–392
Whitehouse L (2003) Corporate social responsibility, corporate citizenship and the global compact a new approach to regulating corporate social power? Glob Soc Policy 3(3):299–318
Williams OF (2007) The UN Global Compact: the challenge and the promise. Bus Eth Q 14 (4):755–774
World's Most Admired Companies. http://fortune.com/worlds-most-admired-companies/, 30 Aug 2015

Author Biographies

Arzu Özsözgün Çalişkan is an Associate Professor in Accounting and Finance area of Business Administration Department of Faculty of Economics and Administrative Sciences at Yildiz Technical University, Istanbul, Turkey. She completed her master's degree in Business Administration from Yildiz Technical University. She earned her Ph.D. in Accounting and Finance at Marmara University, Turkey. Her research interests include financial and managerial accounting, corporate social responsibility, sustainability management, and accounting.

Emel Esen is an Associate Professor and completed her master's degree in Human Resources Management of Business Administration from Yildiz Technical University. She earned her Ph.D. in Organizational Behavior at Marmara University, Turkey. Her research interests include organizational behavior, human resources management, business ethics, and corporate reputation.

Chapter 4
Are Sustainability Disclosures Fraudulent?

Graham Gal

4.1 Introduction

In 1987, the World Commission on Environment and Development produced a report that provided what has become an accepted definition of sustainability. This report became known as The Brundtland Report (World Commission on Environment and Development 1987) and defined sustainability as providing for the current generation without sacrificing the needs of future generations. This is a difficult definition to deal with for a number of reasons, not the least of which is that the needs of future generations are very hard to determine. Additionally, it is not clear how far in the future one should project a generation's needs. In emerging market countries, the government can still play a major role in economic performance, but as countries become more developed, firms will play an increasing if not a major role in sustainable development and therefore their social responsible activities are critical (Akisik and Gal 2011). As a result, corporate social responsibility (CSR) has become the focus of the debate on sustainability in most developed and developing economies. While corporations must play a major role in producing socially responsible outcomes, other stakeholders will also play important roles. For instance, government officials must verify that corporations adhere to established regulations, customers need to look for socially responsible products when making their purchasing decision, and creditors must take CSR initiatives into consideration when extending their financial support.

There is evidence that each of these stakeholder groups will use different types of information in making decisions concerning whether or not to view a firm as socially responsible. With the passage of the Dodd–Frank legislation (United States Congress 2010) the US regulators must consider the use of conflict minerals in

G. Gal (✉)
Isenberg School of Management, University of Massachusetts,
Amherst, MA, USA
e-mail: gfgal@isenberg.umass.edu

K. T. Çalıyurt and R. Said (eds.), *Sustainability and Social Responsibility of Accountability Reporting Systems*, Accounting, Finance, Sustainability, Governance & Fraud: Theory and Application, https://doi.org/10.1007/978-981-10-3212-7_4

firm's supply chains. The Securities and Exchange Commission (SEC) was charged with establishing rules to assist firms in making this determination (Securities and Exchange Commission 2012); however, even the Commerce Department agreed that this is a particularly daunting task for firms (Chasan and Maxwell 2014a, b). For customers, firms will provide information about their production processes as this stakeholder group has become more concerned that companies incorporate sustainable and socially responsible processes in the production of their products (Homburg et al. 2005; Mohr et al. 2001). Investors are increasingly interested in the possibility that a firm will have an environmental issue which could impact their ability to provide a suitable return or repay their debt (Godfrey et al. 2009; Heyes 1996; Hockerts and Moir 2004), so firms must be prepared to disclose any environmental issues that could arise. Thus, it is clear that stakeholder groups look for different CSR information in evaluating the social responsible performance of firms. This also implies that firms can use different approaches to reach these stakeholders, and each has different levels of veracity.

Firms have increasingly used diverse channels to disclose information about their socially responsible activities to different stakeholder groups. For disclosures to regulators, the format is usually quite restricted, and firms have received some specific guidance on the method, the format, and the content of these communications (Securities and Exchange Commission 2010, 2012). However, in making these disclosures to other groups there are a multitude of channels and formats available. One of the more formal avenues of disclosure is the reports that use the Global Reporting Initiative (GRI) format (Global Reporting Initiative 2006, 2011). There is evidence that these disclosures can have an impact on financial performance (Akisik and Gal 2014; Cochran and Wood 1984; Dhaliwal et al. 2012). Therefore, firms have an incentive to provide a favorable information in GRI reports. In fact, there is evidence that firms make certain disclosures to counteract and to preempt any possible adverse publicity (Perks et al. 2013; Vanhamme and Grobben 2009). There is also evidence that not all the information disclosed is accurate (Time 2010). This points out two problems with CSR disclosures; there is not any universally agreed upon report or disclosure channel, and there is not any agreed upon method to review the information contained in many CSR disclosures (Adams and Narayanan 2007; O'Dwyer 2011). However, if managers and owners are producing information with the intent of inducing stakeholders to provide support to their firm and the information may have material errors, then the first two criteria for considering these disclosures to be fraudulent seem to be met. It is the purpose of this paper to expand on issues that arise when considering whether or not CSR disclosures are fraudulent, what the implications for these types of disclosures are, and whether there are any unintended consequences of this concern over social responsibility.

4.2 What Does a Socially Responsible Firm Look like?

For a disclosure to be considered materially misstated, there must be a measure of what the true value would look like. Specifically, for a fraud to have taken place two initial conditions must exist. First, the entity making the disclosure must know a true value, and second, the information provided must be materially different from this value. Many pieces of information are used by stakeholders to determine that a firm is financially healthy. Similarly, many pieces of information are used to determine that firm is socially responsible. Different stakeholder groups put different weights on the available information in making a conclusion that for them this is a socially responsible firm. So a few questions remain, what does a socially responsible firm look like, how far away from a perfectly responsible firm is this firm, and perhaps more importantly, can we tell the difference.

In order to tell the difference between a socially responsible firm and one that is not, a stakeholder must have an idea of what exactly makes a firm perfectly or reasonably responsible. This could entail values for specific attributes: carbon emissions below a certain threshold. Or, it could include information about certain practices: this firm provides excellent workplace training. The problem then is assessing how a firm looks on relevant measures and then somehow measuring its distance from the ideal. In this case, and many others, the problem is one of placing the firm on a continuum and then measuring semantic distance.[1] This decision is similar to other measurement issues confronted by management and other stakeholders.

For instance, Fig. 4.1 looks at possible criteria a stakeholder might consider in evaluating a company. On each criteria, firm A and firm B have different subjective values, so the difference is really a semantic difference. Without objective criteria for "Good Hiring" practices, the placement of the value along the continuum is the result of a stakeholder or stakeholder group's perceptions. When a person (or assurance provider) evaluates hiring practices their placement of the firm along the continuum is based on their perception of the semantic distance from either the end point "Good" or "Poor." Further, the distance between companies A and B on each dimension may be considered as material by one evaluator and immaterial by another; i.e., some evaluator may consider point A on the hiring dimension as close enough to the "Good" end to evaluate the firm as having quality hiring practices. Additionally, one evaluator may consider firms A and B to essentially have the same hiring practices while a different evaluator may consider firm A's practices to be materially better than firm B. To form an overall evaluation, each dimension will contribute some weight in the determination of whether a firm is responsible. An evaluator that belongs to a particular stakeholder group may weight hiring as critically important and therefore rate firm B as being further away from "Perfect"

[1] An objective distance would be agreed upon measureable difference, while a semantic distance would be idiosyncratic, "I feel that this firm does a good (or bad) job of using locally sourced produce."

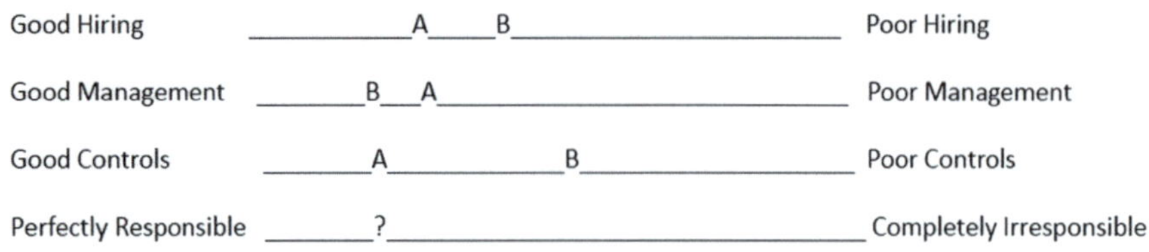

Fig. 4.1 Sustainability criteria

endpoint, while a supplier might consider the quality of management as more relevant and consider B to be much closer to "Perfect" than A. Even if there were only a few criteria to consider when making a determination about a firm's socially responsible or sustainable practices, then the consideration of an overall sustainability or social responsible rating would still be hard; however, there are many criteria that could be considered in making an overall evaluation of a firm.

In Fig. 4.2, the criteria from the (GRI 2011) are listed. Only a few of them might be considered as attributes that could be assigned values, while most are processes.

TABLE 1: CATEGORIES AND ASPECTS IN THE GUIDELINES

Category	Economic		Environmental	
Aspects[III]	• Economic Performance • Market Presence • Indirect Economic Impacts • Procurement Practices		• Materials • Energy • Water • Biodiversity • Emissions • Effluents and Waste • Products and Services • Compliance • Transport • Overall • Supplier Environmental Assessment • Environmental Grievance Mechanisms	
Category	**Social**			
Sub-Categories	**Labor Practices and Decent Work**	**Human Rights**	**Society**	**Product Responsibility**
Aspects[III]	• Employment • Labor/Management Relations • Occupational Health and Safety • Training and Education • Diversity and Equal Opportunity • Equal Remuneration for Women and Men • Supplier Assessment for Labor Practices • Labor Practices Grievance Mechanisms	• Investment • Non-discrimination • Freedom of Association and Collective Bargaining • Child Labor • Forced or Compulsory Labor • Security Practices • Indigenous Rights • Assessment • Supplier Human Rights Assessment • Human Rights Grievance Mechanisms	• Local Communities • Anti-corruption • Public Policy • Anti-competitive Behavior • Compliance • Supplier Assessment for Impacts on Society • Grievance Mechanisms for Impacts on Society	• Customer Health and Safety • Product and Service Labeling • Marketing Communications • Customer Privacy • Compliance

Fig. 4.2 GRI criteria

For instance, the attribute "human rights investment" might have a single dollar amount for its value, while for the "society anti-corruption" an evaluation might entail assurance that has a process in place to review areas of the company susceptible to offering bribes. The Dodd–Frank legislation (United States Congress, 2010) requires companies to ensure that they do not have conflict minerals in their product and to ensure they follow socially responsible practices with respect to their supply chain. Because the review of a firm's entire supply chain can be quite difficult, SEC (2012) recommends that companies follow OECD guidelines with respect to conducting their reviews with due diligence (OECD 2013). If a single reporting framework is used, the problem of having multiple reports is alleviated (Adams and Narayanan 2007; Fornaro 2011; Securities and Exchange Commission 2010); however, the weighting of each attribute (Clarkson 1995) still depends on different stakeholders (or groups) perceptions of what exactly is important and coming to a sustainability measure.

4.3 What Measures of Social Responsibility Are Important?

Each group of stakeholders has a different set of information they use to conclude whether or not to support the firm. Some of this information does not come directly from formal reports, but from informal information channels. For instance, Madden et al. (2012) found that consumers making purchase decisions look at the characteristics of one of the firm's products and project these characteristics to the firm's other products. While Maignan and Ferrell (2001) and others (Öberseder et al. 2013) have found that being perceived as a good corporate citizen can be an important marketing tool. For creditors, there is a concern that the firm will be held responsible for an environmental problem which would impact the firm's ability to repay their debts (Heyes 1996). Therefore, many banks use CSR reports with environmental data when considering loan rates (Thompson and Cowton 2004). For employees, there is evidence they use CSR information when considering prospective employers (Backhous et al. 2002) and that employer social responsibility practices increase the satisfaction of employees (Bauman and Skitka 2012; Riordan et al. 1997; Turban and Greening 1996). Finally, there is also evidence of a "halo" effect as quality financial statements have been shown to impact stakeholders' perceptions of the quality of the overall CSR report (Akisik and Gal 2014). Given the importance that various stakeholders place on the firm's social responsibility and sustainability information, there is a question of what values should be considered most important and whether firms should produce a single comprehensive report.

The disclosure of CSR and sustainability information does change the perception that stakeholders have of a corporation. However, they may not use the information contained in a CSR report directly in making a conclusion about the firm. There is evidence that stakeholders consider the CSR reports, particularly in GRI format, too complicated and therefore use reviews of these reports rather than the information in the report (Akisik and Gal 2014). With evidence that different stakeholder groups use different information in making their evaluation, it raises the question of which information is most important. Is it the credibility attached to the company simply as a result of the release of CSR information (Herzig and Schaltegger 2006)? Is it the review of the reports that have accepted coverage of CSR attributes (Akisik and Gal 2014)? Or is it the release of information through other channels such as marketing communications (Madden et al. 2012) or government disclosures (Khanna and Quimio 1998)? If each of these methods of disclosure impact different stakeholders' perceptions of the firm, then it is important to consider how values for each of these types of disclosure are derived.

Firms have started to produce CSR information because it makes them appear to be a legitimate member of society (Hooghiemstra 2000).[2] So perhaps they make efforts to produce this non-financial information simply to appear as a good citizen. Information from GRI indicates that not all firms seek to have a review of their CSR reports prepared under their guidelines. This implies that firms do recognize the importance of simply producing a CSR report. There are also firms which do take the additional step to have their reports reviewed, but reviews of GRI reports are based on the degree of topics covered and not on the quality of the information. Thus, there are incentives to firms to simply make CSR information available to stakeholders. While there is also evidence that stakeholders use information which is not strictly released by a firm, it is clear that information released by a firm is used by stakeholders. This research seems to satisfy the first two conditions for a fraud to have occurred: Is there evidence that the firm considers CSR to have a material impact on stakeholders' decisions? Or in other words, firms do intend that stakeholders use this information for making a financially relevant decision (Silverstone and Sheetz 2007).[3] If firms do intend for stakeholders to use this information, then the next question is whether the irregularities in the information disclosed by corporations can be measured and attributed to intentional actions of the firm. The next section will look at this issue.

4.4 How Can We Measure Irregularities in These Communications?

For financial information, we have a standard to judge whether the information is not correct. The concept of materiality (Financial Accounting Standards Board 2008) applies to the overall accuracy of the statement. Any difference or omission

---

[2]Initiating a process of communicating CSR information may backfire if the firm stops producing this information or if the release is temporally proximate to some irresponsible event (Morsing et al. 2008).

[3]Even if CSR information is not quantitatively material if it can be shown to be used it may be qualitatively material (Securities Exchange Commission 1999).

in a financial statement that would cause a user to change their decision or perception would be considered material. Given that CSR information does impact stakeholder decisions about whether to loan funds, to buy products, or to seek employment, it is clear that the information is relevant. In addition, there seems to be evidence that certain CSR information is not completely accurate (Time 2010). However, there is little evidence to establish the size of the difference that would cause stakeholders to change their decisions.

There is evidence that certain information classified as CSR or non-financial does have financial relevancy, and that stakeholders might find this information relevant in making decisions. For instance, BP settled the claims in the Deepwater Horizon oil spill for $18.7 billion. From the available information, it is clear that BP and Haliburton could have taken steps to either eliminate or alleviate some of the impact of this spill and mitigate both the financial and the environmental impacts. At the minimum, it seems that it would have been appropriate for these firms to disclose the cost savings that resulted from not using methods that might have mitigated the impact of the spill. Certainly this information would be hard to disclose in traditional financial statements. However, BP has produced sustainability reports using the GRI framework for a number of years and they were reviewed by external parties (2007 report had an A+ rating). Their A+ rating indicates a high level of coverage of the GRI categories. So the question can be raised by all stakeholders: Could not the fact that steps were not taken to protect the financial health of the firm and the environmental health of the Gulf of Mexico be considered a material? Would stakeholders have made different decisions or induced BP to take different decisions had they known this information? It probably can be argued that the answers to these questions are yes; shareholders and other stakeholders would have considered this information in their decisions and therefore it was material information and not disclosed. This satisfies conditions for a fraudulent disclosure; it is material, they intended people to rely on reports that had material information omitted; there were material omissions of fact, and there were damages. While this situation seems to be quite obvious, for other situations the determination of whether a CSR disclosure has irregularities is not as straightforward.

In addition to GRI reports, such as the one filed by BP, firms use other methods to communicate their social responsibility of sustainability intentions. Two important methods used to influence consumers' perceptions of a firm are through product labels and various types of commercials.

Figure 4.3 shows two products that use the term "Natural" on their label. The purpose of this labeling is to induce consumers to buy these products. Research has shown that information provided on one of a firm's products can induce consumers to attach this attribute to other products from the firm (Madden et al. 2012). This research indicates that not only might this labeling induce consumers to buy this product, but consumers might consider the firms other products as having the same quality. A problem with this labeling is that under US consumer protection statutes there is not an accepted definition of the word "natural," and therefore, a company cannot be held responsible for using this and other similar terms (Federal Trade

Fig. 4.3 Product information

Commission n.d.; Perks et al. 2013). Thus, while there is an intention to have consumers rely on this information in making their purchase decisions, there is no objective method to determine that the term was materially false, and certainly no way to determine damages. Other actions by firms that could probably be considered materially false with respect to the CSR practices are even harder to evaluate.

In some industries, it is the collective actions of all firms that produce non-sustainable practices. One example is the fishing industry. Each firm can use sustainable practices, but the combination of activities for all the firms in the industry can produce a non-sustainable result worldwide (Sala 2014). This result can even occur if countries take certain actions to require firms under their control to take steps they consider sustainable in conflict with perceptions of what other countries consider appropriate. In the fishing industry, this is particularly apparent as Japan has a different view of appropriate fishing practices than that of the USA. While overfishing certainly can be considered as a non-sustainable business practice, there are other actions taken by firms which would also probably not be socially responsible.

Using the categories from the GRI framework, there are other examples of firms' actions or in-actions that would make stakeholders question a firm's CSR. For instance, would stakeholders consider a firm that takes kickbacks from firms that rely on their testing procedures or falsifies background checks to be appropriate (Carreyrou and McGinty 2014; Fitzgerald 2105)? If it were not possible to rely on the results of medical tests, this certainly has implications that are not strictly financial, but would significantly impact other stakeholders. Another issue that has become increasingly important for all stakeholders is the security of firm's information system (Banjo and Yadron 2014). If a firm has not taken all appropriate steps to secure their corporate data, this can lead to loss of trade secrets and consumer information. One of the attributes for CSR communications under the GRI framework is security. While security of consumer information might be included in this category, firms are quite reluctant to disclose information about their information security practices or any information about the information security initiatives at their firm. This means that stakeholders are only informed of the inadequate measures as indicated by a security breach at the firm.

This section has looked at various CSR issues that stakeholders probably would consider to be material; i.e., if they had the information, they would have changed their decisions regarding the firm. There are many situations in which omission of information leads to a material misstatement of information about the firm. So in many cases, there is substantial evidence that there is a basis for a decision that these actions were intentionally misleading: a condition for the action to be considered fraudulent. In the next section, the final part of determining a fraud, damages, will be examined.

4.5 Can We Measure Damages?

The final component of determining whether a fraud has occurred is to determine damages. Without damages there cannot be any compensation to the party that presumably relied on a material misstatement or omission. However, in CSR or sustainability misstatements that are material this is the most problematic factor. For instance, for the Deepwater Horizon oil spill there is an $18.7 billion dollar fine levied against BP. These funds are going to the people whose property was damaged or whose income was disrupted due to the spill. However, it is not clear that all other stakeholders have been compensated (Kent 2015). Shareholders obtained returns that might be higher than the returns had BP taken all steps necessary, and incurred the costs, to avoid the spill. So their reduced returns in the future, due to the fine, may actually not completely offset the higher returns of the past (Clarkson 1995). For debtors, the ability of BP to repay them may not be impaired, but there is evidence that environmental risks usually result in higher loan rates (Heyes 1996), and it is not clear that creditors had the information to adjust the rates. For other omissions or misstatements, the damages are even harder to determine.

For the non-sustainable actions taken by a collection of firms in an industry, the damages might be hard to apportion. In the USA, the impact of pollution from coal-fired power plants has been addressed at the national level, but the damages to individuals is hard to measure and may not be centered on the states where the plants are actually located (Harder and Kendall 2015). Attempts to mitigate the damages from this industry are met with challenges due to the impact regulations will have on certain states and industries that may have to absorb damages not equal to the actions of firms in their jurisdiction (Miller and Smith 2015). Measuring and collecting damages are difficult within single country, but when the actions are felt across international borders the process of enforcement is made almost impossible (Spegele 2015). In these first two cases, there are some actual damages which while difficult conceptually can be measured. However, in other cases damages may not even be agreed upon, let alone calculable.

There is evidence that consumers do make decisions about products based on the types, CSR and sustainability communications. Further, they tend to follow opinion leaders in making certain purchase decisions (Brown and Dacin 1997; Chan and Misra 1990; Homburg et al. 2005). Therefore, the inappropriate use of terms like “Natural” can lead to purchasing behaviors that may not be made if accurate information was delivered. Even if it can be concluded that firms use inaccurate terms meant to induce purchase of a product, determining damages is difficult. An examination of the Federal Trade Commission’s cases does not reveal any actions in these situations (Federal Trade Commission).

By any measure, the number of reported cyberattacks is increasing. When a data breach is reported, firms usually are required to provide some sort of support to individuals whose information is acquired. While this can mitigate the damage to consumers in terms of identity theft and provide support for possible attempts to use their personal information in the future, other stakeholders might have less obvious damages. Providing support for individuals that had their personal data taken deals solely with damages to consumers, but there is evidence that poor information security can result in damages to other stakeholders. If a data breach is related to intellectual property, then the impact is much greater as this information may reduce a firm’s competitive advantage. This loss of competitive advantage could impact both shareholders and employees (Cilluffo and Cardash 2015), and in this situation damages is difficult to determine.

These various actions can impact CSR and sustainability performance of a firm. While there are different stakeholders that could claim to have been damaged in each of these situations, there is a difficulty in making precise calculations. This is certainly a requirement to make a determination that a fraud has occurred. There is a question though that if the calculations of damages are difficult should this alleviate firms from the requirement to disclose information relevant for stakeholders? Would these disclosures allow for stakeholders to make a determination that one company has a better CSR or sustainability record? Finally, if this information is relevant in decision making for stakeholder groups should this information be reviewed in much the same way that financial information is reviewed? A final issue that has become relevant in this discussion concerns unintended consequences of the importance of CSR and sustainability disclosures.

4.6 Are There Unintended Consequences of Stakeholders Interest in CSR Information?

There is certainly ample evidence that firms recognize the importance different stakeholders place on CSR and sustainability information (Lin and Chasan 2015). However, there is also evidence that these requirements are creating unintended consequences. One example is the impact of the requirement of the Dodd–Frank Act to produce information on conflict minerals (United States Congress 2010) as firms have run up extensive costs to investigate their supply chains (Chasan and Maxwell 2014a, b). This cost may be one reason that firms have gone to court to eliminate the requirement to disclose the minerals used in their production processes (Chasan 2015). Other examples of some consequences include the manipulations and misreporting of the trading of carbon credits (Henning 2015), and labeling products such as salt as being "GMO" free (Brat 2015). Finally, there is some evidence that firms are buying finished goods from certain suppliers so they can claim that they have no knowledge of the production process. This gives them a measure of plausible deniability in their use of processes that are not sustainable or socially responsible; instead, there is a possibility that some unknown supplier used non-sustainable processes. Stakeholders' interest in the disclosure requirements may be inducing firms to move part of their operations to locations that do not have the same regulations and disclosure mandates.

4.7 Conclusions

Stakeholders are concerned with the social responsibility and sustainability practices of both firms and governments. As economies become more developed, the practices of firms become paramount as governments play a greater role in developing and enforcing regulations. If a firm recognizes that producing favorable CSR and sustainability information can enhance different stakeholders perceptions about the firm and its products, then they have an incentive to produce this information. If their actual practices match the information contained in these disclosures, then stakeholders can take appropriate decisions related to their support of the firm. However, there is evidence that in some cases the information disclosed (or omitted) is materially different from their actual activities. These two conditions providing information that is materially different from the firm's actual CSR and sustainability actions combined with an intent to have stakeholders use this information in making decisions that are favorable to the firm meet conditions for a conclusion that the firm's actions are fraudulent. However, there is also a requirement that damages be determined for an action to be considered fraudulent. This is perhaps the most problematic as in most situations the calculation and appropriation of damages to specific stakeholders is extremely difficult. Instead, regulators impose fines which, while meant to punish firms, clearly do not find their way to the parties that relied on the material misstatement or omission. While there is concern by various stakeholders that firms use responsible and sustainable practices, there are problems with agreeing what practices are most important. Additionally, stakeholders need to have knowledge of sustainable and responsible practices that are not necessarily restricted to those within certain borders. For stakeholders to provide support to those firms whose practices they consider appropriate, CSR information must be readily available and as accurate as possible. Until this happens, firms have an incentive to disclose information that is most advantageous to their success.

References

Adams C, Narayanan V (2007) Standardizing sustainability reporting. In: Unerman J, Bebbington J, O'Dwyer B (eds) Sustainbility accounting and accountability. Routledge, London, pp 70–85

Akisik O, Gal G (2011) Sustainability in business, corporate social responsibility and accounting standards: an empirical study. Int J Account Informat Manag 19(3):304–324

Akisik O, Gal G (2014, December). Financial performance and reviews of corporate social responsibility reports. J Manag Control 25(3–4):259–288

Backhous KB, Stone BA, Heiner K (2002) Exploring the relationship between corporate social performance and employer attractiveness. Bus Soc 41(3):292–318

Banjo S, Yadron D (2014, September 8). Home depot confirms data breach. Wall Street J

Bauman CW, Skitka LJ (2012) Corporate social responsibility as a source of employee satisfaction. Res Organ Perform 1–24

Brat I (2015, August 21) Food Goes 'GMO Free' with same ingredients. Wall Street J B1

Brown TJ, Dacin PA (1997) The company and the product: corporate associations and consumer product responses. J Market 61(1):68–84

Carreyrou J, McGinty T (2014, September 8) A fast-growing medical lab tests anti-kickback law. Wall Street J

Chan KK, Misra S (1990) Characteristics of the opinion leader: a new dimension. J Advert 19 (3):53–60

Chasan E (2015, August 18) Court decision could affect conflict minerals audits. Wall Street J

Chasan E, Maxwell M (2014a, September 16) Supplier maze. Wall Street J

Chasan E, Maxwell M. (2014b, September 16) The big number. Wall Street J

Cilluffo FJ, Cardash S (2015, August 17) Economic espionage: a case for why the U.S. needs to push back. Wall Street J

Clarkson MB (1995) A stakeholder framework for analyzing and evaluating corporate social performance. Acad Manag Rev 20(1):92–117

Cochran PL, Wood RA (1984) Corporate social responsibility and financial performance. Acad Manag J 27(1):42–56

Dhaliwal DS, Radhakrishnan S, Tsang A, Y Y (2012) Nonfinancial disclosure and analyst forecast accuracy: international evidence on corporate social responsibility disclosure. Account Rev 87 (3):723–759

Federal Trade Commission (n.d.) Cases and proceedings. http://www.ftc.gov/enforcement/cases-proceedings. Accessed 5 May 2014

Financial Accounting Standards Board (2008) Statement of financial accounting concepts no. 2 qualitative characteristics of accounting information. Financial Accounting Foundation, Norwalk, CT USA

Fitzgerald P (2105, August 21). U.S. settles fraud case with background screener altegrity. Wall Street J B3

Fornaro JM (2011) SEC Guidance on disclosure related to climate change. J Account 211(1):42–47

Global Reporting Initiative (2006) Sustainability reporting guidelines. Global Reporting Initiative, Amsterdam

Global Reporting Initiative (2011) Sustainability reporting guidelines version 3.1. Global Reporting Initiative, Amsterdam, The Netherlands

Godfrey PC, Merrill CB, Hansen JM (2009) The relationship between corporate social responsibility and shareholder value: an empirical test of the risk management hypothesis. Strag Manag J 30(4):425–445

Harder A, Kendall B (2015, Aug 9) Industry, states set to fight EPA greenhouse gas rules. Wall Street J

Henning E (2015, Aug 13) Deutsche bank employees charged in emissions trading case. Wall Street J

Herzig C, Schaltegger S (2006) Corporate sustainability reporting: an overview. In: Bennett M, Burritt R, Schaltegger S (eds.), Sustainability accounting and reporting (pp. 301–324). Dordrecht, London

Heyes AG (1996) Lender penalty for environmental damage and the equilibrium cost of capital. Economica 63(250):311–323

Hockerts K, Moir L (2004) Communicating corporate responsibility to investors: the changing role of the investor relations function. J Bus Ethics 52(1):85–98

Homburg C, Koschate N, Hoyer WD (2005) Do satisfied customers really pay more? A study of the relationship between customer satisfaction and willingness to pay. J Market 69:84–96

Hooghiemstra R (2000) Corporate communication and impression management—new perspectives why companies engage in corporate social reporting. J Bus Ethics 27(1/2):55–68

Kent S (2015, July 28) BP swings to second-quarter loss on lower oil price, deepwater horizon deal. Wall Street J

Khanna M, Quimio WR (1998) Toxics release information: a policy tool for environmental protection. J Environ Econom Manag 36(3):243–266

Lin K, Chasan E (2015, August 5) In conflict minerals, ethical investors gain ability to rank companies. Wall Street J

Madden TJ, Roth MS, Dillon WR (2012) Global product quality and corporate social responsibility perceptions: a cross-national study of halo effects. J Int Market 20(1):42–57

Maignan I, Ferrell OC (2001) Corporate citizenship as a marketing instrument—concepts, evidence and research directions. Eur J Mark 35(3/4):457–484

Miller JW, Smith R (2015, Aug 3) Impact of EPA's emissions rule on industry to vary. Wall Street J

Mohr LA, Webb DJ, Harris KE (2001) Do consumers expect companies to be socially responsible? The impact of corporate social responsibility on buying behavior. J Consumer Affairs 35(1):45–72

Morsing M, Schults M, Nielsen KU (2008) The "Catch 22" of communicating CSR: findings from a Danish study. J Market Commun 14(2):97–111

O'Dwyer B (2011) The case of sustainability assurance: constructing a new assurance service. Contemp Account Res 28(4):1230–1266

OECD (2013) OECD duc dilligence guidance for responsible supply chains of minerals from conflict-affected and high-risk areas, 2nd edn. OECD Publishing, Paris

Öberseder M, Schlegelmilch BB, Murphy PE (2013) CSR practices and consumer perceptions. J Bus Res 66:1839–1851

Perks KJ, Farache F, Shukla P, Berry A (2013) Communicating responsibility-practicing irresponsibility in CSR advertisements. J Bus Res 66(10):1881–1888

Riordan CM, Gatewood RD, Bill JB (1997) Corporate image: employee reactions and implications for managing corporate social performance. J Bus Ethics 16:401–412

Sala E (2014, July 7) On the future of the oceans. Wall Street J

Securities and Exchange Commission (2010) Commission guidance regarding disclosure related to climate change; final rule 17 CFR parts 211, 231, 241. Securities and Exchange Commission, Washington, DC

Securities and Exchange Commission (2012) 17 CFR Parts 240 and 249b RIN 3235-AK84 Conflict Minerals. US Government Printing Office, Washington, DC

Securities Exchange Commission (1999) Staff accounting bulletin no. 99. United States Government, Washington, D.C

Silverstone H, Sheetz M (2007) Forensic accounting and fraud investigation for non-experts, 2nd edn. Wiley, Hoboken, NJ

Spegele B (2015, July 20) China war on pollution benefits from economic slowdown. Wall Street J

Thompson P, Cowton C (2004) Bringing the Environment into Bank Lending Implications for Environmental Lending. British Account Rev 36:197–218

Time (2010, Nov 8) The world. Time, 19

Turban DB, Greening DW (1996) Corporate social performance and organizational attractiveness to prospective employees. Acad Manag J 40(3):658–672

United States Congress (2010) Dodd-Frank wall street reform and consumer protection act. U.S. Government Printing Office, Washington, DC

Vanhamme J, Grobben B (2009) Too good to be true! The effectiveness of csr history in countering negative publicity. J Business Ethics 85(2):273–283

World Commission on Environment and Development (1987) Our common future. Oxford University Press, Oxford

Author Biography

Graham Gal is an associate professor of accounting at the Isenberg School of Management at the University of Massachusetts in Amherst, Massachusetts. The department of accounting is ranked #1 in the world for behavioral audit research and #4 in accounting information systems research. He conducts his research in the areas of information security, corporate social responsibility, and business ontologies. His recent paper entitled SECURQUAL: An Instrument for Evaluating the Effectiveness of Information Security Programs is being reviewed by the AICPA's task force on development of cybersecurity assurance standards. His work on ontologies includes a forthcoming monograph for the American Accounting Association entitled The REA Ontology. He is currently a council member of the American Accounting Association and is on the editorial board for the Journal of Information Systems.

Chapter 5
Complexity of Sustainable and Resilient Building Design and Urban Development

Shahin Vassigh

5.1 Introduction

Recent scientific research has established that climate change is primarily due to human activities that produce heat-trapping gas emissions. These emissions are mostly a result of burning fossil fuels, changing land use, deforestation, and other activities. Research also shows that among all human activities contributing to climate change, the construction and operation of buildings are among the most energy, pollution, and resource intensive. In the USA alone, buildings and their operations consume three billion tons of raw materials, 40% of the nation's total energy, and 77% of its electricity use each year. Materials utilized in constructing buildings have high embodied energy, high carbon emissions, and high levels of toxins and pollutants in their production cycle (UNEP 2007). It is estimated that buildings contribute as much as one-third of total global greenhouse gas (GHG) emissions primarily through the use of fossil fuels during their operational phase (UNEP 2009).

It is widely recognized that climate change impacts the natural and the built environment leading to grave socioeconomic and health problems (Portier et al. 2010). The impact on natural environments has multiple dimensions ranging from stressing the vulnerable ecosystems to water and food resources, eventually affecting all living things. The impact on the built environment is also substantial. This includes deterioration of buildings and urban infrastructure due to extreme events, high temperatures, and sea level rise leading to loss of life and destruction of public and private property. Impacts occurring now affect water, energy, transportation, agriculture, ecosystems, and health, but they are expected to intensify and increase in the future (Karl et al. 2009).

S. Vassigh (✉)
Associate Dean for the College of Communication,
Architecture and the Arts, Florida International University, Miami, USA
e-mail: svassigh@fiu.edu

K. T. Çalıyurt and R. Said (eds.), *Sustainability and Social Responsibility of Accountability Reporting Systems*, Accounting, Finance, Sustainability, Governance & Fraud: Theory and Application, https://doi.org/10.1007/978-981-10-3212-7_5

Given the sizable contribution of the building industry to greenhouse gas emissions, enhancing the capacity of the building industry to mitigate climate change is critical. Sustainable design and development strategies can lead to significant reductions in energy consumption as well as minimizing the carbon footprint of buildings. Using the National Institute of Building Sciences definition, this article considers sustainable development as design and construction processes that reduce or completely avoid depletion of critical resources like energy, water, and raw materials; prevent environmental degradation caused by facilities and infrastructure throughout their life cycle; and create built environments that are livable, comfortable, safe, and productive (NIBS 2012).

Sustainable design and development is a complex undertaking requiring collaborations among many experts from diverse disciplinary backgrounds, significant investments in buildings and their infrastructure, and developing advanced design and decision support tools. In addition, sustainable development in itself will not ensure safety of our future. The existing GHG levels in the atmosphere will remain high for many years to come. Scientists from the National Oceanic and Atmospheric Administration have concluded that the current level of GHG in the atmosphere will remain 1000 years after stopping emissions (McGregor et al. 2013, 117). This clearly indicates that mitigation strategies to reduce GHG have been difficult to implement and will not eliminate our significant challenges.

Therefore, it is equally important to acknowledge the need for addressing the unavoidable climate change consequences by acting to manage risks and working to create a resilient built environment. Creating flexibility in design to accommodate anticipated conditions will reduce the vulnerability to impact. However, efforts and strategies for adapting to climate change should not undermine mitigation efforts for stabilizing GHG emissions. Sustainability and resiliency approaches and strategies can be enhanced when they are *mutually considered* and incorporated in the design and construction in the early stages of the process.

The following sections of this chapter provide an overview of the complex issues, current design, development processes, and barriers in achieving goals of sustainable and resilient built environments. The specific objectives of the chapter are to: (1) examine and reveal the scale and complexity of challenges in sustainable design and development, and identify a range of broad mitigation strategies, (2) examine vulnerabilities of buildings and their infrastructure to climate change and extreme events, broadly outlining adaptation strategies for resilience, (3) highlight synergetic benefits and conflicts between sustainable and resilient design strategies, and (4) describe traditional building design development and examine how new practices and technologies can foster the sustainability and resiliency of the built environment.

5.2 Sustainable Building Design and Construction

5.2.1 Climate Change Challenges

Recent design and construction standards for energy efficient and sustainable buildings are enhancing the practice of sustainable building design and development in the USA. However, the widespread and large-scale adoption of sustainable strategies has been slow. This slow rate is a consequence of a number of issues. First is the increase in demand for buildings in response to population growth. For example, the number of households in the USA grew nearly 40% (from 80 to 113 million) from 1980 to 2005, and the total area requirement for commercial buildings grew 35% from 1985 to 2004. These represent a combined increase of 70% in energy demand (US DOE 2008). The increased demand for building construction left little room for building industry to consider sustainability as a major element.

The second factor is that buildings with a high degree of energy efficiency in the USA are generally designed by a small group of elite architectural and engineering firms. Limited internal expertise, high cost, and time constraints are among major barriers to a wider adoption and use of sustainable design strategies for small and midsize companies. The third factor is the weakness of the current evaluation, rating systems, and benchmarking for sustainability of buildings. US rating systems, such as Leadership in Energy & Environmental Design (LEED), have been criticized on failing to significantly reduce energy consumption and do not compare well against other international rating systems (Spiegelhaulter 2008).

Finally, the current building design process is mostly reliant on the experience and expertise of the architects and the engineers involved in the process without access to any comprehensive decision support tools. Many design strategies are based on what has worked in the past without an examination of a wide range of other alternatives and possibilities. In addition, computer simulations to predict building performance are often carried out by fragmented simulations of various building systems in isolation, without a holistic approach or integration. This fragmented approach and the lack of adequate decision support system often lead to disregarding design strategies that may be significantly more appropriate and effective for sustainability (Hopfe 2009; Olusegun et al. 2001).

5.2.2 Mitigation Strategies

There are numerous strategies that can be used to reduce energy consumption and minimize the carbon footprint of buildings. However, these strategies are sometimes in conflict or may not align well with broader building objectives such as owners' priorities, building location, or the financial constraints of the project. This makes the process of building design a balancing act that requires input and guidance from multiple recourses.

To create an overall understanding of possible strategies to mitigation, Table 5.1 provides a series of design measures in relation to building design, urban form, and landscape systems. In this table, the strategies for building design are categorized into two subgroups of building configuration, and materials and assemblies.

Table 5.1 Sustainable design strategies

Building design		Strategies
Configuration	Building shape	Reduce surface to volume ratio, appropriate plan shapes for solar radiation, reduce exposed surface area
	Climate responsive design	Appropriate building orientation and siting, access to natural light and natural ventilation
Materials and assemblies	Low energy efficiency	Utilize thermally efficient materials and insulation, seal connections and joinery, use climate responsive facades and shading systems
	Low carbon footprint	Use low embodied energy and low embodied water materials
Urban form		*Strategies*
Density	Dense construction	Reduce vehicular travel miles, change zoning to discourage sprawl, provide incentives for living close to work, enhanced public transportation, use heat recovery systems
Diversity	Mixed-use building	Reduced vehicular travel miles, revise land use designations, provide incentives for high density and infill development, provide amenities in living and work proximity
Landscape systems		*Strategies*
Thermal efficiency	Solar heat gain moderation	Shield from solar heat using canopy shading, vegetated surfaces, green walls, green roofs, and earth sheltering
	Wind control	Landscape wind breaks, foundation planting, wind deflectors, and channels
	Pollution control	Use vegetated filter strips and suitable plants to remove water, soil and contaminants, and air pollution
Thermal efficiency	Solar heat gain moderation	Shield from solar heat using canopy shading, vegetated surfaces, green walls, green roofs, and earth sheltering
	Wind control	Landscape wind breaks, foundation planting, wind deflectors, and channels
	Pollution control	Use vegetated filter strips and suitable plants to remove water, soil and contaminants, and air pollution
Hydrological efficiency	Water conservation	Use low irrigation plant and efficient irrigation mechanisms
	Runoff mitigation	Use pervious pavements, green roofs, storm water planters, bioswales, detention and retention basins
	Wastewater management	Utilize surface and subsurface flow wetlands, use bioremediation systems

Table information is based on Best Practices in Sustainable Design authored by Vassigh et al. (2013), and Urban Form and Climate Change, Hamin and Gurran (2009)

Building configuration involves decisions about building geometry, volume, orientation, and the exposed surface area to the environment. Appropriate strategies for building configuration place a high priority on climatic conditions of the building site often leading to significant energy saving. These strategies prioritize the use of natural cooling, heating, and ventilation (passive controls) over the use of mechanical systems (active controls). They also emphasize the use of natural light over artificial lighting. For example, a building located in a cold climate with an elongated shape along the east and west axis and openings on the south side can utilize solar heat and access daylight, thus reducing energy demand.

Contrarily when designing in hot and dry climates, minimizing the building dimensions in the east–west direction reduces solar heat gain. In addition, placing building services such as elevators and stairs in the east–west direction blocks direct sunlight and creates buffer zones. Shallow floor depths in these climatic conditions provide ample daylight and maximize cross-ventilation and night cooling if the building openings are located on the long sides of the building to utilize prevailing winds.

Building materials and assemblies are another important factors in determination of building performance. Materials with high thermal efficiency used in building enclosures control heat gain and heat loss significantly. For example, wood has a higher resistance to heat transfer than concrete and steel. Therefore, using wood in building facades could be an effective strategy in particular climatic conditions. Some materials such as concrete, masonry, or stone have the capacity to absorb and store solar heat. When properly used, they can absorb heat energy deep into their mass during the day and slowly release it during nighttime.

There are also new technologies and materials such as phase change material (PCM) that can store energy and release it at a later time. PCM can be incorporated into wallboards, roofs, ceiling, and floors to passively cool or heat buildings (Vassigh et al. 2013). It is critically important to have all building connections sealed off to prevent a higher rate of heat transfer at connections, particularly in cold climatic zones. Using airtight connections and placing insulation materials in vulnerable areas often achieve this. Using airtight connections also helps with endurance of the building exterior materials as it prevents moisture accumulation at the connection vicinity where the hot and cold air meets.

Another important aspect of material use in buildings is the evaluation of their environmental impact. Construction materials use energy and water in their production and transportation to the building site. Embodied energy is defined as the energy used during the entire life cycle of a material including the energy used for manufacturing, transporting, and disposing (Lippke et al. 2004). Similarly, embodied water indicates the amount of water used to produce, transport, and dispose of a material. As indicated in Table 5.1, selecting materials with lower embodied energy and embodied water will reduce the carbon footprint of buildings. Unfortunately, embodied energy and water are often overlooked in lieu of other considerations.

The next category of strategies for sustainable development addresses the larger context of development in the urban form. Table 5.1 subdivides urban form into two closely related subcategories of dense construction and mixed-use buildings. Constructing buildings, neighborhoods, and larger communities in densely configured patches has multiple benefits. Density reduces energy used for commuting significantly. When properly coupled with designing mixed-use building strategies, it creates incentives for people to commute less as they are able to walk to work and amenities. In addition, dense development makes the use of public transit more feasible. However, to achieve this, the zoning codes and planning priorities should be significantly revised and incentives for developers and all other involved parties should be expanded. Dense development should be carefully planned as it may be in conflict with other strategies that prioritize reducing traffic and air pollution.

The last section of Table 5.1 lists some of the numerous and effective sustainable strategies that can be provided by landscape systems. Divided into thermal efficiency and hydrological efficiency subcategories (Vassigh, Ozer, Spiegelhalter 2013), these strategies can be applied at the small scale of individual buildings as well as the large scale of the urban environment and beyond. Landscape systems can shield buildings from solar heat. Using canopy shading, vegetated surfaces, green walls, and roofs can moderate solar heat gain. In addition, landscape systems protect buildings from wind and facilitate natural ventilation.

Landscape systems can be used to mitigate air, water, and soil pollution. For example, large-leaved indigenous evergreens mitigate airborne pollution. Vegetative filter strips such as orchards, vineyards, and row crops remove pollutants from runoff water while providing some degree of resistance to soil erosion. Certain species of plants remove or degrade contaminates from soil and water through their internal process, thus providing an economically viable method to control pollution (Kumar et al. 2013).

Significant freshwater conservation can be achieved by incorporating hydrological sensitive landscape design solutions. Using low irrigation plants and efficient irrigation mechanisms in buildings and urban environments can lead to significant water saving. Recycling wastewater generated through buildings' functions (gray water) for watering garden and landscapes is also another increasing viable method for water conservation. Furthermore, landscape strategies can be used to develop ecological habitats for wildlife, absorb floodwaters, provide added recreational amenities, and improve aesthetics (Vassigh et al. 2013).

5.3 Resilient Building Design and Construction

5.3.1 Climate Change Challenge

Climate change is presenting new challenges to the built environment by increasing both the intensity and frequency of extreme events. High temperatures, sustained high winds, weather fluctuations, flooding, drought, and sea level rise set the context in which our buildings and their infrastructure must exist and remain usable.

These events generate significant stresses such as intensified wind impact on building structures, wind-driven rain intrusion into buildings through facades, storm surge, and intense flooding. In addition, the consequences of sea level rise on building systems, materials, and foundations can be devastating.

Generating public sector support in order to develop the appropriate actions for adaptation to climate change impacts has been difficult for a number of reasons: first, the public's disbelief and the lack of recognition of the risks and threats; second, the absence of appropriate risk assessment and decision-making support tools; third, the anticipated high cost of long-term benefits with little or no immediate payback; and finally, the lack of adequate and enforceable policies for building in new conditions.

Three sections of Table 5.2 provide an overview of a series of adaptation strategies for climate change. It categorizes various adaptive approaches for three major climate change impacts including rising temperature, storms and hurricanes, and sea level rise. Measures for addressing each impact are subdivided into three interconnected scales of buildings, community, and the urban environment.

Table 5.2 lists a number of strategies for combating higher temperatures at the building scale. These strategies revolve around extensive use of green walls and green roofs, trees, and vegetated surfaces, in order to provide thermal insulation and shade to reduce temperature. Designing to maximize natural ventilation in buildings

Table 5.2 Resilient Design and Development for Buildings

Climate change impact	Community strategies
Rising temperature	✓ Design for Natural Ventilation and Passive Cooling ✓ Use Green walls, Green roofs, Trees and Vegetated Surfaces ✓ Provide Thermal Insulation, and Canopy Shading ✓ Minimize the Exterior Surface Area
Storms and hurricanes	✓ Enhance and Reinforce Building Foundations to Provide Resistance to Hydrostatic Pressure ✓ Use Rigid Connections and Reinforce Joinery to Increase Resistance to Wind load ✓ Use Simple Building Shapes and Plan to increase Wind Resistance ✓ Use Structural Separation to Divide Building to Wings Which Act independently Under Wind Load ✓ Minimize Exposed Surface Area to Prevailing Winds ✓ Water Proof Building Foundations to Provide Protection from Storm Surges and Flooding ✓ Use Water Resistant Materials in Building Facades to Pro-tects Against Wind Driven Rain and High Humidity ✓ Design Buildings Ground Level to Allow Passage of Flood Water
Sea level rise	✓ Use Flood Walls, and Compact Earth Fills ✓ Raise Buildings on Piles Above Flood Levels to Protects Water Damage ✓ Move Building Service Equipment to Higher Floor ✓ Encourage Multistory Construction to Provide Additional Space if Necessary to Abandon Ground Levels

is another way of combating high temperatures. However, as the temperature rises, the use of outside air for cooling building's interior space becomes less feasible.

Measures for resilient construction for extreme events such as storms and hurricane for buildings include simpler configurations that offer better resistance to high winds. Minimizing exposed surface area and using continuous joinery and connections in buildings are among other strategies to increase resistance to the wind impact. Measures to combat water from storms and hurricanes in buildings include water-proofing foundations, use of water-resistant materials in building facades to protect against wind-driven rain, and designing ground levels to allow passage of floodwater. Methods to address the impact of sea level rise in buildings include construction of sea walls, using compacted earth fills and raising buildings on piles above the flood levels. In addition, relocating all building services and mechanical equipment to higher floors eliminates water damage in storm surge or flooding.

The measures at the community scale are listed in Table 5.3. Using landscape strategies, reflective roofs, and reduced impervious surfaces are among measures to remediate high temperature. To control the impact of storms and hurricanes, clustered planning of buildings can be very effective. Grouping buildings in close proximity in staggered patterns reduces wind-tunneling effect, thus controlling damage.

High-density development, listed in Table 5.1 as a sustainability measure, is also a highly effective resiliency approach to manage storm water. Dense construction can reduce impervious surfaces such as roads, parking lots, and paved sidewalks that cannot absorb the storm runoff and can be easily flooded. Measures for combating sea level rise in low-lying and vulnerable areas include moving entire communities to higher elevations or retreat from the area.

Table 5.4 addresses appropriate measures at the urban scale. The urban environment has a microclimate condition called urban heat island effect, which is a local increase in temperature due to high density of buildings with hard surface, high density of transportation activities, and generation of wasted heat from

Table 5.3 Resilient design and development for community

Climate change impact	Community strategies
Rising temperature	✔ Use reflective roofs and street pavements ✔ Reduced impervious surfaces by grouping buildings in close proximity ✔ Utilize trees to provide canopy shading
Storms and hurricanes	✔ Promote clustered planning to reduce wind-tunneling effect ✔ Utilize detention basins to hold storm ✔ Water
Sea level rise	✔ Elevate buildings and infrastructures ✔ Retreat from low-lying areas

Table 5.2 information is based on Best Practices in Sustainable Design authored by Vassigh et al. (2013), and Urban Form and Climate Change, Hamin and Gurran (2009)

buildings. As temperature rise heightens this condition, utilizing trees and green belts moderates the heat island effect. In addition, using heat recovery systems to remove wasted heat from buildings and converting usable energy is increasingly a technologically and economically viable solution.

To control the impact of storm and hurricane-generated water, the reduction of impervious surfaces can control runoff water. In addition, constructing treatment wetlands for cleansing storm water and placing green space along flood lanes are appropriate measures.

Among strategies to protect the urban environment from the impact of sea level rise in the costal zones reestablishing sand dunes is critical. According to FEMA, due to over development some sand dunes have been completely destroyed. Rebuilding sand dunes and preserving them with coastal vegetation can protect large areas further inland, which enhance the appearance of the beaches (FEMA 2007). Other measures include creating earthen levees, beach nourishment to replace eroding beaches, increased coastal set back requirements, and elevating critical infrastructure (Hamin and Gurran 2009).

The discussion above offers a range of possible mitigation and adaptation strategies for climate change. However, providing an expansive list of measures to address every impact of climate change on the built environment is not the ultimate goal and is beyond the scope of this article. The objective here is to reveal the scale and complexity of issues.

The following sections shift the focus on building design and development processes and examine how to implement these strategies.

5.3.2 Mitigation Strategies

Three sections of Table 5.2 provide an overview of a series of adaptation strategies for climate change. It categorizes various adaptive approaches for three major climate change impacts including rising temperature, storms and hurricanes, and sea level rise. Measures for addressing each impact are subdivided into three interconnected scales of buildings, community, and the urban environment.

Table 5.2 lists a number of strategies for combating higher temperatures at the building scale. These strategies revolve around extensive use of green walls and green roofs, trees, and vegetated surfaces, in order to provide thermal insulation and shade to reduce temperature. Designing to maximize natural ventilation in buildings is another way of combating high temperatures. However, as the temperature rises, the use of outside air for cooling building's interior space becomes less feasible.

Measures for resilient construction for extreme events such as storms and hurricane for buildings include simpler configurations that offer better resistance to high winds. Minimizing exposed surface area and using continuous joinery and connections in buildings are among other strategies to increase resistance to the wind impact. Measures to combat water from storms and hurricanes in buildings include water-proofing foundations, use of water-resistant materials in building facades to protect against wind-driven rain, and designing ground levels to allow passage of floodwater. Methods to address the impact of sea level rise in buildings include construction of sea walls, using compacted earth fills and raising buildings on piles above the flood levels. In addition, relocating all building services and mechanical equipment to higher floors eliminates water damage in storm surge or flooding.

The measures at the community scale are listed in Table 5.3. Using landscape strategies, reflective roofs, and reduced impervious surfaces are among measures to remediate high temperature. To control the impact of storms and hurricanes, clustered planning of buildings can be very effective. Grouping buildings in close proximity in staggered patterns reduces wind-tunneling effect, thus controlling damage.

High-density development, listed in Table 5.1 as a sustainability measure, is also a highly effective resiliency approach to manage storm water. Dense construction can reduce impervious surfaces such as roads, parking lots, and paved sidewalks that cannot absorb the storm runoff and can be easily flooded. Measures for combating sea level rise in low-lying and vulnerable areas include moving entire communities to higher elevations or retreat from the area.

Table 5.4 addresses appropriate measures at the urban scale. The urban environment has a microclimate condition called urban heat island effect, which is a local increase in temperature due to high density of buildings with hard surface, high density of transportation activities, and generation of wasted heat from buildings. As temperature rise heightens this condition, utilizing trees and green belts moderates the heat island effect. In addition, using heat recovery systems to remove wasted heat from buildings and converting usable energy is increasingly a technologically and economically viable solution.

To control the impact of storm and hurricane-generated water, the reduction of impervious surfaces can control runoff water. In addition, constructing treatment wetlands for cleansing storm water and placing green space along flood lanes are appropriate measures.

Table 5.4 Resilient Design and Development for the Urban Environment

Climate change impact	Community strategies
Rising temperature	✓ Use Trees and Green Belts to Create Shade ✓ Utilize Heat Recovery Systems to Remove Wasted Heat from Buildings and Convert to Usable Energy
Storms and hurricanes	✓ Reduce Impervious Surfaces to Control Runoff Water ✓ Utilize Constructed Treatment Wetlands for Cleaning Storm Water ✓ Use Green Space Along Flood Lanes
Sea level rise	✓ Reestablishing Sand Dunes and use Earthen Levees ✓ Use Beach Nourishment to Enhance Eroding Beaches ✓ Increase Coastal Set Back Requirements ✓ Elevate Critical Infrastructure ✓ Retreat From Low Lying Areas

Among strategies to protect the urban environment from the impact of sea level rise in the costal zones reestablishing sand dunes is critical. According to FEMA, due to over development some sand dunes have been completely destroyed. Rebuilding sand dunes and preserving them with coastal vegetation can protect large areas further inland, which enhance the appearance of the beaches (FEMA 2007). Other measures include creating earthen levees, beach nourishment to replace eroding beaches, increased coastal set back requirements, and elevating critical infrastructure (Hamin and Gurran 2009) (Table 5.4).

The discussion above offers a range of possible mitigation and adaptation strategies for climate change. However, providing an expansive list of measures to address every impact of climate change on the built environment is not the ultimate goal and is beyond the scope of this article. The objective here is to reveal the scale and complexity of issues.

The following sections shift the focus on building design and development processes and examine how to implement these strategies.

5.4 Design and Development Process: The Case for Data-Driven Integrated Practice

Building design, development, and construction is an interdisciplinary effort. Architects, engineers, planners, construction experts, landscape designers, and other stakeholders engage in a process that involves understanding many issues, making difficult decisions, and balancing a number of competing concerns. The overlay of sustainable and resilient design considerations creates another layer of complexity that makes it difficult to address with the existing processes and tools. For successful outcomes, experts are in need of appropriate practice processes, decisions support tools, and access to readily usable data.

The traditional process in the design, engineering, and construction of buildings follows a linear pattern, moving the building project from one expert to another (Toth et al. 2009). Most midsize to large building projects begin with an agreement between the client and an architectural firm. Architects, traditionally in charge of building design, begin with tackling the client's needs and critical requirements such as building program and function, siting considerations, aesthetic goals, and the financial aspects of the design. Often, this involves investigation of a range of possible alternatives-based precedent and the experience of the firm or the architect. Possible alternatives are discussed, examined, and analyzed using computer simulation applications, and a single design proposal is selected. At this stage, the critical decisions such as building form, orientation, materials, and systems are mostly concluded and the project is turned over to the engineers. Engineers follow to resolve technical issues and design various building systems including structural, mechanical, and electrical systems. Once the engineering stage is completed, the project is passed to the construction experts.

Decisions made in the earliest stage of design have the greatest impact on building performance, construction, operation cost, and the environmental footprints of buildings (Toth et al. 2009). When structural engineers, mechanical engineers, and construction experts get involved after significant decisions have been made, their contributions are reduced to problem solving rather than providing innovative insights. Without collaborative engagement of all experts from the beginning of the project and input from various perspectives, innovative design possibilities are squandered and many opportunities to create synergetic benefits are lost. Integrating design and engineering decisions at the early stages when the proposal is still malleable (Tavares and Martins 2007) is critical to the building performance and sustainability.

Recent research by the National Institute of Building Sciences and others shows that the most resource efficient, best performing, and environmentally sustainable buildings are designed using integrated practice. Integrated practice is the process by which engineers, architects, construction experts, and other stakeholders begin working together at the conception of a project to create synergy among various building systems and improve overall building performance. When all experts collaborate early and effectively at the start of a building project, their collaboration produces better designed, more efficient, and lower cost buildings (NIBS 2008). Integrated practice also leads to design of resilient buildings. Early planning through integrated practice can reduce the impact of a disruptive event and the duration of their impacts (NBIS 2015).

Promoting integrated practice has been recognized by the American Institute of Architects (AIA) as one of the central challenges facing the profession and one of the most important ways to improve building performance, cost, and environmental impact. The AIA 2030 Commitment challenged the profession to achieve the goal of designing carbon neutral or no greenhouse gas emitting energy, buildings in the USA and *identified the practice of Integrated Design as the primary vehicle to attain this goal* (AIA 2007).

However, moving toward integrated practice has been very slow. There are no comprehensive and effective communication and decision support tools to facilitate this process. Although there are numerous computer applications used for performance simulation, documentation, management, and project delivery, there has not been much effort toward developing tools that can assess the interdependency and dynamic interactions of various decisions and discipline-specific constraints. As strategies are selected or proposed, there is a need to evaluate and compare their competing requirements based on concrete and validated data (McCarney 2009).

In addition, there is also a lack of access to the relevant and critical information that could facilitate decisions made by groups of experts. Current codes, standards, and practices use existing data that assumes the future will be similar to the past (Larsen et al. 2011). Immediate access to curated data on regional climate and its impacts on the environment is a key element for integrated practice

Technological advances in hardware, storage, and software have significantly increased the ability to capture, curate, analyze, and visualize vast amount of data. Recent technologies offer new possibilities to use data for fundamentally changing the way buildings and urban environments are designed and functioned. This is particularly true of climate change data such as predictions of storms, temperature changes, humidity, and sea level rise. In addition, compiling data from pervious buildings and their performance can highlight what has worked in the past and inform decisions for the future based on validated data and informed projections, thus providing a new way of using precedents and past experiences.

5.5 Conclusion

The impact of climate change will significantly challenge the built environment. The impact is expected to continue and intensify in the future, substantially changing our way of life. This chapter described some of these major challenges and provided an overview of strategies and measures to mitigate major impacts. Focused on buildings, sustainability, and resiliency of the built environment was discussed in three related scales of buildings, communities, and urban environments. By highlighting and examining a range of key issues, vulnerabilities, strategies, and processes, the article revealed the complexity of design and development of the built environment, demonstrating the need for decision support tools and a data-driven approach.

As discussed, building design, development, and construction is an interdisciplinary endeavor and effective collaboration among various domain experts is critical to the sustainability and resiliency of the environment. The architectural profession identified integrated practice as the appropriate venue for interdisciplinary collaboration to enhance building performance, foster innovative solutions, and realize synergetic benefits from combining resources in buildings. However, integrated practice must be supported with appropriate tools in order to make it a feasible practice for the majority of design and construction firms. Developing decision support tools based on captured and curated data is a necessary but missing element in the success of integrated practice. With the increasing role of data in environmental sciences and technological advances in simulations and data visualization, developing intelligent decision support tools is within reach.

Integrated practice appropriately supported can move the building design process beyond relying on the experience and expertise of a singular firm, architect, or engineer by utilizing data for validation of the approach. With climate change in full swing, tools that inform practical decisions and facilitate collaborative problem solving must be central to any step forward in moving toward a sustainable and resilient built environment.

References

AIA (2007) Architecture 2030 will change the way you look at buildings. American Institute of Architecture http://www.architecture2030.org. Accessed 3 Aug 2015

Faniran OO, Love PED, Treloar G, Anumba CJ (2001) Methodological issues in design construction integration. Logistics Inf Manage 14 (5/6): 421–428 http://dx.doi.org/10.1108/EUM0000000006254. Accessed 26 Apr 2015

FEMA (2007) Design guide for improving hospital safety in earthquakes, floods, and high winds: providing protection to people and buildings, Washington, DC

Hamin EM, Gurran N (2009) Urban form and climate change: balancing adaptation and mitigation in the US and Australia. Habitat Int 33(3):238–245

Hopfe CJ (2009) Uncertainty and sensitivity analysis in building performance simulation for decision support and design optimization. Eindhoven University, PhD diss

Karl T, Melillo J, Peterson T (2009) Global climate change impacts in the United States, Cambridge University Press

Kumar R, Arumugam T, Balakrishnan S, Rajavel DS (2013) Online ISSN 2277–1808, Bull. Env. Pharmacol. Life Sci. vol 2[2] January 2013: 52-63, 2012, Academy for environment and life sciences, India bulletin of environment, pharmacology and life sciences. http://www.bepls.co. (Accessed 23 Mar 2015)

Larsen L, Rajkovich N, Leighton C, McCoy K, Calhoun K, Mallen E, Bush K, Enriquez J, Pyke C, McMahon S, Kwok A (2011) Green building and climate resilience: understanding impacts and preparing for changing conditions, University of Michigan. USA, Green Building Council

Lippke B, Wilson J, Garcia JP, Bowyer B, Mei lJ (2004) Life-Cycle environmental performance of renewable. J For Prod Mater. http://buildingsdatabook.eren.doe.gov/TableView.aspx?table=Notes. Accessed 3 Jun 2015

McCarney P (2009) City indicators on climate change: implications for policy leverage and governance. In: World Bank's 5th urban research symposium cities and climate change: responding to an urgent agenda, Marseille, France

McGregor A, Roberts C, Cousins F (2013) Two degrees: the built environment and our changing climates routledge, 1st edn. London and New York, p 177

NIBS (2012) National Institute of Building Sciences annual report. http://c.ymcdn.com/sites/www.nibs.org/resource/resmgr/docs/nibs_2012_annualreport_sm.pdf . Accessed 5 May 2015

Portier CJ, Thigpen Tart K, Carter SR, Dilworth CH, Grambsch AE, Gohlke J, Hess J, Howard SN, Luber G, Lutz JT, Maslak T, Prudent N, Radtke M, Rosenthal JP, Rowles T, Sandifer PA, Scheraga J, Schramm PJ, Strickman D, Trtanj JM, Whung P-Y. (2010). A human health perspective on climate change: a report outlining the research needs on the human health effects of climate change. Research Triangle Park, NC: Environmental Health Perspectives/National Institute of Environmental Health Sciences. https://doi.org/10.1289/ehp.1002272 Available: www.niehs.nih.gov/climatereport

Speigelhaulter T (2008) Global Benchmarking: Taking a Critical Look at Sustainable Design in the U.S., the journal of the AIA California Council 9.3

Tavares P, Martins A (2007) Energy efficient building design using sensitivity analysis: a case study. Energy Build 39(1):23–31

Toth B, Fernando R, Salim F, Drogemuller R, Burry J, Burry M, Frazer J (2009) Modeling sustainable and optimal solutions for building services integration in early architectural design: confronting the software and professional interoperability deficit. In: Proceedings of cumulus 38 degrees south, Hemispheric Shifts Across Learning, Teaching and Research, Swinburne, University of Technology and RMIT, Melbourne, Victoria

Vassigh S, Özer E, Spiegelhalter T (2013) Best practices in sustainable building design +interactive learning environment. J. Ross, Fort Lauderdale

UNEP PH (2007) Building and Climate Change. Status Challenges and opportunities, United Nations, Environment Program, Sustainable Consumption and reduction Branch, illustrated edition

UNEP DTIE Sustainable Consumption & Production Branch (2009) Buildings and Climate Change: a Summary for Decision-Makers. Paris, France: UNEP. Retrieved by CAKE http://www.cakex.org/virtual-library/885

U.S. Department of Energy (2008) Energy efficiency trends in residential and commercial buildings, http://apps1.eere.energy.gov/buildings/publications/pdfs/corporate/bt_stateindustry.pdf, Accessed Aug 2015

Author Biography

Shahin Vassigh is a Professor of Architecture and an Associate Dean for the College of Communication, Architecture and the Arts at Florida International University (FIU). She has built a nationally recognized body of research work focused on sustainable building design education through developing alternative pedagogies. Her educational research work has been supported by major federal grants from the National Science Foundation and the US Department of Education. She is the author of "Interactive Structures: Visualizing Structural Behavior" (2005), and the lead author of "Building Systems Integration for Enhanced Environmental Performance" (2011) and "Best Practices in Sustainable Design" (2013).

Chapter 6
The Place of Women in Employment: Turkish Case

Fatma Cesur

6.1 Introduction

The most efficient use of production factors is very important, in terms of growth and development the economy of the country. Labor, in the first place of production factors, is in the front row in employment in favor of men in our country as in the world. Women in the world had begun working for a fee along with the industrial revolution. Almost in every country of the world, women, constitute a significant portion of the population; have assets in the labor market in the past, both in our day behind men, remains limited with the status of "**secondary labor**." The secondary role of women in the labor market is related to the traditional division of labor highly. That gender-based division of labor, though at different levels in every society basically; such as bearing children and growing, doing household chores, physiological and sociological aspects of women's basic tasks, while earning money by working in the market has been recognized as the main role of men.

The factor that pushes woman into the labor market in Turkey is men's participation in World War I, 1915. It is seen that during the years of war, women's participation of labor force has increased. Before 1950, women were working as unpaid family workers in rural areas. Years of the 1950s were urban transformation years. In these years women, left unpaid family labor in rural areas, have migrated to urban areas. That's why, employment had decreased in agriculture and non-agricultural labor force participation had been in real terms, after 1950 urbanization. Women had entered the industry or the services sector by urban migration, but could not have taken important way to go because of being non-educated.

Over time in labor market, women's position and working forms have changed. How the change is in terms of industry is an important issue. The sectoral

F. Cesur (✉)
Faculty of Economics Administrative Science, Trakya University, Edirne, Turkey
e mail: fatmacesur@trakya.edu.tr

K. T. Çalıyurt and R. Said (eds.), *Sustainability and Social Responsibility of Accountability Reporting Systems*, Accounting, Finance, Sustainability, Governance & Fraud: Theory and Application, https://doi.org/10.1007/978-981-10-3212-7_6

distribution of employment in a country is an important indicator of its development level. With development, employment increases in the agricultural sector when decreases in non-agricultural sector. This situation is also current for female employment. In developing countries and regions, female workforce in agricultural sector intensifies, when the service sector is the sector in which women have intensive work in developed countries. Accordingly, the well-paid employment women's labor takes place of the unpaid family labor in developed countries (Tansel 2002: 5).

Especially in developing countries, women's low labor force participation rate attracts attention and importance in the provision of development comes to the fore. Greater participation of women in economic life requires their gaining a greater share from development and growth and ensuring position recovery in the family. Eventually, ignoring or remaining dormant of women's labor force in production factors is economical loss. Women's contribution to labor force thus to the economy, is a gain for all countries, will be an important factor for accelerating development and balancing growth in a structure (Özdemir et al. 2012: 115). There are several reasons to push women to the subordinate position in economic and social areas. The reasons, related to the structural features of society, are as follows (Kocacık and Gökkaya 2005):

1. Discrimination in society, based on "male dominated" culture (in all areas),
2. Women's limited educational opportunities,
3. Physiological differences between men and women,
4. Shortcomings and inaccuracies in the legal regulations.

In achieving development, women's labor force employment case is an important issue that developing countries should deal with it. Today, it is seen that women cannot benefit from employment opportunities as equal to men in many areas in the world. Women are not at the forefront of a society, but they are members of a society, who have significant impact on the advancement. How effective and productive women in society that is so advanced (Kurtsan 2011; Karabiyik 2012).

6.2 The Concept of Employment

Employment is defined in different ways. With the simplest definition, employment is used to mean using, operating, and commissioning (Özaydın 2000: 5). In its broadest sense, the concept of employment is defined as all factors of production used in the production process in order to produce goods and services (Uysal 2007: 55). Employment, as a concept in the dictionary of the Turkish Language Institution (TDK), is defined as operating, using in a job, a task (TDK 2005: 989). As a word, employment is executing a person in order to the fulfillment of a particular job or task. Economic sense, employment including goods and services actively in the production process in order to perform the production or achieve domestic output in a country (Ardıç 2006: 175). However, employment, as content, has much broader meaning and whatever the level of development, it takes an important place in the country's economic problems (Karakayalı 2007: 401). Women's employment is gaining importance at this point (Özmen 2012: 111).

In a country, in working age between 15 and 65 years, the total of the employed and the unemployed is defined as "labor force." In the current period, as well as those who were employed, unemployed people, who wish to be employed, are counted from the labor force (TSI 2009: 14). Labor participation rate is defined as the ratio of labor force in the age 15 and older population (TSI 2011a, b: 175).

This ratio, which reflects certain age, gender, and race of the person showing the probability of being in the labor force and labor force participation decisions of individuals, is one of the main indicators in the implementation of economic policy under consideration. For example, to create and implement policies aimed at ensuring full employment of labor in the society, it must be able to determine how many people want to work; for that, as named as economic activity rate, participation rate of labor force is necessary to known (Biçerli 2009: 53).

6.3 Women Employment and Importance

Women, constitute half of the world population, are less employed than men in all countries and are working for lower wages in general. In World War I and World War II, with recruitment of the male labor force, women had begun to occur in the working area. After these wars and the economic crisis, governments began to expand individuals' (men–women) economic and social life participation fields. By industrialization, new fields were created to women, and women's new roles, within the family and society, had begun to be installed. Women's first use of labor for a fee started with industrial revolution (Kocacık and Gökkaya 2005: 196) and with the process of industrialization, women willingness to participate and necessity in working life, on the other hand the need for employment accelerated women's employment (Özdemir et al. 2012: 115). During World War I and World War II, female labor force took the place of the recruited population of male labor in the arms industry (Altan and Ersöz 1994: 32). Women had worked with low wages and poor working conditions, in the first period of industrialization (Directorate General on the Status of Women, DGSW 2000: 4).

The industrial revolution is considered as the most important historical development, which led to the emergence of the paid female labor force concept, with its current meaning and for the first time. In other words, especially England in the nineteenth century, including many in Western countries, a significant portion of the total labor force was consisted of women (Hobsbawm 2003). However, from the middle of the nineteenth century, policies were begun to be implemented, as law limiting working hours in Western countries, banning women workplaces and businesses with protective laws (Altan and Ersöz 1994: 28–30). In other words, labor exploitation of women in working life also was a factor on the birth and development of the social policy science (Kocacık and Gökkaya 2005: 198). Toward the end of the nineteenth century, rapid developments in the metallurgy, chemistry, and automotive industry had limited women's labor force largely in comparison with past, in production process (Altan and Ersöz 1994: 32). During this period, the growth in the public and service sectors had increased the proportion of women in the total labor force rapidly (Kocacık and Gökkaya 2005: 198). Nowadays, it is known that, as well as developments in the service sector, many interrelated factors are effective in increasing number of women in the labor force. These factors are mainly listed as follows (Koray et al. 2000: 214–215).

Increasing in preventive and supportive laws and practices for working women worldwide, demographic developments, increasing educational facilities and emergency nonstandard (atypical) working ways, decreasing in marriage rates, whereas increasing in divorcing rates, attitudes occurring in positive developments for women's work in society, improvements in child care and other services, women's productivity and efficiency are important for economic development and progress of society. Increasing in female employment can allow to overcoming for women in family and society, who are exposed to many problems (domestic violence, economic pressure, etc.). Also, by increasing family income, women can obtain living standards better.

Women's entrance to working life in agricultural sector and out of home had started with the necessity of supporting decreasing labor force, as a result of the most male population participation to wars in the early twentieth century [Directorate General on the Status of Women (DGSW)]. Female employment in Turkey had been a problem as expected to be resolved since the early years of the Republic. At this point, when considering the historical process, gender-based division of labor, migrations to the city, thaw in the agricultural structure, weakening of the traditional family structure, the difficulties in balancing family and working life, and low levels of women's education were considered as important elements of the causes, which cause to women's lower employment levels (Hotar 2011: transferred from 84 to 86; Karabıyık 2012: 232). After the Republic, the equality of men and women, education and vocational rights for women, with accelerating industrialization, urbanization, and migration, had led to the opening of new business areas (Ersöz 1993: 42).

Women's labor force participation is more active based on 1950s (Kocacık and Gökkaya 2005: 201); although in recent years, in contrast to the general trend with lower increasing rates in the world, women's labor force participation rates had fallen steadily, starting from the mid-1950s; the Confederation of Turkish Trade Unions (TURK-IS 2005: 4). Its reasons are economic basement on agricultural production in the economy of Turkey until the late 1950s (TSI 2004), changes in economic structure, and accompanying social transformations (TSI 2000). In 1950, female labor force participation rate fell from 81.5 to 72% in 1955, in 1965 to 56.2% (Doğramacı 1989: 8; Dülger 1984: 95), in 1990 to 34.1%, in 2000 to 26.6%, in 2005 to 23.3%, but in 2010 increased by 4.3 points and rose to 27.6%. In last 10 years, female employment in Turkey had the lower increasing rate in 2010, although it had declined continuously in general (Karabiyik 2012: 231, 256; International Labour Organization (ILO) 2011; TSI 2010; Karabiyik 2012: 234). According to 2010 data, women employment rate is 24.0% in Turkey, when on average it is 58.2% in 27 EU countries (European Commission 2010). This situation shows that Turkey is in back compared to many EU countries in women employment.

Important part of the female employees is working out of record. One of the most obvious reasons to working out of record is flexibilization. Flexibility is referred as changes in the labor markets, technology, and adapting to changes in production structure. Due to the problems such as unemployment and not creating jobs economy, the inelasticity of the labor market increases the informality by widespread flexible production and flexible working conditions. Flexible working may be in different formats like part-time (35 h or less per week) working, project-based work, on-call working, working from home, connected working to contractors system, and home-based working. It can be said that from the 1970s, widespread flexible working conditions have been shaped by the gendered division of labor. In particular, almost all home-based workers are women. "Home-based workers" term covers piecework, domestic workers dependent on a fee in their homes and contracted employees, without being bound to any employer, self-employed and employees on order. Undeclared work in women's employment rate is quite high related to home-based working, which is one of the common flexible working. Home-based working, which can be addressed within the framework of informal employment elasticity of women's labor relation, is the most intense experiencing informality in flexible forms of working. Home-based working is usually done by women. Especially for women, by reasons such as limited working conditions in outside paid and secure jobs, and caring jobs in home done by home-based working women's responsibility, this type of working women can be preferable. However, women's are defining themselves as "workers," result of home-based working is seen as an extension of household chores and considered as a contribution to the household budget. Home-based women's working fields are extensively in textiles and clothing, manufacturing, domestic service in Turkey (Durusoy Öztepe 2013: 11–48). Women, as a large majority of home-based employees, are working with low wages, very long hours and often work in the trade unions without organizing (Şahin 2011: 99).

6.4 Women's Labor Force Participation in Turkey

It is known that, in comparison with men, women's labor force participation is down and from year to year women's labor force participation is experiencing a steady decline. Working life does not only provide economic freedom to women, but also it increases their confidence and social dignity and improves their position in the family. Although there is no distinction to women's labor force participation from legal perspective, in contrast there is a positive distinction to it; women's responsibilities are heavy in their families, from the role which is loaded by society to women. Women's responsibilities in family life lead to a preference for working or not working. To reconcile working life and family life, sharing responsibilities which are carried by women between their husbands in family and support of government with legislation have great importance. Turkish Government appointed various targets to increase women's labor force participation in the scope of development objectives. "National Action Plan for Gender Equality," prepared by Government, agrees that women's labor force participation is much more behind than men's in our country. The point emphasized by the report is that women's overall social and economic development is closely associated with labor force participation. Closer relationship that exists between women's economic and social development with participation is due to employment, which saves not only women's economic independence, but also increases their self-confidence and position improvements in their families by increasing social prestige.

Basically, three objectives were identified for ensuring gender equality. By determining organizations to realize these three objectives with cooperating institutions, the division of labor had been made and these objectives were identified in a detailed manner as subtitles in order to achieve effective results. The most important reasons that prevent women from the labor market have been identified, and solutions have been developed for the removal of these reasons. Increasing women entrepreneurship, promoting child and elderly care services, reducing extent of the traditional structure, ensuring gender equality, eliminating any discrimination to women, experienced in working life, is one of the forefront case for national action plans. This tabulated National Action Plan for Gender Equality is given below:

Objective 1: Acceleration of efforts to increase women's employment

1.1 Increasing the women's employability through education, vocational training, and entrepreneurship.

1.2 Dissemination of child and elderly care services.

1.3 Increasing social awareness to reduce the prevalence of traditional structures.

Objective 2: Improvement of women's economic position in rural areas

2.1 Promotion of women entrepreneurship in agriculture.

2.2 Implementation of projects, income-generating and intended to improve working conditions for women in rural areas.

Objective 3: Struggling with gender discrimination in the labor market

3.1 Addition of the provisions about gender equality to law, by revising the current Law of Labor.

3.2 Creation of data related to differences in income between men and women, performing similar works.

3.3 Taking the necessary precautions against to all forms of discrimination faced by women in working life.

6.4.1 Woman's Work Life Place in Turkey

According to the Organization for Economic Cooperation and Development (OECD) countries in 2011, the employment rate of women is the highest in Iceland (77.3%) and the lowest rate is 27.8% in Turkey. While the ratio of males' labor force participation is 70.3% in 2004, this ratio has increased to 71% in 2012. The labor force participation ratio of females has increased from 23.3 to 29.5% in the same period. Around one-third of working females is employed as unpaid family worker in the year 2012. While the ratio of females is 54.3% in regular employee and casual employee, 10.8% in own account worker, the ratio of males is 66.5% in regular employee and casual employee, 22.3% in own account worker.

While the ratio of workers in agricultural jobs decreased for both sexes, the ratio of workers in non-agricultural jobs increased for both sexes in 2004–2011. In 2004, while the ratio of female workers is 50.8% in agriculture, this ratio decreased to 39.3% in 2011. In 2004, while the ratio of male workers is 21.6% in agriculture, this ratio decreased to 18.4% in 2012 (Fig. 6.1).

The unemployment ratio of females is higher than that of males. In 2004, while the unemployment ratio is 11% of females, this ratio is 10.8% in 2012. The unemployment ratio is 10.8% of males in 2004; this ratio has decreased to 8.5% in 2012. The unemployment ratio is decreased for both sexes in 2004–2010. The unemployment ratio of 15–24 age groups females is higher than that of males in the same age groups. In 2012, 19.9% of 15–24 age groups females and 16.3% males are unemployment in the same age groups. The start of women's non-agricultural employment had accelerated with the continuing increase of migration to urban areas, but according to TSI data, this rate had begun to decline from 1980s and declined to 20% after 2001 crisis (Fig. 6.2).

The most important factor in this great decline is employment most of the women in the field of agriculture and dwindling of the agricultural employment. Due to most of the women are employed in the agricultural sector, urban labor market participation rates of women are very low compared to rural participation. As a result of the decrease in the employment rate in the agricultural sector,

The distribution of employment by agriculture and non-agriculture

Years	Total employment	Agriculture	Non agriculture	Agriculture (%)	Non agriculture (%)
TÜRKİYE-TURKEY					
2004	19 632	5 713	13 919	29,1	70,9
2005	20 067	5 154	14 913	25,7	74,3
2006	20 423	4 907	15 516	24,0	76,0
2007	20 738	4 867	15 871	23,5	76,5
2008	21 194	5 016	16 178	23,7	76,3
2009	21 277	5 254	16 023	24,7	75,3
2010	22 594	5 683	16 911	25,2	74,8
2011	24 110	6 143	17 967	25,5	74,5
2012	24 821	6 097	18 724	24,6	75,4
Kadın-Female					
2004	5 047	2 565	2 482	50,8	49,2
2005	5 108	2 367	2 741	46,3	53,7
2006	5 258	2 295	2 963	43,6	56,4
2007	5 356	2 288	3 068	42,7	57,3
2008	5 595	2 354	3 241	42,1	57,9
2009	5 871	2 446	3 425	41,7	58,3
2010	6 425	2 724	3 701	42,4	57,6
2011	6 973	2 944	4 029	42,2	57,8
2012	7 309	2 872	4 437	39,3	60,7
Erkek-Male					
2004	14 585	3 148	11 437	21,6	78,4
2005	14 959	2 787	12 172	18,6	81,4
2006	15 165	2 613	12 552	17,2	82,8
2007	15 382	2 578	12 804	16,8	83,2
2008	15 598	2 663	12 935	17,1	82,9
2009	15 406	2 808	12 598	18,2	81,8
2010	16 170	2 959	13 211	18,3	81,7
2011	17 137	3 199	13 938	18,7	81,3
2012	17 512	3 225	14 287	18,4	81,6

Source: TurkStat, Household Labour Force Survey

Fig. 6.1 Distribution of employment by agriculture and non-agriculture. *Source* Republic of Turkey Ministry of Development (2009: 5)

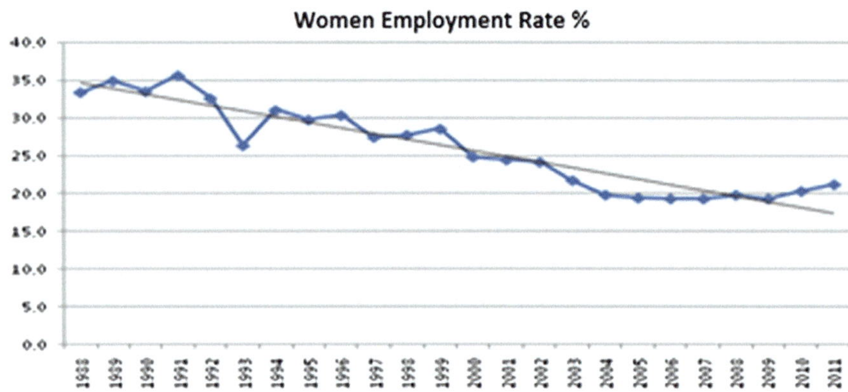

Fig. 6.2 Women employment rate. *Source* TSI household labor force survey

unemployed women in the cities cannot provide the required qualifications for the jobs; remain out of the workforce (Kızılgöl 2012: 87–102).

Considering the rate of women employment to total employment, from October 2008 to present, employment rates are rising. When the ratio of employment is concerned, it is seen that there is seasonality. Employment rates are highest during the winter months (December, January, February) and decrease in the summer and fall, especially in August (Fig. 6.3). Looking at male and female employment trends in terms of years, it is observed that both types of employment also showed a

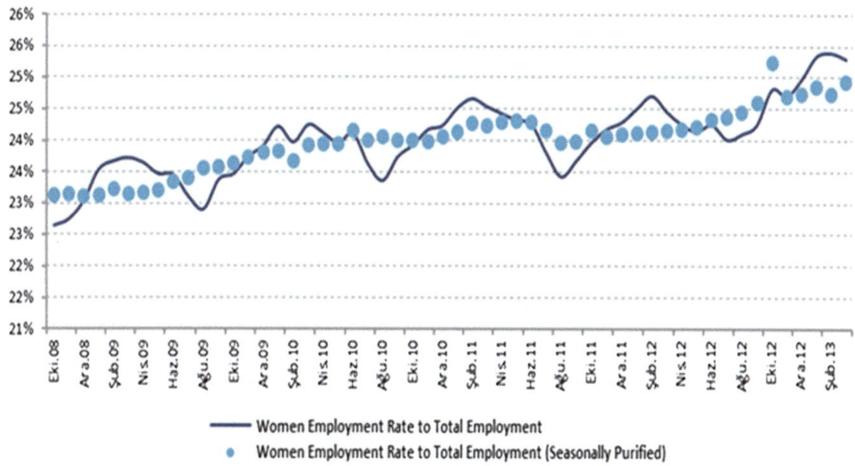

Fig. 6.3 Women employment rate to total employment. *Source* TSI household labor force survey

parallel trend. Analyzing male employment, falling months of the women's employment, although it shows a parallel decline according to women's employment, it fluctuates less and it grows less than women's employment rate in years. Female employment shows a steep drop in the autumn months. From January 2008 until May of 2013, 34% increase had been recorded in female employment which is higher than the increasing male employment rate.

Women's more active participation in working life and their promotion in terms of career have great importance in terms of the economic development of Turkey. Low labor force participation rate of Turkey stems from women's less places in working life. According to TSI, the labor force participation rate in Turkey in 2012 amounted to 50%, and this percent is composed of percent of men and 29.5% of women. Employed female population stays in 26.3%, while the male population has risen to 65%. As women's labor force participation rate is low, unemployment rate is high. This ratio is 8.5% for men and 10.8% for women. The result of low participation in the labor market, women are being dependent on men. Researches show that the inadequacy of services related to child and elderly care, assumptions related to women's work and therefore low career opportunities, inability of education level and gender-based division of labor are the most important causes of women's low labor force participation. These barriers are not only in employment, but also in entrepreneurship, social and political life stands in front of women (Fig. 6.4).

A recession in 2009, which is closer to 5%, although there was an increasing in women's employment, in 2010 and 2011 closer to 9% growth had been experienced close to the domestic market, and staying 2.2% growth in 2012, women's employment had increased and non-agricultural women employment had been closer to 4.9 million. Almost 1.5 million of this 30% is "illegal" working women out of record. Even though, it means an increase in women's share of

Rate of Women's Laborforce Participation %

Year	Rate of Laborforce Participation	Unemployment Rate	Employment Rate	Urban Rate of Laborforce Participation	Rural Rate of Laborforce Participation
1990	34.1	8.5	31.2	17.0	52.0
1995	30.9	7.3	28.7	16.8	49.3
2000	26.6	6.3	24.9	17.2	40.2
2005	23.3	11.2	20.7	18.7	33.9
2010	27.6	13.0	24.0	23.7	36.3
2011	28.8	11.3	25.6	24.8	37.5
2012	29.5	10.8	26.3	26.1	36.9
2013/06	31.9	10.8	28.5	28.6	39.0

Fig. 6.4 Rate of women's labor force participation percentages. *Source* TSI household labor force survey

Table 6.1 Change of women employment rate from 2009 to 2013

Increase in women employment	Total women	Non-agriculture	%
June 2009	6,256,000	3,416,000	54.6
June 2010	6,883,000	3,749,000	54.5
June 2011	7,386,000	4,066,000	55.0
June 2012	7,688,000	4,461,000	58.0
June 2013	8,018,000	4,872,000	60.8
Gap between June 2013 and 2012	330,000	411,000	

Source TÜİK Hanehalkı İşgücü Anketi, (TSI Household Labour Force Survey), http://www.tuik.gov.tr (1 July 2013)

non-agricultural employment from 20 to 25%. Out of agriculture, only 25% of women are working in manufacturing industry. Women, who find jobs in manufacturing industry, work in mostly based on cheap labor, food, garment, textile manufacturing sectors. These are mostly in Istanbul and closer industrial cities as Tekirdag, Kocaeli and Bursa. In June 2012–2013 period, 20% of 330 thousand increasing in women's employment outside agriculture realized, and it also consisted of one-quarter of the jobs created in the industry. Sectors, providing jobs to women, had been education, health and tourism sectors with services sector (Table 6.1).

6.5 Conclusion

The female employment rate in our country has increased from the 1950s until the 1980s and has begun to decline rapidly in the 1980s; in 2000s, it has settled in the last place by reaching an average rate of 24% in OECD countries. According to the result of "Barriers and Opportunities for Women's Introduction to the Labor Market" named study, which is done by the collaboration of Employment Agency and Ministry of Labour and Social Security, women are willing to participate in the labor force and the majority of employers also have a bright view of employing women.

According to the United Nations Development Plan (UNDP) Millennium Development Goals Report 2011, paid women's employment rate, working in non-agricultural sectors, is still quite lower than non-agricultural employment rate in our country. A majority of women, working as unpaid family workers, are engaged in agricultural activities. Women' beginning to work in non-agricultural sectors will increase the proportion of women in wage employment (United Nations Development Programme (UNDP) Human Development Report 2010: 31). In 2011 EU Progress Report, it is indicated that women's rights and gender equality were given wide coverage and limited progress was recorded. Some measures to increase women's employment have been received but the scope and impact of these measures remain at low levels. Also in the report, it is underlined that women take place as limited in senior management positions in relation to education (politics, education, government in management positions in the prefectural authorities, political parties, and trade unions) (TSI 2011a, b). As a result, despite the importance of women's employment in the economic development, women's employment is seen at very low levels in Turkey. We can say that this situation stems from many factors like gender, education, policy-making, family life.

References

Altan S, Ersöz A (1994) Kadının Çifte yükümlülüğü, Kadın ve Sosyal Hizmetler Müsteşarlığı Kadın Statüsü ve Sorunları Genel Müdürlüğü Bülteni, Sayı: 2

Ardıç O (2006) Mikro İktisat, Seçkin Yayıncılık, 4.B, Ankara

Biçerli K (2009) Çalışma Ekonomisi. Beta Yayınları, İstanbul

Directorate General on the Status of Women (DGSW) (Kadın Statüsü Genel Müdürlüğü—KSGM) (2000) Kadın İstihdamı İçin Yeni Perspektifler Ve Kadın İşgücüne Muhtemel Talep, Başbakanlık Kadın Statüsü ve Sorunları Genel Müdürlüğü Yayınları, Ankara. http://www.kandinstatusu.aile.gov.tr

Doğramacı E (1989) Türkiye'de Kadının Dünü ve Bugünü. Ankara, İş Bankası Yayınları

Dülger I (1984) Türkiye'de Şehirde Yaşayan Kadınların Siyasi Haklarını Kullanma Eğilimleri. DPT Yayınları, Ankara

Durusoy Öztepe N (2013) Atölyeye Dönüşen Evler: Denizli Tekstil Sektöründe Ev Eksenli Çalışma

Ersöz GA (1993) Yönetici Kadınların Ve Eşlerinin Ev İçi İş Bölümü Konusundaki Tutum Ve Davranışlarına İlişkin Sosyolojik Bir Araştırma, Hacettepe Üniversitesi Edebiyat Fakültesi

European Commission (2010) Employment in Europe 2010. Publications Office of the European Union, Luxembourg

Hobsbawm EJ (2003) Sanayi Ve İmparatorluk (Trans.: Ersoy A) Ankara: 2.B., Dost Kitabevi Yayınları

Hotar N (2011) Ekonomik Toplumsal Kalkınma ve Kadın İstihdamı, Türk-İş Dergisi, Sayı: 392, Ankara, pp 84–86
International Labour Organization (ILO) (2011) Global Employment Trends. International Labour Office, Geneva
Karabıyık I (2012) "Türkiye'de Çalışma Hayatında Kadın İstihdamı" Marmara Üniversitesi İİBF Dergisi, CİLT XXXII, Sayı I, İstanbul, pp 231–260
Karakayalı H (2007) Ekonomi Kuramı: Mikro ve Makro Çözümleme, Emek Yayınları, 7.B, Manisa
Kızılgöl ÖA (2012) Kadınların İşgücüne Katılımının Belirleyicileri: Ekonometrik Bir Analiz. Doğuş Üniversitesi Dergisi 13(1):88–101
Kocacık F, Gökkaya VB (2005) Türkiye'de Çalışan Kadınlar ve Sorunları. Cumhuriyet Üniversitesi İktisadi Ve İdari Bilimler Dergisi 6(1):195–196, 201
Koray M, Demirbilek S, Demirbilek T (2000) Gıda İşkolunda Çalışan Kadınların Koşulları ve Geleceği. T.C. Başbakanlık KSGM, Ankara
Kurtsan M (2011) İş Hayatında Kadının Yeri ve Karşılaştığı Engeller. http://www.Ba.Metu.Edu.Tr/Manclub/Yayinlar/Glokal/İnsan_Kaynaklari/Kadin.Html. Accessed 5 May 2016
Özaydın MM (2000) Türkiye ve Avrupa Birliğinde İstihdam Politikalarının Genel Görünümü, Karşılaşılan Problemler ve Çözüm Arayışının Mukayeseli Analizi, Ankara: Gazi Üniversitesi Sosyal Bilimler Enstitüsü, Master Thesis
Özdemir Z, Yalman G, Bayrakdar S (2012) Kadın İstihdamı ve Ekonomik Kalkınma: Geçiş Ekonomileri Örneği, In: International Conference on Eurasian economies, 11–13 October, Almaty-Kazakhstan
Özmen F (2012) Türkiye'de Kadın İstihdamı ve Mikro Kredi. Süleyman Demirel Üniversitesi Vizyoner Dergisi 3(6):109–130
Republic of Turkey Ministry of Development (Kalkınma Bakanlığı) (2009) Türkiye'de Kadınların İşgücüne Katılımı: Eğilimler, Belirleyici Faktörler ve Politika Çerçevesi, Beşeri Kalkınma Sektörü Avrupa ve Orta Asya Bölgesi, Rapor No: 48508-Tr
Şahin M (2011) Kayıt Dışı İstihdam ve Esnek Üretim Sürecinde Kadın Emeğinin Durumu: Türkiye'de Ev-Eksenliçalışma. http://www.Kadininstatusu.Gov.Tr/Upload/Kadininstatusu.Gov.Tr/Mce/Eski_Site/Pdf/Uzmanlik_Tezleri/Sahin_Metin_Tez.Pdf. Accessed 5 May 2015
Tansel A (2002) İktisadi Kalkınma ve Kadınların İşgücüne Katılımı: Türkiye'den Zaman-Serisi Kanıtları ve İllere Göre Yatay Kesit Kestirimleri. ERC working papers in economics, 01/05T, May. (http://Erc.Metu.Edu.Tr/Menu/Series01/0105T.Pdf). Accessed 15 Apr 2015
The Confederation of Turkish Trade Unions (TURK-IS) TÜRK-İŞ (2005) Türkiye'de Emek Piyasasında Kadınların Durumu. Ankara, TÜRK-İŞ Yayınları
Türk Dil Kurumu (TDK) (2005) Türkçe Sözlük, Türk Dil Kurumu Yayınları, 10. Baskı, Ankara
Turkish Industry and Business Association (TÜSİAD) (2000) Kadın-Erkek Eşitliğine Doğru Yürüyüş: Eğitim, Çalışma Yaşami ve Siyaset, İstanbul, TÜSİAD Yayınları, Yayın No: TÜSİAD-T/2000-12/290
Turkish Industry and Business Association (TÜSİAD) (2004) Türkiye'de işgücü Piyasasının Kurumsal Yapısı ve işsizlik. İstanbul, TÜSİAD Yayınları, Yayın No: 2004-11/381
Turkish Statistical Institute (TSI) TÜİK (2009) İşgücü, İstihdam ve İşsizlik İstatistikleri Sorularla Resmi İstatistikler Dizisi-1. T.C. Başbakanlık Türkiye İstatistik Kurumu, Ankara
Turkish Statistical Institute (TSI) TÜİK (2010) İstatistik Göstergeler 1923–2009, TÜİK Matbaası, Yayın no: 3493, Aralık 2010, Ankara
Turkish Statistical Institute (TSI) TÜİK (2011a) Kadın İstihdamı Raporu. http://www.tuik.gov.tr. Accessed 1 Sept 2013
Turkish Statistical Institute (TSI) TÜİK (2011b) Hane Halkı İşgücü Araştırması, Ankara
Turkish Statistical Institute (TSI) TÜİK (2013) Hanehalkı Anketi. http://www.tuik.gov.tr. Accessed 1 Sept 2013
United Nations Development Programme (UNDP) Human Development Report (2010). http://www.tr.undp.org. Accessed 20 July 2014

Uysal D (2007). Türkiye'de İstihdam, İşsizlik ve İstihdam Politikaları Türkiye Ekonomisi Makroekonomik Sorunlar ve Çözüm Önerileri, Ed. Ahmet Ay, Çizgi Kitabevi Yayınları, Konya (s: 8; 55–97)

Author Biography

Fatma Cesur is Assistant Professor at Department of Economics in Faculty of Economics and Administrative Sciences. She has graduated from Ph.D. Programme on Economics in Istanbul University in 2000. Her thesis subject is about "Relation Between Money Supply and Inflation: Case of Turkey." Her research fields are Macroeconomics, Monetary Theory, Monetary Policy, Applied Econometrics, Business Cycles.

Chapter 7
Corporate Social Responsibility in the Retail Sector: A Case from Turkey

Onur Kiziltas and Kıymet Tunca Çalıyurt

7.1 Introduction

Corporate Social Responsibility (CSR) is basically the strategies developed and projects made in order to, first and foremost, draw the attention to the sensitivities of the public as well as to create awareness and find solutions to issues that are waiting to be resolved in a society where a brand is a living breathing individual. CSR projects and strategies, which are a golden opportunity to bind with the consumer besides the products and services of the corporations, significantly aid the brand in the matter of sustainability as well. CSR strategies can add positive values, especially in the improvement of brand image and consumer trust.

In this day and age, the term corporate social responsibility is one of the popular words of the modern business world. The changes that happened in both the society and in some organizations are a very big reason and have a lot of importance in the emergence of the term corporate social responsibility, which is commonly used by many individuals and corporations. Also, globalization has helped the term to improve in a social sense, because the communication and information technologies that come with it makes individuals reach information easily, so any positive or negative developments in any corner of the world can be followed effortlessly. Therefore, the development of the information society with the help of increasing levels of education creates a social consciousness. In this sense, the consciousness of protecting the environment, sensitivities to social events and criticism of economic, social and political events increase in today's societies. Furthermore,

O. Kiziltas · K. T. Çalıyurt (✉)
Trakya University, Edirne, Turkey
e-mail: kiymetcaliyurt@trakya.edu.tr

O. Kiziltas
Migros, Edirne, Turkey
e-mail: onurk@migros.com.tr

K. T. Çalıyurt and R. Said (eds.), *Sustainability and Social Responsibility of Accountability Reporting Systems*, Accounting, Finance, Sustainability, Governance & Fraud: Theory and Application, https://doi.org/10.1007/978-981-10-3212-7_7

this consciousness that is developing in the society is reflecting upon the consumption choices of individuals because these individuals expect the organizations in business to act similar to themselves. In other words, today's consumers expect the companies they acquire services from to care about the matters they themselves care about, such as protecting the environment and helping orphans.

In the viewpoint of the organizations, the countless scandals which happen in companies all over the world play a big role in the term corporate social responsibility gaining importance. Examples such as the companies' falsifying their financial reports, them hiring child workers, their misleading marketing activities and the damage they cause to the environment during production cause a big uproar with the help of the media and negatively affect the consumers' choice towards them. In a similar way, nongovernmental organizations which are among the most important cornerstones of our age's democratic society play the key role in increasing the expectance of corporate social responsibility of the companies by educating the consumers. All these developments clearly point out the importance of the phenomenon of corporate social responsibility for the companies.

While the term corporate social responsibility has become fashionable in the business world only in the recent years, it would be wrong to describe it as new. As a matter of fact, the interest on social matters of the business world dates as far back as eighteenth century. In the book written by Adam Smith entitled "Wealth of Nations" at this time, Smith establishes a framework about the relationship between the business world and the society (Nord 2006: 10). Contemporary usage of the notion corporate social responsibility is first seen in the book written by Howard R. Bowen in 1953 entitled as "Social Responsibility of the Businessman" (Carroll 1979: 497). An analysis of the relevant literature shows that from this date on, there are different opinions about corporate social responsibility notion. Two approaches are observed at discussions about the importance and content of the notion.

> First of these approaches embodies the view that corporate social responsibility is unnecessary. This view comes to light in 1962, when Milton Friedman defines corporate social responsibility doctrine as "disruptive in essence". According to Friedman; the business does have purely and simply one responsibility; being engaged in activities which improve profitability by utilizing economic resources; as long as it is in line with the rules of a fair game based on open and free competition. Joseph McGuire emphasized the priority of economic matters in 1963; however in his study he pointed out that the social responsibilities of companies should encompass a wider scale. (Carroll 1979: 497)

In the second approach defending the significance and necessity of the notion corporate social responsibility, Carroll states that the companies not only have responsibilities to stakeholders but also to the whole society. In the same study, Carroll deals corporate social responsibility notion conceptually and builds a model related to the topic. The model named "corporate social responsibility Pyramid" has four levels. These consequently involve economic, legal, ethical and humanitarian responsibilities of the companies. Along with academic studies, the legal developments in employee rights, consumer rights and nature conscious production busted with the advancements in human rights and democracy, contributed to the evolution of corporate social responsibility notion.

7.2 Definition of Corporate Social Responsibility

There exist today many definitions of the term corporate social responsibility and its scope which are made by both scholars and international institutions. For example, in its corporate social responsibility report published in 2000, the Guild of Business World and Sustainable Development expresses the term as promises given by the corporations to cooperate with the employees, their families, the local populace and the society in WBCSD (2010: 10). This is also the definition of corporate social responsibility recommended by the World Bank.

Another definition regarding corporate social responsibility is made by the institution named Business in the Community (BITC). BITC explains corporate responsibility as "the management of the positive effect of the company upon the society and the environment with the help of the interaction between the workings of the company, its products or services and key shareholders such as employees, customers, investors and suppliers".

A broader definition of the term is made by the International Organization for Standardization. According to ISO, an organization taking responsibility for the effect of their decisions and activities on the society and environment, aiding the health and well-being of the society as well as sustainable development by transparency and ethical behaviour, taking into account the expectations of its shareholders in accordance with the current laws and norms of international behaviour, and implementing all these with the organization and using them in their relations is defined as corporate social responsibility (Dodds and Jacqueline 2010: 222).

The various definitions that discuss the term corporate social responsibility reveal that corporations have responsibilities in many different aspects. These various responsibilities branch out as internal and outer of the corporation. In other words, the corporation, first and foremost, is responsible to itself and its shareholders, executives and employees. However, since the corporations are a part of society, they are also responsible to individuals, its customers, its suppliers, competitors, local populace, the environment and both the current and future society (Argandona 2010: 14). In other words, corporate social responsibility is a term about the integration of environmental, social and economical matters within business strategies and applications (Jones et al. 2007a: 582).

7.3 General Information About the Retailing Sector

Retailing is the intermediary services that provide the conveying of the goods between the producer and the consumer. With other words, it comprises overall activities related to marketing the goods and services directly to the ultimate consumer; without commercializing or reselling, neither utilizing them for personal needs (Tek 1984: 46). Among the retailing organizations, there are independent stores (grocery and the like), conjoint retailers (cooperatives, chains, etc.), non-store retailers (direct selling, in-home retailing, etc.), hypermarkets (Migros, Belpa and the like), discount stores (e.g. Vakko Outlet), chain stores (same type of retailer store groups) and shopping malls.

The starting point of contemporary retailing (in Turkey) dates to the years 1954–1957. Even though there have been some work related to the sector following Migros and Gima, there is no significant progress recorded. In 1980s, Turkey is introduced to "customer-oriented sale" concept. Marketing sense being the next level, retailer from abroad started coming to Turkey in 1990s; thus, 1990 has been accepted as the start of retailing era in Turkey, thereby "Customer Satisfaction" and "Relational Marketing" type of concepts sprung.

At the time 2000s have been reached an increased chaining type of retailing came to the agenda; where a growing competition came up, which was in compliance with consumer wants, and a consequent dominance passage from producer to the consumer had been observed. Major hypermarkets in Turkey are Tansaş, Migros, Carrefoursa, Bim, Makro Market, Beğendik, Yimpaş, Kipa, Metro, etc. (Gavcar and Didin 2007: 25–26).

The progress of retailing as a sector has been improved as the number of working women in Europe, migration to urban areas and number of nuclear families increased. Changes in consumers' shopping habits, migration towards big cities, proliferation of usage of credit cards, promotions, rigidity in consumers' time spent for shopping, the increasing number of car owners, the advantage of finding any kind of products at the same place and the like are among important factors impacting the preferability of big retailing companies (Özgüven 2011: 151). While back in the old days, the function of retailing was procurement of manufacturer's products, carrying out some kind of marketing activities and supplying to the consumers; in our day, retail business comes out in a different way. Now, customer-oriented retailing practices like customer satisfaction, quality of service, etc., have already started; along with these, more goods under retailers' brands are marketed to the markets and consumers (Gavcar and Didin 2007: 24).

Huge metamorphoses have been lived especially since 2002. During this development process, several types of retailers were formed and successfully sustained. Hypermarkets, supermarkets, chain markets and discount markets have an important place among these formats. This situation considerably changed consumers' shopping habits and costs. Huge retailers appeared against small retailers. Market share of these big retailers increased rapidly. Moreover, advantages of these companies against manufacturers are unarguable. In fact, global retailing giants' revenues (e.g. Wallmart 244 Billion Euros) multiplied against revenues of a few big manufacturers (Nielsen 2005). Along with these progresses, retailers having reached saturation in Europe and USA moved towards less-developed countries (Azabağaoğlu and Dursun 2008: 2).

Retailing sector in developing countries like Turkey showed huge progress in late years. Retail store businesses established both by Turkish companies and foreign partner entities are continuously adding new rings to their chain stores in order to increase their market shares; thus, their market shares increase (Özgüven 2011: 151). Both from population and consumer spending points, Turkish retailing sector shows an outstanding potential. Being seventh from consumption expenditures aspect, Turkish retailing sector is fifth in food expenditures and eight in non-food expenditures in Europe (https://www.izto.org.tr). Considering the retailing sector as a whole the expected integrated growth rate between 2015 and 2020 is 10% (https://www.atig.com.tr).

7.4 Corporate Social Responsibility Projects in the Retailing Sector

It is known in the recent years that big corporations that operate in the retail sector continuously increase their market shares. As in all sectors, against the social consciousness that increases because of the controversial economical, social and environmental effects of the operations in the retailing sector, the retailers emphasize on corporate social responsibility projects and show their devotion in this matter (Jones et al. 2007a: 591).

Profitability is the basis of a corporation and the reason of its existence, by its nature. For this reason, it is a priority to make profit in the retail sector. In a similar manner, continuity is also a priority. Providing social benefits can be considered an indirect goal. However, nongovernmental organizations do not possess a direct goal of profitability. Making profit only means to acquire a needed way to continue their operations in a field they feel they are responsible in. Continuity is also important in order for the operations to continue (Turgut 2010: 39). Retailers, in a strategical level, integrate corporate social responsibility practices into their core operations not only to secure long-term growth and their financial security but also to keep their positions and reputations in the market (Jones et al. 2007c: 33).

Retailing is a dynamic and innovative sector which changes constantly. The fact that investments being done all the time on people and places in the retailing sector provides a suitable environment for social policies and activities (Jones et al. 2007b: 21). Corporate social responsibilities of the firms which operate in the retail sector consist of the sum of some of their responsibilities. Among these responsibilities are following desirable policies for the people, making decisions and following actions (Turgut 2010: 39). For example, environmental problems, which is one of the important social matters that threaten the retailers in the recent years, has become an important field for corporations that operate in it to act in a socially responsible manner. Some retailer companies such as Tesco have managed to earn a good image in the corporate sense and reputation with their corporate social responsibility policies towards the protection of the nature (Piacentini et al. 2000: 461).

7.5 The Process of Corporate Social Responsibility Projects

Retailing companies have to give effort not only for economical gain but also for their social duties as a corporate citizen. In other words, much like the other sectors, companies that operate in the retailing sector have to execute their corporate social responsibility performances in order to create a positive public opinion (Jones et al. 2007b: 22). The process of corporate social responsibility consists of *four fundamental steps* which are related to and following each other. These steps are told in detail below.

7.5.1 *Situation Analysis*

The first step of the process of corporate social responsibility is situation analysis. As a matter of fact, the whole campaign will be built upon this analysis. The main method that will be used within the context of situation analysis is strength, weakness, opportunities and threats (SWOT) analysis. SWOT analysis is a technique used to determine the strong and weak points of the corporation, technique, process or the settlement and the opportunities and threats caused by the external environment. The purpose of SWOT analysis is to profit from the strong points and opportunities as best as possible and to develop strategies to minimize the effects of threats and weak points by taking into account the internal and external factors. SWOT analysis ensures to focus on areas where being in is strong and large opportunities are waiting to be assessed (Uca Özer and Arıkan 2014: 9). In a general sense, SWOT is a method where the establishment is observed while it is in contact with its environment, in a systematic manner. In this context, the internally strong and weak points of the establishment and the opportunities and threats caused by the external environment are determined. This approach means to analyse the strong and weak points of the establishment and the opportunities and the threats it faces and develop strategies for the future. The operations that are done in the situation analysis can be listed as follows (Özgen 2013: 114–115):

- Identifying and including different shareholders;
- Including different perspectives and sources of information in the process;
- Making an informed decision;
- Determining the conflicting needs and conflict of interests;
- Creating a consensus at the beginning of the project.

The campaign's success depends on the extent of the research. For this reason, research and planning stages should always begin with a situation analysis. Gathering the info to identify the target demographic is the crucial part of the research. The education, traditions, habits, views, beliefs and the local attributes of the target demographic should be known very well. The advantage of these information is its assistance in determining priorities and the composition of messages (Uzun 2010: 38).

7.5.2 *Planning*

The second stage of preparing a campaign is planning. Planning involves the predetermining of the budget required for the campaign, communication tools to use, personnel to work, duration of the campaign, steps to take and the details of the messages which will be served to the masses (Uzun 2010: 39). In the planning stage of the execution of the campaign for corporate social responsibility, it is tried at first to determine how important of a social problem the topic of the project is. The main goal here is to make the senior executives of the corporation to believe that this specific social problem exists. After that, it is researched how much motivation the corporate social responsibility project will be for the employees and therefore if they want to be involved in the campaign or not. In the next stage, specialists about the topic are assigned and the fundamental advantages of the campaign are emphasized (the important thing is not the features of the campaign, but how those features will benefit the society). The topics about the corporate social responsibility project in the planning stage can be listed as follows (Özgen 2013: 116–117):

- Its purpose;
- The advantages it will bring;
- Of whom the campaign crew will consist of;
- The contents of the campaign;
- Its fundamental messages;
- Its target demographic;
- Potential threats;
- Time window;
- Budget;
- Assessment.

7.5.3 *Execution*

In the execution phase which is the third step, all the previous research and planning done on paper are executed (Uzun 2010: 39). After the situation analysis, purpose and the planning stages of the CSR projects are defined, the applicability of the project is reviewed and execution stage is reached. For the CSR project to succeed, the execution should be followed actively, the project's message should be clear—understandable—and to relay the information about the project in regular updates will help immensely in the execution stage (Mermutlu 2009: 38). In the execution stage, pre-defined messages are delivered to the people and organizations that are chosen as the target for the duration of the campaign with various communication tools. The image of the firm is delivered to the public opinion by using communication tools such as media announcements, exhibits, brochures, trips, organization logos and award ceremonies. However, the messages need to be in certain patterns, easily repeatable, catchy and understandable.

7.5.4 Assessment

The assessment of the corporate social responsibility campaign and the evaluation of the results are important. Putting up measurable targets is important in achieving results or to ascertain the non-achieved ones. It is a necessity to determine the assessment criteria and to apply these depending on the content and topic of the campaign. It is also an obligation to do the assessment in terms of accountability towards the society. Doing the SWOT analysis before starting the campaign, doing the pre-test according to the determined content and doing post-tests afterwards, measuring perceptions are important in reviewing the results (Özgen 2013: 121).

7.6 The Execution Methods of Corporate Social Responsibility

It is possible to mention three fundamental methods in the execution of corporate social responsibility projects. These are partnership with a nongovernmental organization, directly going for the result and the mixed method.

7.6.1 Partnership with a Nongovernmental Organization

The first method of executing corporate social responsibility projects for a corporation is to partner up with a nongovernmental organization (NGO) which is related to the field it is in. As it is known, NGOs are organizations that aim to meet a specific need or several which are determined depending upon an information at a specified location and time, which serve without the aim of profit, thus staying in the administration of the public (Ural 2013: 90–91). Whichever subject or project is invested upon, it provides many benefits to partner up with nongovernmental organizations which are specialists at that matter. First of all, the nongovernmental organizations are the source of correct information. Not finishing projects that are created with missing or false information effects the reputation of the corporation negatively. Secondly, strengthening the nongovernmental organizations is for the benefit of the society. On one hand producing projects, nongovernmental organizations will also create communication platforms about the society looking at said project in a sensitive way (Özgen 2013:116). In many situations, the NGO itself can be a known brand and can increase the recognizability of the corporate social responsibility project. The NGO is the expert in the field it operates in, and its voluntary potential can help for the company to expand its network of shareholders. In our country, the primary NGOs that the companies work with on corporate social responsibility projects are Association for Supporting Contemporary Life, Educational Volunteers Foundation of Turkey and Mother Child Education Foundation. The companies usually work with a single NGO which is involved in the subject, such as Turkcell's "Snowdrops (Kardelenler)" project with Association for Supporting Contemporary Life (Ural 2013: 90–91).

7.6.2 Directly Going for the Result

It means the company determining a suitable social goal which is appropriate for its field and executing the project by itself. In the recent years where we come upon directly going for the result, the company executes all the activities itself, from determining the social goal to its execution. For this method, OPET's "Clean Toilets Campaign" can be shown as an example. (Ural 2013: 92). The biggest advantage for the companies who prefer the going for the result method and who makes successful attempts at these will be the success of executing the entirety of CSR activities by itself and the reflection of this success upon the public opinion (Mermutlu 2009: 38).

7.6.3 Mixed Method

Sometimes the resources of the company can be limited and the suggested approach in this situation is to, rather than using those resources on an issue which exists worldwide, to go for a local platform where the whole society can benefit from and where the efforts can be combined with the other aid organizations in the country (Ural 2013: 92–93). For this method, the companies have three paths to choose. These are (Mermutlu 2009: 39):

1. Companies improving a lesser known, less active NGO;
2. Creating a new organization to operate in a new field and doing activities; and
3. Developing a project with an NGO whose area of effect is wide and organizing a CSR activity.

With the mixed method applications, the companies cannot only determine a small but idealist NGO and support a social project, but also can organize campaigns in fields which have not been looked into by an official guild and can cause new ones to be formed by brand improvement work (Ural 2013: 92–93).

7.7 Research About the Understanding of Corporate Social Responsibility of Migros Trading Incorporated and Its Projects

In this section of the research, there are in-depth interviews and results of reviewing documents to assess the projects in order to determine the corporate social responsibility understanding of Migros Trading Inc. and information about their analysis.

7.7.1 The Goal and the Importance of the Research

The main goal of this research is to put forth the understanding of corporate social responsibility of Migros Trading Inc. the scope of this core goal, it is aimed to review, analyse and assess the corporate social responsibility projects which Migros Trading Inc. has conducted in the past terms and still is.

7.7.2 The Method of the Research

The qualitative research approach has been taken in this research. Qualitative research is defined as "a research where qualitative data collection methods such as observation, interview and document analysis are used, where a qualitative process is being used in order to put perceptions and events in a natural environment in the open as a whole and in a realistic manner" (Yıldırım and Şimşek 2011: 39). In the project, two different data collection techniques were used. These techniques are primary data collection and secondary data collection techniques. In the study, in-depth interview method, which is one of the methods of qualitative research also known as the researchers' way of reaching genuine data he needs, was used. In-depth review is also called face-to-face interview, and it is the research that is done by talking to the concerned person or group, asking questions and recording received information. In the research, the topics that will be taken in the reviews have been shaped according to the status of the individual that is being reviewed. Thanks to this, first-hand information was received and reviewed. Sound recordings were taken in some interviews, besides that notes were taken and different questions were asked about the topic in appropriate places to try to receive broad and in-depth information. In choosing the in-depth interview method, advantages it brings such as it being possible to infer more detailed information compared to group discussions, being able to reach more detailed information by interviewing senior executives who are hard to bring together and being able to discuss more complex and technical topics were important. However, it was conducted during face-to-face interviews. The form which is used in the context of in-depth review is present in Attachment 1.

For the secondary data sources, literature and the publications of institutions that are directly related to the topic were used (Reports, news in the media about corporate social responsibility projects, the official Website of the institution, etc.). The secondary data collection method, which is also known as "Literature search", is a method about examining and searching every sort of document which were pre-defined, written, printed, published or non-published. The main secondary data used in the research were obtained from printed publications and from the Internet. Thesis search was done at the Institution of Higher Education Website and theses which are thought to be helpful were reviewed and relevant sections were used as secondary data. Magazines, articles, newspapers and television news which are accessed through online databases were searched and used as secondary data sources. Secondary data were frequently used while outlining the concept of the research and in the preface, theory and methodology sections, also these data aided in the research by guiding the formation of the application stage of the study.

7.7.3 Data Collection Tools and Collecting Datum

The research datum was gathered from interviews done with officials of Migros Corporation department of Corporate Communication of Turkey, the documents presented to the researcher during these interviews, the sustainability reports and the corporate Website of Migros Corporation. During the interviews, an interview form which questions topics such as the general corporate social responsibility strategies of Corporation, its point of view towards the notion of corporate social responsibility, projects that were done and are still being done, the criteria for selecting and reviewing projects, the process of the project, the application methods of the project, etc., was created to be conveyed to the executives. The aforementioned interview form was created by the researcher himself as a result of the datum acquired by literature searching and the guidance of the officials of department of corporate communications. The questions that are on the interview form are designed as a question–answer format in a way that would make gathering findings about the purpose of the study possible. In other words, these questions were prepared in the light of the theoretical knowledge about corporate social responsibility, designed taking into account the contents of successful corporate social responsibility projects and were prepared paying attention not to make them pointed and leading. In addition to this, the sample datum from the awareness surveys about corporate social responsibility projects towards the consumers, and their results were included (Attachment 2). These data are the ones that are acquired as a result of marketing research done to measure the awareness of the consumers towards the corporate social responsibility projects done by Migros Corporation and on which fields these projects were realized on, as well as the perception of other competitor retailing companies towards corporate social responsibility projects.

In the context of the research, a meeting was held in 02.11.2015 with officials from Migros Trading Inc. corporate communications department and the questions on the questionnaire which are prepared beforehand were relayed. Since the results cannot be explained using any statistical method, they were just interchanged and then interpreted.

7.7.4 The Findings of the Research

In this section, there is the analysis of the information gained about the corporate social responsibility projects of Migros Trading Inc. as a result of the qualitative research conducted. In this context, general information about Migros Trading Inc. is given first, then its understanding of corporate social responsibility and projects that are realized are reviewed.

7.8 General Information About Migros Trading Inc.

Today, Migros Trading Inc., which is the pioneer in the modern retailing sector of Turkey, in its stores which have vast areas of usage provides all the needs of its customers with its departments such as cosmetics, glassware, domestic appliances, books and clothing besides food and necessities. The company, which was formed by the municipality of Istanbul in 1954, provided the best prices and quality to the public under the control of the municipality. In 1975, Koç Group, which is one of the most important groups in Turkey, took control of the majority of the shares of Migros with the guidance and desire of its founder, Vehbi Koç, beginning the process of opening chain retail stores which began in Istanbul and quickly spread around to embrace all the consumers in Turkey. By the end of 1989, it began providing services with its 34 stores which are located in 2 metropolises (https://www.migroskurumsal.com).

Migros started the practice of department store by the end of 1990, opening MM and MMM Migros stores. During this process Migros, which is the company that brought the concept of part time employment into Turkey, brought into life its personnel training programs. Migros, which was made public in 1991, created Şok, the first discount brand of Turkey. In addition, Migros, which started for the first time in Turkey its "Migros in the eyes of the customer" with its customer satisfaction surveys, in its 40th year of foundation, became available for the customer in 5 regions with its 75 stores. Migros, which came together with the consumers in Erzurum in 1996, opened its first store abroad, Bakü Ramstore, later in Moscow in the same year. Since the year 1997, it also created the term "Migros Shopping Centre", which provides a new environment for shopping to its customers. Again in the year 1997 Migros, pioneering the online shopping realized Migros Digital Market. In the year 1998, Migros Club Card, the first loyalty card application, was brought into existence. With its pace of launching two stores a week, in the year 2000 Migros opened 128 stores in various locations both domestic and abroad raised its store count to 450 (https://www.migroskurumsal.com).

Migros in the year 2005, with a significant progress bought out the retailing chain Tansaş, reinforcing its leadership in the sector and increased its store count to 722. After the merger of Tansaş, Migros Trading Inc. increased its ability to stay close to its customers with the brands of Migros, Tansaş, Şok, Macrocenter and Sanal Market. In the 2008 report of Global Powers of Retailing which is prepared by Deloritte annually, Migros entered the list from the 236th place, which is a first for Turkey. Migros Trading Inc. between the years 2001 and 2006 ranked as 12th among 50 fastest growing companies. Migros Trading Inc., which reinforces its fast growth plan with innovative practices that provide value for its customers, in the year 2009 started the bag that can dissolve in nature for the first time in Turkey and supported this practice with a usable cloth bag. "Jet Registers" with its fun and easy use that provide the customers a different shopping experience was brought together with the Turkish customers for the first time by Migros. In the year 2010s January, it brought into life its "Clean Farming Practices" with the leadership of the Ministry of Food, Agriculture and Livestock. In the year 2011 with the desire to reach its customers from everywhere, it put into service the "Mobile Market" which provides the possibility of shopping with scanning a barcode on mobile devices. In August 2011, it ceded ownership of Şok Discount Markets and Migros-Jets took their place in the sector as the most practical and fastest form of supermarkets (https://www.migroskurumsal.com).

In the year 2014 Migros, which celebrated its 60th year, succeeded in relaying its understanding of "The New Generation of Retailing" to every part of society with its increasing ratio of penetration, its effective operation management which leads investments in productivity and with innovations that is befitting to its pioneer role. Migros with its vision of "Better Future", taking leading steps in sustainability studies and topics such as environment, people and a better life, succeeded in earning the title of the only retailing corporation that entered the sustainability index of BİST (Istanbul Stock Exchange) (https://www.migroskurumsal.com).

7.9 The Corporate Social Responsibility Vision of Migros Trading

Migros Trading Inc. is the only retailer that appeared in the Sustainability Index of BIST two years in a row. The index puts into light how the companies approach matters such as global warming, biodiversity, effective use of natural resources, employment, supply chain, the companies corporate governance which are about sustainability and are important for both Turkey and the rest of the world and bases itself on sharing these performances with the public opinion in a transparent manner. Migros Trading Inc. while developing joint projects not only for its customers, but also for its employees, workers, suppliers and shareholders, assist in today's depletable resources with sustainable projects. It determines the areas that are needed for the society to advance and collaborates with various foundations, associations and nongovernmental organizations.

Migros, which received the "The Most Beloved Retailing Company of Turkey" prize for the 11th consecutive time in 2014, which came first in the Turkey's Lovemarks 2014 research in the retailing sector, realizes practices that will be looked upon by the new generation of retailing with its "Better Future" motto.

7.10 The Corporate Social Responsibility Projects and Campaigns of Migros Trading Inc.

Migros Group conducts studies on corporate social responsibility projects that are shaped in the context of "sustainability" and concern the future of the society that will be a model and provide hope for the whole society in case a solution is reached. With all the projects it creates, Migros works together with various foundations, associations and nongovernmental organizations to spread the consciousness of social sensitivity with the involvement of its business partners, customers and employees.

For the last five years, Migros Trading Inc. created the "Sustainability Committee" which is in the body of the corporation and is lead by the senior executives in order to coordinate its processes of sustainability studies from a single location. The sustainability committee provides the measurement and evaluation of the sustainable values such as sustainability, productivity, use of natural resources which include all the functions of the company, with tangible criteria. Computer-assisted measurement methods are used for the supervision of all the said sustainability factors. The corporate social responsibility projects on which Migros Trading Inc. is collaborating with nongovernmental organizations are explained in the section below.

7.10.1 Corporate Social Responsibility Projects About the Environment

- Migros conducts various studies with the Environmental Protection and Packaging Waste Recovery and Recycling Foundation (ÇEVKO) on raising environmental consciousness and awareness. For years, it has organized informing studies for its customers about "**Recycling and Packaging Waste Recovery**" in its stores. Also with the assistance of ÇEVKO and Turkish Marine Environment Protection Association, a variety of clean environment projects are put into practice where Migros personnel are contributing and studies about environmental consciousness are carried out. Besides this, Migros works together with Educational Volunteers Foundation of Turkey and Mother Child Education Foundation about recycling wastes which emerge because of the operation with the "Integrated Waste Management Plan".
- Migros also together with Turkish Marine Environment Protection Association —TURMEPA, works on cleaning our seas by systematically collecting "**Waste Vegetable Oils**" in the stores. In this project where the customers are also contributors, vegetable oils that are gathered thanks to the waste oil cans in the stores are brought back into the economy.
- Since 2007, the olives that have been produced by Aegean Forest Foundation have been put to sale in Migros Group stores, and the received revenues are used to create new **forest areas** instead of the burned and damaged ones. Until this day, 529 thousand saplings have been planted in the Aegean region.
- For the purpose of collecting waste batteries, Migros Group placed waste battery bins to its stores with the collaboration of TAP (Foundation of Manufacturers and Importers of Portable Batteries). The batteries that are gathered with the help of these bins are sent to TAP foundation regularly, and they are being assisted in recycling them back into the economy.
- Another practice regarding the environment is "Recycling-Kiosks". Customers contribute to recycling by throwing the paper, glass, plastic, metal packing wastes and batteries into separate boxes prepared beforehand after scanning their barcodes. Besides that, with the help of World Wild Life Fund (WWW) Turkey, customers adopt endangered sea turtles, which have been living more than 110 million years by using the "Environment Points" earned from waste recycling.
- It is seen that Migros took very important steps for green retiling. The first store earning LEED GOLD certificate is Bodrum Maya Migros store. Leadership in Energy and Environmental Design (LEED) Certificate issued by US Green Buildings Council is the utmost recognizable and admittable green building certificate.
- For the electronic wastes, Macrocenter, 5M Migros, MMM Migros, MM Migros and Maxi Tansaş, Midi Tansaş format stores collect all kinds of electrical and electronic equipment wastes from big and small home appliances to lighting fixtures, from sporting goods to information technology equipments; send these

wastes to the Ministry of Environment licensed recycling facilities within the "**Electronic Waste Collection Project**" and this way enables recycling at an optimum rate.

7.10.2 Corporate Social Responsibility Projects About Education

- There are lots of practices in "Education". In 2013 "**Book for All Foundation**" stood up stands in five Migros stores and collected books were conveyed to people all over Turkey waiting for them via "**Book for All Foundation**". The project widened in 2014 and applied at Migros stores in 70 cities. Customers dropped books they purchased at a discount from these stores or books taken from their houses into "Book for All Foundation Boxes". Through this campaign, 47,000 books have been collected.
- There are many educational projects Migros and Educational Volunteers Foundation of Turkey (TEGV). At the year end, some part of the revenue earned from specific branded goods for sale at Migros stores is transferred to TEGV for children's education. Besides, every year during the whole week of *April 23 National Sovereignty and Children's Day* with the help of **TEGV Money Boxes** in Migros Group stores, books, stationery and toys purchased and dropped to these boxes are transmitted to TEGV Parks and shared with children.
- With periodical campaigns, Migros supports nongovernmental organizations. According to this, some part of the Mother–Baby catalogue goods sale revenue earned during October–November 2014 has been donated to Turkish Foundation for Children in Need of Protection. This way Koruncaklar (children to be protected) are enabled to have education by developing their personal skills and supported to become a good member of the society.
- In 2014 and 2015 by sending school stationery sets to, "Migros gave support to the education of **children living in disadvantageous areas**".
- In order to support "**1 Million Books for Our Martyrs**" campaign started by Çanakkale Onsekiz Mart University, Migros sent 700 books to Çanakkale Onsekiz Mart University Library.

7.10.3 Culture-Art CSR Projects

- For the last 21 years, Migros collaborates with State Theatres in culture-art areas. According to this, during *April 23 National Sovereignty and Children's Day* week Migros purchases children theatre play tickets in 11 cities and distributes them free of charge. This way **half a million kids** have been enabled theatre plays.

- With "Hands-in-Hands to the Future" slogan Migros Children's Theatre the longest sustained social responsibility project in Turkey, brought 300,000 children in 53 different cities with the fairy world of theatre. On its tenth anniversary in 2014–2015 theatre season, **Migros Children's Theatre** visited seven regions during seven months and played.

7.10.4 Health and Sports CSR Projects

- Migros Group adding value to the lives of Turkish consumers with its pioneering implementations in retailing sector for 61 years combined healthy nutrition and activity under the slogan "Good Living" within "**Look Lively Project**". The project found life with "Get Move" call and everybody choosing the city they live from the application "Get Move" won as they walked. Sport fans showed high interest to the project and at the end of competition, fitness parkours were established in Erzincan and Sakarya provinces.
- Another implementation of Migros is "**Young Players Project**", and it became an important project where children learnt embracing sports as a lifestyle. Within the project, amateur sport teams composed by 11–12-year-old boys and girls were trained in TEGV Training Parks for sports ethics understanding-based football. Besides, existing football fields were renewed. At the end of six-year lasting project, at 10 training parks 4997 children from 11 provinces received Turkish Football Federation certificated football training. Number of volunteering trainers became 245.
- For the last ten years with the "**Special Support for Special Athletes Campaign**" every year at a specific period, part of the revenue earned from P&G products is transferred to Special Olympics Turkey Organization and mentally challenged young people are supported for sporting activities. Since 2004 with the help of the project encompassing the consumers willing to support special athletes and sports, 7.3 million Migros customers helped supporting near 5,000 special athletes to hold on to life. Special athletes earned 124 medals from several national and international events.
- With the application started in 2011 at Tansaş format under the name "**No Barriers in Shopping**" is continuing with an increasing interest and liking. Disabled citizens coming to Tansaş stores shop with the assistance of personnel. Another project again at Tansaş format is "**Let Us Carry**". Under this project, customers aged over 65 are companioned and they are helped in carrying bags to their houses. Besides, with the "Healthy Days with Tansaş" activity, six days a week sporting activities are supervised by trainers. Totally cost-free activity gains popularity day by day.

7.10.5 *Social Aid* CSR *Projects*

- According to the protocol signed with HAYTAP (Animal Rights Federation) applying to specific stores mentioned in the protocol, Migros hands goods, the last consumption date of which are nearing or the expires the same day, to HAYTAP authorities within social aid frame. This way Migros supports nourishment of street animals. The project having started with 65 pilot stores in 2014, reached 205 stores in 2015.
- Again within social aid frame under "**Clothing Donation Campaign**", Migros in collaboration with Ariel bestowed new and clean clothing to more than 500,000 children. Customer intensely supporting this campaign dropped outgrown clothing of their children to donation boxes in Migros stores, and at the end of the campaign clothes are cleaned by Ariel and via several foundations they are sent to children in need.

7.11 General Assessment of Corporate Social Responsibility Projects of Migros Corporation

As a result of completed and ongoing corporate social responsibility projects and interviews done with executives of Migros Corporate Communications department, the general profile and projects of the company can be assessed as follows.

As it was summarized in Table 7.1, the corporate social responsibility projects of Migros Trading Inc. are carried out by a committee which consists of the CEO, senior executives and the staff from the corporate communications department. The CEO and the senior executives have the say in the planning and supervision stages of corporate social responsibility projects which are coordinated and executed by the corporate communications department.

Migros Trading Inc. works together with institutions that it is a member of at the stage of selecting corporate social responsibility projects. At the same time, one of the most important factors in deciding projects is to choose areas that involve the society and is beneficial to it. At this stage, topics that alongside customers, personnel and nongovernmental organizations can include themselves in are prioritized. Individual help efforts (such as doing renovations on a school in Van) are not included in the topics of corporate social responsibility projects.

First thing to do during the process of executing corporate social responsibility projects is planning studies about the application of the project. In this context, details such as which nongovernmental organizations to collaborate with and on how the customers and employees can aid the project are formed. At the same time, further planning is done in line with goals given to the stakeholders. For example,

Table 7.1 General structure of corporate social responsibility projects of Migros Trading Inc.

Structure of the CSR department	• A committee consisting of the CEO, senior executives and the corporate communications department
Creation of CSR projects	• Suggestions from institutions that Migros is a member of topics that are involving the society
Execution of CSR projects	• Joint applications with nongovernmental organizations
CSR process	• Receiving offers and starting studies • Division of labour • Planning towards goals
Assessment of the effects of CSR projects upon the consumers	• Market and customer behaviour questionnaires • Comparing goals with numerical datum

goals, such as a company water savings this year will be …m^3/h, are given. During planning, these sorts of goals are taken into account. In the second stage, execution begins without delaying the offers with the involvement of nongovernmental organizations.

To assess the effects of corporate social responsibility projects on the consumers, the research unit which is located within the body of Migros conducts questionnaire research upon market and customer behaviour. In these questionnaires, questions about social responsibility project topics are asked to the customers. Usually, consumers' perceptions and awareness about the said projects are tried to be measured. In Attachment-2, there are some examples and datum about the aforementioned questionnaires. Many questionnaire studies show that the customer awareness towards corporate social responsibility projects towards Migros Ticaret A.Ş. is much higher than other retailing firms. The results of the corporate social responsibility projects which are defined by the committee are also assessed by the committee. In the assessment stage, the goal ratios are compared to the actual numerical datum, and thus it is determined if the goals are reached or not. The goals of corporate social responsibility projects are not ones that are beneficial to the company such as sales, the ones focused are the ones that are completely for the benefit of the society.

7.12 Discussion

How they shape their company image is as important as the companies for their products and their advertising methods. A good, successful and lasting image is paramount in gathering customers, binding them for a long time and protecting the current customer portfolio. However, on the other side, a possible negative image can pose serious troubles for the future of the company. For this reason, the time and budget spent on creating an image increased in importance over the last years. Usually, firms try to come up with new products and try to advertise these in different methods for image arrangement. Most times, even though the new products are interesting and loved by the people, the fact that these are not long lasting and not the only factor as they used to be in creating customer loyalty has lead the companies to create alternatives. At this point, corporate social responsibility projects that find themselves on company lists in agendas have a major importance for the companies to protect their image. If a firm is able to describe its social responsibility projects well to those who do not buy their products, it will be successful.

The fundamental purpose of this research is to define the corporate social responsibility understanding of Migros Ticaret A.Ş. In the context of this purpose, past and ongoing corporate social responsibility projects of Migros were examined and data gathered by in-depth reviews with department executives were analysed. When the corporate social responsibility projects of Migros Ticaret A.Ş. are examined, it is seen that lots of projects in various fields are undertaken. The said fields can be classed as "environment", "education", "culture and arts", "health and sports" and "social aids".

The first of the most important of findings that are acquired from interviews is that a majority of the corporate social responsibility projects are towards the environment that take into consideration the principle of sustainability. Migros Ticaret A.Ş. prioritizes the environmental problems in its corporate social responsibility projects. It is also observed that nongovernmental organizations are usually partnered with on the realization of said projects.

According to the findings gathered from the interview results, Migros Ticaret A.Ş. conducts projects that are beneficial to the society in many different fields and is aware of the sensitivity of its consumers towards public opinion and social responsibility projects. In this sense on one hand creating plus value with applications that are beneficial to the society, on the other hand it increases its image value by what the company accomplishes with volunteer work and how important the works it does is. With this indirectly increasing image value, the profit rates of the company increase as well as the general viewpoint of the society towards the company in a positive way. At the same time, Migros Inc. while sharing the services conducted with the public opinion constantly, it enables people to know about the importance of the studies done. This situation is better understood from the consecutive customer satisfaction rewards the company has received, and it is seen how the activities of the company reflect positively.

In the topic of customer loyalty, Migros Ticaret A.Ş. reaps the reward of creating a positive image in its customers' minds in terms of corporate social responsibility projects by not putting financial concerns as the basis of its studies. Migros Ticaret A.Ş. never once until this day declared how projects are done completely from their own finances in any of its commercials or messages and have not answered any questions regarding the matter. Corporate social responsibility projects are topics that are prone to manipulation and receive all kinds of criticism all over the world. For this reason, if it is informed that the work is voluntary and there is no expectation in each step of the projects, it gains clarity and removes the questions that the consumers have. Thus, it becomes possible to form a loyal customer base.

In this project study, it has been tried to assess the corporate social responsibility projects of Migros Ticaret A.Ş. The most important limitation of the research is that the said applications are assessed by the executives of the corporate communications department of the company. Since in the case where the corporate social responsibility applications of Migros Ticaret A.Ş. are reviewed with the point of view of the consumer it is possible to arrive at different results, the findings of the research cannot be generalized. It would be significantly beneficial to the literature for more detailed field researches where the aforementioned projects are looked at in the perspective of the consumers. It is believed that this project research can shine a light to more detailed researches in the future.

Attachment 1. Interview Questions

1. From whom does your firm's corporate social responsibility department consist of? What kind of organization structure does it have?
2. How are corporate social responsibility projects created? How are project offers received and reviewed?
3. How are corporate social responsibility projects executed? Are partnership with other organizations made? Does the company take charge of the projects by itself?
4. How does the process of executing corporate social responsibility projects proceed? How are planning studies conducted?
5. How are the effects of corporate social responsibility projects measured upon the consumers?
6. How is it measured if the completed corporate social responsibility projects reached their targets? How are the results assessed?

Attachment 2. Sample Datum about Awareness Surveys of CSR Projects towards Consumers Conducted by Migros Ticaret A.Ş. and Their Results

See Tables 7.2, 7.3 and 7.4.

Table 7.2 Findings about consumer awareness towards the fact that Migros Ticaret A.Ş. is conducting corporate social responsibility projects

(MIGROS) conducts social responsibility projects	Total (%)
I completely agree	22.7
I agree	37.6
I neither agree nor disagree	10.4
I disagree	4.2
I completely disagree	1.2
No comment/no answer	23.8
Total	100

Table 7.3 Findings about what is known by the consumer about CSR projects conducted by Migros Ticaret A.Ş. and competing retailer companies

	KS1b. Known about MİGROS CSR projects (%)	KS1b. Known about CARREFOUR CSR projects (%)	KS1b. Known about BİM CSR projects (%)
Support to protecting the nature and environment	7.6	1.6	2.2
Supporting sports	3.8	2.5	0.9
Support given to art and culture-related activities	2.2	1.9	0.6
Support given to education	4.3	1.9	1.5
Support given to health and health services	3.1	2	1.2
Support given to NGOs or unions for development of the society	2	1.9	0.4
Contribution to awareness rising of customers	2.2	1.2	0.9
Appreciating and equally treating the employees and contributing work safety	2	1.3	1.2
Food aid for people in need	1.8	1	0.9
Operations according to Ethics and moral values	2.1	0.9	1
Giving support to historic preservation	0.3	0.1	0.3
Activities directed to human rights	0.7	0.5	0.1
Giving support to projects combating domestic violence women rights children rights	0.7	0.3	0.2
Do not remember/no idea	67.2	82.8	88.5
Total	100	100	100

Table 7.4 Findings about consumer awareness about the content of Migros coordinated CSR projects

	Support to protecting the nature and environment	Supporting sports	Support given to art and culture-related activities	Support given to education	Support given to health and health services	Support given to NGOs or unions for development of the society	Contribution to awareness rising of customers
Basis	**112**	**56**	**33**	**64**	**46**	**29**	**33**
2 Arbour	1.8	0	0	0	0	0	0
4 Recycling	5.4	0	0	0	0	0	3
6 Environment friendly bags	7.1	0	0	0	0	0	0
8 Protecting environment	1.8	0	0	0	0	0	0
13 For disabled people	0	5.4	0	0	0	0	0
14 National team sponsorship	0	10.7	0	1.6	0	0	0
15 Being a basketball sponsor	0	3.6	0	0	0	0	0
19 Other	3.6	1.8	0	3.1	2.2	0	3
20 April 23 Sponsorship	0	0	0	1.6	0	0	0
21 Student grants	0	0	0	10.9	0	0	0
23 Collecting books	0	0	0	3.1	0	0	0
24 Supporting LÖSEV	0	0	0	0	13	10.3	0

(continued)

Table 7.4 (continued)

	Support to protecting the nature and environment	Supporting sports	Support given to art and culture-related activities	Support given to education	Support given to health and health services	Support given to NGOs or unions for development of the society	Contribution to awareness rising of customers
25 Campaigns for collecting clothing	0	0	0	0	0	0	0
31 TEMA	1.8	0	0	0	0	0	0
32 Father Send Me to School	0	0	0	1.6	0	0	0
33 Kardelen	0	0	0	1.6	0	0	0
36 Support to Kızılay	0	0	0	0	0	6.9	0
44 Aid campaigns	0	0	0	0	0	0	0
45 Çevko project	4.5	0	0	0	0	3.4	0
46 Haytap	0	0	0	0	0	0	0
48 Petrol Ofisi	0	0	0	0	0	0	0
49 Vodafone Istanbul Marathon	0	5.4	0	0	0	0	0
50 Cinema activity/project	0	0	3	0	0	0	0
51 Koç University/Koç group	0	0	0	6.3	0	0	0

(continued)

Table 7.4 (continued)

	Support to protecting the nature and environment	Supporting sports	Support given to art and culture-related activities	Support given to education	Support given to health and health services	Support given to NGOs or unions for development of the society	Contribution to awareness rising of customers
52 Girls to school	0	0	0	3.1	0	0	0
53 Distributing glass bottle to support breast cancer	0	0	0	0	0	0	6.1
54 Friendship food	0	0	0	0	0	0	0
57 Free entry to children's theatre	0	0	3	0	0	0	0
58 Art exhibition	0	0	6.1	0	0	0	0
59 Support to opera	0	0	3	0	0	0	0
998 Do not remember	74.1	73.2	84.8	67.2	84.8	79.3	87.9

	Appreciating and equally treating the employees and contributing work safety	Food aid for people in need	Operations according to EthicsEthics and moral values	Giving support to historic preservation	Activities directed to human rights	Giving support to projects combating domestic violence women rights children rights	Names of CSRCSR projects
Basis	**29**	**27**	**31**	**4**	**11**	**10**	**34**
2 Arbour	0	0	0	0	0	0	0
4 Recycling	0	0	0	0	0	0	0
6 Environment friendly bags	0	0	0	0	0	0	0

(continued)

Table 7.4 (continued)

	Appreciating and equally treating the employees and contributing work safety	Food aid for people in need	Operations according to EthicsEthics and moral values	Giving support to historic preservation	Activities directed to human rights	Giving support to projects combating domestic violence women rights children rights	Names of CSRCSR projects
8 Protecting environment	0	0	0	0	0	0	2.9
13 For disabled people	0	0	0	0	0	0	0
14 National team sponsorship	0	0	0	0	0	0	0
15 Being a basketball sponsor	0	0	0	0	0	0	0
19 Other	6.9	0	0	0	0	0	5.9
20 April 23 Sponsorship	0	0	0	0	0	0	0
21 Student grants	0	0	0	0	0	0	0
23 Collecting books	0	0	0	0	0	0	0
24 Supporting LÖSEV	0	0	0	0	0	0	2.9
25 Campaigns for collecting clothing	0	0	0	0	0	0	2.9
31 TEMA	0	0	0	0	0	0	0

(continued)

Table 7.4 (continued)

	Appreciating and equally treating the employees and contributing work safety	Food aid for people in need	Operations according to EthicsEthics and moral values	Giving support to historic preservation	Activities directed to human rights	Giving support to projects combating domestic violence women rights children rights	Names of CSRCSR projects
32 Father Send Me to School	0	0	0	0	0	0	0
33 Kardelen	0	0	0	0	0	0	0
36 Support to Kızılay	0	0	0	0	0	0	0
44 Aid campaigns	0	18.5	0	0	0	0	0
45 Çevko project	0	0	0	0	0	0	0
46 Haytap	0	0	0	0	0	0	2.9
48 Petrol Ofisi	0	0	0	0	0	10	2.9
49 Vodafone Istanbul Marathon	0	0	0	0	0	0	0
50 Cinema activity/project	0	0	0	0	0	0	0
51 Koç University/Koç group	0	3.7	0	0	0	0	0
52 Girls to school	0	0	0	0	0	0	0
53 Distributing glass bottle to support breast cancer	0	0	0	0	0	0	0

(continued)

Table 7.4 (continued)

	Appreciating and equally treating the employees and contributing work safety	Food aid for people in need	Operations according to EthicsEthics and moral values	Giving support to historic preservation	Activities directed to human rights	Giving support to projects combating domestic violence women rights children rights	Names of CSRCSR projects
54 Friendship food	0	0	0	0	0	0	14.7
57 Free entry to children's theatre	0	0	0	0	0	0	0
58 Art exhibition	0	0	0	0	0	0	0
59 Support to opera	0	0	0	0	0	0	0
998 Do not remember	93.1	77.8	100	100	100	90	64.7

References

Argandona A (2010) The Tourism Industry: some lessons from Spanish experience. Working Paper 844, University of Navara

Azabağaoğlu MÖ, Dursun E (2008) Tüketicilerin Modern Gıda Perakendecilerine Karşı Davranışının Analizi. Tekirdağ Ziraat Fakültesi Dergisi 5(1):1–12

Carroll AB (1979) A three-dimensional conceptual model of corporate performance. Acad Manag Rev 4(4)

Dodds R, Jacqueline K (2010) Among canadian mass tour operators: good awareness but little action. Int J Contemp Hosp Manag 22(2)

Gavcar E, Didin S (2007) Tüketicilerin "Perakendeci Markalı" Ürünleri Satın Alma Kararlarını Etkileyen Faktörler: Muğla İl Merkezi'nde Bir Araştırma. ZKÜ Sosyal Bilimler Dergisi 3(6): 21–32

Jones P, Comfort D, Hillier D (2007a) Marketing and within food stores. Br Food J 109(8): 582–593

Jones P, Comfort D, Hillier D (2007b) What's in store? Retail marketing and corporate social responsibility. Mark Intell Plan 25(1):17–30

Jones P, Comfort D, Hillier D (2007c) A case study of the top ten global retailers. EuroMed J Bus 2(1):23–35

Mermutlu, FG (2009) Türkiye'de Kurumsal Sosyal Sorumluluk Uygulaması: Kardelen Projeleri. Istanbul University Institute of Social Sciences, unpublished master thesis

Nielsen AC (2005) Perakende ve Hızlı Tüketim Ürünleri Pazarı Değerlendirilmesi. Raporu, Istanbul

Nord T (2006) In the hotel industry: a cross cultural perspective. Stockholm University, unpublished master thesis

Özgen E (2013) Kurumsal Sosyal Sorumluluk. In: Öztürk MC (ed) Kurumsal Sosyal Sorumluluk Projeleri. Açıköğretim Fakültesi Yayınları, Eskişehir. Publication No: 1973, pp 112–130

Özgüven N (2011) Kriz Döneminde Küresel Perakendeci Aktörlerin Performanslarının Topsis Yöntemi İle Değerlendirilmesi. Atatürk Üniversitesi İktisadi ve İdari Bilimler Dergisi 25(2): 151–162

Piacentini M, MacFadyen L, Eadie D (2000) Corporate social responsibility in food retailing. Int J Retail Distrib Manage 28(11):459–469

Tek ÖB (1984) Perakende Pazarlama Yönetimi. Üçel Yayıncılık, Izmir

Turgut N (2010) Yönetsel Süreçte Kurumsal Sosyal Sorumluluk. Hacettepe University Institute of Social Sciences, unpublished doctoral thesis

Uca Özer S, Arıkan VI (2014) Turizm Destinasyonlarında Sürdürülebilirliğe Yönelik Yeni Bir Yaklaşım: "Sakin Şehirler (Slow Cities)" - Zeytinbağı (Trilye)'na Yönelik Bir Uygulama Önerisi, Turizm ve Qonaqperverlik Tedqiqatları – Tourism and Hospitality Studies, No 4, pp 5–15

Ural ZG (2013) Kurumsal İletişim Çalışmalarının Sürdürülebilirliği Açısından Kurumsal Sosyal Sorumluluk Uygulamaları. Istanbul Kültür University Institute of Social Sciences, unpublished master thesis

Uzun B (2010) Kurumsal Sosyal Sorumluluk Projesi Olarak "Gönül Köprüsü" Projesinin Değerlendirilmesi. Gazi University Institute of Education Sciences, unpublished master thesis

Yıldırım A, Şimşek H (2011) Sosyal Bilimlerde Nitel Araştırma Yöntemleri. Seçkin Yayıncılık, Ankara

Internet Sources

https://www.atig.com.tr/arastirma/raporlar/tr/perakende_sektor_raporu.pdf. Retrieved 12 Nov 2015
https://www.izto.org.tr/portals/0/argebulten/perakendesekt%C3%96r%C3%9C_g%C3%96zdesev%C4%B0lm%C4%B0%C5%9E.pdf. Retrieved 04 Oct 2015
https://www.migroskurumsal.com/Icerik.aspx?IcerikID=43#. Retrieved 02 Nov 2015
WBCSD (2010) World Business Council for Sustainable Development, corporate social responsibility: making good business sense. https://www.wbcsd.org/includes/getTarget.asp?type=d&id=MzE0. Retrieved: 28 Mar 2015

Author Biographies

Onur Kiziltas has graduated from Mechanical Engineering Department and works in Migros Corporation. He has master's degree in Business Administration, Social Graduate School, Trakya University.

Kıymet Tunca Çalıyurt, CPA, CFE, graduated from the Faculty of Business Administration at Marmara University, Istanbul, Turkey. Her master's and Ph.D. degrees are in Accounting and Finance Programme from the Social Graduate School, Marmara University. She worked as auditor in Horwath Auditing Company, manager in McDonalds and finance staff in Singapore Airlines. After vast experience in private sector, she has started to work in academia. She is holding CFE and CPE titles. Her research interests are in accounting, auditing, fraud, social responsibility, corporate governance, finance and business ethics, with a special interest in aviation management and women rights in business. She is the founder of the International Group on Governance, Fraud, Ethics and Social Responsibility (IGonGFE&SR) and the president of the National-International-Students' Conference Series on Governance, Fraud, Ethics and Social Responsibility (IConGFE&SR). In 2009, she also founded the International Women and Business Group, which organizes a global, annual conference. Kiymet has published papers, chapters and books both nationally and internationally on fraud, social responsibility, ethics in accounting/finance/aviation disciplines and NGOs in Springer and Taylor Francis Routledge, some titles are Emerging Fraud (with Sam Idowu), Corporate Governance: An International Perspective (with Sam Idowu), Women and Sustainability in Business: A Global Perspective, Sustainability and Management: An International Perspective (with Ulku Yuksel), Globalization and Social Responsibility (with David Crowther). She is regular speaker at International Economic Crime Symposium in Jesus College, Cambridge University. She is a member in editorial board Social Responsibility Journal, Journal of Financial Crime, International Journal of Law and Management.

Chapter 8
The Role of Empathy in Sustainable Development and Corporate Social Responsibility of Multinational Enterprises in China

Maria Lai-Ling Lam

8.1 Introduction

Although corporate social responsibility (CSR) and sustainable development are both "essentially contested concepts," much research has discovered that multinational enterprises' corporate social responsibility can contribute to sustainable development when multiple stakeholders are engaged in their process of policy development and implementation (Husted and Allen 2007; Jo and Harjoto 2012; Laszlo 2008; Moon 2007). "In essence, CSR can be viewed as an extension of the firm's efforts to foster effective CG <corporate governance>, ensuring the firm's sustainability via sound business practices that promote accountability and transparency not only to shareholders, but also to the greater society" (Jo and Harjoto 2012:54). When multinational enterprises (MNEs) adopt CSR practices, they must overcome these four explicit challenges: "the developing of well-performing CSR projects and programs, building competitive advantages based on CSR, responding to local stakeholder issues in the host countries, and learning from different CSR experiences on a worldwide basis" (Cruz and Boehe 2010). Managers are expected to know how to engage multiple stakeholders and respond to social, moral, and economic needs of multiple stakeholders before they can meet the interest of shareholders (Freeman 1984). They need to use the empathetic communication with multiple stakeholders which is recommended to foster organizational justice and better corporate performance (Dutton 2003; Dutton et al. 2006; Ehrenfeld 2008; Eshelman et al. 2012; Kanter 2009; Krueger 2008; Inkpen and Tsang 2005; Lam 2007; Pruzan 2008; Vaill 1989, 1996, 2007; Wood and Kaufman 2007; Young 2004). The effective way to engage local stakeholders is to practice the "ethic of care" (Simola 2007). The "ethic of care" allows the participants to listen,

M. L.-L. Lam (✉)
Research Department, AJ-Great Limited, Flat 607, 6/F, Kwai Cheong Centre,
50 Kwai Cheong Road, Kwai Chung, Hong Kong, China
e-mail: 19710901marialam@gmail.com

K. T. Çalıyurt and R. Said (eds.), *Sustainability and Social Responsibility of Accountability Reporting Systems*, Accounting, Finance, Sustainability, Governance & Fraud: Theory and Application, https://doi.org/10.1007/978-981-10-3212-7_8

understand, and establish trust during the engagement process. Simola said "It is when respect for, and empathic engagement with, local communities and their needs occur that other native capabilities such as the facilitation of voice, and development of trust can occur" (Simola 2007:135). Simola's concept of empathetic engagement in multinational enterprises is necessary for the formation of empathetic organization culture and must include the process of development of organizational capabilities for social reflections and resilience. *In this chapter, the organizational process of the development of empathetic engagement with different stakeholders is advocated to be an essential element in the CSR programs.* This process will be aligned with our innate human capacity and the moral ecology of the capitalist system (Novak 2004). I will describe how empathy, embedded in a culture with care and justice, allows organizations to be sustainable and be aligned with the values of market economy when companies implement their CSR programs with humanistic approaches. I will also describe the CSR context in which multinational enterprises operate in China. Then I will describe how two multinational enterprises develop their moral progresses through empathetic engagement with their stakeholders in their CSR programs.

8.2 Relationships Between Empathy and Sustainable Development

When I reflect on my ongoing research work about corporate social responsibility of foreign multinational enterprises in China, I find that empathy is aligned with the best corporate social responsibility practices (Lam 2014). I define empathy as a process to consider a particular perspective of another person, to feel as another person feels, and to take action for the needs of another person. Empathy is our innate ability. Empathy, embedded in a culture of care and justice, has been validated to promote better common good (Batson 2011; Hoffman 2000). The practice of empathy is related to the provision of space for all individuals to exercise their power of being human in a market economy. The moral of free market economy is to empower individuals to exercise their rights of being human. Practicing empathy can increase a participant's responsiveness to specific needs of people in a particular context. The practice also respects individual autonomy and justice in each interpersonal relationship. Thus, the practice of empathy, embedded in a culture of care and justice, allows organizational actors to be more deeply informed with multiple frames of references and more reflections about the contingent solutions. When companies are facing many disruptive innovations and many unknown competitors, they need to cultivate the process of engaging many different stakeholders in their CSR programs if they want to be sustainable. Through the empathetic engagement with different stakeholders, they can be open to their limitations and develop social capacities for reflections. They have to be open to change their approaches and develop strong relationships with their customers, employees, community, environment, shareholders, and other stakeholders while they contribute to the moral ecology of the capitalist system.

> Moral ecology is the sum of all those conditions—ideas, narratives, institutions, associations, symbol systems, prevailing opinions and practices, and local dispensers of shame and praise—that teach us the habits necessary for human flourishing and support us in their practice (Novak 2004, p. 31).

The recent economic crises and numerous business scandals really shake our faith in the capitalist system. What kinds of moral ecology do we need in the future when capitalism is being seriously criticized in the world? Businesses are called to be innovative and uphold the moral values to protect environment and respect human lives in the process of seeking long-term financial returns if they want to sustain the best of the capitalist system (Bower et al. 2011). If there is no action to sustain the capitalist system, the rising power of populists will request their government to do more interventions and destroy the capitalist system that generates greater common good. Business needs to be committed concerning the principles of their CSR practices and be innovative if they want to sustain the capitalist system that enables the companies to flourish. In the process of the development of moral capacities, companies need to respect human lives as the ends, not the means for financial return. When companies are called by the community to solve social and environmental problems in a digitized global market economy, the more effective way is to cultivate the habit of empathy, embedded in a culture of care and justice (Lam 2015). The practice of empathy, embedded in a culture of care and justice, allows organizations to collaborate with the respect of human dignity and common good. Corporate social responsibility leading sustainable corporate development and the capitalist system is possible when companies are committed to incorporate the process of empathetic engagement with different stakeholders. Practicing empathy with the principles of care and justice allows companies to develop their moral strength and capacities for social reflections and resilience. Managers can understand the interconnectedness of lives in a global market economy and realize the consequences of their daily choices on other people's lives.

Given so much disruptive innovations in the current capitalist system, it is increasingly important for corporations to be more deeply informed, and to develop multiple scenarios of future and multiple normative framework if they want to be sustainable (Porter and Kramer 2006; Sarewitz 2016; Schepers 2006). Many researchers have endorsed empathy as the essential element for the development of multiple framing, reflective exploration of meaning, and practical reasoning in the process of engaging local stakeholders in win–win collaborative activities (Dutton 2003; Dutton et al. 2006; Ehrenfeld 2008; Eshelman et al. 2012; Pruzan 2008; Salovey and Mayer 1990; Vaill 1989, 1996, 2007; Young 2004). Empathy is stated as "the fundamental competence of social awareness" (Goleman et al. 2002:50; Goleman 2006). It is also the foundation for the practice of partnership and justice (Auroi 2003; Beji-Becheur et al. 2008; Boyd et al. 2007; Crul and Zinkhan 2008; Drake and Schalachter 2007; Laczniak and Murphy 2008; Lam 2012a; Tate et al. 2009).

Empathy is also advocated as a major contributor in human relationships and the organization process for sustainability (Aguilera et al. 2007; Nidumolu et al. 2009; Lyon 2004; Mirvis and Googins 2006; Laszlo 2008; Zadek 2004). It is also considered to be one key component of servant leadership (Walumbwa et al. 2010) or effective leadership (Ashkanasy et al. 2002; Kellett et al. 2006). It relies on active listening and a secure space for the practice of vulnerability in collaboration (Cook et al. 2013; Vaill 1989). Thus, in the journey toward sustainable development, organizations need to embrace empathy as their corporate culture (Lyon 2004; Vaill 1996) and practice empathetic communications with their suppliers (Ehrenfeld 2008; Kanter 2009; Krueger 2008; Inkpen and Tsang 2005; Lam 2007; Pruzan 2008; Vaill 1996, 2007; Wood and Kaufman 2007; Young 2004). The literature about empathy and market-based approaches in the management literature also shows that empathy can be another paradigm to explain why some companies choose to empower the insignificant partners to access the market and become producers (Lam 2012a, 2013b; McKague and Oliver 2012). The emphatic engagement with stakeholders allows the companies to develop its moral values that enable organizations to flourish in the capitalist system and have financial return from their CSR projects. Thus, the organizational practice of empathy, embedded in a culture of care and justice, can enable the companies to sustain themselves, the stakeholders, and the moral ecology of the capitalist system.

8.3 Research Methodology

This chapter is based on my reflections of my 20 years' study of sustainability and corporate social responsibility practices of multinational enterprises in China (Lam et al. 2010; Lam 2000, 2002, 2004, 2005, 2006, 2007, 2008, 2009a, b, 2010a, b, c, d, 2011a, b, c, d, 2012a, b, c, d, 2013a, b, c, 2014, 2015). I have extensively reviewed the literature about moral ecology of the capitalist system, business ethics, and empathy in a digitalized global market economy. I mediate the power of the capitalist system on our lives and the changes of China since she moved from communist system to market economy in 1979. With many disruptive innovations and contingent managerial solutions in a world of unprecedented changes, I question how to use the logic of market efficiency to solve social and environmental problems in many CSR programs. During my fieldwork in China (2006–2016), I attended many CSR conferences and wanted to find whether CSR activities led by multinational enterprises were workable or not.

I have conducted my research in eleven cities in China: Beijing (2006, 2008, 2009, 2010); Dalian (2006), Shanghai (2006, 2007, 2010, 2016); Hangzhou (2007, 2010); Guangdong (2011), Tianjin (2009), Qingdao (2007), Nanjing (2007), Chongqing (2006, 2007, 2009), Wuhan (2012, 2013), and Hong Kong (2006–2016). I interviewed thirty Chinese executives from twenty different foreign multinational enterprises which are classified as global corporate citizens (Logsdon and Wood 2005). Eighteen foreign corporations in the study have earned corporate citizens' awards from the Chinese government during the past ten years. Fifteen interviewees were responsible for corporate social responsibility programs, while the others were working for sales, marketing, purchasing, human resources, and software development. Sixteen companies were in the areas of information technology, electronic, and plastic industries. Two companies were in the pharmaceutical industry. One was in consumer packaged goods industry, and another one was in the apparel industry. I applied the process model of organizational sense making explaining how the Chinese managers, who are working for foreign multinational enterprises in China think, discuss, and perform with their key stakeholders and the world (Basu and Palazzo 2008). The data for the perception of these Chinese executives about their corporations' sustainability practices were collected through semi-structured, in-depth personal interviews during 2006–2016. Several interviewees were interviewed twice during this ten-year period. Each one was conducted in the interviewee's native tongue and lasted from 1hour to 3 hours. The interview instrument included four major parts: personal experiences, internal organization practices, impact of the companies' corporate social responsibility programs, and the expectations and recommended changes in their companies' corporate social responsibility programs. I also validated the data and my interpretations by evaluating the interviewees' corporate reports, their American and Japanese headquarters' interviews, published Chinese documents, articles, and Chinese students' dissertations about corporate social responsibility and multinational enterprises (Huberman and Miles 1984; Glaser and Strauss 1967). I also used feedback from different professional communities in the USA, France, Japan, and China to validate my findings.

8.4 CSR Context in China

Many multinational enterprises (MNEs) in China are often encouraged by the Chinese government and international non-government organizations to pursue sustainable development through corporate social responsibility activities (Prasad 2015). The recent study about corporate social responsibility development and trends in China shows that many CSR programs of MNCs in China are limited to philanthropy and short-term projects even though the CSR knowledge and performance of MNEs is better than that of companies by other ownership types (Embassy of Sweden and CSR Asia 2015). They mainly focus on economic issues and the compliance of labor laws in the workplace labor issues. CSR activities are not fully integrated in their strategies and daily decision-making process. The focus of CSR program is on operational efficiency and legal compliance. As the Chinese market is exceedingly price competitive within weak institutional environments, MNEs are proposed not to invest in the CSR even though these CSR activities are defined as no harm activities to the stakeholders (Campbell 2007). When there are more and more external government regulations and international non-government organizations to scrutinize the activities of MNEs in China, firms tend to maintain minimum CSR investment to comply with the external requirements (Bansal 2005). Many multinational enterprises (MNEs) in China adopt evasive compliance with the external industry code of conduct in their supply chain management

(Lam 2012a). A few powerful multinational enterprises are criticized for their use of their corporate social responsibility activities to mask their labor and environmental abusive programs (Abdul-Gafaru 2009; Ellram et al. 2008; Gugler and Shi 2009; Harney 2008; Murdoch and Gould 2004; Lam 2007, 2009a; Lund-Thomsen 2008; Rondinelli 2006; SACOM report 2010; Stiglitz 2006; Sum and Ngai 2005; Tate et al. 2009; Visser 2008).

In my field work in China, eighteen companies (80% of companies in this study) just want to gain legitimacy and to minimize their operating costs in China through corporate social responsibility programs (Lam 2010a). They are not committed to long-term strategic CSR practices in China even though these companies have received global corporate citizenship awards and have listed their global CSR visions, values, and principles in their CSR reports. They do not invest in the management capability in the area of stakeholders' engagement. They select the suppliers based on cost and production efficiency rather than CSR performance. They use many evasive compliance-oriented mechanisms (i.e., monitoring, evaluating, reporting, and sanctioning) over Chinese suppliers (Lam 2012a). There is lack of internal alignments between commercial and responsible supply chain objectives. The foreign multinational enterprises' global buyers can demand quick delivery at the expense of the Chinese suppliers' workers' basic health and safety rights. The CSR reports about sustainable supply chain activities and the fulfillment of the international code of conduct will not disclose the abuse of labor in China. It is quite easy for the Chinese suppliers to fake the compliance of the global buyers' international code of conduct such as Social Accountability 8000 standard (SA 8000) at the expense of labor's welfare. One interviewee told me the company had to cover up the cost of submitting the SA 8000 report by reducing the salary of its workers. Thus, many global CSR reports do not reflect their response to the needs of local stakeholders. Several interviewees told me their CSR reports were used for the global investors and to support the stock prices of their companies in the US stock market. Their CSR reports are quiet similar and their activities in China appeared to comply with the societal requirements. They tend to adopt similar CSR structures and practices. Their CSR practices are described as "isomorphic" as these companies conform to other foreign enterprises in China which deal with similar situation (DiMaggio and Powell 1983).

8.5 Two Pioneers

During the Spring, 2016 semester, I asked 177 undergraduate students at Hong Kong Polytechnic University to investigate the CSR practices of those companies that had been chosen as leaders in their own industry according to the Sustainability index; many students still were surprised to know these well-represented companies still could not implement their global CSR strategy and programs in China. It is still very challenging for many MNEs to localize their global CSR strategy in China and to integrate CSR practices in their key decision-making process even though these

MNES are named as exemplars in many international CSR reports. In my 10 years' study of CSR of 30 MNEs in China, only two foreign multinational enterprises in China initiate empathetic engagement with their workers and local Chinese suppliers and develop first-hand understanding about the needs of local stakeholders. Their CSR officers are very dedicated and practice empathetic communication with selected stakeholders. Their empathetic engagement with stakeholders gradually becomes part of the organization culture. The process of empathetic engagement, with the culture of care and justice, allows these two companies to initiate industry codes of conduct that are trustworthy. Through their experience of interacting with local stakeholders in China, they have encouraged the headquarters to develop a global CSR strategy and apply it in other areas. They can use their global presence in China to experiment various sustainable practices for the competiveness of their firms and the well-being of multi-generations (Abdul-Gafaru 2009; Aguilera et al. 2007; Berstein and Greenwald 2009; Kenrick 2011; Philipp 2009). Thus, the process of empathetic engagement with stakeholders provides opportunities to develop trust relationships and opens the door to other opportunities.

Case A—Empathetic Engagement with Labors

One Japanese multinational company's CEO is committed to improve the workers' welfares in his subsidiaries in China after he received a report about the horrible labor conditions in China in 2005. He established CSR offices in Tokyo, Japan, and Shenzhen, China in 2006. The Japanese CSR officer is under CEO in the headquarters while the Chinese CSR officer has already many years of working experience in Dailian where there are numerous Japanese investments. They both have empathy about the Chinese workers and want their corporations to provide many social programs that should be provided by the Chinese government because they know many Chinese workers coming from rural areas have to struggle to adapt to factory conditions in an urban city. They successfully convinced CEO to invest two US dollars for each worker's training in the area of public health, education, and social security, and then they relied on a local labor consulting organization to train their local workers to be empowered in a factory. They both practice empathy with the principle of care and justice. They also have developed disciplinary programs and incentives to encourage workers to participate in daily operations.

After many years of empathetic engagement with workers, the two CSR officers transfer their experience to selected Chinese suppliers to know how to empower their workers through many workshops and training in China. The company and her suppliers develop trusting relationships and share norms of social and environmental practices and common codes of conduct in their industries. The codes of conduct are specific and enforceable. Members will not join the codes of conduct just for window dressing activities as they have already shared the norms of CSR practices in their daily engagement process. Through the empathetic engagement process with its own workers and then with its Chinese suppliers, the company can easily develop some institutionalized codes of conduct based on years of trusting relationships. These codes of conduct have been further elaborated and complied with other industry codes of conduct in the global market. Thus, the empathetic engagement with workers and suppliers leads to enforceable codes of conduct in its own industry. The company gradually can transfer its CSR practices and experience in China back to its headquarters. Since 2009, the company established its universal CSR policy and different global organizations in the headquarters to managing CSR practices in other parts of the world, and the company has made moral progress and knows how to integrate CSR strategy in the daily decision-making process. The company is also one of the few Japanese companies which had not encountered labor strikes in 2011 and also named as a pioneer in the CSR practices in China. Thus, the empathetic engagement with local employees and suppliers allows the Japanese executives to have first-hand understanding about the local situation and incorporate the voice of local stakeholders in the global CSR strategies.

Case B—Empathetic Engagement with Suppliers
A Japanese multinational company is commended for its environmental policy in the entire global supply chain and requests the suppliers around the world to fulfill the requirements of the three-year green certificates whose environmental performances are much higher than the shared environmental standards in the industry. One Japanese expatriate has many years of experience in many foreign countries and is an active member in the CSR society in Hong Kong. He adopts empathetic engagement with local Chinese suppliers. He has empathy about the fear of Chinese suppliers who would like to get the contracts and have no confidence of fulfilling the requirements of the three-year green certificates. He also knows that that some Chinese suppliers perceive that these environmental standards are used to reduce their competitiveness. He has to persuade his supervisors to invest more money in the education and training of selected Chinese suppliers in the green certificate program. He also initiates a provision for more ongoing education rather than just using a survey to ask whether the Chinese suppliers comply with the green requirements. He knows that the self-assessment in the form of a survey as part of the compliance mechanism in the industries in China is not valid since the Chinese suppliers tend to have a more positive assessment on their environmental performance in the self-assessment surveys. He also knows that there are poor concepts of environmental stewardship between Chinese suppliers and many Chinese employees. He prefers to provide numerous training workshops, elaborate the requirements in-depth, develop progressive objectives, and manage the performance of these suppliers through a three-year comprehensive green certificate program. As he practices empathy toward these Chinese suppliers and enhances their capability in reaching the requirements in the green certificates through many consultative face-to-face interactions, the selected suppliers are motivated to continue learning and be monitored if they want to renew their green certificates issued by this reputable global company. These selected suppliers also learn new practices and increase other buyers' confidences in their environmental capabilities as they earn green certificates. The practice of empathy is embedded in the principle of care and justice. Later, the Chinese suppliers learn and adopt higher standards. The empathetic culture is generated through many inter-organization communications. Thus, the empathetic engagement with local selected suppliers provides an

incentive to develop trusting relationships with their suppliers and practice procedural justice and enhance the internal alignment between commercial and responsible supply chain objectives in the company. Later, the company passes this experience to other suppliers in Thailand and is committed to develop a CSR standard much higher than the industry standard.

8.6 Conclusion and Discussion

In the above two pioneers' CSR practices, the process of empathetic engagement includes the empowerment of insignificant partners such as workers and suppliers. The process is initiated by the leaders and then diffused as institutional practices in and outside their companies. The process of empathetic engagement with employers and suppliers is fruitful when the leaders from these two exemplars are committed to their companies' CSR values and are willing to be connected with these Chinese workers and suppliers through training and development. They legitimate the rights and power of these stakeholders who were once weak or insignificant and could be ignored by powerful foreign multinational enterprises. They empower these weak parties and invest in their capacities to be partners in their corporate social responsibility programs through ongoing training and support. They select the best suppliers who could be aligned with their companies' social, environmental and economical values. They chose to practice empathy with the principle of care and justice. Later, the process of empathetic engagement is embraced by many employees and becomes part of the organizational culture through many trainings and seminars. Consequently, the partnership approaches in their relationships with their selected suppliers generate better codes of conduct and CSR practices that are related to the sustainable development of the entire industry. The two pioneers learn how to transfer their local CSR experience from China to the headquarters and other subsidiaries. The institutionalization of the process of empathetic engagements with their local stakeholders become part of their global CSR practices and organization culture. These two pioneers are engaged in institutional dialogues with their employees, suppliers, and communities even though they are working in very price-competitive and weak institutional environments in China. The process of empathetic engagement with the local stakeholders allows companies to know how to localize their CSR strategy and programs in China and learn to develop trusting relationships with their stakeholders. Companies can learn how to be innovative in their CSR programs when they are willing to be open to include the voices of insignificant partners with empathy. They respect human dignity and are willing to develop trusting relationships with others through wealth creation activities. The values behind the process of empathetic engagement with different stakeholders in the CSR programs are trust, cultural humility, human dignity and solidary in a community. These values are claimed to be the virtues of moral ecology of a global market economy (Novak 2004). When the capitalist system is at risk, many citizens may use their voting power to ask their government to strictly regulate the business for better social and environmental returns. It is better for companies to be proactive and be creative agents to reduce all negative externalities on people's lives and environment as soon as possible. The process of empathetic engagements with various stakeholders allows companies to adopt humanistic approaches that are related to our innate human capacity—empathy and to the core values of moral ecology of a capitalist system that allows people to flourish in the community. The practice of empathy with the principle of care and justice can also develop virtues of trust, cultural humility, and solidarity in the community. Companies need to be innovative in their CSR programs that can sustain themselves and the virtues of the moral ecology of the capitalist system. Thus, CSR can contribute to sustainable development of companies and the market system when there are empathetic engagements with the local stakeholders in the policy and organization culture.

The acceleration of globalization of multinational enterprises (MNEs) also causes the proliferation of corporate social responsibility initiatives in the global market. Many MNEs have to learn how to develop empathetic engagement with their local stakeholders such that their CSR practices can contribute to sustainable development. They need to cultivate the process of including many stakeholders and be open to multiple frames of the future and multiple interpretations through empathetic practices with the principle of care and justice. They need to be committed to develop the process of empathetic engagement in their organizational culture. More managers need to cultivate the skills of empathetic communication with multiple stakeholders when they want to be effective spokespeople for the multiple stakeholders and builders for multiple coalitions in their CSR programs. Empathetic engagement with various stakeholders can foster trusting relationships and organizational justice among stakeholders. It is necessary to incorporate the process of empathetic engagement with multiple stakeholders when companies develop innovative CSR programs that can sustain themselves and the moral ecology of the capitalist system. The process of empathetic engagement will enable managers to be sensitive to the needs of their stakeholders, have compassion toward their stakeholders, and choose a wise path to enable their companies to be sustainable in the current global market economy through their CSR programs. Thus, the process of empathetic engagement also empowers managers to be open to many changes and seeks better social, economic, and environmental returns in their CSR programs that achieve sustainable development of their companies and stakeholders. The process also enhances the organizational capabilities for reflection and resilience in a world of permanent white water. This moral progress allows the companies to seek economic, social, and environmental returns in their CSR programs while they are open to many changes. Thus, the process of empathetic engagement with various stakeholders allows the companies to develop their moral progress that is grounded on our innate human capacities and moral ecology of the capitalist system when companies are seeking sustainable development through their CSR programs.

Acknowledgements The author thanks Dr. Martha J. B. Cook, Dr. Georgia L. Eshelman, Dr. Peter. B. Vaill, Alice Lam, and 200 interviewers in this project.

References

Abdul-Gafaru A (2009) Are multinational corporations compatible with sustainable development? The experience of developing countries. In: Ivanaj, McIntyre (eds) Multinational enterprises and the challenge of sustainable development. Edward Elgar, Cheltenham, UK, pp 50–72

Aguilera R, Rupp D, Williams C, Ganapathi J (2007) Putting the "S" back in corporate social responsibility: a multilevel theory of social change in organizations. Acad Manag Rev 32 (3):836–863

Ashkanasy NM, Hartel CEJ, Daus CS (2002) Diversity and emotion: the new frontiers in organizational behavior research. J Manag 28(3):307–338

Auroi C (2003) Improving sustainable chain management through fair trade. Green Manage Int 43:25–35

Bansal P (2005) Evolving sustainably: a longitudinal study of corporate sustainable development. Strateg Manag J 26(3):197–218

Basu K, Palazzo G (2008) Corporate social responsibility: a process model of sensemaking. Acad Manag Rev 33(1):122–136

Batson CD (2011) Altruism in humans. Oxford University Press, New York

Beji-Becheur A, Pedregal VD, Ozcaglar-Toulouse N (2008) Fair trade—just how "fair" are the exchanges? J Macromarketing 28(1):44–52

Berstein A, Greenwald C (2009) Benchmarking corporate policies on labor and human rights in global supply chains. Pensions and Capital Stewardship Project Labor and Worklife Program, Harvard Law School, Boston, MA. http://www.law.harvard.edu/programs/lwp/pensions/publications/occpapers/occasionalpapers5.pdf. Accessed 14 Apr 2013

Bower JL, Leonard HB, Paine LS (2011) Capitalism at risk: rethinking the role of business. Harvard Business School Publishing, Boston, MA

Boyd DE, Spekman RE, Kamauff JW, Werhane P (2007) Corporate social responsibility in global supply chains: a procedural justice perspective. Long Range Plan 40:341–356

Campbell J (2007) Why would corporations behave in socially responsible ways? An institutional theory of corporate social responsibility. Acad Manag Rev 32(3):946–996

Cook M, Lam M, Klemann A (2013) Active listening and vulnerable collaboration as foundational elements in the education for sustainability. In: Proceedings of 2013 North American management society conference

Crul L, Zinkhan G (2008) A theory of the firm perspective on marketing and distributive justice. J Macromarketing 28(1):12–23

Cruz L, Boehe DM (2010) How do leading retail MNCs leverage CSR globally? Insights from Brazil. J Bus Ethics 91:243–263

DiMaggio PJ, Powell WW (1983) The iron cage revisited: institutional isomorphism and collective rationality in organizational fields. Am Sociol Rev 48:147–160

Drake MJ, Schlachter JT (2007) A virtue-ethics analysis of supply chain collaboration. J Bus Ethics 82:851–864

Dutton JE (2003) Breathing life into organizational studies. J Manage Inq 12(1):5–19

Dutton JE, Worline MC, Frost PJ, Lilius J (2006) Explaining compassion organizing. Adm Sci Q 51(1):59–96

Ehrenfeld J (2008) Sustainability by design: a subversive strategy for transforming our consumer culture. Yale University Press, New Haven, CT

Ellram LM, Tate WL, Billington C (2008) Offshore outsourcing of professional services: a transaction cost economics perspective. J Oper Manage 26:148–163

Embassy of Sweden and CSR Asia (2015) A study on corporate social responsibility development and trends in China. http://www.swedenabroad.com/ImageVaultFiles/id_29016/cf_347/CSR-development-and-trends-in-China_WEBB.PDF. Accessed 26 July 2016

Eshelman G, Lam M, Cook M (2012) Three contributing factors to effective utilization of technology in management education and practice: personhood, mindfulness, and meditation. J North Am Manag Soc 6:24–34

Freeman R (1984) Strategic management: a stakeholder approach. Pitman Publishing Inc, Massachusetts

Glaser BG, Strauss AL (1967) The discovery of grounded theory: strategies for qualitative research. Aldine, Chicago, IL

Goleman D, Boyatzis R, McKee A (2002) Primal leadership. Harvard Business School Press, Boston, MA

Goleman D (2006) Social intelligence: the new science of human relationships. Bantam Dell, Random House Inc, New York

Gugler P, Shi J (2009) Corporate social responsibility for developing country multinational corporations: lost war in pertaining global competiveness? J Bus Ethics 87:3–24

Harney A (2008) The China price. The Penguin Press, New York, NY

Hoffman ML (2000) Empathy and moral development: implications for caring and justice. Cambridge University Press, New York

Huberman AM, Miles M (1984) Data management and analysis methods. In Denzin, Lincoln (eds) Handbook of qualitative research. Sage, Thousand Oaks, CA, pp 428–444

Husted B, Allen D (2007) Strategic corporate social responsibility and value creation through large firms: lessons from the Spanish experience. Long Range Plan 40:594–610

Inkpen A, Tsang E (2005) Social capital, networks, and knowledge transfer. Acad Manag Rev 30 (1):146–165

Jo H, Harjoto MA (2012) The cause effect of corporate governance on corporate social responsibility. J Bus Ethics 106:53–72

Kanter R (2009) Supercorp: how vanguard companies create innovation, profits, growth, and social good. Crown Business, New York, NY

Kellett JB, Humphrey RH, Sleeth RG (2006) Empathy and the emergence of task and relations leaders. Leadersh Q 17:146–162

Kenrick V (2011) CEOs and investors embrace sustainability. http://site.destinationgreen.com/?p=985. Accessed 14 Apr 2013

Krueger D (2008) The ethics of global supply chains in China—convergence of East and West. J Bus Ethics 79:113–120

Laczniak G, Murphy P (2008) Distributive justice: pressing questions, emerging directions, and the promises of Rawlsian analysis. J Macromarketing 28(1). http://epublications.marquette.edu/cgi/viewcontent.cgi?article=1014&context=market_fac&sei-redir=1#search="Laczniak,+1999. Accessed 14 Apr 2013

Lam M, Lam A, Lam L (2010) The importance of non-Government organizations in the corporate social movement in China. The International Journal of Humanities 7(12):101–114

Lam MLL (2000) Working with Chinese expatriates in business negotiations: portraits, issues, and applications. Quorum Books, Westport

Lam MLL (2002) Globalization and Asian Christians. In: Proceedings of the 18th annual christian business faculty association conference

Lam MLL (2004) Reflections on integrating faith and marketing education. In: Proceedings of the 20th annual christian business faculty association conference

Lam MLL (2005) Redemptive business education in the age of globalization. In: Proceedings of the 21st annual christian business faculty association conference

Lam MLL (2006) A study of the transfer of corporate social responsibility from multinational Enterprises to Chinese Subsidiaries: implications for Christian business educators. In: Proceedings of the 22nd Christian business faculty association annual conference. Cedarville University, Dayton, Ohio, USA

Lam MLL (2007) A study of the transfer of corporate social responsibility from well-established foreign multinational enterprises to Chinese subsidiaries. In: Hooker J, Hulpke J, Madsen P (eds) Controversies in international corporate responsibility (International Corporate Responsibility Series, vol 3. Carnegie Mellon University, Pittsburgh, PA, pp 343–363

Lam MLL (2008) Being innovative by doing good. In: Proceedings of academy of innovation and entrepreneurship 2008. Tsinghua University, Beijing, China

Lam MLL (2009a) Beyond credibility of doing business in China: strategies for improving corporate citizenship of foreign multinational enterprises in China. J Bus Ethics 87:137–146

Lam MLL (2009b) Sustainable development and corporate social responsibility of multinational enterprises in China. In: McIntyre JR, Ivanaj S, Ivanaj V (eds) Multinational enterprises and the challenge of sustainable development. Edward Elgar, Cheltenham, UK, pp 230–244

Lam MLL (2010a) Political implications of the corporate social responsibility movement in China. J Int Bus Res Pract 4:125–134

Lam MLL (2010b) Managing corporate social responsibility as an innovation in China. In: Al-Hakim L, Chen J (eds) Innovation in business and enterprise: technologies and frameworks. IGI Global, Hershey, PA, pp 224–238

Lam MLL (2010c) Beyond legal compliance: toward better corporate citizenship of foreign multinational enterprises in China. J Biblical Integr Bus 13:100–109

Lam MLL (2010d) Sustainable development in a global market economy—a compassion-oriented approach. In: Proceedings of post-Christian business faculty association conference

Lam MLL (2011a) Becoming corporate social responsible foreign multinational enterprises in China. J Int Bus Res Pract 5:47–61

Lam MLL (2011b) Successful strategies for sustainability in China and the global market economy. Int J Sustain Dev 3(1):73–90

Lam MLL (2011c) Becoming corporate social responsible foreign multinational enterprises in China. J Int Bus Res Pract 5:47–61

Lam MLL (2011d) Challenges of sustainable environmental programs of foreign multinational enterprises in China. Manag Res Rev 34(11):1153–1168

Lam MLL (2012a) An alternative paradigm for managing sustainability in the global supply chain. Int J Soc Ecol Sustain Dev 3(4):1–12

Lam MLL (2012b) A best practice of corporate social responsibility: going beyond words on a page and a check. In: Jaworski J (ed) Advances in sociology research, vol 13. Nova Science, New York, pp 157–164

Lam MLL (2012c) Corporate social responsibility movement in China: what can foreign corporations' corporate social responsibility programs in China do to universal values? In: Wang K (ed) Dialogue among cultures: peace, justice and harmony. Foreign Language Press, Beijing, China, pp 221–234

Lam MLL (2012d) Toward sustainability through innovation. In: Proceedings of inaugural international conference on innovation and entrepreneurship: theory and practice relevant to China, Wuhan, China

Lam MLL (2013a) An educator as a contemplative practitioner in business education. J High Educ Theory Pract 13(2):84–93

Lam MLL (2013b) Being Chinese: a reflective study of foreign multinational corporations' sustainable development and global talent programs in China. In Proceedings of the NAMS (North American Management Society) of MBAA international conference, U.S.

Lam MLL (2013c) A case study of the challenges of sustainable business development in China. In Proceedings of the 2013 AIB-Midwest conference, U.S.

Lam MLL (2014) Empathy as a major contributing factor to sustainability in the global supply chain. In Khosrow-Pour (ed) Inventive approaches for technology integration and information resources management. IGI Global Publications, Hershey, PA, USA, pp 53–67

Lam MLL (2015) Moral ecology in a digitized global market economy through empathetic practice. In: Proceedings in the North American Management Society conference, Chicago, U.S.

Laszlo C (2008) Sustainable value: how the world's leading companies are doing well by doing good. Stanford University Press, Stanford, CA

Logsdon JM, Wood DJ (2005) Global business citizenship and voluntary codes of ethical conduct. J Bus Ethics 59(1–2):55–67

Lund-Thomsen P (2008) The global sourcing and codes of conduct debate: five myths and five recommendations. Dev Change 39(6):1005–1018

Lyon D (2004) How can you help organizations change to meet the corporate responsibility agenda? Corp Soc Responsib Environ Manag 11:133–139

Mckague K, Oliver C (2012) Enhanced market practices: poverty alleviation for poor producers in developing countries. Calif Manag Rev 55(1):98–129

Mirvis P, Googins B (2006) Stage of corporate citizenship. Calif Manag Rev 48(2):104–126

Moon J (2007) The contribution of corporate social responsibility to sustainable development. Sustain Dev 15:296–306

Murdoch H, Gould D (2004) Corporate social responsibility in China: mapping the environment (a study commission by the global alliance for communities and workers). GA Publication Series, Baltimore, MD

Nidumolu R, Prahalad CK, Rangaswami MR (2009) Why sustainability is now the key driver of innovation. Harv Bus Rev 87(9):56–64

Novak M (2004) The universal hunger of liberty. Basic Books, New York

Philipp B (2009) Multinationals' sustainable supply chains and influence on suppliers inside and outside the U.S.: a comparative approach. In: McIntyre JR, Ivanaj S, Ivanaj V (eds) Multinational enterprises and the challenge of sustainable development. Edward Elgar, Cheltenham, UK, pp 141–163

Porter M, Kramer M (2006) Strategy & society: the link between competitive advantage and corporate social responsibility. Harv Bus Rev 84(12):78–92

Prasad E (2015) The path to sustainable growth in China. Brookings Institution. http://www.brookings.edu/research/testimony/2015/04/22-sustainable-growth-china-prasad. Accessed 30 June 2015

Pruzan P (2008) Spirituality as a firm basis for corporate social responsibility. In: Crane A, McWilliams A, Matten D, Moon J, Siegel D (eds) The Oxford handbook of corporate social responsibility. Oxford University Press, Oxford, UK, pp 552–559

Rondinelli D (2006) Globalization of sustainable development? Principles and practices in transnational corporations. In: Paper presented at MESD International Research Colloquium in the Georgia Tech, Atlanta, GA

Salovey P, Mayer JD (1990) Emotional intelligence. Imagination Cogn Pers 9(3):185–211

Sarewitz D (2016) Presentation at the sixth ISBEE world congress in Shanghai, China on 14 July 2016

Schepers D (2006) The impact of NGO network conflict on the corporate social responsibility strategies of multinational corporations. Bus Soc 45(3):282–299

Simola SK (2007) The pragmatics of care in sustainable global enterprise. J Bus Ethics 74:131–147

Stiglitz JE (2006) Making globalization work. W. W. Norton, New York, NY

Students & Scholars Against Corporate Misbehavior (SACOM) (2010) Dying young: suicide & China's booming economy. http://sacom.hk/wp-content/uploads/2010/05/dying-young_sucide-chinas-booming-economy.pdf. Accessed 14 Apr 2013

Sum NL, Ngai P (2005) Globalization and paradoxes of ethical transnational production: code of conduct in a Chinese workplace. Compet Change 9(2):181–200

Tate WL, Ellram LM, Bals L, Hartmann E (2009) Offshore outsourcing of services: an evolutionary perspective. Int J Prod Econ 120:512–524

Vaill PB (1989) Managing as a performing art. Jossey-Bass, San Francisco, CA

Vaill PB (1996) Learning as a way of being: strategies for survival in a world of permanent white water. Jossey-Bass, San Francisco, CA

Vaill PB (2007) Organizational epistemology: interpersonal relations in organizations and the emergence of wisdom. In: Kessler E, Bailey J (eds) The handbook of managerial and organizational wisdom. Sage, Thousand Oaks, CA, pp 327–355

Visser W (2008) Corporate social responsibility in developing countries. In: Crane A, McWilliams A, Matten D, Moon J, Siegel D (eds) The Oxford handbook of corporate social responsibility. Oxford University Press, Oxford, UK, pp 473–502

Walumbwa FO, Hartnell CA, Oke A (2010) Servant leadership, procedural justice climate, service climate, employee attitudes, and organizational citizenship behavior: a cross-level investigation. J Appl Psychol 95(3):517–529

Wood CH, Kaufman A (2007) The communication of corporate social responsibility (CSR) through the supply chain: an SME perspective. In: Susman IG (ed) Small and medium-sized enterprises and the global economy. Edward Elgar, Cheltenham, UK, pp 140–153

Young IM (2004) Responsibility and global labor justice. J Polit Philos 12(4):365–388

Zadek S (2004) The path to corporate responsibility. Harv Bus Rev 82(12):125–132

Author Biography

Maria Lai-Ling Lam is currently a senior consultant. She has been a Professor of Marketing at Point Loma Nazarene University, San Diego, California, and Malone University, Canton, Ohio, in the USA for fourteen years. She also has been a visiting scholar at several prominent universities in China. She holds a Ph.D. in marketing and organization behavior from George Washington University, a M.A. degree in Religion Studies, a M.B.A. degree in Marketing and International Business, and a B.B.A. degree in Marketing from the Chinese University of Hong Kong. She has published one book and more than 70 peer-reviewed articles.

Chapter 9
Sustainable Tax Behavior on Future and Current Emerging Markets: The Case of Romania and Brazil

Larissa Batrancea, Anca Nichita, Ioan Batrancea, Ana Maria Roux Valentini Coelho Cesar and Denis Forte

9.1 Introduction

With regard to education, Kofi Annan, a former United Nations Secretary-General and recipient of the 2001 Nobel Peace Prize, once stated that it is "a human right with immense power to transform. On its foundations rest the cornerstones of freedom, democracy and sustainable human development." Hereby, the international diplomat indicated a strong link between education and sustainability, for which he continued to advocate (among others) during his leading UN position (1997–2006). As a result, in 1999 Annan proposed the creation of the United Nations Global Compact (UNGC) to the World Economic Forum participants. Officially launched one year later, the UNGC is an international organization mandated by the UN to endorse the principles of sustainability and social

L. Batrancea (✉) · A. Nichita
Faculty of Business, Babes-Bolyai University, Cluj-Napoca, Romania
e-mail: lm.batrancea@tbs.ubbcluj.ro

A. Nichita
e-mail: ancaramona.nichita@gmail.com

I. Batrancea
Faculty of Economics and Business Administration,
Babes-Bolyai University, Cluj-Napoca, Romania
e-mail: ioan.batrancea@econ.ubbcluj.ro

A. M. R. V. C. Cesar
Graduate School of Accounting, Applied Social Sciences Center,
Mackenzie Presbyterian University, São Paulo, Brazil
e-mail: rouxcesar@mackenzie.br

D. Forte
Ph.D. Program, Strategic Finance Department,
Mackenzie Presbyterian University, São Paulo, Brazil
e-mail: denis.forte@mackenzie.br

K. T. Çalıyurt and R. Said (eds.), *Sustainability and Social Responsibility of Accountability Reporting Systems*, Accounting, Finance, Sustainability, Governance & Fraud: Theory and Application, https://doi.org/10.1007/978-981-10-3212-7_9

responsibility, but also to advance education around the world. For that matter, the organization has been labeled the "largest corporate sustainability action," as it includes 12,000 companies and nonbusinesses which voluntarily adhered to its principles. The UNGC framework is represented by a set of ten principles targeting four major domains such as human rights, labor, environment, and anti-corruption. Figure 9.1 displays this framework.

According to the UNGC, compliance with principles that promote the fundamental human rights, labor freedom, environmentally friendly business practices, and the enhancement of anti-corruption measures is crucial when aiming to increase sustainability levels worldwide. If corporate taxpayers are educated to value sustainability and more lucrative and non-lucrative entities around the world consequently embrace the UNGC framework in the upcoming years, societies will thrive in the long run.

Giving the rapid development of nowadays societies and markets interconnectivity, taxpayers are called not only to comply with sustainability principles, but also with national and international tax regulations. For that matter, compliance is a key aspect in the field of tax behavior, where it manages to draw the line between more and less thriving societies.

Among the aspects previously stated, the following set of questions arises: Is there a link between sustainability and tax behavior? To what degree can a tax behavior be considered sustainable? How do the traits of such tax behavior alter under the dynamics of future and current emerging markets? The following chapter will address this set of questions and will approach matters from the perspective of Romania and Brazil, two countries that share similarities by being closely related to the concept of emerging market. The former aims to obtain the status in the nearest future, while the latter is already an established emerging market and member of the well-known BRICS association. The structure of the chapter is the following. Section 9.2 offers general considerations on tax behavior and its link to the "sustainability" notion. Section 9.3 comprises a detailed comparison of Romania and Brazil in terms of sustainable tax behavior. Section 9.4 draws conclusions.

9.2 General Considerations on Sustainable Tax Behavior

As stated in the introduction, this section will explain the link between tax behavior and sustainability and will present the features of a sustainable tax behavior, from our point of view.

By quantifying Internet searches, it can be stated that the terms "sustainability" and "tax" have been stirring a rising interest during the last six years. Table 9.1 displays the regional interest and searches related to these terms (i.e., "associated phrases"), as listed by Google Trends. When analyzing "sustainability," one can see that the areas registering the highest number of searches were located in Australia, Oceania, and Southeast Asia. Moreover, associated phrases were generally centered

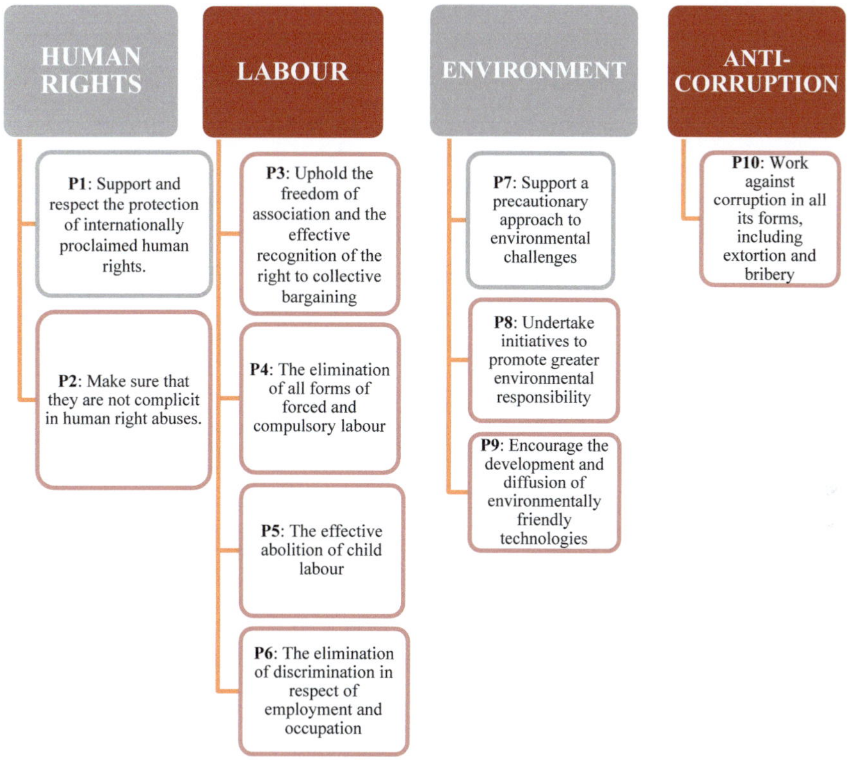

Fig. 9.1 Ten principle framework of the United Nations Global Compact (UNGC). *Source* Designed based on https://www.unglobalcompact.org/what-is-gc/mission/principles

on the environment, the definition of the term, sustainability reports, energy concerns, business, management, social aspects, or work.

When analyzing "tax," it can be seen that the areas of interest were located in Europe, South Asia, Australia, North America, Africa, and Southeast Asia. Hence, a more extensive regional preoccupation was registered compared to the case of the former term. The related searches referred to different types of direct and indirect taxes, standard tax documents, computations and computation tools, refunds, crediting, or taxpaying methods.

After taking notice of the online search interest produced by the terms "sustainability" and "tax," we will focus on answering to the subsequent question: To which degree is there a link between tax behavior and sustainability? By tax behavior, we mean the actions undertaken by corporate and individual taxpayers while activating in a tax system.

As stated in an OECD (2014: 91–92) report, tax money constitutes an essential ingredient for financing the actions of national/federal, state, and local/municipal authorities that can be further used to enhance all three sustainability pillars

Table 9.1 Interest for the two terms contingent on regional interest and related search

Interest for the term "sustainability"		Interest for the term "tax"	
Regional interest	Related search	Regional interest	Related search
Australia	"sustainable"	Ireland	"income tax"
Uganda	"environmental sustainability"	UK	"tax return"
Zimbabwe	"definition sustainability"	India	"calculator"
New Zealand	"what is sustainability"	Australia	"tax calculator"
Kenya	"sustainability report"	USA	"sales tax"
South Africa	"energy sustainability"	Canada	"property tax"
Ghana	"business sustainability"	New Zealand	"tax refund"
Singapore	"sustainability management"	Singapore	"tax credit"
Tanzania	"social sustainability"	South Africa	"tax online"
Hong Kong	"sustainability jobs"	Hong Kong	"tax car"

Source Based on data provided by Google Trends for the period January 2011–July 2016 (www.google.com/trends)
Note The information is listed in descending order, starting with the highest number of searches *Regional interest* highlights the areas that registered the highest number of searches *Related search* highlights the associated phrases that registered the highest number of searches

(i.e., economic, social, environmental). Specifically, while shaping tax policies for national economies (Schratzentaller 2015) and designing public goods systems, authorities can also incorporate the sustainability perspective to ensure a high-quality lifestyle for their citizens and to target a long-term thriving society.

This integrative approach is equally important for both developed and developing countries around the world. Nevertheless, developing and emerging countries are called to make additional tax efforts in order to achieve their sustainability goals and mitigate their dependence on external financing (OECD 2014: 92). For instance, according to the same report, ensuring environmental sustainability is one of the eight UN Millennium Development Goals that can be achieved by developing countries, provided they manage levying taxes worth 20% of their GDP. By comparison, OECD countries succeed directing nearly twice as much taxes toward their state budgets, i.e., 34% of the GDP. With respect to the economic level, sustainability can be achieved by developing markets if tax authorities establish a cooperative compliance approach within tax systems (van der Enden and Baisalbayeva 2015), fostering interactions with taxpayers based on two main standpoints: (1) trust and transparency; (2) predictability and certainty (PricewaterhouseCoopers, the World Bank, and International Finance Corporation, 2015: 83). Social sustainability can be increased through a more equal distribution of income and wealth (Stancil 2010) and through a reduction of gender gaps (OECD 2016; Schratzentaller 2015).

Starting from the aforementioned aspects, it can be stated that the relationship between tax behavior and sustainability is straightforward. Namely, in addition to tax authorities' actions, the behavior of taxpayers is also a major determinant of a country's tax revenues and ultimately sustainability levels. If taxpayers decide to pay their fair share, tax revenues amass and authorities are able to support sustainability projects by using part of these revenues.

What are the tax behavior patterns? According to the tax behavior literature (Kirchler 2007), the taxonomy of mandatory revenue reporting is centered on the notions of compliance and non-compliance. Relative to this, Franzoni (2000: 55) defines a tax compliant behavior by means of four traits: (1) accurate disclosure of taxable income; (2) precise calculation of tax due; (3) tax return filing in due time; (4) tax liability payment in due time. A taxpayer's behavior is considered to be compliant as long as it incorporates all the aforementioned traits. When the behavior misses even a single attribute, it is immediately categorized as non-compliant.

Regarding the tandem compliance/non-compliance, in-depth empirical research has elicited that a compliant tax behavior can be voluntary or enforced (e.g., Kirchler et al. 2008) and that a non-compliant behavior can be avoidant or elusive. In the first case, voluntary tax compliance emerges when taxpayers credit authorities with high trust, while enforced tax compliance emerges when taxpayers credit authorities with high power. In the second case, avoidance falls out when taxpayers take advantage of the legislative loopholes in order to lessen their tax burden; evasion occurs when taxpayers purposely disregard tax regulations in order to cut out their tax burden.

In our view, a *sustainable tax behavior* cannot be other than a tax compliant behavior. Namely, a tax behavior that internalizes legal, ethical, moral, fairness, and sustainability considerations, that contributes to the benefits of the society and that facilitates the achievement of economic, environmental, and social sustainability levels. After all, taxpayers are drafting the societies in which they live and determining the extent to which the existence of such societies can be sustainable in days to come.

9.3 Sustainable Tax Behavior Under the Dynamics of Emerging Markets: Romania Versus Brazil

In this section, we will investigate the degree to which a sustainable tax behavior alters under the dynamics of future and current emerging markets, with special focus on the case of Romania and Brazil. The two countries were chosen due to their proximity to the emerging market concept: Romania targets to be listed among the emerging countries in the near future; Brazil has been benefiting from this status for quite a while and activating within the BRICS association.

With respect to encouraging sustainable economic activity, Romania and Brazil have already shown commitment in this direction. In 2016, together with other 178 nations, both countries signed the so-called Paris Agreement pertaining to the United Nations Framework Convention on Climate Change (UNFCCC). This is the first covenant focused on climate changes that will enter into force after its ratification by at least 55 of the signatory countries, responsible for producing 55% of the total greenhouse gas emissions. Among the goals of this agreement, two highly important ones are capping the increase of global temperature at 1.5 and mitigating global emissions in the shortest period. Therefore, corporate taxpayers activating in Romania and Brazil, which are motivated to display a sustainable tax behavior, will have to respect the aforementioned agreement and design tax strategies that incorporate cost cuts, energy risks, and environmentally friendly business practices (Deloitte 2012).

The first element we assessed is taxpayers' adherence to sustainability principles. As mentioned in the introduction, the UNGC gathers 12,000 member entities from 170 countries, which number over 58 million employees. Of this total, at the moment the UNGC includes 52 entities (i.e., companies and nonbusinesses) from Romania and 1090 entities from Brazil. The distribution of the companies depending on the activity sector is presented in Figs. 9.2 and 9.3.

In the case of Romania, the activity sectors registering the highest number of taxpayer members are "NGOs, foundations, and associations," followed by "technology" and "financial services." In the case of Brazil, "NGOs, foundation, and associations," "industrial goods and services," and "health care" are the most represented sectors. As can be seen, the entities that primarily emphasize sustainability principles on both emerging markets are NGOs, foundations, and associations, which are generally inclined to support initiatives of improving living standards. Nevertheless, the number of taxpayers compliant with UNGC principles is still insignificant compared to the number of registered corporate taxpayers in both countries (namely, 1,185,703 in Romania and 5,392,234 in Brazil). Sustainability goals would be achieved earlier if more entities would guide their activities based on such principles.

Due to the market dynamics, taxpayers and authorities interact continuously and their interests are often intertwined. Consequently, sustainability-driven goals may appear on their agendas, as they serve the interests of both. It goes without saying that corporate and individual taxpayers can display easier a sustainable tax behavior if authorities set up a tax framework to achieve green policy objectives. The characteristics of this framework (i.e., tax incentives and tax penalties) are captured by the KPMG Green Tax Index 2013, which ranks 21 of the most important world economies (KPMG 2013). Ranging on a scale from 0 to 50, the index is meant to inform corporate taxpayers of the facilities and sanctions implemented by governments in order to promote sustainable business practices. Results indicate that emerging economies register the highest number of tax incentives in terms of renewable energy and fuels.

Out of the two countries included in our study, only Brazil was considered for listing because of its noticeable green tax system. The country ranked 18th among the 21 surveyed economies, with an overall score of 10. With respect to the 11 parameters that make up the index, Brazil was listed half of the times. Namely, it ranked 3rd in green innovation, 6th in material resources and waste, 8th in ecosystem and pollution, 12th in tax incentives, and 15th in vehicles. According to the Green Tax Index 2013 (KPMG 2013: 6), Brazil belongs to the fourth quartile of

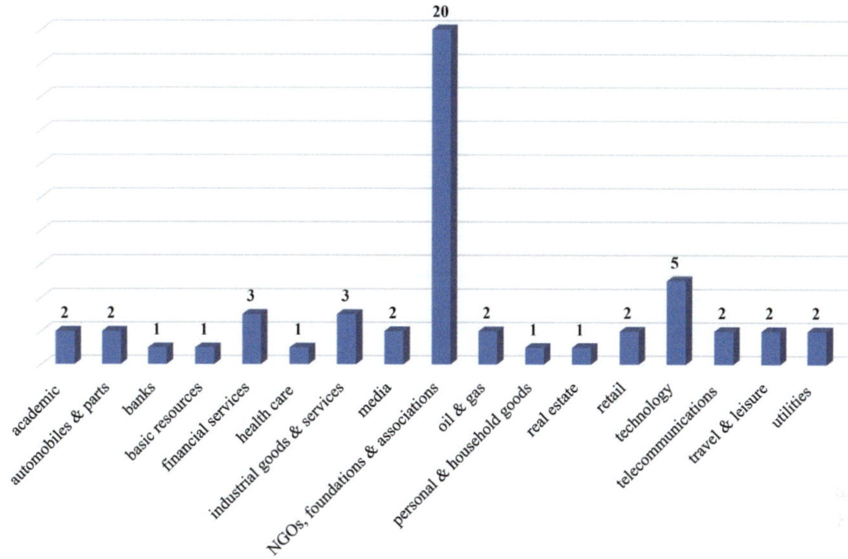

Fig. 9.2 Entities from Romania adhering to the United Nations Global Compact (UNGC) principles. *Source* Designed based on data retrieved from https://www.unglobalcompact.org

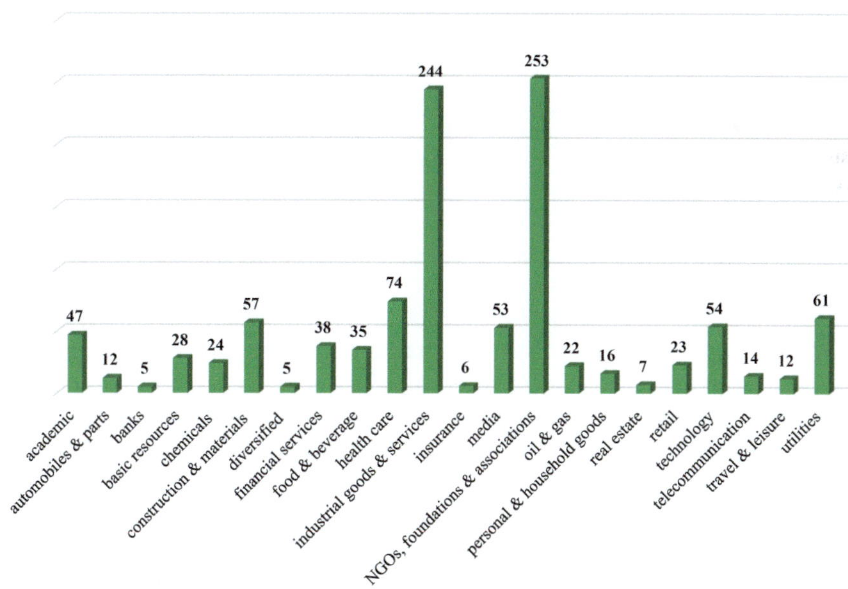

Fig. 9.3 Entities from Brazil adhering to the United Nations Global Compact (UNGC) principles. *Source* Designed based on data retrieved from https://www.unglobalcompact.org

countries, registering the following marks: (a) reduced use of taxes as green policy instruments; (b) lack of green tax penalties; and (c) available funding programs for sustainability projects, i.e., the FUNTEC R&D grants (Amman and Baer 2002). Starting from the fact that Brazil occupies a leading position in incentivizing green innovation on the wind, solar, and biofuel markets (Afionis et al. 2014; World Bank 2012: 67), it can be forecasted that a higher number of corporate taxpayers activating on these markets will adopt a sustainable tax behavior in the future.

The presence of Brazil within the green tax landscape is understandable given that the country possesses considerable resources (Clusener-Godt and Sachs 1995) and has been manifesting interest for projects enhancing sustainability for more than three decades (i.e., Law no. 6938/1981). In Romania, similar approaches have been tackled more recently (i.e., Law no. 137/1995). The disparities between the two countries hold up also in the case of the results produced by the Happy Planet Index.[1]

Ranging from 0 to 100, the composite indicator estimates sustainable well-being by determining the degree to which country residents employ natural resources to experience long, happy, and sustainable lives.

Figure 9.4 displays the evolution of the Happy Planet Index overall scores for Romania and Brazil. As it can be seen, Brazil has scored higher during the entire period, which translates into a greater care for natural resources from corporate and individual taxpayers. A similar conclusion can be drawn from Fig. 9.5. The index component termed "ecological footprint" is measured in global hectares (i.e., 10,000 m^2), and it indicates the land area available for the production of resources and services to be consumed by the general population. Though both countries exceeded the levels compatible with environmental sustainability, Romania puts a higher demand on its natural resources than Brazil. In order to decrease the country's ecological footprint, corporate taxpayers in Romania could invest more in technologies decreasing carbon emissions and could also limit the consumption of non-renewable resources while developing their businesses.

As a rule, monitoring tax compliance behavior is an intricate process that requires complex efforts from tax authorities. On the other side, it is also true that monitoring compliance requirements within tax systems entails substantial efforts from contributors who aim to display a sustainable tax behavior. Nevertheless, both matters seem to find answers in international publications. Yearly, the *Paying Taxes* reports issued by PricewaterhouseCoopers and the World Bank Group offer detailed insights into tax systems around the world. Moreover, these reports track the evolution of analyzed tax systems by means of a standard indicator framework, which assesses the ease of taxpaying for corporate contributors and thus facilitates benchmarking.

---

[1]For the analyses of this chapter, we have considered the previous version of the Happy Planet Index (2006–2012), which encompassed "life expectancy," "experienced well-being," and "ecological footprint," in order to present its evolution. The 2016 version of the composite index is slightly changed, as "life expectancy" and "experienced well-being" are adjusted for "inequality of outcomes."

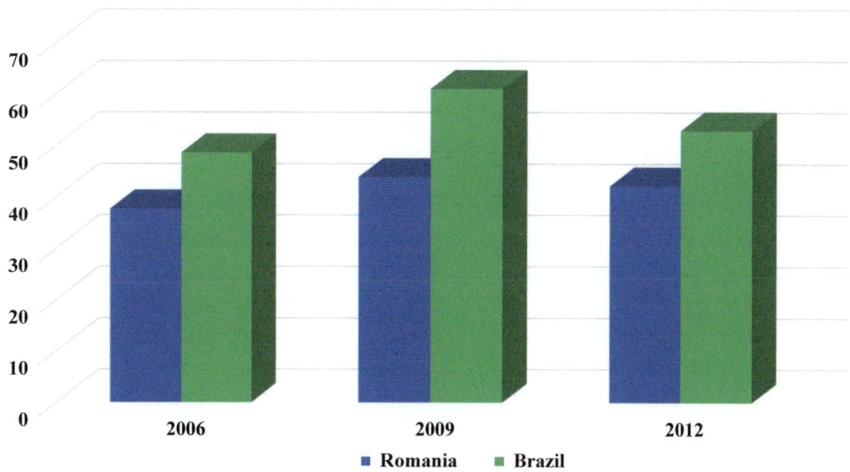

Fig. 9.4 Happy Planet Index overall rankings for Romania and Brazil. *Source* Based on data retrieved from the Happy Planet Index reports (New Economics Foundation 2006, 2009, 2012)

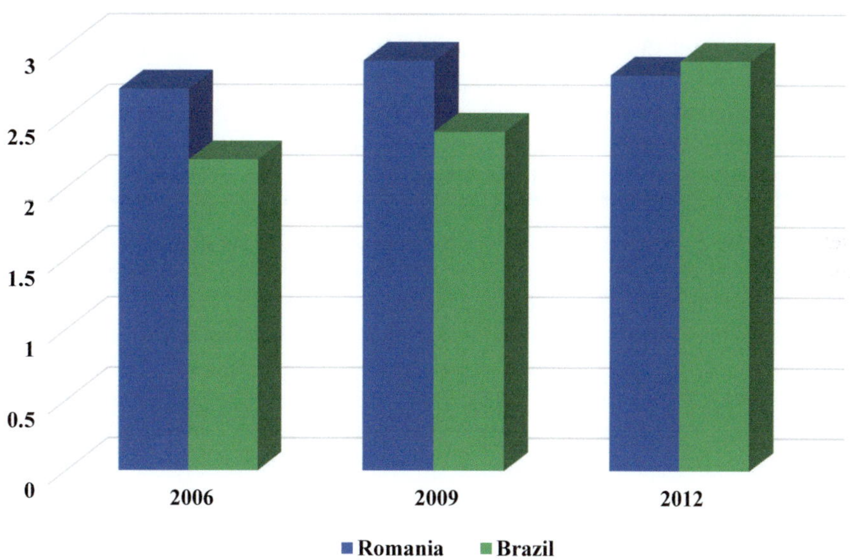

Fig. 9.5 Ecological footprint scores for Romania and Brazil. *Source* Based on data retrieved from the Happy Planet Index reports (New Economics Foundation 2006, 2009, 2012)

The framework comprises the following three indicators (Paying Taxes 2016: 9): (a) *total tax rate*, capturing the amount of taxes as a percentage of the commercial profit; (b) *time to comply*, indicating the number of hours needed to compile, file, and pay three main types of taxes (i.e., corporate income, labor and mandatory contributions, and consumption); (c) *number of payments*, quantifying the rate with which a corporate taxpayer is expected to file and pay different taxes through the tax year.

In the following, we will briefly examine the evolution of the standard indicators for Romania and Brazil,[2] based on data covering a ten-year period (i.e., 2005–2014).

Figure 9.6 highlights considerable differences between the two tax systems in terms of total tax rate. If corporate taxpayers activating in Romania have been subject to an average tax rate of 45%, their counterparts have been expected to direct on average 69% of their commercial profit to the Brazilian authorities. In addition, while the tax burden in Romania has been constantly decreasing from 48% to 42% along the years, in Brazil it has remained almost unchanged. For that matter, the differences are understandable, given the fact that Brazil is one of the countries with the highest tax rates in the world, a skewed income distribution, onerous tax regulations for private businesses, a rising effective tax rate (Freitas Azevedo and Marsiglia Fasolo 2015), and a higher reliance on consumption taxation than Romania (for more information, see Brazil's tax guide).

The intricacy of Brazilian tax regulations stems primarily from the fact that taxes are levied at different levels: federal, state, and municipal (OECD 2015). Considering sales taxes for instance, while Romania taxes consumption of goods and services only through its value-added tax (VAT) applied at national level, Brazil levies multiple sales taxes, such as: tax on industrialized products (IPI) at federal level; tax on sales and services (ICMS) at state level; tax on services provided to third parties (ISS) at municipal level. Secondly, tax rates differ considerably within the same level. For instance, each of the 26 Brazilian states has different rates for the same tax.

Consequently, the high tax burden and the complex tax system have resulted in lower tax-to-GDP ratios for Brazil than for Romania. For example, in 2012 Brazil registered a rate of 14.1%, while Romania registered 18%.

The differences between the two tax systems remain considerable in terms of the time to comply and the number of payments indicators. As can be seen from Figs. 9.7 and 9.8, the Romanian tax system is characterized by less red tape than the Brazilian one. On average, a corporate taxpayer registered in Romania makes around 74 tax payments throughout the fiscal year and fulfills all the administrative tasks connected to such payments in about 8 days (i.e., 198 h). Overall, the values of both indicators have decreased with the passing of time.

On the other side of the globe, corporate taxpayers in Brazil are requested to make only 11 tax payments, yet the time needed to fulfill authorities' regulations

[2]In the case of Brazil, the last two editions of the *Paying Taxes* reports have determined the three indicators for its two leading cities (Godfrey 1999), São Paulo and Rio de Janeiro; the former is the most important financial center in Latin America, and the latter is deemed the cultural capital of the country. Consequently, we displayed the standard indicators for both cities. When the reports indicated only overall country values, we considered them to be identical for São Paulo and Rio de Janeiro.

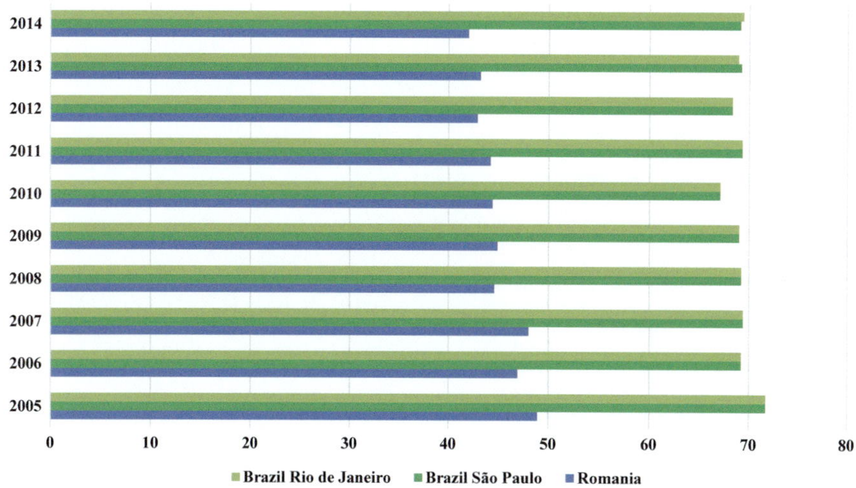

Fig. 9.6 Evolution of the PwC total tax rate indicator for Romania and Brazil. *Source* Based on data retrieved from the PwC *Paying Taxes* reports released in the period 2006–2015

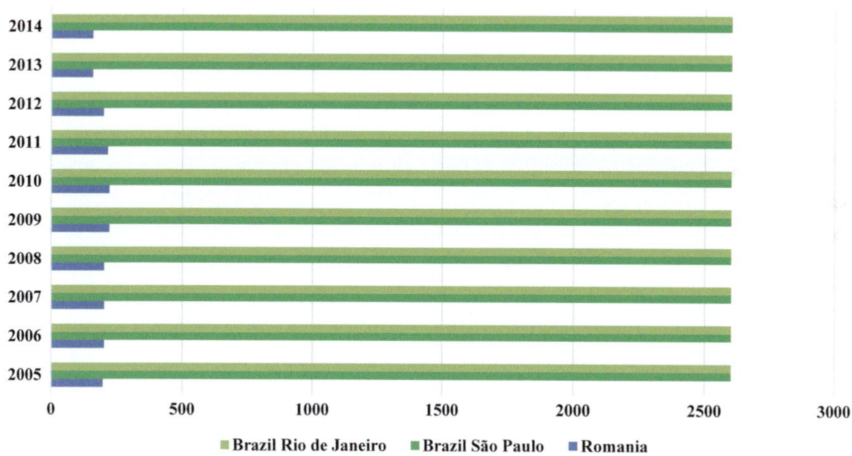

Fig. 9.7 Evolution of the PwC time to comply indicator for Romania and Brazil. *Source* Based on data retrieved from the PwC *Paying Taxes* reports released in the period 2006–2015

covers one-third of a fiscal year (i.e., 2600 h). The tax payment rate has remained relatively stable (except for the year 2005), with only São Paulo municipality registering a slight increase from 9 to 10 payments. The time spent by taxpayers to comply has remained unchanged for a decade.

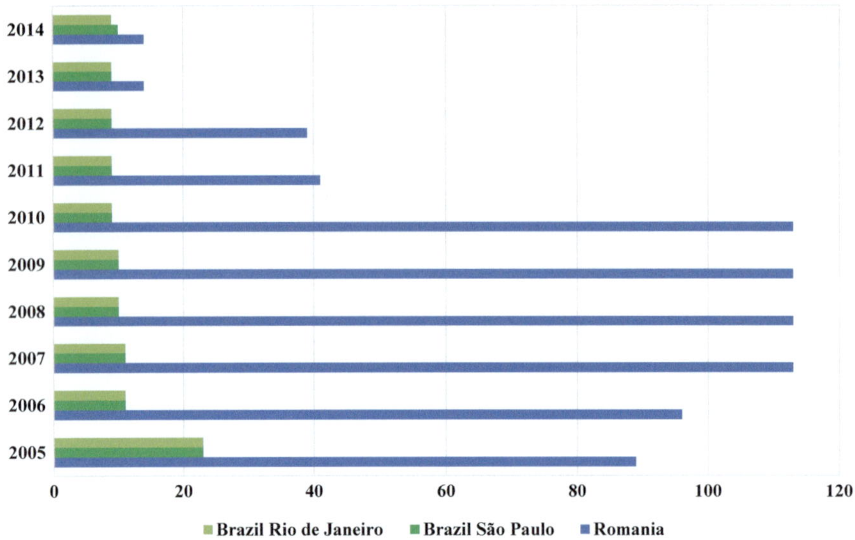

Fig. 9.8 Evolution of the PwC number of payments indicator for Romania and Brazil. *Source* Based on data retrieved from the PwC *Paying Taxes* reports released in the period 2006–2015

Considering the country features of the standard indicator framework, Brazilian authorities should undertake substantial efforts in simplifying tax requirements to make contributors display a sustainable tax behavior and to attract more investors, as Brazil is the largest recipient of foreign direct investment in Latin America.

Besides respecting customary tax regulations, a sustainable tax behavior involves also an increased concern for the environment, awareness regarding the negative impact of pollution, and a thorough knowledge of aspects like green taxation (Kreiser et al. 2012a; OECD 2006; Von Weizsacker and Jesinghous 1992; Zhou and Segerson 2012). In this respect, corporate and individual taxpayers from Romania and Brazil are (at least in theory) familiarized with the topic of green taxation, as national tax systems stipulate the levying of various environmental taxes (e.g., on energy, pollution, transportation), among which the so-called eco-tax on plastic bags. In Romania, this type of tax was introduced in 2008, it has a value of 0.2 RON (approx. 0.04 Euros) and is intended to collect additional resources to the Environmental Fund (which finances the environment protection since 2005), and it also targets to decrease the demand of bags made from non-biodegradable materials. According to a study within the "Pre-waste" European partnership project conducted on the Romanian market, the second aim of this eco-tax has still not been reached. Taxpayers seem indifferent between using bags from biodegradable and non-biodegradable materials, and therefore, the consumption of plastic bags has increased over the years.

On the Brazilian market, taxpayers are encouraged to reuse bags after shopping and not purchase new ones. For example, in 2015 a law banning retailers from providing traditional plastic bags (made of petroleum-based plastic) to their customers was enacted by the municipal authorities of São Paulo. Consequently, since then it is mandatory for retailers to provide only plastic bags made from sugarcane ethanol (i.e., a sustainable bioplastic containing at least 51% renewable material), which could be three times more expensive than the petroleum-based ones. Regarding this issue, Avallone et al. (2012) conducted a study on Brazilians' conscious consuming and reported that subjects attributed median importance to the use of plastic bags and were inclined toward reusing them in their households.

9.4 Conclusions

The opening paragraphs in Chap. 2 of the volume "Where is the Wealth of Nations?" (World Bank 2005: 19) state the following: "Economic theory tells us that there is a strong link between changes in wealth and the sustainability of development—if a country (or a household, for that matter) is running down its assets, it is not on a sustainable path." Amid the intensification of the economic activity on worldwide developed, emerging, and developing markets, the increasing world population, and the slow resource depletion, the question of sustainability under its different forms (i.e., economic, social, environmental) remains much debated in the literature.

The importance of endorsing sustainable economic projects is one of the primary issues found on the agendas of international organizations (International Monetary Fund, Organisation for Economic Co-operation and Development, United Nations and World Bank 2011; OECD 2008, 2010; United Nations 2015; United Nations Economic and Social Commission for Asia and the Pacific 2016; United Nations Global Compact 2014), established professionals and researchers (Carroll and Buchholtz 2014; Frieders 2015; Garcia-Diaz and Raidbard 2016; Goldin and Winters 1995; Grubb 2014; Kreiser et al. 2012b; Murty 2009; Nelson et al. 2015; Nordhaus 2010; Pearce 1991). The majority of the studies convey the same message: Integrating the sustainability perspective into business strategies has become a necessity for societies aiming to increase citizens' well-being in the upcoming years. For this reason, sustainable behavior in general (Manning 2009; McKenzie-Mohr 2011) and sustainable tax behavior in particular should be considered by an increasing number of world citizens.

The present chapter tackles the concept of sustainable tax behavior on future and current emerging markets, with particular interest on the Romanian and Brazilian economies. We define the sustainable tax behavior as a tax compliant behavior. In other words, a market conduct is displayed by a corporate or individual contributor who understands that paying the fare share to national/federal, state, or municipal authorities (according to the tax law in force) finances not only the quality of his lifestyle, but also secures a sustainable well-being. Going further, one could state that any deviation from tax compliance (i.e., tax avoidance or tax evasion) ultimately affects sustainability levels.

Using data retrieved from reports provided by international organizations and companies like the International Monetary Fund, KPMG, New Economics Foundation, OECD, United Nations Global Compact, World Bank, and country-specific sources (i.e., Romanian National Trade Register Office, Brazilian Institute of Geography and Statistics, Brazil Tax Guide), we investigate the attributes of sustainable tax behavior of contributors from Romania and Brazil by targeting adherence to UNGC sustainability principles, the dynamics of sustainability level, the characteristics of tax systems and compliance requirements, and also aspects related to green taxation.

According to the analyses, both countries have taken steps forward on the way to encouraging sustainable economic activity, with Brazil registering noticeable progress especially in sustainability levels and green taxation. The assessment of the tax systems via the PwC standard indicator framework (i.e., total tax rate; time to comply; number of payments) reveals that authorities in both countries need to make additional progress in incentivizing citizens to display a sustainable tax behavior, particularly Brazil which requires a considerable simplification of its tax requirements.

Acknowledgements This work was supported by a grant of the Babes-Bolyai University through the Grants for Young Researchers Program, project no. GTC 31780/01.04.2016.

References

Afionis S, Stringer LC, Favretto N, Buckeridge M (2014) Unpacking Brazil's leadership in the global biofuels arena: Brazilian ethanol diplomacy in Africa. Sustainability Research Institute, Paper no. 74

Amman E, Baer W (2002) The development of Brazil's technology capabilities in the post war period. Lat Am Bus Rev 3(1):1–29

Avallone IV, de Giraldi JME, de Oliveira SVWB (2012) Conscious consumption: a study on plastic bags' consumers in Brazil. Int J Psychol Stud 4(1):122–134

Brazil tax guide. Volume 1: strategic and practical information. International Business Publications, Washington, DC

Carroll AB, Buchholtz AK (2014) Business and society: ethics, sustainability, and stakeholder management, 9th edn. Cengage Learning, Stamford, CT

Clusener-Godt M, Sachs I (1995) Brazilian perspectives on sustainable development of the Amazon region, vol 15. United Nations Educational, Scientific and Cultural Organization, Paris

Deloitte (2012) Tax data management: a foundation for sustainable tax compliance, planning, and examination support

Franzoni L (2000) Tax evasion and tax compliance. In: Bouckaert B, De Geest G (eds) Encyclopedia of law and economics, vol 14. Edward Elgar Publishing, Cheltenham, pp 51–94

Freitas Azevedo C, Marsiglia Fasolo A (2015) Effective tax rates on consumption and factor incomes: a quarterly frequency estimation for Brazil. In: Banco Central do Brasil Working Paper 398

Frieders DM (2015) Foundations of sustainable development: law, regulation, and planning. ABA Publishing, Chicago, IL

Garcia-Diaz D, Raidbard N (2016) Promising practices for tax initiatives that address sustainable development goals: A U.S. case study from the GAO audit of the low-income housing tax credit program (LIHTC). In: Paper presented at the 30th annual international training conference, Miami, FL
Godfrey BJ (1999) Revisiting Rio de Janeiro and São Paulo. Geograph Rev 89(1):94–121
Goldin I, Winters LA (1995) The economics of sustainable development. Cambridge University Press, Cambridge
Grubb M (2014) Planetary economics: energy, climate change and the three domains of sustainable development. Routledge, New York, NY
http://data.worldbank.org/indicator/GC.TAX.TOTL.GD.ZS. Accessed 1 July 2016
http://www.brazil-for-foreigners.com/tax-rates-in-brazil/. Accessed 1 July 2016
https://www.google.com/trends. Accessed 1 July 2016
http://unfccc.int/paris_agreement/items/9444.php. Accessed 10 June 2016
http://www.happyplanetindex.org. Accessed 10 June 2016
http://thebrazilbusiness.com/article/the-16-most-common-brazilian-taxes. Accessed 2 Aug 2016
http://www.un.org/millenniumgoals/bkgd.shtml. Accessed 2 July 2016
https://www.unglobalcompact.org/what-is-gc/mission/principles. Accessed 2 May 2016
http://thebrazilbusiness.com/article/recycling-of-waste-in-brazil. Accessed 3 Aug 2016
http://www.oecd.org/brazil/greeninnovationintourismriodejaneiro.htm. Accessed 3 Aug 2016
http://www.prewaste.eu/index.php?option=com_k2&view=item&id=249&Itemid=94. Accessed 3 July 2016
http://theglobalgrid.org/city-of-sao-paulo-brazil-launches-ban-on-traditional-plastic-bags/. Accessed 6 June 2016
https://treaties.un.org. Accessed 8 Sept 2016
http://ec.europa.eu/clima/policies/international/negotiations/paris/index_en.htm. Accessed 3 July 2016
http://thetaxdialogue.org/articles/responsible-corporate-tax-behavior/. Accessed 2 May 2016
http://www.ibge.gov.br/home/estatistica/pesquisas/pesquisa_resultados.php?id_pesquisa=9. Accessed 1 Sept 2016
http://www.kpmg-institutes.com/institutes/global-energy-institute/articles/2013/05/kpmg-green-tax-index.html. Accessed 3 Aug 2016
http://www.onrc.ro/index.php/ro/statistici?id=243. Accessed 9 Sept 2016
http://www.rightingfinance.org/?p=1459. Accessed 11 June 2016
http://www.sustainablecitiescollective.com/global-site-plans-grid/1071541/city-s-o-paulo-brazil-launches-ban-traditional-plastic-bags. Accessed 3 Aug 2016
International Monetary Fund, Organisation for Economic Co-operation and Development, United Nations, World Bank (2011) Supporting the development of more effective tax systems: a report to the G-20 development working group by the IMF, OECD, UN and World Bank. International Monetary Fund, Organisation of Economic Co-operation and Development, United Nations, Washington DC/Paris/New York
Kirchler E (2007) The economic psychology of tax behaviour. Cambridge University Press, Cambridge
Kirchler E, Hoelzl E, Wahl I (2008) Enforced versus voluntary tax compliance: the "slippery slope framework". J Econ Psychol 29(2):210–225
KPMG (2013) The KPMG green tax index 2013. An exploration of green tax incentives and penalties
Kreiser L, Yábar Sterling A, Herrera P, Milne JE, Ashiabor H (eds) (2012a) Green taxation and environmental sustainability: critical issues in environmental taxation, vol XII. Edward Elgar Publishing, Cheltenham
Kreiser L, Yábar Sterling A, Herrera P, Milne JE, Ashiabor H (eds) (2012b) Carbon pricing, growth and the environment, 1st edn. Edward Elgar Publishing, Cheltenham
Law no. 6938/31.08.1981. Dispõe sobre a Política Nacional do Meio Ambiente, Seus Fins e Mecanismos de Formulação e Aplicação, e dá Outras Providências. Legislação Federal, Controle de Poluição Ambiental. Série Documentos. São Paulo: CETESB

Law no. 137/29.12.1995. Environmental Protection Law. Published in the Official Gazette no. 304/30.12.1995
Manning C (2009) The psychology of sustainable behavior: tips for empowering people to take environmentally positive actions. Minnesota Pollution Control Agency, Saint Paul, MN
McKenzie-Mohr D (2011) Fostering sustainable behavior: an introduction to community-based social marketing, 3rd edn. New Society Publishers, Gabriola Island
Murty MN (2009) Environment, sustainable development, and well-being: valuation, taxes, and incentives. Oxford University Press, Oxford
Nelson J, Jenkins B, Gilbert R (2015) Business and the sustainable development goals: building blocks for success at scale
New Economics Foundation (2006) The happy planet index: an index of human well-being and environmental impact
New Economics Foundation (2009) The happy planet index 2.0: why good lives don't have to cost the earth
New Economics Foundation (2012) The happy planet index: 2012 report. A global index of sustainable well-being
Nordhaus WD (2010) Carbon taxes to move toward fiscal sustainability. Econ Voice 7:1–3
OECD (2006) The political economy of environmentally related taxes. OECD Publications, Paris Cedex
OECD (2008) Promoting sustainable consumption: good practices in OECD countries. OECD Publications, Paris Cedex
OECD (2010) Taxation, innovation and the environment: executive summary. OECD Publications, Paris Cedex
OECD (2014) Tax revenues as a motor for sustainable development. In: Development co-operation report 2014: mobilising resources for sustainable development. OECD Publishing, Paris Cedex
OECD (2015) Brazil. In: Taxing energy use 2015: OECD and selected partner economies. OECD Publishing, Paris
OECD (2016) OECD employment outlook: how does Brazil compare? OECD Publishing, Paris Cedex
Pearce D (1991) The role of carbon taxes in adjusting to global warming. Econ J 101:938–948
PricewaterhouseCoopers, World Bank, International Finance Corporation (2006) Paying taxes 2007: the global picture
PricewaterhouseCoopers, World Bank, International Finance Corporation (2007) Paying taxes 2008: the global picture
PricewaterhouseCoopers, World Bank, International Finance Corporation (2008) Paying taxes 2009: the global picture
PricewaterhouseCoopers, World Bank, International Finance Corporation (2009) Paying taxes 2010: the global picture
PricewaterhouseCoopers, World Bank, International Finance Corporation (2010) Paying taxes 2011: the global picture
PricewaterhouseCoopers, World Bank, International Finance Corporation (2011) Paying taxes 2012: the global picture
PricewaterhouseCoopers, World Bank, International Finance Corporation (2012) Paying taxes 2013: the global picture
PricewaterhouseCoopers, World Bank, International Finance Corporation (2013) Paying taxes 2014: the global picture
PricewaterhouseCoopers, World Bank, International Finance Corporation (2014) Paying taxes 2015: the global picture. The changing face of tax compliance in 189 economies worldwide
PricewaterhouseCoopers, World Bank, International Finance Corporation (2015) Paying taxes 2016. Ten years of in-depth analysis of tax systems in 189 economies. A look at recent developments and historical trends
Schratzenstaller M (2015) Sustainable tax policy. Concepts and indicators beyond the tax ratio. Revue de l'OFCE, pp 557–577

Stancil JL (2010) Taxes and sustainability. In: Stoner JAF, Wankel C (eds) Global sustainability as a business imperative. Palgrave MacMillan, New York, NY, pp 147–164

United Nations (2015) UNCTAD: investing in sustainable development goals. Action plan for private investments in SDGs. United Nations Publication

United Nations Economic and Social Commission for Asia and the Pacific (ESCAP) (2016). The Asia-Pacific tax forum for sustainable development (AP-TFSD): a proposal. First high-level follow-up dialogue on financing for development in Asia and the Pacific, Incheon, Republic of Korea, 30–31 Mar 2016, Discussion Paper

United Nations Global Compact (2014) Guide to corporate sustainability: shaping a sustainable future

van der Enden E, Baisalbayeva K (2015) The relevance and sustainability of co-operative compliance models for tax in African countries. In: Paper presented at the African Tax Research Network (ATRN), 1st annual congress, Contemporary Tax Challenges for African Countries, Cape Town, South Africa

Von Weizsacker EU, Jesinghous J (1992) Ecological tax reform: a policy proposal for sustainable development. Zed Books, London

World Bank (2005) Where is the wealth of nations? Measuring capital for the 21st century. World Bank Publications, Washington, DC

World Bank (2012) Inclusive green growth: the pathway to sustainable development. Washington, DC

Zhou R, Segerson K (2012) Are green taxes a good way to help solve state budget deficits? Sustainability 4(6):1329–1353

Author Biographies

Larissa Batrancea is an Assistant Professor at Babes-Bolyai University, Cluj-Napoca, Romania, where she has been an academic since 2003. She received her Ph.D. in Economics from Babes-Bolyai University in 2009, after graduating from two B.A. and two M.Sc. programs (economics—class valedictorian; mathematics) at the same institution. From 2011 to 2013, she was a postdoctoral researcher within a program coordinated by the Romanian Academy and completed it with the highest GPA. She was invited to be a lecturer at Mackenzie Presbyterian University, Brazil (2015), the University of Brescia, Italy (2008–2011), and a visiting researcher at Mackenzie Presbyterian University, Brazil (2015), the University of Vienna, Austria (2011–2014), and the University of Brescia (2007–2008). She specialized in Economics and Neuroeconomics at the University of Amsterdam, the University of Bologna, Colorado State University, the University of Copenhagen, Heidelberg University, Humboldt University of Berlin, National Research University—Higher School of Economics, Moscow, Pompeu Fabra University, and the University of Economics, Bratislava. Her research interests are centered on cross-cultural tax behavior, experimental economics, neuroeconomics, and financial analysis. Her publication record comprises 23 books and chapters, plus over 75 scientific articles covering topics from the aforementioned fields. She translated the book "The Economic Psychology of Tax Behaviour" (Cambridge University Press, 2007) into Romanian, authored by Erich Kirchler and released in 2013 under the title "Psihologia Economica a Comportamentului Fiscal" (Risoprint Publishing). She activated as a principal investigator and a member of ten international and national research grant teams. She was awarded ten prizes for excellence in research and teaching.

Anca Nichita is currently a Research Assistant at Babes-Bolyai University, Cluj-Napoca, Romania. She received her Ph.D. in Finance with honors (summa cum laude) from Babes-Bolyai University, Cluj-Napoca, Romania, after graduating with a B.A. (class valedictorian) and an M.Sc. in Economics from the same university. She was a visiting researcher during the years 2011–2014 at the University of Vienna, Austria. She pursued research training at various universities from Denmark, Germany, Italy, the Netherlands, and Russia. She was a postdoctoral researcher in the realm of tax behavior, within a program coordinated by the Romanian Academy (2014–2015). Her research interests stem from over 25 published articles and books revolving around public finance, experimental economics, neuroeconomics, and financial analysis.

Ioan Batrancea is currently a Professor of Finance at Babes-Bolyai University, Cluj-Napoca, Romania, where he has been an academic since 1979. He received his Ph.D. in Political Economy from Babes-Bolyai University in 1992 and completed advanced programs in Economics at the University of Oslo (Norway—1991), in Management at the Wharton School, University of Pennsylvania (Philadelphia, USA—1993), and in Marketing at Kellogg School of Management, Northwestern University (Chicago, USA—1993). In 2000, he became the Chair of Economic and Financial Analysis at the Babes-Bolyai University. He benefited from 11 international and national research grants financed by the World Bank, the Romanian government, and various Romanian companies, either as principal investigator or as a member. He has published 48 books and course handbooks as well as around 150 scientific articles on the topics of economic and financial analysis, financial and managerial accounting, auditing, public finance, and informatics.

Ana Maria Roux Valentini Coelho Cesar is an Associate Professor of Decision Making, Organizational Behavior, and Multivariate Statistics at Mackenzie Presbyterian University, Graduate School of Accounting, São Paulo, Brazil. Her academic background is the following: Postdoctoral Fellow at Spalding Rehabilitation Hospital, Harvard University (2010); Ph.D. (2004) and master's (1999) degrees at the University of São Paulo (USP), Business School; B.A. in Psychology (1975) at the Pontificia Universidade Católica (PUC). Her scientific activity is dedicated to studying the topics of economic decision making, neuroeconomics, neuroaccounting, and behavioral economics. She has published several articles in international journals and chapters about decision making and strategy. She acts as reviewer for various international academic journals. She participated in many Brazilian and international conferences as invited speaker or regular presenter.

Denis Forte is an Assistant Professor at the Strategic Finance Department of Post Graduation Program in Business Administration at Mackenzie Presbyterian University, São Paulo, Brazil. He obtained a Ph.D. in Finance at Mackenzie Presbyterian University in 2007, with a thesis on capital structure, and an M.Sc. in Finance at FGV/HEC (Paris) in 1999, with a dissertation on activity-based costing. He is a former international executive for consultancies (Accenture, Coopers), manager (Lada), and a controller director (Intel Security). Currently, he is responsible for teaching behavioral finance at the doctoral program. He has published many scientific papers in Brazil and has been acting within advisory boards in selecting papers for academic congresses and local journals (e.g., Brazilian Administrative Review, RAC).

Part II
Corporate Social Responsibility

Chapter 10
An Empirical Research on the Impact of the Perceptions of Female Employees About Corporate Social Responsibility on Their Organizational Commitment

Seniz Ozhan, Nevin Altug, Yasemin Koldere Akin and Duygu Talih Akkaya

10.1 Introduction

Nowadays, social responsibility concept which provides a basis for public service applications has an ever-increasing importance. Increasing competition due to the globalization and developments at information technologies lead to differentiation in the desires and expectations of customers. Customers are no longer interested in only the quality and price of the goods and services; they are also interested in whether the producing company has ethical values and serve to the public in order to fulfil the social responsibility. Additionally, the increase in the awareness of the society causes the emergence of service expectancy in the society from the organizations. In this way, a growing number of institutions become aware of the social responsibility and behave accordingly (Saran et al. 2011: 3734). In our day, many organizations reinforce their relation with all of the stakeholders, including customers, investors, governments, suppliers and even employees. By this means, they ensure minimum conflict and maximum loyalty at their relations with all of their stakeholders (Imran et al. 2010: 2796). Moreover, owing to the corporate social

S. Ozhan (✉)
Department of Business Management, Çorlu Vocational School,
Namik Kemal University, Tekirdag, Turkey
e-mail: serdem@nku.edu.tr

N. Altug
Department of Business Administration, Management and Marketing,
Faculty of Economics and Administrative Sciences, Trakya University, Edirne, Turkey

Y. Koldere Akin
Department of Econometric, Faculty of Economics and Administrative Sciences, Trakya University, Edirne, Turkey

D. Talih Akkaya
Department of Marketing, Yalova Vocational School, Yalova University, Yalova, Turkey

K. T. Çalıyurt and R. Said (eds.), *Sustainability and Social Responsibility of Accountability Reporting Systems*, Accounting, Finance, Sustainability, Governance & Fraud: Theory and Application, https://doi.org/10.1007/978-981-10-3212-7_10

responsibility (CSR) activities, competitive advantage arises because CSR fosters better relations between the socially responsible company and two sets of key stakeholders, customers and employees (Madison et al. 2012: 2).

Corporate social responsibility (CSR) is a concept that emphasizes a company's social and environmental accountability beyond business economics through its operations, products or services, and through its interaction with key stakeholders such as employees and local communities. In other words, CSR is a mechanism whereby businesses embrace their role to positively impact the environment and the community at large for future generations (Smith and Kumar 2013: 50). CSR is not just only an effort to create positive image or reputation; instead of these, it is a concept which should become an apparent understanding at all of the actions of an organization. For instance, it is a problematic issue that to what extent a CSR activity, which is conducted by an organization which does not treat fairly and honestly to its employees, does not create a value for the society, causes unfair competition, damages the environment and uses child labour, is effective and beneficial. Therefore, the understanding of corporate social responsibility must be permanent in an organization and make itself feel to all stakeholders of the organization and the public (Varol 2010: 52). Due to these reasons, today's organizations attach importance to CSR concept more than ever. Here, the foresight that organizations will obtain significant gain by means of CSR concept has a strong influence (Aktan et al. 2007: 19).

On the other side, organizations consist of people who comes together so as to realize certain objectives and human factor, which is one of their most important resources for the organizations should be effectively used by them in order to be adapted to the rapid changes and developments of our age and maintain their continuity in the competitive world. One of the most important factors at balancing individuals' aims and organization's objectives, reducing labour force turnover rate and enhancing employee productivity efficiently, is organizational commitment levels of the employees (Yazicioglu and Topaloglu 2009: 4). Organizational commitment concept reflects the interest, loyalty and the belief of the employee towards organization and its values which are important for the success of the organization (Kaya 2008: 126). For the organizations, the most important feature of the organizational commitment behaviour is that it enables organizations to benefit from the talented human resources ideally. Commitment of the employees is seen as the most critical factor to reach organizational success and then organizations are aiming to improve its members' commitment, just because organizational commitment transforms employees into problem-solver ones, rather than problem-maker ones. If organizations want to maintain their existence and live well, they must absolutely ensure their member's commitment (Bozkurt and Yurt 2013: 126). Although emergence of the organizational commitment concept was very long time ago, it is still at the centre of attention (Erdem 2007: 67). Many researches have been conducted about organizational commitment concept after it comes into prominence and gains admission as an indispensable administrative approach for businesses (Bozkurt and Yurt 2013: 122). In this study, the impact of the perceptions of employees about corporate social responsibility on their organizational commitment is examined. Data which is gathered from the female employees in two different universities via survey is analysed, and the effect mentioned above is tried to be explained.

10.2 Corporate Social Responsibility

When corporate social responsibility is mentioned, it is usually understood as the production activity of a business by taking necessary precautions in order to preserve the nature and environment within the frame of sustainable growth objective. In fact, it is an incomplete definition. A business has responsibilities towards not only the environment and society, but also all of the stakeholders which are in relation with the business, affected by the activities and decisions of the business directly or indirectly (Aktan et al. 2007: 13). Corporate social responsibility concept took part in the book of an American economist, Howard Bowen, named "*Social Responsibilities of the Businessmen*" in 1953 for the first time. In that book, Bowen emphasized that businesses must follow policies which are in line with the values of the society (Saran et al. 2011: 3734–3735).

With a plain expression, corporate social responsibility (CSR) refers to companies taking into account the interests of stakeholders beyond shareholders (Hofman and Newman 2014: 631). Corporate social responsibility is also defined as all of the liabilities of a company towards its stakeholders which arise while the company works in an economical and environmental way. Furthermore, this concept is beyond protecting the own benefits of the company and shows itself as being beneficial to the society in various ways and looking after societies' interest (Varol 2010: 52–53). Corporate social responsibility, which is based on voluntariness, prompts organizations to fulfil their environmental and social responsibilities and also influences their marketing strategies. Here the significant point is the voluntary contribution of organizations for a better society and environment. These voluntary activities, which are carried out with social responsibility consciousness, gather public institutions and non-governmental organizations together and orient them to act in unison for a specific purpose. Finally, positive results of these activities are shared by the society (Saran et al. 2011: 3734–3735).

Foundation of corporate social responsibility is based on Industrial Revolution. Industrial Revolution provided an intense production at mining, textile, iron–steel, automobile sectors and then "Scientific Management Principles" which were manifested by Taylor, directed companies and played a key role at shaping process of the business world during the twentieth century. Addition of corporate social responsibility concept to the agendas of the companies was not voluntary; conversely, many companies involved with this concept after facing unexpected reactions from society about the issues of which they did not accept as a part of work responsibility in the past (Saran et al. 2011: 3735). At the end of nineteenth century, new acts were legislated concerning that investments were required to be made for shareholders' interest rather than public interest, and in 1970s, academicians in America and Europe started social accounting movement for organizations. Thereafter in 1980s as stock market gained importance, social responsibility evaluation reports of companies decreased in number; however in 1990s with the emergence of globalization and privatization, quality and mutual gain concepts, social and information sharing responsibilities became crucial for organizations and international institutions (Tatari 2003: 2).

Corporate social responsibility is a requirement in today's competitive market environment as well as a strategical tool in order to respond expectations of a great number of stakeholders (Maden et al. 2012: 656). Therefore, organizations should aim to apply issues intended for both internal and external environment of the organizations; including improving life quality, providing local development, easing social life, protecting natural life at every phases of investment and production and at the same time creating new natural areas, contributing to every field of education, supporting healthcare with the understanding of human life's preciousness, preserving cultural properties and handing them down to future generations by means of corporate social responsibility concept (Varol 2010: 53).

10.3 Organizational Commitment

Organization concept can be defined as an administration function at which individual's efforts are coordinated in the direction of specific objectives, or as a system at which technology dimensions are nested or as a structure which has a distinctive culture and shows the relation between work and employees (Bozkurt and Yurt 2013: 122). Commitment as a concept and understanding format exists at anywhere where society feeling exists, and also it is an emotional expression style for the instinct of the society (Gunes et al. 2009: 485). Organizational commitment concept which is consisting of commitment and organization means the desire of an employee to stay within the organization and strive for it. Also it means adopting the aims and objectives of the organization and in the meantime identifying with the value judgment of the organization and meanwhile feeling the responsibility to achieve the goals of the organization without expecting a benefit from the organization in return (Ergun Ozler et al. 2008: 42). In spite of the fact that organizational commitment concept is defined differently by various authors, their common point is the strive of the individual to stay within the organization (Bozkurt and Yurt 2013: 123). Organizational commitment is the relative strength of an individual's identification and involvement within a particular organization (Wang et al. 2014: 26).

Organizational Commitment subject was firstly handled by Whyte in 1956. In his study named "Organization Man", he mentioned the risks of extreme commitment and defined the man working in an organization not only as an employee but also as an individual who belongs to that organization. From this aspect, organizational commitment is a necessity for an individual and that individual would work in all fields of his/her life to satisfy this need (Yazicioglu and Topaloglu 2009: 6).

During recent years, in conjunction with the technological developments, organizations became more complicated and ultimately organizational commitment subject grow in importance. Nowadays organizations expect their employees to put forth more effort, be motivated and take initiative. Success of an organization is not only dependent on how the organization improves the skills of its employees, but also dependent on how the organization encourages its employees to commit to the organization (Ozutku 2008: 79–80). One of the most important objectives of businesses is obtaining maximum yield from employees and increasing their commitment to the organization by enhancing their abilities and skills (Ergun Ozler et al. 2008: 42). For this reason, it is extremely important for the managers to exhibit attitudes and behaviours in such a way that employees' organizational commitment level will increase (Bagci 2013: 168). It is seen that employees who have higher level organizational commitment participate to organizations and production more, perform better in the organization, build good relationships with other members of the organization and have higher work satisfaction levels, with respect to the ones who have lower level organizational commitment (Ergun Ozler et al. 2008: 42).

Based on the existing literature, Meyer and Allen conceptualized organizational commitment as affective commitment, continuance commitment and normative commitment, and they defined measurable attributes for each of the subconcepts. *The affective commitment* refers to "the employee's emotional attachment to the organization, identification with and involvement in this". Identification occurs when the employees' values are congruent with the values of the organization, when the organization internalizes its values and assumes its objectives (Rusu 2013: 193). Affective commitment which attaches people to the organization emotionally and ensures their happiness from being a member of the organization arises from the agreement between the individual and organizational values (Durna and Eren 2005: 211). In general, people who retain in the organization with a strong affective commitment behave like this not because they are required to retain in the organization but because they want to retain in the organization (Colakoglu et al. 2009: 78).

The continuance commitment refers to "the recognition of costs associated with the departure from the organization". The conceptualization of this type of commitment was inspired by the theory of "side-bet" by Becker (1960). The employees calculate their investments in the organization, what they gain if they retain their membership in the organization and what they have to lose if they leave the organization. The persons develop this type of commitment also due to the lack of alternative employment (Rusu 2013: 193). When an employee notices that leaving from the organization has a greater cost than retaining in that organization, then the employee will retain in that organization just because he/she is in need of this (Egriboyun 2014: 32). In this commitment type, it is thought that emotions play a little role in organizational commitment. There are several individual and organizational factors during the formation of the continuance commitment at employees.

It is possible to list the factors which influence continuance commitment as abilities, education, change of location, personal investment, pension liability and society and other options (Bozkurt and Yurt 2013: 125).

Third and the last concept is the normative commitment related to an employee's feelings of obligation to stay with the organization. It is influenced by social norms about whether people should remain committed to their organization and it is likely to develop as a feeling of reciprocation when the employee has a positive experience of their organization (Hofman and Newman 2014: 634). Normative commitment is the responsibility and ethical dimensions of the organizational commitment and reflects the liability feelings of employees with regard to retaining in the organization. Commitment of an employee to his/her organization depends on the social responsibility consciousness of the employee and his/her perception to retain in the organization as a duty. As this commitment type comes out when an employee considers retaining in the organization as correct, it represents a different standpoint for organizational commitment in comparison with the other two commitment types (Bozkurt and Yurt 2013: 125).

When these three commitment types are compared, it is seen that employees with strong affective commitment remain because they want to, those with strong continuance commitment because they need to, and those with strong normative commitment because they feel they ought to do so (Allen and Meyer 1990: 3). In other words, this subject is evaluated in "desire" (affective), "need" (continuance) and "liability" (normative) axes (Durna and Eren 2005: 212). Although common to these different approaches is a link between the employee and organization that decreases the likelihood of turnover, it is clear that the nature of that link differs. Some employees, for example, might feel both a strong need and a strong obligation to remain, but no desire to do so; others might feel neither a need nor obligation but a strong desire, and so on. The "net sum" of a person's commitment to the organization, therefore, reflects each of these separable psychological states (Allen and Meyer 1990: 3–4).

10.4 Relation Between Corporate Social Responsibility and Organizational Commitment

In literature, corporate social responsibility and organizational commitment concepts are examined by many researchers, but they mainly focused on external factors for the business. A number of the research results about the impact of the perceptions about social responsibility on organizational commitment are stated below.

In the research conducted by Brammer et al. (2007), the impact of the perceptions of employees about corporate social responsibility changes according to gender was examined. According to the results of the research, it was found that there is a positive relation between perceptions of employees about corporate social responsibility and their organizational commitment. Furthermore, it was concluded that the impact of the perceptions about corporate social responsibility shows an alteration according to gender, and accordingly female employees give importance to procedural justice and extroversive social responsibility activities more than male employees, and on the other side, male employees attach importance to educational activities more than female employees.

In the study carried out by Turker (2008), the impact of corporate social responsibility activities of businesses on the organizational commitment levels of employees was aimed to examine and in line with this aim, the research is conducted on 280 people working at companies from various sectors in Turkey. At the end of the study, it was identified that perceptions of employees about social responsibility towards social and non-social stakeholders (society, natural environment, future generations and non-governmental organizations), other employees and customers affect their organizational commitment level in a positive way, and at the same time their perceptions towards government do not have any positive impact on their organizational commitment level.

At the research done by Imran et al. (2010) on 371 professionals working in different sectors of Pakistan, the relation between perceptions of employees about corporate social responsibility, organizational commitment and organizational performance level was investigated and it was found that perceptions of employees about corporate social responsibility affect their organizational commitment and performance level in a positive way.

Hasanov (2010) examined the impact of corporate social responsibility activities on organizational commitment from four different viewpoints by conducting a research on 215 people working at Azersun Holding which predominantly operates at food sector in Azerbaijan. According to the results obtained, it was understood that perceptions of employees about legal, ethical and voluntary responsibility have positive effect on their organizational commitment level, but their perceptions about economic responsibility do not have any impact on their organizational commitment. The research carried out by Hofman and Newman (2014) on 280 people working at small- and medium-sized enterprises in Zhejiang and Jiangsu states of China aimed to examine the impact of the perceptions about corporate social responsibility of businesses on affective and normative commitment levels of employees. The acquired results showed that perceptions about corporate social responsibility towards employees have positive impact on affective and normative commitments and only partial impact exists about the perceptions towards government and customers. In addition to all these, when the literature about this topic is studied, it is seen that research conducted with different aspects has investigated whether there are financial payoffs to increased social responsiveness, the influence of perceptions concerning corporate social responsiveness on customers, and the attractiveness of social performance to investors. These studies provide evidence of payoffs to improved social responsibility (Brammer et al. 2007: 1702). An important stakeholder of a firm is its employees. Several studies confirm that corporate social responsibility activities of a company are an important means to attract and engage talented employees. It has been suggested that corporate social responsibility may better position a company to attract higher quality employees due to a more positive public image. Companies with more positive corporate social responsibility ratings may have a competitive advantage to attract higher quality candidates than companies with lower ratings (Smith and Kumar 2013: 51–54).

10.5 Study on the Impact of Perceptions of Female Employees About Corporate Social Responsibility on Their Organizational Commitment

10.5.1 Research Methodology

The aim of this research is to examine the relation between perceptions of female employees about CSR of businesses and their affective organizational commitment. On the basis of this aim, the impact of the perceptions about corporate social responsibility on affective organizational commitment was investigated and the results obtained were analysed and evaluated. This study is based on descriptive research model. The reason why this model was selected is that it is possible to reach generalization by defining the relation between variables in descriptive researches (Islamoglu 2009: 34). First of all, in this research, a theoretical model was developed which asserts that the perceptions of female employees about corporate social responsibility influence their affective organizational commitment. Then, whether the perceptions about CSR of businesses towards social and non-social stakeholders, and employees and customers have an impact on affective organizational commitment was investigated (Fig. 10.1).

10.5.2 Population and Sample

Research population consists of all female personnel working at Trakya University. Although one of the most important stakeholders of businesses is employees, in literature it is seen that several researches were focused on the impact of CSR of businesses on stakeholders external to the business and their impact on stakeholders internal to the business was neglected. Besides that, at today's business world in

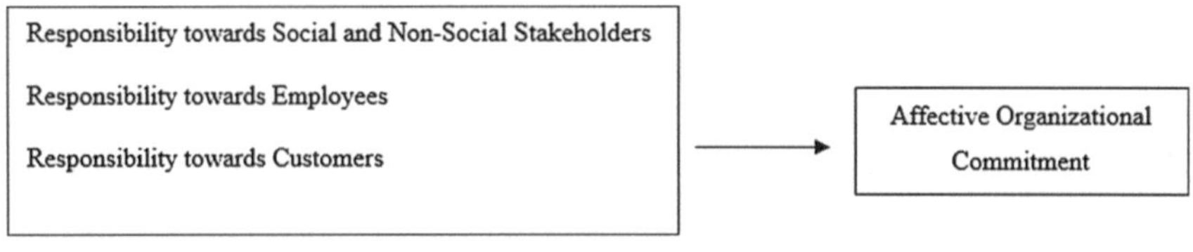

Fig. 10.1 Research model

Turkey, the number of female employees is increasing gradually but it is not at desired level yet. Consequently, social responsibility perceptions of female employees are emphasized in this study. In this framework, by using one of the incoincident sampling methods; convenience sampling method, face-to-face meetings were done through questionnaire form with 99 female employees working in Trakya University and a whole valid questionnaire form was obtained. Thus, the volume of the sample is finalized as 99.

The necessary data for the research was obtained by using face-to-face questionnaire method. Face-to-face questionnaire method was chosen because of the advantages such as its high response rate and the opportunity it provides to make observation. During the data collection phase, corporate social responsibility scale which was developed by Turker (2008) and affective organizational commitment scale which was developed by Mowday et al. were used. As the questionnaire was applied to the employees working in a state university, the statements "Our company pays its taxes always on time in full" and "Our company attaches importance to fulfil its legal obligations against the state on time and completely" were deducted from the scale. All of the statements in the scales were placed as five-point Likert-type scale questions (1 = Strongly Disagree, 5 = Strongly Agree).

Questionnaire consists of three sections. In the first section, there are 16 statements belonging to 3 factors to measure perceptions of employees about CSR of businesses. These factors are responsibility towards social and non-social stakeholders, employees and customers. In the second section, there are 9 statements to measure the impact of the perceptions of employees about corporate social responsibility activities on their affective organizational commitment. In the third part of the questionnaire form, there are demographic and socio-economic questions which provide descriptive information about the respondents of the questionnaire.

10.5.3 Variables of the Research

Independent variables of the research are responsibility towards social and non-social stakeholders, employees and customers which consist of employee's perceptions about CSR of businesses. As for dependent variable, it is set as affective organizational commitment.

10.5.4 Hypotheses of the Research

By means of hypotheses which were based on the conducted literature review, the relationships between perceptions of employees about CSR of businesses and their affective organizational commitment were tested.

H_1 There is a positive relation between perceptions of female employees about CSR of businesses towards social and non-social stakeholders and their affective organizational commitment.

H_2 There is a positive relation between perceptions of female employees about CSR of businesses towards employees and their affective organizational commitment.

H_3 There is a positive relation between perceptions of female employees about CSR of businesses towards customers and their affective organizational commitment.

10.5.5 Data Analysis

In this part, questionnaire results were evaluated based on the information obtained from the literature and statistical operations were done by using SPSS 17 software. Demographic and socio-economic features of respondents were summarized by using frequency and descriptive statistics, and also factor analysis was done in order to see the dimensions and number of these dimensions at where proposals would gather and then reliability values of these factors were calculated. Thereafter, relationships between variables were tested by using correlation analysis and then the results obtained were interpreted.

10.5.6 Reliability

Reliability is the extent to which a test or scale yields the same results on repeated trials in a consistent way. The more a test or scale is reliable, the more obtained data is reliable (Altunisik et al. 2010: 122). Reliability values are changing between 0 and 1, and value 0 means that the scale is not reliable, on the other side value 1 means that the scale is definitely reliable.

Reliability values of factors which are used to identify the perceptions of attendants are shown in Table 10.1. According to the founded α values, all of the factors have high degree of reliability.

10.5.7 Validity

Validity is the degree to which a test or a scale succeeds in measuring what it wants to measure (Altunisik et al. 2010: 121). As, during the research, scales which were developed by scientific methods were used, it was thought that scales are valid from the aspect of content validity. Before using these mentioned scales at research, they

Table 10.1 Reliability values of factors and their statement counts

Factors	Cronbach's alpha	Statement count
Responsibility towards social and non-social stakeholders	0.942	8
Responsibility towards employees	0.902	5
Responsibility towards customers	0.933	3
Affective organizational commitment	0.921	8

were assessed by discussing with various academicians and experts and it was deduced that each of the participants infers the same meaning from the same question. By this way, it was concluded that these scales are suitable for the face validity aspect as well.

10.6 Findings

When the frequency distribution of female employees' age information was analysed, it is understood that 11.1% of them are in age between 21 and 25, 32.3% are in age between 26 and 30, 19.2% are in age between 31 and 35, 12.1% are in age between 36 and 40, 19.2% are in age between 41 and 45 and lastly 6.1% are in age between 46 and 50. According to the data, it can be said that the university subject to our research has a young female employee profile. When it comes to total working period of participants, it is seen that most of them have been working in the university for 2–6 years. When the monthly family income of the participants was analysed, it is stated that 5.1% of them earn more than 7.000 TL, 30.3% earn between 1.000 and 2.500 TL, 31.3% earn between 2501 and 4000 TL, 22.2% earn between 4001 and 5500 TL and lastly 11.1% earn between 5501 and 7000 TL in a month. Finally, according to the data about the educational backgrounds of the participants, the majority of them are postgraduate and the majority of them are working as academic staff in the university (Table 10.2).

10.6.1 Factor Analysis

Factor analysis is a multivariate analysis technique which can reduce the number of variables by using the relationships between variables (Islamoglu 2009: 228). The general purpose of the factor analysis is to form a new and combined "less dimensions and factors set" with minimum information loss, by summarizing the cumulative information obtained from a large number of original variables (Gegez 2010: 316). In this analysis technique, eigenvalues which will be examined are gathered together as smaller linear combination groups without losing their

Table 10.2 Findings about demographic and socio-economic features of participants

Age	*f*	%	Educational background	*f*	%
21–25	11	11.1	Primary	5	5.1
26–30	32	32.3	Secondary	4	4.0
31–35	19	19.2	Undergraduate	17	17.2
36–40	12	12.1	Graduate	29	29.3
41–45	19	19.2	Doctorate	36	36.4
46–50	6	6.1	*Monthly family income*	*f*	%
Total working period in organization	*f*	%	1000–2500 TRL	30	30.3
<2 years	21	21.2	2501–4000 TRL	31	31.3
2–6 years	42	42.4	4001–5500 TRL	22	22.2
7–11 years	7	7.1	5501–7000 TRL	11	11.1
12–16 years	14	14.1	7000 TRL >	5	5.1
<16 years	15	15.2	*Position in organization*	*f*	%
			Academic	64	64.6
			Administrative	26	26.3
			Other	9	9.1

significance. Therefore, basic characteristic of factor analysis is to abbreviate and summarize the information and at the same time all of the variables are included in the scope of the analysis (Yukselen et al. 2011: 199). Before applying factor analysis to the data in question, KMO and Bartlett tests were performed to evaluate the adequacy of data. The Kaiser-Meyer-Olkin (KMO) test shows whether the sample number is sufficient to apply factor analysis, and Bartlett sphericity test shows whether the relation between variables is adequate enough to apply factor analysis (Islamoglu 2009: 234). For KMO value, values between 0.5 and 1.0 were taken as acceptable, whereas values below 0.5 were the indicator of the inconvenience of factor analysis for the dataset. However in general, minimum KMO value that is considered satisfactory for researchers is 0.7 (Altunisik et al. 2010: 266).

As it is seen in Table 10.3 where KMO and Bartlett tests results exist, 0.927 value from the KMO test indicates that sample size is sufficient and also approximate chi-square value 2068.475 and $p = 0.00$ from the Bartlett test is found as significant at confidence level. Consequently, it can be concluded that data is suitable for factor analysis. After it was understood that statements in questionnaire were suitable for factor analysis, factor analysis was completed in order to determine the dimensions and number of dimensions at which these statements will be gathered. Subsequently, the statement in the affective commitment scale "I am extremely pleased to choose this organization instead of other organizations when I was going to start my career" was extracted from the scale because it took part in another factor and it also impaired conceptual meaning. Then again a factor analysis

Table 10.3 KMO and Bartlett tests results

KMO and Bartlett's test		
Kaiser-Meyer-Olkin measure sample conformance test		0.927
Bartlett test	Approximate chi-square	2068.475
	Df	276
	Sig.	0.000

was done on the data. As the result of the analysis, statements were gathered under four factors. Factor groups, statements corresponding to each of the factor groups and related statistical values are shown at Table 10.4. In conclusion, it was founded that the model is valid (suitable for the 4-factor structure), and results are consistent, in other words reliable, for the application.

As it is seen in the table, the first factor *responsibility towards social and non-social stakeholders* explains 55.522%, the second factor *responsibility towards employees* explains 5.514%, the third factor *responsibility towards customers* explains 3.764% and finally the fourth factor *affective organizational commitment* explains 8.768% of the total variance. Moreover, it is founded that total variance explanation per cent of these four factors is 73.477%.

10.6.2 Correlation Analysis

On the purpose of asserting the relation between the factors obtained, correlation analysis is used. Primarily, distribution of the variables must be tested to make correlation analysis. For that purpose, Kolmogorov–Smirnov test which is a test to identify the distribution of the factors is applied firstly (Table 10.5).

When the table above is examined, it is seen that the factors corporate social responsibility towards social and non-social stakeholders, corporate social responsibility towards employees and corporate social responsibility towards customers are normally distributed as the significance value is greater than 0.05 for them, which is the limit value for statistical significance calculations. On the other hand, affective organizational commitment factor turns not to be normally distributed (0.042 < 0.05). Accordingly, Spearman's rank correlation coefficient is used to present the relation between factors. Spearman's rank correlation coefficient which is a nonparametric method is calculated to examine the relation between variables in cases that distribution is not known or variables do not show a normal distribution (Altas 2013: 132) (Table 10.6).

According to the correlation analysis, it was found that there is a positive, at a level of 64.2% medium-level relation between the affective organizational commitment level and the perceptions about corporate social responsibility towards social and non-social stakeholders ($r = 0.642$; $p = 0.000 < 0.05$). Thus, the hypothesis H_1 which formulates that there is a positive relation between perceptions

Table 10.4 Factor analysis results for participants' perceptions

Statements	Factor loads	Eigen values	Variance explained (%)	Cronbach's alpha
Corporate social responsibility towards social and non-social stakeholders		13.325	55.522	0.967
Our organization, attaches great importance to its social responsibilities towards the society	0.690			
Our organization contributes to organizations and projects which will benefit to the society	0.745			
In our organization, various programs are put into practice to reduce harmful effects to the environment	0.591			
Our organization actively participates to the activities aiming at protecting and enhancing natural environment	0.772			
Our organization aims sustainable growth which also takes care of future generations	0.707			
Our organization attempts to make social investments which are oriented to future generations	0.813			
In our organization, every employee is encouraged to participate in voluntary work and charity activities	0.713			
Our organization promotes various associations and foundations working at several areas	0.780			
Affective organizational commitment		2.083	8.678	0.921
In order to help my organization's success, I am ready to make a great effort more than expected normally	0.723			
I say to my friends that this organization is a very good place to work	0.660			
I would accept almost every duty so as to go on working in this organization	0.780			
I think that my values and my organization's values are very similar	0.653			
I am proud of saying that I am a part of this organization	0.748			
This organization encourages me well about work performance	0.625			
I really care about this organization's destiny	0.775			
In my opinion, this organization is the best one among the other organizations that I can work	0.664			

(continued)

Table 10.4 (continued)

Statements	Factor loads	Eigen values	Variance explained (%)	Cronbach's alpha
Corporate social responsibility towards employees		1.323	5.514	0.902
Our organization supports the employees who want to take education	0.710			
Our organization has encouraging policies on developing employees' talents and careers	0.761			
Our organization applies flexible policies which enables employees to balance their private life and business life	0.735			
Our organization has a management which places importance to employees' requests and needs	0.700			
The decisions of the management on the employees are usually fair	0.606			
Corporate social responsibility towards customers		0.903	3.764	0.933
Our organization presents exact and true information about its services to students/patients	0.637			
Our organization has an awareness about student/patient rights beyond legal regulations	0.728			
Our organization gives great importance to student/patient satisfaction	0.702			

of female employees about CSR of businesses towards social and non-social stakeholders and their affective organizational commitment was accepted, and it was found that employee's responsibility perceptions towards social and non-social stakeholders affect employees' affective commitment positively. When the relation between the perceptions of attendants about responsibility towards employees and employees' affective commitment levels was examined, it was seen that there is a positive and medium-level relation between ($r = 0.651$; $p = 0.000 < 0.05$). According to this result, it was concluded that perceptions of employees about corporate social responsibility activities of businesses affect employees' affective commitment levels in a positive way, and hence, the hypothesis H_2 was accepted.

According to the result of correlation analysis to reveal the relation between employees' responsibility perceptions towards customers and employees' affective commitment level, again it was found that there is a positive, medium-level relation ($r = 0.667$; $p = 0.000 < 0.05$). So, this situation supported the proposed hypothesis that perceptions of female employees about responsibility towards customers have a positive impact on their affective organizational commitment, and hence, the

Table 10.5 Kolmogorov–Smirnov test

		Corporate social responsibility towards social and non-social stakeholders	Corporate social responsibility towards employees	Corporate social responsibility towards customers	Affective organizational commitment
N		99	99	99	99
Parameters	Average	3.2348	3.4545	3.2694	3.4523
	Standard deviation	0.84332	0.93713	0.96266	0.88009
Kolmogorov–Smirnov		0.969	1.096	1.390	0.816
Sig.		**0.305**	**0.181**	**0.042**	**0.251**

Table 10.6 Correlation analysis

		Affective organizational commitment
Corporate social responsibility towards social and non-social stakeholders	*r*	0.642
	P	0.000
	N	99
Corporate social responsibility towards employees	*r*	0.651
	P	0.000
	N	99
Corporate social responsibility towards customers	*r*	0.667
	P	0.000
	N	99

hypothesis H_3 was accepted and it was deduced that positive perceptions affect affective commitments positively. At Table 10.7, the results of hypotheses which were constituted for the research model are presented all together.

10.7 Discussion

The aim of this study is to examine the relation between perceptions of female employees about corporate social responsibility activities of businesses and their affective commitment. The sample of the study was comprised of 99 female employees working at Trakya University. Questionnaire form which was prepared in accordance with the aim of the study was applied to the attendants, and the data obtained from the answers were analysed and interpreted.

Table 10.7 Results of the hypotheses belonging to research model

Hypotheses	Result
H_1: There is a positive relation between perceptions of female employees about CSR of businesses towards social and non-social stakeholders and their affective organizational commitment	Accepted
H_2: There is a positive relation between perceptions of female employees about CSR of businesses towards employees and their affective organizational commitment	Accepted
H_3: There is a positive relation between perceptions of female employees about CSR of businesses towards customers and their affective organizational commitment	Accepted

At the end of the study, factor analysis was conducted to define the dimensions and number of the dimensions in which statements in the questionnaire would gather. *Results of that factor analysis* are as follows:

- Before applying factor analysis to the data in question, KMO and Bartlett tests were performed so as to evaluate the convenience of the data for factor analysis. The resulting value of KMO test which shows whether the sample number is sufficient to apply factor analysis was 0.927. Meanwhile, the Bartlett test which shows whether the relation between variables is adequate enough to apply factor analysis, resulted in 2068.475 and $p = 0.00$ which were interpreted as significant at confidence level. Consequently, it was concluded that the data is suitable for factor analysis. After it was understood that statements in questionnaire were suitable for factor analysis, factor analysis was completed in order to determine the dimensions and number of dimensions at which these statements will be gathered. At the end of the analysis, 24 statements in the scale were gathered under four factors and it was founded that model is valid (suitable for the 4-factor structure), and results are consistent, in other words reliable.
- *Responsibility towards social and non-social stakeholders* factor explains 55.522%, *responsibility towards employees* factor explains 5.514%, *responsibility towards customers* factor explains 3.764% and finally *affective organizational commitment* factor explains 8.768% of the total variance regarding to the perceptions of female employees about corporate social responsibility activities of businesses and their affective commitment.

Correlation analysis was performed to test the hypotheses developed in the research. As a result of the analysis, *the data obtained and the results of the hypotheses* are as follows:

- Before making correlation analysis, Kolmogorov–Smirnov Z test which is used for identifying the distribution of the variables was applied first. According to this test's results, it was seen that the factors corporate social responsibility towards social and non-social stakeholders, corporate social responsibility towards employees and corporate social responsibility towards customers are normally distributed as the significance value is greater than 0.05 for them, which is the limit value for statistical significance calculations. On the other hand, affective organizational commitment factor turns not to be normally distributed (0.042 < 0.05). For this reason, Spearman's rank correlation coefficient was used to present the relations between factors.

According to the conducted correlation analyses, it was found that there is a positive, medium-level relation between perceptions of female employees about responsibility towards social and non-social stakeholders, perceptions of female employees about responsibility towards employees, perceptions of female employees about responsibility towards customers and their affective organizational commitment level, and finally all of the hypotheses were accepted.

10.7.1 Restrictions of the Research

This research is restricted to female employees working at Trakya University, and other universities left out of scope. Furthermore, usage of convenience sampling method during data collection and the fact that research was done only in Turkey are restricting the generalizability of the results. Additionally, only corporate social responsibility activities and their affective commitment concepts were examined in the research; the other commitment types, normative and continuance commitment types, were not included to the research. In conclusion, the research is limited with the questions in questionnaire and answers of the participants. Conclusion and generalizations which are deduced in the light of the findings obtained are only valid in the research population.

10.7.2 Administrative Effects

On the basis of the findings which are obtained as a result of the research, corporate social responsibility activities affect the affective commitment of female employees working in the university in question. Considering this point, recommendations listed below can be offered to businesses about corporate social responsibility activities in order to improve affective commitment levels of their employees:

- Businesses should be aware of the importance of corporate social responsibility activities for female employees and take this fact into account.
- Businesses should take the ideas and expectations of female employees who are internal stakeholders into consideration while they are conducting corporate social responsibility activities.
- Businesses should share the information with their employees about their corporate social responsibility activities.

- Businesses should effectively evaluate the perceptions of female employees about corporate social responsibility activities for the success of these activities.

10.7.3 Recommendations for Future Researches

Based on the academic value of the study, recommendations for the researches that will be conducted in the future about this topic are presented below:

- A study which uses random sampling method and collects data from both public and private university employees will enable generalization of the results. Furthermore, a comparative study can be performed by including employees working at the universities abroad.
- In the researches that will be done in the future, different scales may be used and the results obtained may be compared with these ones obtained here.
- The model, which is developed by means of questionnaire method within the context of this study, can be used at the experimental studies in the future, and this is thought to contribute to the literature.
- Apart from the perceptions of employees about corporate social responsibility activities, measurement of demographic variables which can affect affective organizational commitment level will be helpful to enlighten much further the research topic.
- In this study, the impact of the perceptions of female employees about corporate social responsibility activities on their affective organizational commitment was emphasized. In the future studies, the impact of the perceptions of employees about corporate social responsibility on employees' organizational commitment can also be examined by including other organizational commitment types.

References

Aktan CC, Boru D, Kurumsal SS, Kurumsal SS (2007) Isletmeler ve Sosyal Sorumluluk, IGIAD Yayinlari: 4, Istanbul

Allen NJ, Meyer JP (1990) The measurement and antecedents of affective, continuance and normative commitment to the organization. J Occup Psychol 63:1–18

Altas D (2013) Istatistiksel Analiz Teknikleri. Beta Yayincilik, Istanbul

Altunisik R, Coskun B, Recai Y, Serkan E (2010) Sosyal Bilimlerde Arastirma Yontemleri SPSS Uygulamali, Gelistirilmis 6. Baski, Sakarya Yayincilik, Sakarya

Bagci Z (2013) Calisanlarin Orgutsel Adalet Algılarının Orgutsel Bagliliklari Uzerindeki Etkisi: Tekstil Sektorunde Bir Inceleme. Uluslararası Yonetim Iktisat ve Isletme Dergisi 9(19):163–184

Becker HS (1960) Notes on the concept of commitment. Am J Sociol 66(1):32–40

Bozkurt O, Yurt I (2013) Akademisyenlerin Orgutsel Baglilik Duzeylerini Belirlemeye Yonelik Bir Arastirma. Yonetim Bilimleri Dergisi 11(22):121–139

Brammer S, Millington A, Rayton B (2007) The contribution of corporate social responsibility to organizational commitment. Int J Hum Resource Manag 18(10):1701–1719
Colakoglu U, Ayyildiz T, Cengiz S (2009) Calisanlarin Demografik Ozelliklerine Gore Orgutsel Baglilik Boyutlarinda Algilama Farkliliklari, Kusadasi'ndaki Bes Yildizli Konaklama Isletmeleri Ornegi. Anatolia: Turizm Arastirmalari Dergisi 20(1):77–89
Durna U, Eren V (2005) Uc Baglilik Unsuru Ekseninde Orgutsel Baglilik. Dogus Universitesi Dergisi 6(2):210–219
Egriboyun D (2014) Ortaogretim Okullarinda Gorev Yapan Yonetici ve Ogretmenlerin Orgutsel Destek ve Orgutsel Bagliliklari Arasindaki Iliski. Gumushane Universitesi Sosyal Bilimler Elektronik Dergisi 9:25–52
Erdem R (2007) Orgut Kulturu Tipleriyle Orgutsel Baglilik Arasindaki Iliski: Elazig Il Merkezindeki Hastaneler Uzerinde Bir Calisma. Eskisehir Osmangazi Universitesi Iktisadi ve Idari Bilimler Fakultesi Dergisi 2(2):63–79
Ergun Ozler D, Giderler Atalay C, Dil Sahin M (2008) Mobbing'in Orgutsel Baglilik Uzerine Etkisini Belirlemeye Yonelik Bir Arastirma. Dumlupinar Universitesi Sosyal Bilimler Dergisi 22:37–60
Gegez AE (2010) Pazarlama arastirmalari beta yayinlari. Istanbul
Gunes I, Bayraktaroglu S, Ozen Kutanis R (2009) Calisanlarin Orgutsel Baglilik ve Tukenmislik Duzeyleri Arasindaki Iliski: Bir Devlet Universitesi Ornegi. Suleyman Demirel Universitesi Iktisadi ve Idari Bilimler Fakultesi Dergisi 14(3):481–497
Hasanov V (2010) Calisanlarin Isletmelerin Sosyal Sorumluluklarina Iliskin Algilamalarinin Orgutsel Bagliliga Etkisi. Gazi Universitesi Sosyal Bilimler Enstitusu, Basilmamis Doktora Tezi, Ankara
Hofman PS, Newman A (2014) The impact of perceived corporate social responsibility on organizational commitment and the moderating role of collectivism and masculinity: evidence from China. Int J Hum Resource Manag 25(5):631–652
Imran A, Kashif U, Rehman SI, Ali JY, Maria Z (2010) Corporate social responsibility influences, employee commitment and organizational performance. Afr J Bus Manag 4(12):2796–2801
Islamoglu AH (2009) Sosyal Bilimlerde Arastirma Yontemleri, Beta Yayincilik, Izmit, Temmuz
Kaya H (2008) Kamu ve Ozel Sektor Kuruluslarinin Orgutsel Kulturunun Analizi ve Kurum Kulturunun Calisanlarin Orgutsel Bagliligina Etkisi. Maliye Dergisi 155:119–143
Maden C, Arikan E, Telci EE, Kantur D (2012) Linking corporate social responsibility to corporate reputation: a study on understanding behavioral consequences. Proc Soc Behav Sci 58:655–664
Madison TF, Ward S, Royalty K (2012) Corporate social responsibility, organizational commitment, and employer-sponsored volunteerism. Int J Bus Soc Sci 3(1):1–14
Ozutku H (2008) Orgute Duygusal, Devamlilik ve Normatif Baglilik ile Is Performansi Arasindaki Iliskinin Incelenmesi. Istanbul Universitesi Isletme Fakultesi Dergisi 37(2):79–97
Rusu R (2013) Affective organizational commitment, continuance organizational commitment or normative organizational commitment? Manag Econ 2(70):192–197
Saran M, Coskun G, Inal Zorel F, Aksoy Z (2011) Universitelerde Sosyal Sorumluluk Bilincinin Gelistirilmesi: Ege Universitesi Topluma Hizmet Uygulamalari Dersi Uzerine Bir Arastirma. J Yaşar Univ 22(6):3732–3747
Smith S, Kumar A (2013) Impact of corporate social responsibility on employee organizational commitment within the gaming industry. Adv Hosp Leisure 9:49–67
Tatari B (2003) Sirketlerin Toplumla İliskisinde Yukselen Deger: Kurumsal Sosyal Sorumluluk, Izmir Ticaret Odasi Yayini, Aralik, pp 1–11
Turker D (2008) The impact of employee perception of corporate social responsibility on organizational commitment: a scale development study. Dokuz Eylul Universitesi Sosyal Bilimler Enstitusu, Basilmamis Yuksek Lisans Tezi, Izmir
Varol A (2010) Hedef Kitlelerin Kurumsal Sosyal Sorumluluk Degerlendirmesi: Universite Genclerine Yonelik Bir Arastirma. Paradoks Ekonomi, Sosyoloji ve Politika Dergisi 6(1):49–64
Wang X, Ma L, Zhang M (2014) Transformational leadership and agency workers' organizational commitment: the mediating effect of organizational justice and job characteristics. Soc Behav Pers 42(1):25–36

Yazicioglu I, Topaloglu IG (2009) Orgutsel Adalet ve Baglilik Iliskisi: Konaklama Isletmelerinde Bir Uygulama. Isletme Arastirmalari Dergisi 1(1):3–16
Yukselen, Cemal, Pazarlama Arastirmalari, Yenilenmis 5. Baski, Detay Yayincilik, Ankara (2011)

Author Biographies

Seniz Ozhan is Lecturer of Business Management at Namık Kemal University, Corlu Vocational School, Turkey. She received BA, MA, and Ph.D. degrees in Business Administration from Trakya University. Her research interests are corporate social responsibility; consumer behaviour; service quality; service marketing; healthcare marketing; marketing research and contemporary issues in marketing.

Nevin Altug Ph.D. was born in Edirne in 1967. Nevin Altuğ has been an Assistant Professor of Marketing at Trakya University in Turkey for thirteen years. She holds a Ph.D. in Marketing and International Business from Istanbul University, a M.B.A. degree in Marketing and International Business, and a Bachelor's degree in Economics from the Marmara University. She has more than twenty publications in international academic journals.

Yasemin Koldere Akin is Assistant Professor of Econometrics at Trakya University School of Economics, Edirne, Turkey. She joined Trakya University in 1994, and following this she completed her M.Sc. in Econometrics at Marmara Üniversity in 1996. Dr Koldere Akin holds a Ph.D. in Econometrics from Marmara Üniversity which she obtained in 2009. Her several research works have been published in peer-reviewed articles.

Duygu Talih Akkaya is Assistant Professor of Marketing and Advertising at Yalova University, Yalova Vocational School, Turkey. Her scientific activity is dedicated to study the themes of Social Media Advertising, Consumer Behaviour, Online Consumer Behaviour, Service Quality. She has written several articles in Turkish and International Journals. She has participated in many Turkish and International Conferences.

Chapter 11
The Role of Corporate Social Responsibility in Modern Business in the Republic of Serbia

Danijela Sarcevic

11.1 Introduction

A large number of researchers suggest that corporations of twenty-first century can derive enormous benefits when perceived as being socially responsible by their stakeholders (Crowther 2003; Idowu and Towler 2004). Concept of CSR promotes ethical concerns which are integrated into the strategic visions of corporations: it is manifestation of effectively managed the impact of social and ethical issues in and out of business area. Generally, this concept could be defined as the corporation way for integration of social, environmental and economic perspectives into their values, culture, decision-making and strategy of transparency and responsibility. Therefore, they could have better managed within organization, create wealth and prove social responsibility, which are not obligate to carry out and which are in accordance with law, in order to bring the whole community and society profits. The synergy of social and economic concerns, as well as concern for the environment, based in the organizational culture, decision-making, strategy, transparent operations and responsible behaviour, contributes and shows desire to preserve both natural and social, and human resources. The actions carried out in this regard are not casual, but involve long-term, planned activities, about which organizations have to plan well and took stand (Sarcevic 2011). CSR is of high relevance for all business companies and has strong impact and high dependence on the economy, the environment and the society. It may be defined as the commitment of business to contribute to sustainable economic development, working with employees, their families, the local community and society at large to improve quality of life (World business council for sustainable development 2004). For companies, it is essential not only to develop and implement socially responsible initiatives, but to promote them in effective way as well. Basic element of contemporary free market is

D. Sarcevic (✉)
Institute of Meat Hygiene and Technology, Belgrade, Republic of Serbia
e-mail: danijela.sarcevic@inmes.rs; danisar3@gmail.com

K. T. Çalıyurt and R. Said (eds.), *Sustainability and Social Responsibility of Accountability Reporting Systems*, Accounting, Finance, Sustainability, Governance & Fraud: Theory and Application, https://doi.org/10.1007/978-981-10-3212-7_11

transparency and availability of social relevant information upon which others, like stakeholders, may create their opinions and attitudes. According to this, promoting companies' social goals must be continuous process by which a lasting dedication to socially responsible business activities is explicitly expressed and not just the completion of some ad hoc activity (Durovic and Randjic 2011).

11.2 Development of the Concept of Corporate Social Responsibility in the Republic of Serbia

The Republic of Serbia, as a country in transition, is a specific case in relation to other countries in Central and Eastern Europe, which have been going through this process. This has been affected by the historical circumstances in which the country found itself in the early 1990's of the last century. Until year 2000, the business was based on illegal flows and non-market transition that were a function of personal interests and corruption. Business in Serbia has constantly faced two problems: uncertainty due to non-compliance with laws and weak institutions and unable to form a strong market. The monopoly over the market has been kept by a few strong organizations that have held the position through bribery and corruption of weak state institutions. One important feature of Serbian society and culture is the low ranking of responsibility as a respected value. That is why any initiative that introduces a modern, universal and enlightened value of such responsibility was very important for the Republic of Serbia. The concept of corporate social responsibility began to develop and to be promoted over the past ten years. Given that this is a concept that requires a certain level of social and political consciousness; it can be said that the Republic of Serbia, a country with many economic and political problems, initially has recognized this type of responsibility, mainly as a benefit to the organization, because it builds good corporate image to the public. Later, as a consequence that economic activity may have on the environmental situation in the country, the topics that are basic to the concept of corporate social responsibility are identified.

According to the reports of the European Union, in Serbia, the greatest attention is paid to the involvement of companies in solving problems in the community. Most companies examine the needs of the local community on which to base the activities and support programmes. Programmes are mostly one-time occurring and periodical, and among all, a very small number of companies are operating long term and strategically. A strategic cooperation was observed between companies and universities or research centres, through continued support to science and education, in the implementation of projects in the field of health care in collaboration with the local government. Considerably, more companies are supporting sporadic and unplanned specific projects to improve the community such as park maintenance and support to implementation of infrastructure projects, such as building roads. In addition, a large number of companies are providing support for education and the arts, culture and sports sponsoring sporting events, etc. (Hayiyev 2008). Companies pay a lot of attention to the environmental dimension of corporate social responsibility. Many companies have introduced some of the environmental standards (usually ISO 14 001) for environmental management. In this area, “ad hoc” programmes that are mainly related to cleaning, landscaping in urban areas and in the protected areas such as national parks, are much more frequent. Only foreign companies operating in the market of the Republic of Serbia present data on the ecological dimension through a special report made public and attach considerable importance to it, but it is still lower than in the countries of the European Union (Martinovic and Damjanovic 2009). Surveys conducted in Serbia in the period 2005–2008 show that the public awareness of the need for applying the concept of the corporative social responsibility has gradually increased. On the other hand, they show that most people do not understand the essence and importance of the concept. Poor level of awareness of the CSR concept is also exhibited by managers who believe that social issues should be concern of the state, and for this reason, no great importance is attached to the organization of business in a socially acceptable way. Even those who perceive the concept of CSR as important mostly associate it with different forms of one-time financial assistance, such as sponsorship of cultural, sport events and other non-profit events, donating money or equipment to hospitals and charities that help vulnerable groups of the population, as in the opinion of managers, the sponsorship and donations are the most visible forms of CSR which enhance the company’s reputation (Mazurkiewicz 2007). In the surveys carried out by managers, elements such as women’s rights, minority rights, the rights of different social groups, discrimination were not considered as categories of corporate social responsibility (Martinovic 2007). The situation in practice is such that the CSR is recognized as a marketing tool that can be a good form of promotion and a way to build reputation, without attributing any strategic importance to it. According to the data of “Databases of good practice” that includes 68 mostly large companies in Serbia, only five companies have managers for corporate social responsibility, in others the work is performed by directors of foundations, and in others the services for public relations. In addition, the results achieved in the field of social responsibility are not included or entered in reports, but are conveyed to the public via Websites or media (Martinovic and Damjanovic 2009). However, the business and the company’s success in the market do not have to be and are not opposed to its responsibility and ethics in business. Companies are not and cannot be isolated from the society in which they operate, so the development of a society, the quality of education, infrastructure, development of local business, the quality of the public sector are the factors that significantly affect the operations of a company. The multinational companies operating in the Serbian market, in addition to the capital, bring also the business policy and are trying to establish certain business culture, which includes the application of the concept of corporate social responsibility. The following multinational companies operating in Serbia are promoters of social responsibility: “Lafarge”, “Holcim”, “Cisco systems”, “EFG Eurobank”, “Societe General Bank”, “Carlsberg”, “Banca Intesa”, “Mercator”, “Microsoft” and others. NGO “Smart Collective” together with several leading companies operating in the territory of Serbia initiated formation of a database that would include all the case studies related to socially responsible activities of companies in Serbia. The basic idea of creating such a database is to reliably and objectively identify best practices that maximize both the competitive and social benefits. The aim of the initiative is to support companies to intensively measure the impact they have on their business, the wider social and natural environment, as well as to report on their activities in this regard. Above-mentioned companies have established a successful business in Serbia; they have shown a strong will and made an effort to establish a partnership with the environment that enabled a successful business by investing in the local community and thus becoming its "corporate citizen". Also, companies have recognized that the application of the concept of CSR contributes to long-term stability of business operations, increased sales and greater loyalty and motivates employees, but also improves the company's reputation. On the other hand, the above study has shown (Smart Kolektiv 2007) that the greatest obstacle to the implementation of CSR is implementation of legislation in this area, followed by human factor and factors of the economic nature. The content of the CSR concept has been analysed through actors, transparency of operations, code of conduct, social projects, to the protection of the environment. As a means of CSR in Serbia, the following are recognized: the transparency of operations, preserving the health of employees, avoiding the use of child labour and protection of the environment. In this context, companies recognize also tax payment, creating new jobs, providing of job security, listening to stakeholders and providing voluntary income (Smart Kolektiv 2007). The obstacles and risks, categorized by the size of the experienced risk in the implementation of the concept of corporate social responsibility in companies in Serbia, are following: increased operational costs, increased demands of stakeholders, increased involvement of regulatory authorities, lagging behind the competition, reduced productivity, the negative impact on profitability, negative impact on the quality of goods and services. The promotion of CSR is actively exercised by the Serbian Chamber of Commerce, which has since 2007 established a National Award for Corporate Social Responsibility. The prize is awarded in two categories (large enterprises and small and medium enterprises) based on a complex methodology in five key areas of CSR. The jury consists of representatives of relevant ministries, chambers of commerce, universities, non-governmental organizations, the media and international organizations. At the initiative of 14 leading companies in Serbia, the Business Leaders Forum Serbia was founded in 2008, as the first exclusively business coalition with a mission to stimulate the development of CSR and to establish lasting and stable practice of CSR in the Serbian business sector.

For the purpose of harmonization with the EU acquis, the Government of the Republic of Serbia in 2010 passed the "Strategy for the development and promotion of CSR in Serbia in the period from 2010 to 2015", which comprehensively assesses the situation in the field of CSR in the country. As a country that aspires to join the European Union, the Republic of Serbia is obligated to accept the standards and practices of the European Union, which includes the recognition and promotion of CSR and its contribution to social harmony and sustainable competitiveness and development. Business justification for the implementation of the concept of CSR operates on three levels:

- *pressure of the environment and protection of the reputation*—pressure from NGOs, consumers, media, government and others leading to appropriate action to avoid potential financial losses and protect brand image;
- *profitability—tangible financial gains* (e.g. increasing productivity and reducing energy and material inefficiency;
- *strategic level*—CSR as an essential part of the development strategy of the company, such as a substantial change in products, CSR as an integral part of the brand identity, or as a path towards learning and innovation. The comprehensive vision of CSR according to the above-mentioned strategy aims to promote sustainable business growth development that promotes social inclusion and prevent harm to the environment.

11.3 Materials and Methods

The survey of the application of the concept of corporate social responsibility in companies operating in the Republic of Serbia was carried out in 2012–2013. The survey was organized on the basis of a questionnaire specially composed for the sample of respondents—company managers/directors. The aim of the study was to determine the presence of the elements of the CSR concept in business practices of companies from the perspective of the company manager. The sample was designed to 50 units. For statistical analysis of data, the usual procedures of descriptive statistics and inference statistics were used: techniques of descriptive statistics (mean and standard deviation). All statistical analyses were performed with the statistical package SPSS 17.0 (Statistical Package for Social Science for Windows). The study was set up so that the survey data were processed according to the following control variables: company size, ownership structure, business field, manager position in the company, the level of educational attainment.

11.3.1 Results and Discussion

The Republic of Serbia has in the past gone through multi-layer transformations in the areas of legislation, property rights, market economy, the organization of business and technology development. It has significantly contributed to the improvement of operation of domestic companies. The research conducted for this study included 50 companies that are on the market of the Republic of Serbia. Figures 11.1 and 11.2 show the representation of companies in the sample examined in relation to the size of the company and ownership structure.

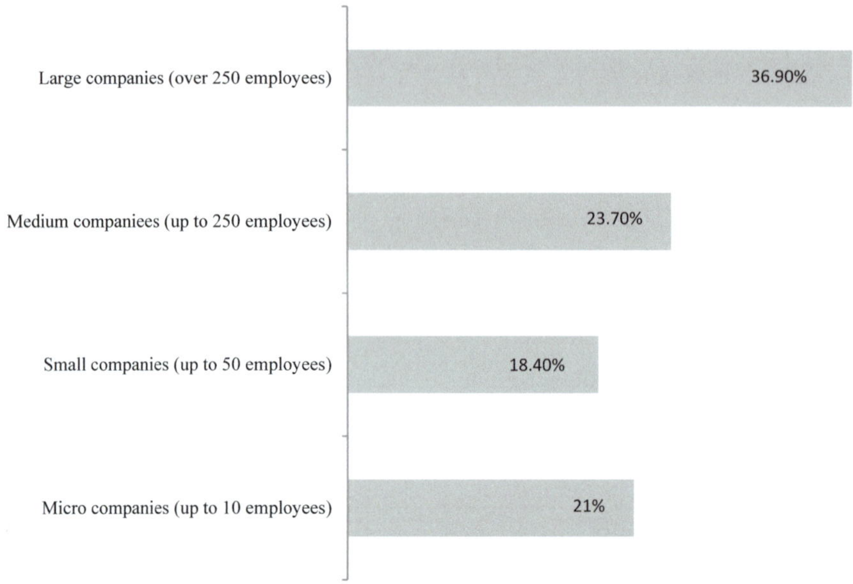

Fig. 11.1 Representation of companies in the sample examined in relation to the size

Fig. 11.2 Sample examined in relation to the ownership structure

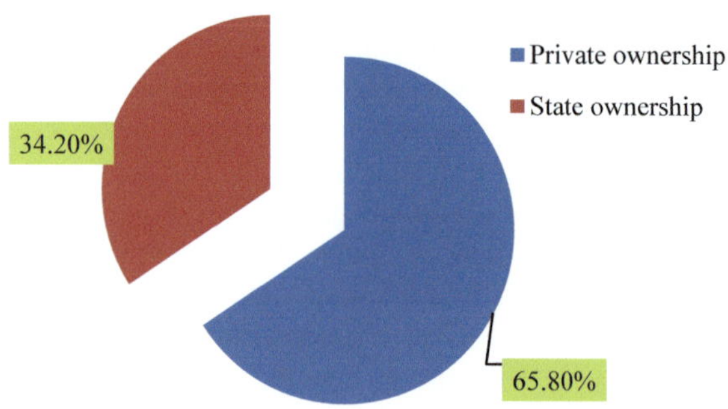

This study mostly included large companies 36.9% (with over 250 employees) and the lowest percentage of medium-sized companies (up to 50 employees) 18.4%. The survey covered 65.8% of the companies in private ownership, and 34.2% state-owned. Results pertaining to the present areas of operations (Fig. 11.3) show that the service sector is present with 26.3%, trade with 21%, finance with 18.4%, transport and telecommunications with 13.2% and the lowest percentage education with only 2.6%. These data indicate that in the Republic of Serbia, the service sector and trade employ almost half of the economy market, and the industry is represented in only 10.6%.

The survey was completed by managers of companies, which were in the same percentage of 36.7% directors and managers/directors of the sector (Fig. 11.4).

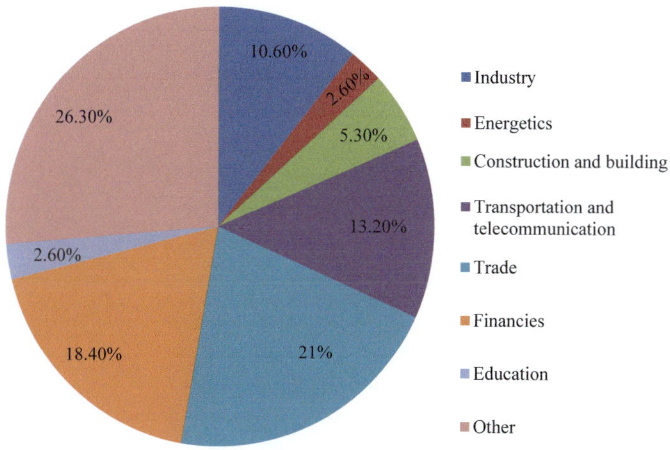

Fig. 11.3 Representation of the business area in the examined sample

Fig. 11.4 Respondents' position in the company

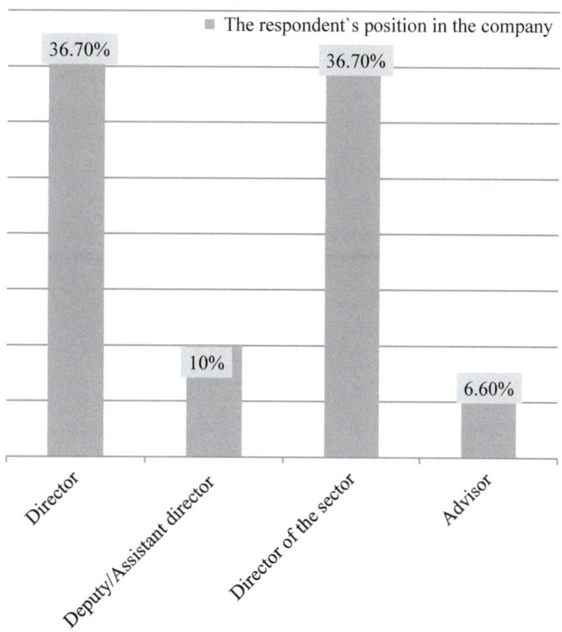

Figure 11.5 shows the education level of the respondents, according to which we can see that half of the respondents completed postgraduate (specialist) studies, 23.7% master studies, 7.9% doctoral (Ph.D.) studies, and only 2.6% have a high school diploma.

When asked whether they had encountered in the practice the term corporate social responsibility, the majority of respondents 77.8% answered that in their

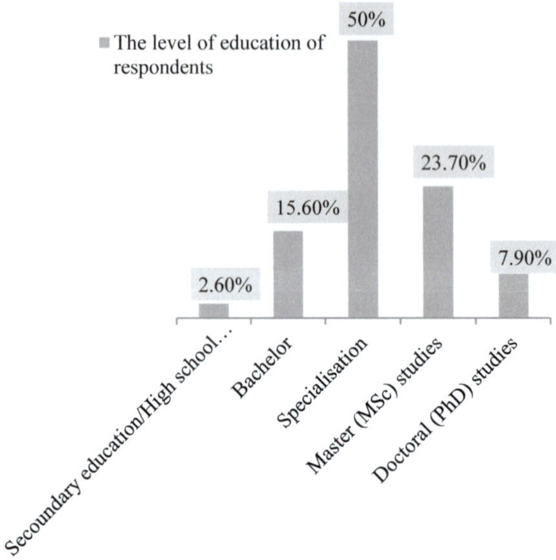

Fig. 11.5 Level of education of respondents

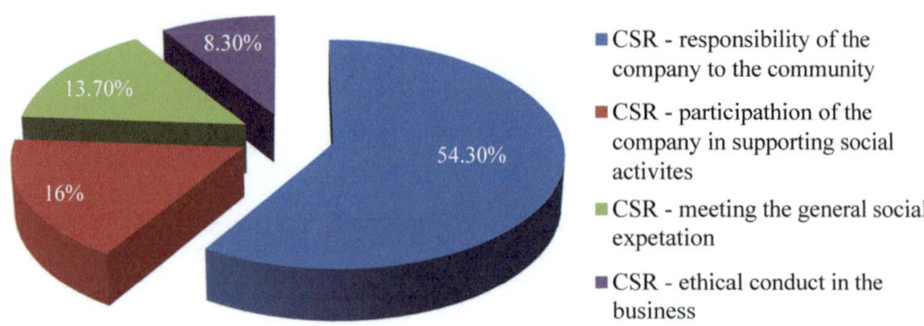

Fig. 11.6 Definition of corporate social responsibility, given by 77.8% of respondents in this survey

activities they had encountered the term corporate social responsibility, while 22.5% had not. Figure 11.6 shows the definitions of the terms stated by 77.8% of respondents, who recognized the corporate social responsibility as a responsibility of the company to the community 54.3%, as participation in support of the social activities 16%, meeting the general social expectations 13.7% and the lowest percentage of 8.3% as ethical conduct in the business.

Based on the presented data, it can be concluded that awareness and knowledge of corporate social responsibility in companies in the period from 2005 to 2013 show growing trend, as the directors of the company have shown by defining CSR a better understanding of the concept that goes beyond compliance with legislation, as initially this concept was interpreted. Also, these data suggest that managers of companies perceived social responsibility in the sphere of the community, which shows much wider perception angle of activities and resources, as compared to initial views on this subject. In one of the first studies conducted in the Republic of Serbia on identifying and understanding the concept of CSR in 2006, the most of the companies, 67% of them, were engaged in environmental projects. A third of respondents in this survey stated they had carried out the programme of recycling. This percentage is much higher among those who are engaged in production and large companies. Comparing these studies, we can see that the area of CSR recognition has extended to the community as a whole, support and fulfilment of social expectations that go beyond the obligation to meet legal requirements and environmental protection.

When asked whether the concept of CSR was applied in their companies, 81% of respondents answered that they believed that corporate social responsibility was applied in their companies, while 19% did not see the application of CSR in their companies. Figure 11.7 shows respondents' attitudes about the application of CSR in their companies.

The highest percentage of respondents 46.9% showed the attitude that CSR in their companies was applied partially, 21% that CSR was part of integrated management systems and 25% that it was implemented within the marketing project, while only 6.2% of respondents had attitude that CSR was applied independently as a concept.

For the application of the concept of CSR in companies, according to respondents, usually the cabinet/office of the general manager/director is responsible 53.3%, several organizational units within the company 23.3%, public relations 13.3% and marketing sector 10.1%. As a possible problem with the application of the concept of CSR, the fact can be observed that socially responsible activities are associated with the general manager/director (53.3%). When it comes to planning social responsibility activities in the companies, the opinions and attitudes are divided. Turning towards the public interest creates conditions for increasing customer and consumer loyalty, profiling data about them, their long-term bonding and building brand value. Socially responsible initiatives directly affect the improvement of the image and therefore the overall level of competitiveness of domestic companies. The data we obtained indicate that 50% of

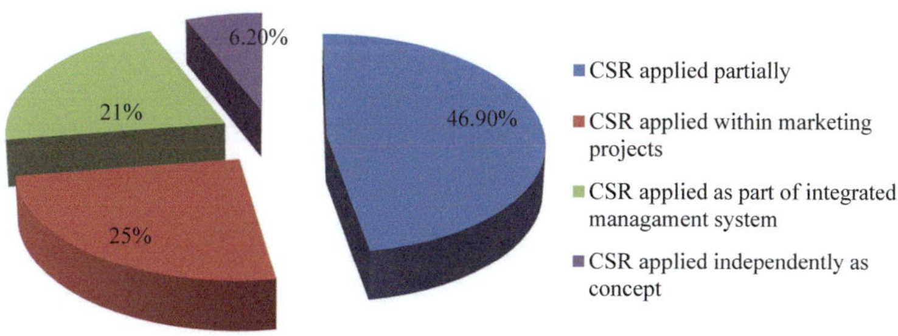

Fig. 11.7 Attitudes of 81% of respondents on the application of CSR in their companies

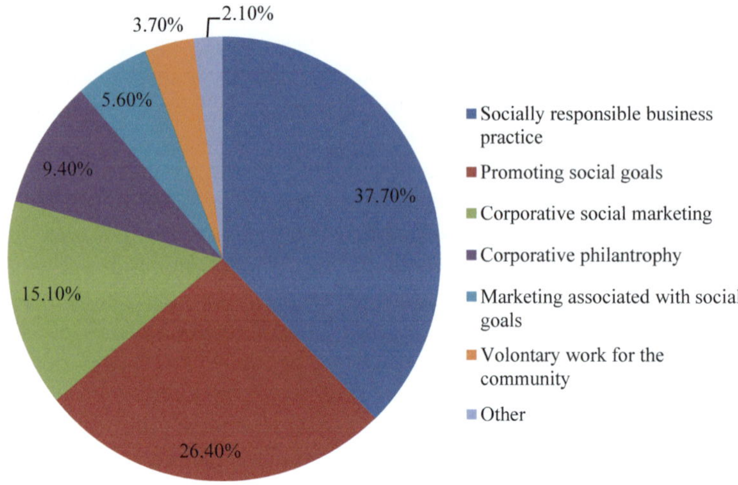

Fig. 11.8 Most prevalent socially responsible actions in companies

directors believe that CSR actions are planned, and the other half stated that such actions are not planned, but realized when possible. Managers/directors who implement these activities in a planned way, according to the respondents, they do so on an annual basis as a percentage of 71.4%; at 3 months, 14.3%, in relation to a project 14.3%. When it comes to basic approaches in the allocation of funds, 57.1% of respondents believe that there is a possibility of allocating funding (up to 5% of funds—70.6%, from 5 to 10% of funds—23.5%, 10–15% of funds—5.9%). Company managers/directors emphasized the importance of corporate social responsibility initiatives in the wider CSR complex as socially responsible business practices (37.7%), to promote social goals (26.4%), corporate marketing (15.10%) and corporate philanthropy (9.40%). These activities should be the backbone of activity in this area (Fig. 11.8).

As the main factors to improve the business, respondents indicated training of employees—27.6%, improving the quality of business operations—17.3%, the application of modern management methods and techniques—11.2%, the development and application of information technologies—10.2%, increase in business productivity—8.2%, the development of integrated management systems—7.1%, development and implementation of the concept of corporate social responsibility—7.1%, internationalization of the business operations of domestic enterprises—6.1% and improvement of technical and technological base of business operations—5.2%. Figure 11.9 shows the main areas of development and improvement of employees/staff.

The majority of managers/directors, 51.28%, had training in the past year, while 48.72% did not have training. The areas of improvement are: development 34%, quality 18.8%, human resources 15.6%, business communications 12.5%, marketing 12.5%, benchmarking 3.1% and management of technical systems 3.1%.

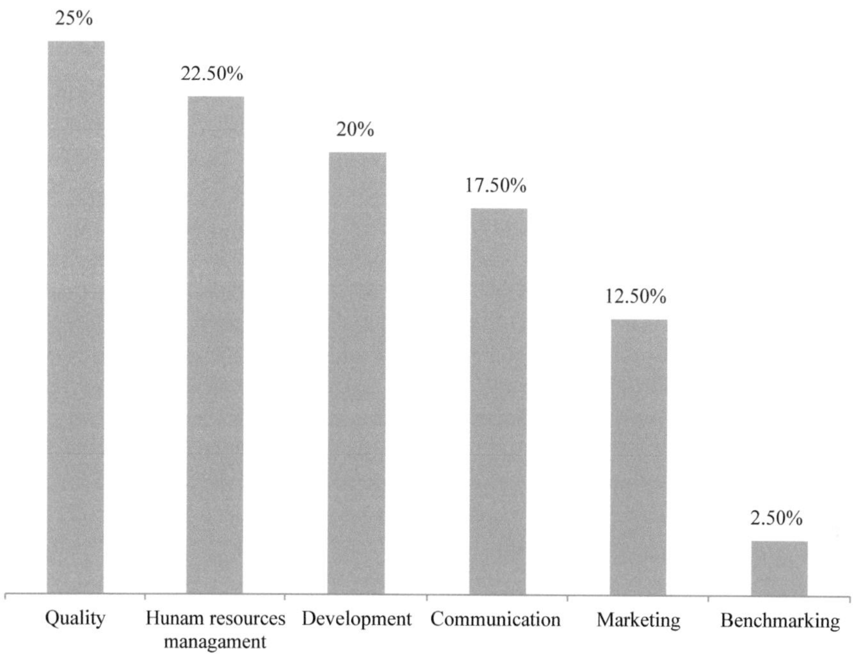

Fig. 11.9 Areas of development and improvement of employees/staff

The most of respondents, 57.1% said that their company has implemented a quality management system according to ISO 9000. The majority of managers/directors believe that there are companies and organizations in their market that could be called business excellent. The results obtained in this study indicate that the concept of CSR is in the development stage, and the main problems associated with a comprehensive systematic approach to the development of the concept are: chronic lack of financial resources, the effects of the global economic crisis and the slow application of the latest achievements in the field of management. Although the effects of the global economic crisis and transitional recession are significant, the lack of resources is not necessary impediment to development. This is confirmed by the experience of the Japanese, who have overcome the problem of resource poverty by improving knowledge, using a confirmed experience of the West, with the aim to improve present concepts and techniques. In this approach, the man as the bearer of work and knowledge was at the centre of attention. In this sense, the proper use of knowledge is the most important direction for improving the competitiveness of companies in the Republic of Serbia, and thus improving the concept of CSR.

11.4 Discussion

If the presence and application of the concept of corporate social responsibility in the Republic of Serbia from 2005 until today are compared, based on the mentioned studies, it can be concluded that there is a positive direction of movement. This means that the main drawback in promoting CSR on business scene in the country, that was not present in 2005, today exist. The state is actively involved in the development of strategies and promoting the concept, in the way it is discussed in the world. In this sense, the concept of CSR refers to all economic entities in the society, company or organization, regardless of size and activity. The survey data presented in the paper showed that the companies with foreign share ownership recognize more the importance and apply the concept of CSR. This may be an indicator for other business organizations and companies in the country to incorporate the elements of strategic CSR and by their example influence other organizations in the community. Synergy participation of many companies and organizations in the welfare of the community and the environment would solve many problems in society and contribute to the social group and the individual to accept and implement the principles of corporate social responsibility. The Republic of Serbia is in the process which may be called the construction of the first generation of socially responsible institutions. The process of globalization and the emergence of new commercial and technological opportunities have shifted the balance between the responsibilities of government and business organizations. Companies are faced with increasing pressure to openly commit to introduce voluntary measures to improve the environment and society despite legal obligations.

References

Crowther D (2003) Corporate social reporting: genuine action of window dressing? In: Crowther D, Rayman-Bacchus L (eds) Perspectives on corporate social responsibility. Ashgate, Aldershot, pp 140–160

Durovic I, Randjic D (2011) The importance of corporate social responsibility in contemporary business. In: 38th national conference of quality

Hayiyev E (2008) Baseline study on CSR practices in the Western Balkans. http://europeandcis.org.data/files/20091012_a_guide_to_CSR_in_europe_final.pdf. Accessed 5 Apr 2015

Idowu SO, Towler BA (2004) A comparative study of the contents of corporate social responsibility reports of UK companies. Manag Environ Qual Int J 15(4):420–437

Martinovic N (2007) Društvena odgovornost predeuzeća u Srbiji—trenutno stanje i moguće postojeće inicijative. www.unido.org. Accessed 16 June 2015

Martinovic N, Damjanovic S (2009) Izveštaj dobre prakse društveno odgovornog poslovanja: analize i preporuke. Tim predstavnika za implementaciju strategije za smanjenje siromaštva—Agencija za strana ulaganja i promociju izvoza

Mazurkiewicz P (2007) Business perspectives about corporate social responsibility attitudes and practice in Serbia and Montenegro. http://siteresources.worldbank.org/extdevcommeng/resources/CSR_in_Serbia_and_Montenegro.pdf. Accessed 14 June 2015

Sarcevic D (2011) Researching importance of CSR concept in scientific-research institution. Ph.D. thesis. Faculty of Organizacional Science, Belgrade, Republic of Serbia
Smart Kolektiv (2007) Poslovne perspective o društvenoj preduzeća, Beograd. www.srbija.gov.rs/vesti/dokumenti_sekcija.phd. Accessed 8 June 2015
World Business Council for Sustainable Development (2004). www.wbscd.org. Accessed 3 Mar 2015

Author Biography

Danijela Sarcevic Ph.D., is researcher in area of organizational science. She works on position of public relation representative in Institute of Meat Hygiene and Technology in Belgrade, Republic of Serbia. She has published widely in more than 30 journals as well as presented on national and international conferences. Her research interests include corporate social responsibility, environmental protection, consumer's perception about attitudes and behavior on safe and quality food. She is member of International Group on Governance Fraud Ethics and CSR and representative of the group in Serbia.

Chapter 12
CSR Communication Through the Lens of New Media

Lina M. Gomez

12.1 Introduction

Today communication plays an important role in our society because it contributes to the creation, development, and improvement of relationships. Thanks to new media (e.g., social media), companies have different opportunities to build and promote communication processes that can contribute to the exchange of ideas and opinions with different groups of stakeholders. Communication is the key for the success of any objective or business strategy, and this should be conceived with passion, fun, and vision (Roddick 2000). For this reason, communication is a fundamental element in the creation, planning, development, and evaluation of CSR initiatives. However, communication should not be ambiguous and manipulative, instead it must be transparent and truthful. Due to the decline of public trust in American corporations, companies must consider different ways to improve their relationships with key stakeholders. One way to achieve this is to promote transparent communication (Rawlins 2009 as cited by DiStaso and Bortree 2012).

CSR communication can be defined as the transmission of information regarding social and environmental initiatives toward different key groups of stakeholders. However, this information should be relevant and interesting in order to generate answers from stakeholders. This could lead to an exchange of CSR ideas that could evoke opinions, collaborations, and changes in attitudes and behaviors. Today, Internet has become a powerful instrument for CSR communication. Many companies have developed websites or sections for the information and communication

L. M. Gomez (✉)
Universidad del Este, Puerto Rico, USA
e-mail: lmgomez@suagm.edu

K. T. Çalıyurt and R. Said (eds.), *Sustainability and Social Responsibility of Accountability Reporting Systems*, Accounting, Finance, Sustainability, Governance & Fraud: Theory and Application, https://doi.org/10.1007/978-981-10-3212-7_12

of CSR practices. However, previous research has indicated that the majority of these websites have presented unidirectional messages, in other words, a one-way communication process (Gomez and Chalmeta 2011; Chaudhri and Wang 2007). On the other hand, social media has altered how companies performed their business, how they market and promote their products and services, and how they develop organizational communication processes (Bilic 2010). Thanks to social media platforms, companies can communicate easily their different CSR initiatives and projects with stakeholders.

Social media platforms like Facebook, Twitter, YouTube, LinkedIn, Pinterest, blogs are based on the principles of interactivity, exchange of ideas, collaboration, participation, dialogue, and commitment. Through different technologies, consumers and different groups of stakeholders are more vigilant regarding organizational actions and decisions that could affect the society and the environment. Thanks to social media platforms any person can create, contribute, and share information and ideas. In addition, these technologies allow companies to attract clients, consumers, and different actors for promoting dialogues regarding different topics (e.g., responsible and sustainable practices) and at the same time, maintain long-term relationships with them (Fieseler et al. 2010; Du et al. 2010). Stakeholders are more attracted to buy products of companies that encourage open and transparent communication. This creates a sense of community and participation (Mangold and Faulds 2009). Therefore, through social media platforms, that sense of community and participation can be reached.

This chapter proposes two theoretical frameworks of CSR communication through Internet (one for corporate websites and one for social media profiles). The frameworks contain different Web and social features (design, content, and interactivity) that are important for an interactive communication process through corporate websites and social media platforms. These guidelines were applied to the top 50 Fortune companies of 2011 through a content analysis of CSR websites and social media profiles (Facebook and Twitter). However, the complete results of this analysis are not presented in this chapter. The key findings will be show in order to propose the theoretical frameworks for effective CSR communication through corporate websites and social media. These frameworks are unique in its nature. There are no current theoretical frameworks regarding CSR online communication that can help and advise companies in what they should really communicate, what Web and social features include, how frequently they should do it, etc.

There is a potential niche in new media platforms (e.g., interactive corporate websites and social media) for engaging audiences in the contribution and commitment of responsible and sustainable practices. Promoting bidirectional and symmetrical CSR communication among organizations and public is crucial. Therefore, we should start looking at CSR communication through the lens of interactive new media. This is perhaps the missing piece for achieving a successful CSR communication process.

12.2 Literature Review

12.2.1 CSR Communication

Today organizations employ different interactive new media resources, like websites and social media profiles, instead of using traditional platforms like newspapers, TV, radio, brochures, bulletin boards, for CSR communication with their stakeholders (Isenmann 2006; Freeman 1984). Dawkins (2005) indicates that is important to provide creative communication (relevant and comprehensible content) at the moment of communicate CSR practices, and this process should be open, specific, and attractive (Lundquist 2010). Furthermore, communication should be credible, informative, and educative (Azevedo 2004 as cited by Wanderley et al. 2008). CSR communication should also be transparent and genuine (Chaudhri and Wang 2007; Golob and Bartlett 2007). Overall, promoting CSR communication could help to generate a positive image among different public, nurturing relationships with them (Ihlen et al. 2011; Morsing and Schultz 2006).

Currently, CSR communication presents two problems: (1) Lack of company interest in communicate CSR practices and (2) stakeholder skepticism (Ihlen et al. 2011; Du et al. 2010; Morsing and Schultz 2006). In spite of the different resources and tools available to facilitate communication, this important element (communication) is still considered as the missing link in CSR strategies of many companies (Capriotti and Moreno 2009; Gomez and Chalmeta 2011). Communication cannot be avoided, because it is unthinkable not to communicate with public (Morsing and Schultz 2006). On the other hand, if corporations communicate frequently, this could bring skepticism among stakeholders. This means that public are not paying attention to CSR practices, because they suspect that there are hidden motives in CSR actions (Du et al. 2010). Therefore, academic research suggests that CSR should be communicated in a way that public do not perceive it like intense (Morsing et al. 2008).

Forehand and Grier (2003) exposed that one way to reduce skepticism is taking into account intrinsic and extrinsic motives of CSR communication. These two problems could also be reduced, with the inclusion of different groups of key actors in the organizational CSR process, in other words to have consultants, employees, customers, bloggers, journalists, economists, politics, etc., participating in the development of CSR strategies and initiating dialogues (Wehmeier and Schultz 2011). Therefore, it is important that organizations should promote informal communication channels, but credible, which could be initiated and maintain by employees and other stakeholders (Dawkins 2005; Du et al. 2010).

There are considerable guidelines and models to report CSR and sustainable practices like (Global Reporting Initiative, Accountability, UN Global Compact, ISO 260006. There are also responsible indexes like Dow Jones Sustainability Index (DJSI), FTSE4Good Index, or Ethibel Sustainability Index (ESI). Although these guidelines and indexes are an excellent resource to show the commitment that companies have for responsible practices, the way these reports are presented and communicated demonstrates lack of interest by companies in initiate stakeholder dialogue and interactivity (Lundquist 2010; Capriotti and Moreno 2009).

Morsing and Schultz (2006) propose three strategies for CSR communication (based in the PR model of Grunig and Hunt 1984). In the first strategy called stakeholder information, communication goes in one way, from the organization to the public. Its objective is purely informational. The second (stakeholder response strategy) and third strategies (stakeholder involvement) are based on two-way communication. However, there is a difference between these two strategies. The first one is a public relations effect in favor of the company, while the second one, proposes dialogues among stakeholders, in which persuasion could occurred by any of the actors involved. According to Morsing and Schultz (2006), there is a lack of evidence that today companies are doing stakeholder involvement strategies. Therefore, it is important that companies understand the power of interactive new media platforms that can transform communication processes and derivate benefits (Crowther 2002). "In other words, communication is inescapable, it is implicated in CSR and business strategies whether management likes it or not… Communication provides the potential to help constitute stakeholder participation and ethical business practices" (Ihlen et al. 2011, p. 11).

12.2.2 CSR Communication Through Corporate Websites

According to Internet Word Stats, in December 31, 2000, there were approximately 360.985.492 Internet users. Fifteen years later, that number increased to 3.035.749.340 (June 30, 2014). These findings confirm that Internet is a media platform of rapid growth, which disseminates more information in an agile way. Internet is also more favorable in economic terms that other traditional media like TV or newspapers.

The principal advantages in using Internet as a communication tool (compared to traditional media like newspapers and magazines) are its low cost, rapid dissemination of information, unlimited space to store information, and liberty to use color, movement, and audio (Williams and Ho Wern Pei 1999; Taylor et al. 2001; Pollach 2003). Information on Internet is persistent, letting users to choose what topics see and how frequently access to them (Wanderley et al. 2008). Thanks to the great benefits that Internet has for CSR communication, companies could promote, measure, and communicate its social, economic, and environmental objectives and initiatives (Brennan and Johnson 2004; Branco and Rodrigues 2006). According to an interview developed by Fleishman-Hillard (2007), Internet has become the principal source for information regarding CSR for Americans. Seventy-three percent of Americans have employ search engines and almost 50% have use websites for looking for information or news regarding social responsibility.

Corporate websites permit companies to initiate and maintain multi-stakeholder dialogues, promoting interactive and constant communication (Kent and Taylor 1998; Esrock and Leichty 1999, 2000), and at the same time, they provide with the opportunity to create and maintain relationships with different groups of public (Wright 1998, 2001). Using an interactive communication approach is a tremendous challenge for the traditional practice of CSR communication which is usually based in a static and sporadic process.

On the other hand, the design and content of a website should be attractive, modern, and accessible (Coope 2004). Websites should be characterized to be simple to use by any person and should pay attention to the diverse interests of audiences (Coupland 2005). Additionally, content and language should be clear and legible. Language contributes to the reproduction and transformation of power relations, (Fairclough 1995), and therefore, language is a fundamental aspect that should be effective developed and presented for initiating a communication process regarding CSR. Usually, Web content features are employed to create a public image of the company and to cultivate relations with stakeholders (Robbins and Stylianou 2003). CSR communication through websites could lead to an innovate communication process, only if companies are taking advantages of the different and unique features that Internet has for enrich the communication process (hyperlink, feedback opportunities, documents downloading, search engines, etc.) (Isenmann 2006).

Kent and Taylor (1998) identified five principles in order to promote dialogic communication with different groups of public through corporate websites: (1) Users should navigate the website with easiness, (2) users should feel animated to navigate and remain in the website, (3) users should be encouraged to come back many times to the website in order to generate relations, (4) Websites should promote useful information to a variety of public, and (5) websites should promote opportunities for answering questions and generating feedback. In corporate websites, there are two basic approaches to communication: (1) diffusion of information (level of interactivity is low, and it is characterized by a unidirectional process of communication), and (2) generation of relations between companies and stakeholders (level of interactivity is high and bidirectional communication processes are presented) (Capriotti and Moreno 2009; Taylor et al. 2001; Esrock and Leichty 1998; Kent and Taylor 1998).

In the last decade, there have been many studies that have demonstrated the growth in the importance of CSR online communication in different parts of the world (Esrock and Leichty 1998; Maignan and Ralston 2002; Snider et al. 2003; Coope 2004; Branco and Rodrigues 2006; Birth et al. 2008; Golob and Bartlett 2007; Chaudhri and Wang 2007; Capriotti and Moreno 2009; Basil and Erlandson 2008; Tang and Li 2009; Gomez and Chalmeta 2011). Overall, these studies have analyzed the presence of CSR information and communication in websites of different organizations around the world. They have concluded that in spite of the great advantages that Internet has for communication, many corporate websites does not utilize all the potential and the available resources, in order to promote a communication process of social practices.

If companies take into account Web design and content, and promote interactivity in their corporate websites, companies could communicate effectively their CSR efforts. For example, companies should report their different CSR initiatives (objectives, achievements, future projects, etc.), and promoting and maintain at the same time, fruitful dialogues with different key groups of stakeholders (Capriotti and Moreno 2009; Rolland and Bazzoni 2009). In that direction, CSR communication through Internet could facilitate balanced relationships among organizations and public, increasing citizen participation (Kent et al. 2003).

12.2.3 CSR Communication Through Social Media

The importance and growth of social media have brought many challenges to the organizational communication practice. Social media is not new; some of the first Internet applications were centered on communication and exchange: "For decades, we've watched the development of new genres of social media—MUDs/MOOs, instant messaging, chat rooms, bulletin boards, etc. (Boyd 2009, p. 1).

Social media can be defined as Web media and mobile technologies for social interaction and communication, and for the creation and exchange of content generated by users (Burkhardt 2009). Social media includes social networks (Facebook, LinkedIn, Google+, etc.), micro-blogging (Twitter, Tumblr, etc.), blogs (Wordpress, Blogger, etc.), location-based services (Foursquare, Facebook places, etc.), video-sharing sites (YouTube, Vimeo, etc.), social bookmarking (Delicious, CiteULike, etc.), and virtual worlds (Second Life, World of Warcraft, etc.), among many others. Social media stimulates exchange of ideas, interactivity, and collaborative knowledge, promoting citizenship and consumer empowerment (Thackeray et al. 2008; Jones et al. 2009). In social media platforms, consumers and citizens present an active role, creating, editing, and sharing content (Burkhardt 2009).

A study developed by Nielsen (2011) found that today, four of five users are Internet active users that use social media. Facebook is the social network most employed by Americans, reaching almost 70% of active users. Other study found that social media permits to create new levels in conversations that were impossible to achieve before (Burson-Marsteller Communications Group 2010). This study analyzed the presence of social media by Global Fortune 100 companies. It found that 79% of global companies and 86% of American companies present at least one social media platform (Facebook, Twitter, YouTube or corporate blogs).

Social media platforms are a vital tool for organizational communication, its effective usage impact relations with customers, workplace, and corporative culture (Creese 2007, as cited by Hearn et al. 2009). The benefits that social media present for companies are: low cost of implementation, credibility, corporate image, reputation, communication in real time, public relations, and the availability of an online archive (Pressley 2006, as cited by Schneider et al. 2007). Additionally, social media presents great potential for creating and maintaining dialogues among different groups of stakeholders, in contrast with static corporate websites (Fieseler et al. 2010). Social media also promotes authentic and durable relationships with many public, creating competitive advantage (Bilic 2010; Fieseler et al. 2010; Mangold and Faulds 2009; Schneider et al. 2007).

Through social media, organizations could evaluate the perceptions that customers, employees, and society have about them, with the purpose of identifying improvement areas (Dou and Krishnamurthy 2007). Therefore, companies could be proactive at the moment of use social media, attracting, and retaining stakeholders, in order to become advocates and messengers of CSR (Du et al. 2010). Word-of-mouth power among consumers has increase recently due to the popularity of social media. Consumers are more attracted to buy certain products or be faithful to certain brands, participating in conversations and constructing a sense of community (Mangold and Faulds 2009).

A survey carried out to 250 people that work in the area of CSR and sustainability found that social media is becoming a fundamental tool to discuss and share CSR information, but organizations are not aware of these resources for CSR communication (Lundquist 2010). One similar study by Custom Communications (2010) analyzed 287 American and European companies by industry type in order to discover if those companies communicate sustainability topics through social media. They found that only 22% of the companies communicate messages regarding sustainability and CSR through social media.

Typically, CSR communication through websites is controlled by the same corporations. However, through social media, companies do not have control of the information and communication that different users (consumers, activists, ONGs, etc.) are producing and sharing regarding the company in non-official social platforms like blogs, social networks. These actors are now informing, communicating, and mobilizing regarding organizations (Du et al. 2010). Companies could not subestimate the power of social media. Specific genres of social media could appear and disappear, but the innate characteristics of social media (participation, sharing, and collaborative knowledge, interactivity) are here to stay.

12.3 Methodology: Theoretical Framework

This chapter proposes theoretical frameworks which consist of different categories and subcategories for the online communication of CSR. Two theoretical frameworks are proposed: one for CSR communication through corporate websites and another for CSR communication through social media. Both frameworks are based through an extensive literature review of studies regarding Internet, social media, and CSR communication. This section will discuss the different categories of the frameworks and the authors that support them. The next section will include the two both completed frameworks after being analyzed on the websites and social media profiles of 50 Fortune companies. The key findings are discussed also in the next section.

12.3.1 Corporate Websites

Three categories were established for the theoretical framework of CSR communication through corporate websites:

(1) Web design: It includes the subcategories of presentation (supporting material like photos, videos) and navigation (hyperlinks, visualization, etc.)
(2) Web content: It encloses the subcategories of CSR commitment (general information objectives, goals, achievements regarding CSR, etc.) and CSR initiatives/resources (CSR initiatives, news, annual reports, etc.)
(3) Web interactivity: It includes the subcategories of basic contact information (email, phones, address of the CSR department or office, etc.), informational tools (RSS News Feed, FAQ, etc.), and communication tools (blogs, social media, chats, etc.).

Table 12.1 presents these categories and subcategories and the respective authors that support them.

In spite of the existence of considerable guidelines for the creation of websites, today there are not any rules or standards to identify the essential elements that a website should have, especially for CSR. Some websites use common features like search engine, feedbacks, maps, security information, and privacy policy (Robbins and Stylianou 2003). According to these authors, there are certain categories required for a website in order to be fully attractive and functional: design, navigation, security, velocity, and tracking. It is also important to include corporate information, communication tools, updates, financial information, employment opportunities, and social topics in the content of a website (Robbins and Stylianou 2003).

Table 12.1 Categories for the theoretical framework of CSR communication through corporate websites

Categories	Subcategories	Theoretical background
Web design	Presentation	Esrock and Leichty (1998), Robbins and Stylianou (2003), Capriotti and Moreno (2009)
	Navigation	Esrock and Leichty (1998), Robbins and Stylianou (2003), Capproti and Moreno (2009)
Web content	CSR Commitment	Esrock and Leichty (1998), Robbins and Stylianou (2003), Capproti and Moreno (2009)
	CSR initiatives and resources	Esrock and Leichty (1998), Robbins and Stylianou (2003), Capproti and Moreno (2009), Birth et al. (2008)
Web interactivity	Basic contact information	Esrock and Leichty (1998), Capproti and Moreno (2009)
	Informational tools	Esrock and Leichty (1998)
	Communication tools	Esrock and Leichty (1998), Capproti and Moreno (2009)

The indicators of each subcategory are described below:

Web design categories permit companies to develop a functional and attractive website (Robbins and Stylianou 2003), for the identification of different resources for CSR information and communication (Capriotti and Moreno 2009). Two Web design subcategories were established: presentation and navigation. Presentation refers to visual appearance and general attractiveness of a website (Robbins and Stylianou 2003). It includes indicators like presence of supporting material like videos, photos, animations, figures, and the presence of available document formats (Word, PDF, JPG) and the presence of interactive documents (including annual reports and other relevant documents). Navigation lets users to found specific information in an easy way inside a website (Robbins and Stylianou 2003). The following indicators were established for the navigation subcategory: presence of a CSR hyperlink in the homepage of the company (this will redirect to the CSR website or section), the presence of a hyperlink of the CSR annual report in the CSR homepage, presence of internal, external, and related hyperlinks, and lastly the correct visualization of hypertext, documents, videos, audio, and animation in all popular browsers: Internet Explorer, Firefox, Opera, Safari y Google Chrome.

Web content category refers to what is included on the website and the different types of information and topics presented (Capriotti and Moreno 2009; Robbins and Stylianou 2003). Content categories for CSR websites are important to be considered because it shows how the companies and top management are committed to CSR, presenting all the relevant information regarding CSR. Two content subcategories were developed: CSR commitment and CSR initiatives and resources. CSR commitment refers to key CSR information and the support of the top management has for CSR. Examples of indicators in this subcategory include: top management's commitment (through a letter, video, blog post, etc.), objectives or purpose of the CSR practice; the presentation and explanation of CSR future plans or projects, the presentation and explanation of partnerships with other institutions, organizations, and causes, the different accomplishments or achievements regarding CSR. CSR initiatives and resources include the different resources that support the CSR practice and permit the dissemination of information (Capriotti and Moreno 2009). This subcategory presents the following indicators: presence and description of internal and external CSR projects or initiatives (by CSR core area), list of key stakeholders, presence of annual reports (current and past years) in PDF and/or interactive format, and the presence of news regarding CSR (up to date).

Lastly, Web interactivity category promotes adequate information and communication with different stakeholders. Three subcategories were developed: basic contact information, informational tools, and communication tools. Basic contact information displays the way public can contact the CSR department or staff (names, postal address, phone, and email). Informational tools permit users to share relevant information regarding CSR, through the following indicators: RSS News Feed, share buttons (email this, share this on Twitter, Facebook, etc.), bulletin boards, mail lists, and FAQ section. Communication tools allow the generation of opinions and dialogues regarding CSR through interactions. The following indicators were established: blogs, chats/forums, contact forms, and social media.

12.3.2 Social Media

The following categories were established for the theoretical framework of CSR communication through social media (especially Facebook and Twitter):

(1) Presentation: It includes supporting material for the CSR content like photos, videos, hyperlinks, and other resources provided by each social platform)
(2) Content: It refers to the different messages regarding CSR core areas (e.g., according to G3 guidelines of the Global Reporting Initiative and other CSR topics)
(3) Interactivity: It encloses the purpose of the message and the frequency of those messages.

Table 12.2 presents the different categories and subcategories and the theoretical evidence that supports them.

Presentation category refers to the different resources and basic and essential information (photos, videos, and basic information of the company) that a company social media profile should present. Additional resources promote and reinforce the companies' presence in social media, for example, hyperlinks or icons of social media profiles in the corporate webpage or CSR website, and the promotion of other social media profiles (LinkedIn, YouTube, Pinterest, Flickr, blogs, etc.) in the corporate website or social media profiles. The framework presented here is dedicated to social media profiles on Facebook and Twitter regarding CSR core areas; however, it could be applied to other social media platforms as well.

The content of a social media profile should include different messages relevant for the company and its stakeholders (general messages, institutional, promotional, news, events, new products and services, etc.). Due to this chapter proposes a framework for CSR communication through social media, in addition to the above types of messages' examples, companies must disclose messages regarding CSR core areas. Therefore, it was selected the core areas of the G3 guidelines of the

Table 12.2 Categories for the theoretical framework of CSR communication through social media

Categories	Subcategories	Theoretical background
Presentation	Supporting material	Waters et al. (2009), Rybalko and Seltzer (2010)
	Additional resources	Waters et al. (2009), Rybalko and Seltzer (2010)
Content	GRI core areas	GRI G3 Guidelines (2009)
	Other CSR topics	Rybalko and Seltzer (2010)
Interactivity	Informational (one-way communication)	Hughes and Palen (2009), Rybalko and Seltzer (2010), Morsing and Schultz (2006), Lovejoy and Saxton (2012)
	Communicational (two-way communication)	Rybalko and Seltzer (2010), Morsing and Schultz (2006), Lovejoy and Saxton (2012)
	Mobilization	Lovejoy and Saxton (2012)

Global Reporting Initiative: economy, environment, labor practices, human rights, society, and product responsibility. Other indicators in this content category are messages regarding annual reports or CSR achievements and messages regarding CSR chats or discussions.

Lastly, interactivity category includes how frequent the messages are posted and the purpose of the message. A message is informational if it promotes one-way communication (dissemination purpose), communication (two-way communication) presents the feedback element and encourages dialogue. Mobilization or action messages motivate users to do something for the company (like, share, comment, attend an event, donate money, etc.).

Both frameworks were constructed based upon contribution of other authors (based on a literature review of CSR communication, social media, and Internet). After developing both frameworks, we tested on a small sample of 5 companies (5 websites and 5 social media profiles) in order to evaluate its efficiency and relevance. After doing this first analysis, other subcategories and indicators were found. Once the frameworks were completed, each one of the indicators and subcategories were applied and analyzed to 50 corporate websites and 50 social media profiles of Fortune companies.

12.4 Theoretical Framework of CSR Communication Through Corporate Websites

Results shown that the evaluated companies (that were analyzed applying the theoretical framework) presented 84% of Web design features, 61% of Web content features, and only 33% of interactive features on CSR websites. Eighty-two percent of the companies (from the 50 analyzed) presented a dedicated website for the information and communication of CSR. These findings show a deficiency among the analyzed companies in present up-to-date and useful information regarding CSR toward audiences. In addition, these websites lacked of information and communication tools that could facilitate a rewarding experience and participative experience to users. Findings indicated that Fortune companies are doing efforts to inform regarding CSR practices; however, they are not creating communication process (two-way communication) in their CSR websites.

Therefore, a theoretical framework of CSR communication through corporate websites is proposed. Frameworks or guidelines are important to minimize subjectivity and to let reviewers evaluate different Web features (Evans and King 1999 as cited by Miranda et al. 2009). The framework proposed includes Web design, content, and interactivity features that must be presented on a CSR website that has the purpose to promote information and communication in an effective way.

After testing the framework on the CSR websites of 50 Fortune companies, other subcategories and indicators were included. Table 12.3 presents the complete framework. Here are particular explanations drawn for the analysis:

Table 12.3 Theoretical framework of CSR communication through corporate websites

Categories	Subcategories	Indicators
Web design	Presentation	• Supporting material • Documents in different formats of easy access and download • Interactive documents
	Navigation	• CSR hyperlink on corporate homepage • Annual report's hyperlinks on CSR homepage • Internal, external, and related links • Correct visualization of the website structure in every popular browser
Web content	CSR Commitment	• Top management commitment CSR objectives • CSR achievements • CSR future plans • Partnerships • CSR awards or recognition
	CSR initiatives and resources	• CSR initiatives (internal level) • CSR initiatives (external level) • List of key stakeholders • Special content for each group of key stakeholders • Up-to-date annual reports • Past annual reports • Up-to-date CSR news
Web interactivity	Basic contact information	• Names of CSR staff • PO Box address— CSR office • Phone numbers— CSR office • Email (CSR staff)
	Informational tools	• RSS News Feed • Participation tools (share bottoms) • Newsletters • Email lists • FAQ section • Calendar of events
	Communication tools	• Blogs • Forums/Chats • Contact formats • Social media

Web design

Presentation: In this subcategory, the supporting material can include the presence of photos, videos, animations, and figures. It is also important to include documents in accessible formats for downloading (e.g., Word and PDF). Interactive documents can include in annual reports or other relevant documents.

Navigation: In this subcategory, the CSR hyperlink presented on the corporate homepage should include the less number of clicks in order to promote a better experience to the user. In addition, the hyperlink of the CSR annual report should be included in the CSR homepage and not hidden. Lastly, hypertext (documents, videos, animations) must be visualized without problems in all the popular browsers (Internet Explorer, Google Chrome, Firefox, Safari,).

Web content

CSR commitment: The top management's commitment regarding CSR should be display as an interactive letter, video, or blog post. This letter is fundamental because it shows the commitment and importance that CSR has for the company (represented by the top management).

CSR initiatives and resources: Annual reports should be presented in both ways (PDF and interactive). The advantage of using interactive reports is that it brings the opportunity to the user to choose the information that he/she wants to read. In other words, each user builds a personal CSR report according to its need and preferences. In addition, it is important to disclose past annual reports (at least from 5 years). News should be up to date. In the analysis performed to companies, there was news from 2 to 3 months ago (only 38% of the companies exhibited news on the websites). If the company has a Twitter account, it could include a widget to show up-to-date information and news from Twitter.

Web interactivity

Communication tools: Regarding the social media indicator, it is important that companies must bear in mind that they must choose the social media platforms that are more adequate according to its CSR objectives and strategies. In other words, companies should have a social media plan for CSR communication. What companies want to achieve? What is the companies' goal of having a social media profile? Companies cannot have a presence in every social media platform just because popularity reasons. Is my audience in these social platforms? These all questions should be asked by companies, once they are answered, they must evaluate if these platforms are adequate and related to their CSR mission and purpose.

This theoretical framework, as stayed before, was applied to 50 websites dedicated to inform and communicate CSR. Companies were employing more Web design and content features. However, several of the Fortune companies were employing all features. In this chapter, we do not disclose the complete results. These findings are published in (Gomez and Chalmeta 2011).

This theoretical framework shows validation to be applied and use by any type of organization. It was developed taking into account studies from other authors, who found different aspects in the presentation of information of CSR in many companies around the world. Therefore, this theoretical framework can help other companies and organizations to create and evaluate CSR websites that contain design, content, and interactivity features. Furthermore, this guideline could help academics and researchers to evaluate the communication of CSR practices in different organizations in diverse countries.

12.5 Theoretical Framework of CSR Communication Through Social Media

Results showed that companies use social media in order to inform or promote about products and services and not for CSR issues. There is a lack of information and communication regarding CSR in social media platforms. Therefore, it is needed a theoretical framework of CSR through Facebook and Twitter for effective use of these platforms for CSR communication.

The framework proposed, as presented before, was applied to 50 official profiles on Facebook and Twitter of Fortune companies. However, only 39 official active accounts were found on Facebook and 43 Twitter official active profiles of Fortune companies were encountered. These active accounts of Facebook and Twitter were analyzed during two months in order to analyze presentational, content, and interactivity features. Companies were not using its social media profiles for CSR information and communication. However, few of the Fortune companies were employing all features and few of them have official profiles dedicated to CSR communication. In this chapter, we do not disclose specific results. These findings are published in (Gomez 2013).

The theoretical framework was developed taking into account studies from other authors, regarding the importance of communication through social media. Therefore, this framework includes different key features that must be presented in official social media profiles (in Facebook and Twitter) for the information, promotion, and communication of CSR messages.

This framework could help companies of any nature, to create a social media profile in CSR or for communication of CSR messages in official general profiles. At the same time, this model can serve as a guideline to help scholars and researchers to evaluate the communication of CSR practices through social media platforms in different types of organizations in many countries. After testing and analyzing the framework on the official social media accounts of Fortune companies, other subcategories and indicators were established. Table 12.4 presents the complete framework.

Here are some key explanations for some indicators:

1. *Presentation*: There are many applications on Facebook to include videos, events, polls, notes, discussions, and ask questions, among other applications. In addition, Twitter let users include photos, videos, and multimedia in messages (tweets). These basic resources can be used when they are relevant and adequate to the CSR message that companies are communicating. This helps to reinforce the CSR message. In addition, other hyperlinks or icons of social media profiles reinforce also the CSR promotion and presence. For example, if a company has a Twitter and Facebook profile dedicated to CSR, both should be promoted in both accounts. This is important in order to support CSR messages in other social media platforms.
2. *Content*: CSR messages must be informative, clear, interesting, respectful, and human (Sweetser 2010). For Twitter, companies must use hashtags (#) for

Table 12.4 Theoretical framework of CSR communication through social media

Categories	Subcategories	Indicators
Presentation	Supporting material	• Photos • Videos • Basic information about CSR (objective, purpose) located in the bio or about section
	Additional resources	• Social media hyperlinks or icons on the corporate homepage • Social media hyperlinks or icons on the CSR homepage • Hyperlinks to other social media accounts
Content	GRI topics	• Messages about economy • Messages about environment • Messages about labor practices • Messages about human rights • Messages about society • Messages about product responsibility
	Other topics	• Messages about annual reports or achievements • Messages about recognitions and awards • Messages about discussions and chat sessions
Web interactivity	One-way communication	• Transmission of messages • Frequency of the messages
	Two-way communication	• Feedback of messages • Presence of dialogues • Frequency of the feedback/dialogues • Presence of hashtags, retweets, and replies • Like and follow other organizations and causes
	Co-mobilization/ action	• Like/follow • Reply • Share/retweet • Comment • Attend • Participate • Donate • Others

keywords like #csr #environment #sustainability, etc., in order to enrich the content of the tweet. Including hashtags promotes that these messages can be viewed by other people that are not followers of the company profile on Twitter. Other supporting topics for creating content are shares and retweets. Shares and retweets should be relevant to the company and the followers/fans. Retweeting/ Sharing is an important practice and it is complimentary to the communication of CSR messages. This means that companies are listening to what others organizations and stakeholders are saying or discussing regarding a particular topic.

3. *Interactivity*: One-way communication includes not only the dissemination of interactive information (that includes supporting material like videos, photos, or hyperlinks) that users could share but also the frequency of the messages (Rybalko and Seltzer 2010). According to Hughes and Palen (2009), a social

media profile is active when companies send at least 1 message per week. Therefore, it is important to send messages at least 2–3 times per week, avoiding being absent no more than 1 week. In addition, it is fundamental to promote two-way communication process, inviting and motivating different groups of stakeholders to dialogue regarding different, projects, initiatives, news, and ideas related to CSR (Morsing and Schultz 2006). In Twitter, hashtags (#) are an excellence resource to create, develop, track, and monitor conversations regarding CSR topics. Another resource that can help to be active in interactive CSR communication is to like or follow other organizations, people, products, or causes relevant to the organization. This action can be beneficial for the organization, because this could led to networking opportunities with the purpose of including stakeholders in other relevant activities of the company. Lastly, the concept of mobilization/action was conceived by Lovejoy and Saxton (2012), mobilization means that companies are empowering customers and fans to do something for them (e.g., share information, attend an event, donate). However, it is fundamental to take into account content that promotes co-mobilization or co-action where all actors in a CSR communication process can mobilize others to take action.

Each social media platform has its advantages and disadvantages, therefore, each company, according to its social media objectives, must select platforms that are beneficial with the purpose of promoting an appropriate communication process. Social media is based on relations, therefore those companies that are ready to have a presence in any social media platform, means that they are ready to invest in people, in other words, in stakeholders and society.

12.6 Conclusions

In 1984, Grunig and Hunt proposed the famous public relations model (press agentry/publicity, public information, two-way asymmetric, and two-way symmetric). By that time, these authors indicated that only 50% of the companies promoted one-way communication (informational messages) toward stakeholders while only 35% of the companies' performed two-way communication process. In that time, few companies promoted two-way communication messages toward its public. Grunig and Hunt could think that after 30 years, companies will be more active in their communication process, but unfortunately the actual trend that predominates (in the public relations, organization communication, and corporate social responsibility world) is a unidirectional pattern. This research has concluded that this predisposition in promoting unidirectional messages has extended to online platforms like corporate websites and social media.

Create, develop, and maintain relationships with different groups of stakeholders are fundamental for effective CSR communication. Thanks to new technologies of information and communication, the importance of stakeholder relationships has increase in value for companies. Today, consumers and citizens are more active online, creating and sharing content, participating in conversations, in fact, trusting more other users than corporations (e.g., in the review of products and services). Technology has let any person around the world to participate in discussions and create content equally. Furthermore, it has also convened and mobilized public opinion, in order to shape a new global solidarity (Aras and Crowther 2011). This "global solidarity" among citizens and active consumers will cause new communication challenges to organizations. Today, different groups of stakeholders are informing and communicating about different CSR issues, sometimes before the companies inform it (problems regarding environment, human rights violation, etc.). Therefore, organizations must be open, honest, and proactive at the moment of CSR communication. Those companies that have good relations with public, that listen and answer to them, to their needs, will have the tendency to survive and prosper in crisis (Paine 2011).

This chapter does not suggest that companies will be more responsible if they inform and communicate CSR messages. However, this research founds vital and important (due to the analysis performed) that the frequency and update of CSR information, the continuous interactive communication and feedback, and the use of all Web features. These all are indictors of effort and commitment to present an adequate CSR online communication process.

As proposed by Ihlen et al. (2011), CSR communication is the corporate use of symbols and languages. Therefore, based on the features of the theoretical framework, this chapter defines CSR online communication as the appropriate use of Web symbols or design/presentational features, which support and reinforces the content. In addition, it is the suitable use of language or content features, which present up-to-date and required information, and the use of interactivity, which promote the creation of dialogues, participation, and collaboration among actors.

Online communication of social responsible practices does not mean to upload a particular video or have a blog or a presence on Facebook, online communication goes beyond that. In other words, online communication of CSR is the combination of all Web and social features that allow the CSR communication puzzle fits. Puzzle pieces do not work alone or isolated, they should remain always together for everything to work adequately and precisely.

The reality is that companies are not using all the potential that interactive new media platforms present, neither for the communication of corporate messages (Rybalko and Seltzer 2010; Waters et al. 2009). We could think that social media is frequently used for communication due to its interactive nature. However, this study found that social media was used particularly as another information channel of products and services, failing to take into account the different interactive resources that social media platforms provide for communication and participation.

Findings indicate a lack of commitment and interest in promote a truly genuine and effective CSR communication process. Therefore, due to the inexistence of theoretical frameworks of CSR through Internet (corporate websites and social media), the frameworks proposed in this chapter can help companies to initiate or to evaluate CSR sections, homepages or websites, taking into account web/

presentation design, content, and interactive features. In addition, it can serve as a guideline for the creation, development, and evaluation of CSR communication through social media (especially Facebook and Twitter). Academics and scholars in the field of CSR and public relations could use these frameworks and applied/evaluated to other different types of companies around the world, in order to discover and analyze the progress of CSR communication.

The correct way to use the different online platforms available for CSR communication is based in understanding the communication needs that each company has in order to choose those suitable tools for reaching its communication purpose. Therefore, the frameworks proposed help as a model or guideline to comprehend the key functions of interactive CSR communication, no matter the strategy or purpose performed in CSR practices.

After 25 years of publishing the public relation model, Grunig (2009) indicates that Internet has the potential to carry out communications more strategically, two-way communication, interactive, and socially responsible. However, he asseverates that communication professionals are using these new technologies “in the same ways they used the old—as a means of dumping messages on the general population rather than as a strategic means of interacting with public and bringing information from the environment into organizational decision-making” (p. 1). We believe this panorama will change once Internet and particularly social media platforms are used for the purpose they were created: to inform, communicate, participate, and co-mobilize.

References

Aras G, Crowther D (2011) Commentary: the view from management. In: Ihlen O, Barlett JL, May S (eds) The handbook of communication and corporate social responsibility. Wiley, Oxford

Basil D, Erlandson J (2008) Corporate social responsibility website representations: a longitudinal study of internal and external self-presentations. J Mark Commun 14(2):125–137

Birth G, Illia L, Lurati F, Zamparini A (2008) Communicating CSR: practices among Switzerland’s top 300 companies. Corp Commun Int J 13(2):182–196

Branco MC, Rodrigues LL (2006) Communication of corporate social responsibility by Portuguese banks: a legitimacy theory perspective. Corp Commun Int J 11(3):232–248

Brennan LL, Johnson VE (2004) Technology management for corporate social responsibility. Technol Soc Mag IEEE 23(1):40–48

Bilic I (2010) Development of web corporate communications function by official web sites and value added ranking: case of Croatia. Bus Rev 15(1):151–158

Boyd DM (2009) Social media is here to stay… Now what? Microsoft Research TechFest. Online http://www.danah.org/papers/talks/MSRTechFest2009.html. Accessed 20 Nov 2012

Burkhardt P (2009) Social software trends in business: introduction. In Tiako P (ed) Software applications: concepts, methodologies, tools, and applications. Information Science Reference, Hershey, PA

Burson-Marsteller Communications Group (2010) The Global Social Media Check-up, white paper. http://www.bursonmarsteller.com/Innovation_and_insights/blogs_and_podcasts/BM_Blog/Documents/Burson-Marsteller%202010%20Global%20Social%20Media%20Check-up%20white%20paper.pdf. Accessed 15 July 2012

Capriotti P, Moreno A (2009) Communicating CSR, citizenship, and sustainability on the web. J Commun Manage 13(2):157–175
Chaudhri V, Wang J (2007) Communicating corporate social responsibility on the internet. A case study of the top 100 information technology companies in India. Manage Commun Q 21 (2):232–247
Crowther D (2002) The psychoanalysis of on-line reporting. In: Homes L, Grieco M, Hosking D (eds) Distributed technology, distributed leadership, distributed identity, distributed discourse: organizing in an information age. Ashgate, Aldershot
Coope R (2004) Seeing the net potential of online CR communications. Corp Responsib Manage 1:25
Coupland C (2005) Corporate social responsibility as argument on the web. J Bus Ethics 62(4):335–366
Custom Communications (2010) SMI special report-social media sustainability index extract: an essential guide to how the world's most sustainable companies are communicating their green convictions and deeds through social media
Dawkins J (2005) Corporate responsibility: the communication challenge. J Commun Manage 9(2):108–119
DiStaso MW, Bortree DS (2012) Multimethod analysis of transparency in social media practices: survey, interviews and content analysis. Pub Relat Rev 38(3):511–514
Dou W, Krishnamurthy S (2007) Using brand websites to build brands online: a product versus service brand comparison. J Advertising Res 47(2):193–206
Du S, Bhattacharya CB, Sen S (2010) Maximizing business returns to corporate social responsibility (CSR): the role of CSR communication. Int J Manage Rev 12(1):8–19
Esrock SL, Leichty GB (1998) Social responsibility and corporate web pages: self-presentation or agenda setting? Pub Relat Rev 24(3):305–319
Esrock SL, Leichty GB (1999) Corporate world wide web pages: serving the news media and other publics. J Mass Commun Q 76(3):456–467
Esrock SL, Leichty GB (2000) Organization of corporate web pages: publics and functions. Pub Relat Rev 26(3):327–344
Fairclough N (1995) Media discourse. Oxford University Press, NY
Fieseler C, Fleck M, Meckel M (2010) Corporate social responsibility in the blogosphere. J Bus Ethics 91(4):599–614
Fleishman-Hillard (2007) National consumers league study. rethinking corporate social responsibility. http://fleishmanhillard.com/wp-content/uploads/2007/05/csr_white_paper.pdf. Accessed 16 July 2011
Freeman RE (1984) Strategic management: a stakeholder approach. Pitman Publishing Company, Boston, MA
Forehand MR, Grier S (2003) When is honesty the best policy? The effect of stated company intent on consumer skepticism. J Consum Psychol 13(3):349–356
GRI G3 Guidelines (2009) Global reporting initiative sustainability report. https://www.globalreporting.org/resourcelibrary/GRI-Sustainability-Report-2009-2010.pdf. Accessed 1 July 2016
Golob U, Bartlett JL (2007) Communicating about corporate social responsibility: a comparative study of CSR reporting in Australia and Slovenia. Pub Relat Rev 33(1):1–9
Gomez L, Chalmeta R (2011) Corporate responsibility in U.S. corporate websites: a pilot study. Pub Relat Rev 37(1):93–95
Gomez L (2013) Me gusta o te sigo: Análisis de la comunicación de prácticas de Responsabilidad Social Corporativa a través de los medios sociales. Correspondencias Análisis 3:89–109
Grunig JE, Hunt T (1984) Managing public relations. Harcourt Brace Jovanich, Orlando, FL
Grunig JE (2009) Paradigms of global public relations in an age of digitalization. Prism 6(2):1–19
Hearn G, Foth M, Gray H (2009) Applications and implementations of new media in corporate communications. An action research approach. Corp Commun Int J 14(1):49–61
Hughes AL, Palen L (2009) Twitter adoption and use in mass convergence and emergency events. Int J Emerg Manage 6(3/4):248–260

Ihlen O, Barlett JL, May S (2011) Corporate social responsibility and communication. In: Ihlen O, Barlett JL, May S (eds) The handbook of communication and corporate social responsibility. Wiley, Oxford

Isenmann R (2006) CSR online: internet based communication. In: Jonker J, White M De (eds) Management models for corporate social responsibility. Springer, Berlin

Jones B, Temperley J, Anderson L (2009) Corporate reputation in the era of Web 2.0. The case of primark. J Mark Manage 25(9–10):927–939

Kent ML, Taylor M (1998) Building dialogic relationships through the world wide web. Pub Relat Rev 24(3):321–334

Kent ML, Maureen T, White WJ (2003) The relationship between website design and organizational responsiveness to stakeholders. Pub Relat Rev 29(1):63–77

Lovejoy K, Saxton GD (2012) Information, community, and action: how nonprofit organizations use social media. J Comput Mediated Commun 17(3):337–353

Lundquist (2010) CSR online awards survey 2010: time to get real-time and personal. Recuperado de http://www.lundquist.it/research/ Accessed 1 Dec 2011

Mangold G, Faulds D (2009) Social media: the new hybrid element of the promotion mix. Bus Horiz 52:357–365

Maignan I, Ralston D (2002) Corporate social responsibility in Europe and the U.S.: insights from businesses self-presentations. J Int Bus Stud 33(3):497–514

Miranda FJ, Sanguino R, Bañegil TM (2009) Quantitative assessment of European municipal web sites. Developing and use of an evaluation tool. Internet Res 19(4):425–441

Morsing M, Schultz M (2006) Corporate social responsibility communication: stakeholder information, response, and involvement strategies. J Bus Ethics 15(4):323–388

Morsing M, Schultz M, Nielsen K (2008) The catch 22 of communicating CSR: findings from a Danish study. J Mark Commun 14(2):97–111

Nielsen (2011) State of the media: the social media report Q3 2011. http://blog.nielsen.com/nielsenwire/social/. Accessed 14 Aug 2012

Paine KD (2011) Measure what matters. online tools for understanding customers, social media, engagement, and key relationships. Wiley, Hoboken, NJ

Pollach I (2003) Communicating corporate ethics on the world wide web: a discourse analysis of selected company websites. Bus Soc 42(2):277–287

Roddick A (2000) Business as unusual. Thorsons, London

Robbins SS, Stylianou AC (2003) Global corporate web sites: an empirical investigation of content and design. Inf Manage 40(3):205–212

Rolland D, Bazzoni JO (2009) Greening corporate identity: CSR online corporate identity reporting. Corp Commun Int J 14(3):249–263

Rybalko S, Seltzer T (2010) Dialogic communication in 140 characters or less: how fortune 500 companies engage stakeholders using twitter. Pub Relat Rev 36(4):336–341

Schneider AM, Stieglitz S, Lattemann C (2007) Social software as an instrument of CSR. Proceedings of ICT, transparency and social responsibility, Lisbon

Snider J, Hill RP, Martin D (2003) Corporate social responsibility in the 21st century: a view from the world's most successful firms. J Bus Ethics 48 (2):175–187

Sweetser KD (2010) A losing strategy: the impact of nondisclosure in social media on relationships. J Pub Relat Res 22(3):288–312

Tang L, Li H (2009) Corporate social responsibility communication of Chinese and global corporations in China. Pub Relat Rev 35:199–212

Taylor M, Kent ML, White WJ (2001) How activist organizations are using the Internet to build relationships. Pub Relat Rev 27:263–284

Thackeray R, Neiger BL, Hanson CL, McKenzie JF (2008) Enhancing promotional strategies within social marketing programs: use of web 2.0 social media. Health Promot Pract 9(4): 338–343

Wanderley LSO, Lucian R, Farache F, Sousa Filho JM (2008) CSR information disclosure on the web: a context-based approach analyzing the influence of country of origin and industry sector. J Bus Ethics 82(2):369–378

Waters R, Burnett E, Lamm A, Lucas J (2009) Engaging stakeholders through social networking: how nonprofits organizations are using facebook. Pub Relat Rev 35(2):102–106

Wehmeier S, Schultz F (2011) Communication and corporate social responsibility. a storytelling perspective. In: Ihlen O, Barlett JL, May S (eds) The handbook of communication and corporate social responsibility. Wiley, Oxford

Williams SM, Ho Wern Pei C (1999) Corporate social disclosures by listed companies on their web sites: an international comparison. Int J Acc 34(3):389–419

Wright DK (1998) Corporate communications policy concerning the Internet: a survey of the nation's senior-level, corporate public relations officers. The Institute for Public Relations, Gainesville, FL

Wright DK (2001) The magic communication machine: examining the internet's impact on public relations, journalism, and the public. The Institute for Public Relations, Gainesville, FL

Author Biography

Lina M. Gomez is Assistant Professor and Researcher in the Digital Communication Program at the School of Social and Human Sciences, Universidad del Este in Puerto Rico. She has a Ph.D. in Business with a concentration in Corporate Social Responsibility and Sustainability from Universitat Jaume I in Spain, M.A. in Communication (University of Puerto Rico—Río Piedras Campus), and B.A. in Communication and Journalism(Universidad del Norte, Colombia). She recently obtained a postgraduate certification in Social Media Management from Universidad Autónoma de Barcelona. Dr. Gómez has also published in prestigious journals and has presented in many international conferences in public relations, corporate social responsibility, and social media. She has been granted with external funding to conduct research projects in the area of social media and health communication, and university social responsibility. Her expertise and research interests are in social media, organizational communication, public relations, corporate social responsibility and sustainability.

Chapter 13
Social Responsibility Reputation of Brands: A Strategic Approach

Ipek Altinbasak-Farina and Bilge Bicer

13.1 Introduction: Social Responsibility and Pro-Social Behavior

Marketing can be very narrowly defined as "satisfying consumer needs" (Kotler and Armstrong 2012, p. 26–29; Graham 1993). However, it has been argued like half a century ago that marketing had a broader definition covering social and ethical issues besides only satisfying consumer needs (Kotler and Levy 1969; Feldman 1971). Kotler and Levy (1969) stated that "marketing is a pervasive societal activity that goes considerably beyond the selling toothpaste, soap and steel" and added that marketing people should enhance their vision and use their skills for broader social activities. Therefore, the broad notion of "the value creation" has been involved in the marketing definition. Furthermore, the "societal marketing concept" emphasizing that a company's marketing decisions should consider not only the company requirements and consumers' wants but also should lead to the improvement of the consumers' as well as the society's long-term interest and welfare (Kotler and Levy 1969; Graham 1993; Hoeffler and Keller 2002).

Throughout the years, the concept proved to increase its importance due to the global changes related to several factors such as growing environment-related problems, population increase, advances in technology, scarcity of resources, wars, increasing awareness. Since 1970s, economic and technological changes have lead to an increase in the production and as well in the consumption of products and services. The urge of protecting and using the world resources in a more conscious

I. Altinbasak-Farina (✉)
Faculty of Economics, Administrative and Social Sciences,
Bahcesehir University, Istanbul, Turkey
e-mail: ipek.altinbasak@hotmail.com

B. Bicer
Graduate School of Social Sciences, Bahcesehir University, Istanbul, Turkey

K. T. Çalıyurt and R. Said (eds.), *Sustainability and Social Responsibility of Accountability Reporting Systems*, Accounting, Finance, Sustainability, Governance & Fraud: Theory and Application, https://doi.org/10.1007/978-981-10-3212-7_13

and responsible way is increasing. Therefore, the consumers and companies together are required to be more sensitive and act more responsibly to the world and societies' welfare (Akyıldız 2007).

The rise of recognition of the social responsibility leads corporations to implement socially responsible activities to their business activities and consumers expect brands to design marketing activities by involving at least one non-economic objective related to social welfare (Hoeffler and Keller 2002). There are several factors contributing to the growing consciousness about social responsibility. Among them, accepting social responsibility as normal good, delivering information about companies' social responsible activities and increasing public awareness about social responsibility can be counted as important drivers for such a trend (Benabou and Tirole 2010).

Social responsibility takes place and is implemented by actors at institutional, organizational, and individual levels. At institutional level, forces like regulation, standards and certification, stakeholders' decisions define social responsibility activities and most times it can be used for improving reputation, customer loyalty, and evaluation of products. At organizational level, companies' values, instrumental reasons such as financial outcomes and strengthening customer relationships identify social responsibility. On the other hand, at individual level, different normative motives, personal values and concerns are definitive for pro-social behavior (Auginis and Glavas 2012).

Standard definition of social responsibility is "sacrificing profits in the social interest" and social responsibility involves being environment-friendly, attentive to ethics, and respectful for communities (Benabou and Tirole 2010). Corporate social responsibility is a managerial perspective and a philosophy that pays attention to society's expectations, needs, values and requests, and it requires acting in accordance with individual and social benefits (Bir et al. 2009). According to Wartick and Cochran (1985), social responsibility concept has two fundamental premises: (1) The methods of operation must be compatible with society's regulations and (2) The corporations should act as a moral agent that reflect and reinforce society's values and welfare.

Pro-social behavior is a form of positive acts such as helping, donating, cooperating, and volunteering to maintain others' well-being. According to Benabou and Tirole (2010), pro-social behaviors "obey a complex mix of interdependent motivations" and are driven by self-esteem and genuine intrinsic altruism. Pro-social behaviors are altruistic behaviors that are performed by individuals and companies with the intention of promoting and delivering welfare and involve helping others and volunteering (Kelley and Hoffman 1997) such as responsible waste handling or careful use of non-renewable energy sources (Gronhoj and Thogersen 2012).

Commonly, one of the most widespread forms of social responsibility is perceived as green marketing. Green marketing can be described as the use of individual consumer power to promote less environmentally damaging consumption, while still satisfying customer needs and demands (Charter et al. 2002). On the company side, according to Polonsky and Rosenberger III (2001), the green marketing concept of today has moved much beyond the simple ecological posturing of years ago and now the true responsible green marketing can be considered as an "integrated strategic tool" for the companies. According to Menon and Menon (1987) (as cited in Polonsky and Rosenberger III 2001) strategic greening should lead to a significant change in corporate philosophy.

Green marketing is for sure very crucial but there are other aspects of social responsibility which also have very significant roles related to the welfare of a society. Several authors (Heikkurinen and Ketola 2012; Zabkar and Hosta 2013; White et al. 2012) define the ensurement of fair trade; environmental protection including the 3R—reproduction, re-using and re-cycling; the prevention of any product-harm; paying attention to a better use of scarce resources; issues related to poverty and education; ethical practices among the most significant aspects related to social responsibility. Furthermore, in all types of socially responsible activities, a holistic approach is considered to be crucial rather than a one-time, short-sided view.

13.2 Consumers' Perspective: Awareness About and Attitude Toward Social Responsibility

Socially conscious consumers can be defined as individuals caring to bring social change by thinking about the consequences of their private consumption (Webster 1975). The trend is that the number of socially responsible consumers eager to buy products of socially responsible companies is increasing. Furthermore, they are willing to pay more for those products while developing negative attitudes and creating negative word-of-mouth for irresponsible brands and companies (Russell and Russell 2010). Socially conscious consumers tend to buy products and services that represent qualities such as "sustainability, social justice, corporate responsibility, or workers' rights" and make pressure on corporations to reconsider the social impact of their business activities (Willis and Schor 2012, p. 162).

Recent research suggests that consumers are increasingly concerned with ethical issues, socially conscious product options, fair trade, and justice for others, and they demand ethical product options (White et al. 2012). Findings suggest that consumers and business environment increasingly tend to reward responsible brands and punish irresponsible ones (Du et al. 2010).

Some people invest in socially responsible funds, help people to sustain their lives, buy and consume green products and devote their times for good causes (Benabou and Tirole 2010). According to Griskevicius et al. (2010), consuming pro-social products is an indicator of being "not pro-self" and showing that the consumer has enough time, energy, and money for preferring those products. The research indicates that there is a group of people with such concerns. They are conscious about spending more for a car to help people and not to harm environment by sacrificing performance features, design, and comfort. Personal norms are translated into behaviors and cultivated by perceptions about social welfare, and an awareness of the results of consumption is created (Osterhus 1997).

The awareness about and attitude toward social responsibility vary from country to country, and research indicates that the level of development of a country is related with the social responsible behavior of its citizens. Regarding Ethical Consumerism Market Report 2013, in UK, ethical market shows strong growth and average spending on ethical products increases from 2000 to 2012 such as cosmetics from 7£ pounds to 21£; energy 20£ to 96£, home products 59£ to 184£.

Furthermore, consumers wish to be informed about socially responsible activities of the brands and they expect firms to involve them in their pro-social behavior. Corporations are required to compensate their operations' negative consequences for the earth and the society and maximize the positive impact. It is argued that pro-social activities of the brands affect the purchase behavior of those consumers (Pomering and Johnson 2009).

Consumers' awareness of pro-social activities constructs favorable beliefs associated with brands and its products (Pomering and Johnson 2009). There are different motivations leading to pro-social behavior.

(1) The intrinsic altruism, which is the desire to make some good and help others.
(2) Material incentives such as tax reductions.
(3) Social and self-esteem concerns, related to self-image (Benabou and Tirole 2010).

As claimed by Henrich and Gil-White (2001), being pro-social without being assertive is associated with status. This is even more valuable as this status is gained through freely conferred deference. Furthermore, the pro-social behavior of an individual for the sake of the other people may result in the selection of this person as a leader and can build social approval feeling (Hardy and Van Vugt 2006; Milinski et al. 2002).

Pro-social behaviors may lead to important functional consequences for individuals such as environmental conservation can build pro-social reputation (Griskevicius et al. 2010). It is implied that buying social prestige is a part of the incentive to engage in pro-social behavior for individuals (Benabou and Tirole 2010). People define themselves and gain emotional pleasure by constructing social interactions such as helping others, buying products that carry social responsible characteristics. It is stated that this behavior also contains a status value, which means self-esteem, honor, or worth (Zabkar and Hosta 2013). The corporations may strengthen the above-stated self-esteem and social approval feeling of the consumer through showing how the consumer involvement contributed to the success of the cause program (Hoeffler and Keller 2002).

Another major outcome of being referred as pro-social in a group is the notion of status and prestige. As a result, those socially responsible people may prefer socially responsible brands over some luxury products to satisfy status motives showing that "they care" (Griskevicius et al. 2010). Also, these consumers have other altruistic and prestige motives than cost concerns (Zabkar and Hosta 2013).

The companies should analyze well the primary motives of their target customers and design their marketing program accordingly.

13.3 Corporations' Perspective: Social Responsibility and Brand Reputation

Brand reputation is defined as a collective representation of a brand's history and ability of delivering value to multiple stakeholders. Furthermore, it is considered to be a stronger and more stable external assessment than brand image. Brand reputation is also accepted as an intangible asset that provides opportunity for competitive positioning. As a key influencer, brand reputation encourages stakeholders' anticipation for the brand's future (de Chernatony 1999).

The corporations are aiming to build good reputation through performing socially responsible activities and promoting them to the targeted publics. Corporate reputation reflects the firm's image in consumers' mind. As the sensitivity of the consumers is observed to increase, the corporations are putting more emphasis on the realization of socially responsible activities. In order to create a strong point of differentiation, corporations position their brands on this platform and promote them accordingly (Pomering and Johnson 2009). Socially responsible reputation of a brand is a multidimensional construct that can be composed of personal and social norms and economic forces (Osterhus 1997); trust and awareness are significant outcomes of this reputation (Osterhus 1997; Griskevicius et al. 2010). According to Formbrun (1996) (as cited in Pomering and Johnson 2009), brands need to develop positive reputations through "innovation, operational excellence or closeness to the customers."

Pro-social behaviors are functional for corporations in terms of contributing to achievement of organizational objectives (Brief and Motowildo 1986). Brands with a pro-social positioning are targeting the socially conscious consumers. Consumers' positive attitudes toward socially responsible companies are observed to enhance firms' desire to continue the socially responsible activities (Osterhus 1997). For the brands, engaging in pro-social behaviors can build pro-social reputation and having reputation can create valuable contribution to competitive strategy (Griskevicius et al. 2010). The trust provides company's reputational capital also known as "goodwill" and this capital strengthens firms' competitive position against its rivals (Pomering and Johnson 2009).

Furthermore, the emotions and judgments created by the socially responsible activities of the company may affect the quality and intensity of the relationship consumers have with the brand. As noted by Hoeffler and Keller (2002), this intensified relationship may lead to the building of brand communities where fellow brand users and customer, or instead, employees or representatives of the company interact. The companies should be aware of the impact of the pro-social behavior on the equity of their brands.

Corporate social responsibility requires brands to implement the broad societal responsibility and meet consumers' and the earth's broader expectations (Pomering and Johnson 2009). As mentioned by White et al. (2012), the major challenge for marketers is that several fair-trade products often entail a unique consumer trade-off between individual-level costs (e.g., higher prices and less accessible distribution) and more societal, other-oriented payoffs (e.g., fair wages and ethical working conditions for producers in developing countries).

In the twenty-first century, branding practices are used to differentiate brands in the market more than ever. Corporate social responsibility can be an influential option to satisfy multiple objectives such as creating differential advantage through a strong corporate image and building emotional, even spiritual, bonds with consumers (Hoeffler and Keller 2002). As an important builder of the brand equity, the socially responsible activities are suggested to be tailored according to the positioning of the brands in a way to create more involvement and bonding with the consumers.

13.4 Final Discussion and Suggestions

Having reviewed the social responsibility and pro-social behavior concepts from the consumers' and the organizations' perspectives, it would not be wrong to say that societal marketing issues that are pointed out in the article of Kotler and Levy (1969) are still valid and even more important in the twenty-first century. According to Benabou and Tirole (2010), there is an increasing demand in the society related to individual and corporate social responsibility.

Social responsibility activities of the brand are effective when they provoke consumers to develop positive attitudes and emotions toward brands (Pomering and Johnson 2009). Although there may be some contradicting evidence, in many instances, consumers take into account corporations' social responsible activities for their purchase decisions and also they are willing to pay more for the brands which are more engaged with social responsible activities (Servaes and Tomayo 2013). As mentioned in the previous sections of this paper, the consumers may have different motivations to get engaged in pro-social activities and support the companies emphasizing that notion. However, independent of the motivation whether it is prestige, self-esteem, search for leadership or altruism, those consumers want their actions to be visible and create word-of-mouth related to the actions taken by the brands/companies. Many times, they are becoming the advocate and promoters of the projects. Therefore, it is suggested to the companies that they identify those consumers and build a relationship with them, get them involved in the projects, receive their ideas and suggestions so that they will feel part of the pro-social behavior of the brand and/or company.

On the company side, social responsibility creates big responsibility for the brands to sustain their activities, which develop and support the brand reputation (Pomering and Johnson 2009). Therefore, corporations are required to provide convergence of social and business interest and assure target audience that their social responsible activities are beneficial for both society and themselves (Du et al. 2010). As emphasized, corporate social responsibility activities may help to build brand equity through increasing brand awareness, eliciting positive associations with the brand, creating a sense of belonging through communities and evoking the desire for spreading out positive word-of-mouth resulting in bonding (Hoeffler and Keller 2002).

However, it should be noted that carrying out socially responsible activities can lead to desired results only when they are communicated to the targeted publics on time. In this context, Internet and social media constitute a very important tool for the companies. Socially responsible behavior of companies is also communicated to masses through social media in a very quick manner.

Social media sites have already become a part of the modern society in many contexts such as social, educational, political, and business (Aleman-Meza et al. 2006). Social media platforms allow brands not only delivering messages but also collecting information about their consumers, gathering deeper insights, and triggering micro-communities to engage the societal issues (Champoux et al. 2012). Furthermore, the audience response can be obtained in real time and be measured.

Social networking sites (SNSs), such as Twitter, Instagram, and Facebook, are very important to increase the effectiveness of the communication strategy and to spread brand statements rapidly and simultaneously (Du et al. 2010). Word-of-mouth has also been a crucial tool to keep consumers updated about the pro-social activities of the corporations. Furthermore, social media provides more data than ever possible in order to understand customers and their behaviors, learning from consumers' expectations and reactions in real-life situations (Champoux et al. 2012).

Strong brands are expected to be proactive in using social media communication to engage their consumers for being their advocates (Du et al. 2010). The point is that social media communication is very delicate and requires huge attention. Although stakeholders claim that they want to be informed about the social responsibility activities of the firm, they sometimes can be doubtful about the brands with which they interact (Du et al. 2010). Once the doubt is felt, this communication can cause a negative reaction about brands' social initiatives; the advocates can create negative contents about social responsibility activities (Du et al. 2010). A well-planned and managed communication strategy may defeat those concerns and may result in the building of trust between the consumer and the company. Furthermore, some firms are criticized for spending too much money on advertising (Hoeffler and Keller 2002). Therefore, the use of social media and Internet may lessen those critics, as they are much less costly.

Consumers perceive social media activities of brand as a distinctive value comparing to others that use old-fashioned marketing activities (Daugherty et al. 2008; Kim and Ko 2012). Brands offering platforms for consumers to share experiences and to communicate friendly with brand and with each other are perceived more positively by the consumers. The possibility of direct communication affects consumer perceptions positively and improves the brand equity (Kim and

Ko 2012). So, it may be desirable for brands to communicate their socially responsible activities via SNSs through clear, transparent, and direct messages, avoiding the doubtful statements that can create undesirable perceptions about brands.

The marketing communication programs also should enhance the social approval feeling of the consumer through symbols, making visible the consumers' participation in the socially responsible activities of the company. This is considered an effective way to build positive consumer imagery.

The last but not least important point is that in order to build sustainable strongbrands, the corporations should put the social responsibility issue as a part of their mission statement. The social responsibility concern is expected to be the philosophy of the company and be incorporated in the mission statement, inspiring its employees and directing all of its activities. This philosophy will affect many strategic decisions such as the technologies used by the company, the investments to be made, the types of need-satisfying products to be produced, the communication style, etc. On the other side for the consumer, the pro-social behavior should be a part of a lifestyle, demanding sacrifice related to costs, performance, and even time. However, the self-esteem and prestige motives are expected to compensate those sacrifices and lead to a satisfaction toward a better world.

To create a better world and be able to sustain our exploited earth, all of the members of the society, not only the consumers and private companies but also the state enterprises and governments, are invited to acknowledge that this is the responsibility of all, and without reasonable sacrifice, it is not possible to achieve favorable results.

References

Akyıldız M (2007) Sosyal Sorumluluk ve Ahlaki Yaklasımlar Çerçevesinde Pazarlamanın Sürdürülebilir Gelismedeki Rolü. Dokuz Eylül Üniversitesi Sosyal Bilimler Enstitüsü Dergisi 9 (1):18–43

Antil JH (1984) Socially responsible consumers: profile and implications for public policy. J Macromarketing 4:18–39

Aleman-Meza B, Nagarajan M, Sheth AP, Arpinar IP (2006) Semantic Analysis on social networks: experiences in addressing the problem of conflict interest detection. WWW '06 Proceedings of the 15th international conference on World Wide Web 407–416

Auginis H, Glavas A (2012) What we know and don't know about corporate social responsibility: a review and research agenda. J Manag 38(4):932–968

Benabou R, Tirole J (2010) Individual and corporate social responsibility. Economica 77 (January):1–19

Bir ÇS, Süher İK, Altınbaşak İ (2009) Corporate social responsibility orientation and employer attractiveness. J Yaşar Univ 4(15):2303–2326

Brief P, Motowildo SJ (1986) Prosocial organizational behaviors. Acad Manage Rev 11(4): 710–725

Charter M, Peattie K, Ottman J, Polonsky MJ (2002) Marketing and sustainability. Centre for Business Relationships, Accountability, Sustainability and Society (BRASS), in association

with The Centre for Sustainable Design, April 2002. http://cfsd.org.uk/smart-know-net/smart-know-net.pdf
Champoux V, Durgee J, McGlynn L (2012) Corporate Facebook pages: when "fans" attack. J Bus Strategy 33(2):22–30
de Chernatony L (1999) Brand management through narrowing the gap between brand identity and brand reputation. J Mark Manage 15(1999):157–179
Daugherty T, Eastin MS, Bright L (2008) Exploring consumer motivations for creating user-generated content. J Interact Advertising 8(2):16–25
Du S, Bhattacharya CB, Sen S (2010) Maximizing business returns to corporate social responsibility (CSR): the role of CSR communication. Int J Manage Rev 2010:8–19
Ethical Consumerism Market Report (2013) Retrieved form http://www.ethicalconsumer.org/portals/0/downloads/ethical_consumer_markets_report_2013.pdf
Feldman LP (1971) New challenge for marketing. J Mark 35(3):54–60
Graham P (1993) Marketing's domain: a critical review of the development of the marketing concept. Mark Bull 4:1–11
Griskevicius V, Tybur JM, den Bergh BV (2010) Going green to be seen: status, reputation, and conspicuous conservation. J Pers Soc Psychol 98(3):392–404
Gronhoj A, Thogersen J (2012) Action speaks louder than words: the effect of personal attitudes and family norms on adolescents' pro-environmental behavior. J Econ Psychol 33(2012): 292–302
Hardy CL, Van Vugt M (2006) Nice guys finish first: the competitive altruism hypothesis. Pers Soc Psychol Bull 32:1402–1413
Heikkurinen P, Ketola T (2012) Corporate responsibility and identity/ from a stakeholder to an awareness approach. Bus Strategy Environ 21(2012):326–337
Henrich J, Gil-White FJ (2001) The evolution of prestige freely conferred deference as a mechanism for enhancing the benefits of cultural transmission. Evol Hum Behav 22(2001):165–196
Hoeffler S, Keller KL (2002) Building brand equity through corporate societal. J Public Policy Market 21(1):78–89
Kelley SW, Hoffman KD (1997) An invastigation of pro-social behaviors and service quality. J Retail 73(3):407–427
Kim AJ, Ko E (2012) Do social media marketing activities enhance customer equity? An empirical study of luxury fashion brand. J Bus Res 65(2012):1480–1486
Kotler P, Armstrong G (2012) Principles of marketing. Pearson, Harlow, ENG
Kotler P, Levy SJ (1969) Broadening the concept of marketing. J Mark 33(January):10–15
Milinski M, Semmann D, Krambeck H (2002) Donors to charity gain in both indirect reciprocity and political reputation. Proc R Soc Lond B 269:881–883
Osterhus TL (1997) Pro-social consumer influence strategies: when and how do they work? J Mark 61(4):16–29
Polonsky MJ, Rosenberger III PJ (2001) Reevaluating green marketing: a strategic approach. Bus Horiz Sept–Oct 2001
Pomering A, Johnson LW (2009) Constructing a corporate social responsibility reputation using corporate image advertising. Australas Mark J 17(2009):106–114
Russell DW, Russell CA (2010) Here or there? Consumer reactions to corporate social responsibility initiatives: egocentric tendencies and their moderators. Market Lett 21(2010): 65–81
Servaes H, Tomayo A (2013) The impact of corporate social responsibility on firm value: the role of customer awareness. Manage Sci 59(5):1045–1061
Wartick SL, Cochran PL (1985) The evolution of corporate social performance model. Acad Manage Rev 10(4):758–769
Webster FE Jr (1975) Determining the characteristics of the socially conscious consumer. J Consum Res 2(3):188–196
White K, MacDonnell R, Ellard JH (2012) Belief in a just world: consumer intentions and behaviors toward ethical products. J Mark 76:103–118

Willis M, Schor JB (2012) Does changing a light bulb lead to changing the world? political action and the conscious consumer. ANNALS Am Acad Polit Soc Sci 644:160. https://doi.org/10.1177/0002716212454831

Zabkar V, Hosta M (2013) Willingness to act and environmentally conscious consumer behaviour/ can pro-social status perceptions help overcome the gap? Int J Consum Stud 37(2013):257–264

Author Biographies

Ipek Altinbasak-Farina is Professor in Marketing and acts as Dean for the Faculty of Economics, Business Administration and Social Sciences in Bahcesehir University. She received her B.A. degree in Business Administration from Bogazici University in Istanbul, Turkey, and her M.B.A. from West Georgia University in the USA. After graduation, she worked as brand manager, marketing manager, and new product development director in the FMCG sector at companies like Unilever and Komili Holding. As a brand manager, she received an award from United Nations with "Rama Cansuyu Project" nominated as the best environmental protection project of the year in 1994. She got her Ph.D. in marketing from Bogazici University and joined Bahcesehir University in 2004. She served as the director of the Social Sciences Institute and established more than 20 master programs at Bahcesehir University. She teaches several courses on Marketing, Brand Management, and research at undergraduate, graduate and Ph.D. levels. Among her research interests are country image/place marketing, brand management, marketing strategy, social marketing, and service marketing. She has been giving training to the representatives of the Ministry of Culture and Tourism of Turkey, and she has been elected as the member of the commission of the Ministry responsible for identifying the worldwide promotion campaigns of Turkey for the two consecutive years, 2011–2012. She has prepared and presented a TV program namely "Branding Adventure" in TRT for several years. She has also worked as strategy consultant in telecommunication, leather, and finance sectors.

Bilge Bicer is a doctoral candidate in Marketing at Bahcesehir University in Istanbul, Turkey. She received her B.A. degree in Chemistry and her M.B.A. from Yildiz Technical University in Istanbul, Turkey. After graduating, she worked as a brand manager in the cosmetics sector and was also a part-time lecturer at Bahcesehir University. She is now working for eBrandValue as a Director of Marketing Science and Product Champion. Her research interests include customer-based brand equity, netnography, social media marketing, marketing research, and sustainability.

Chapter 14
Identifying Commonalities in CSR Definitions: Some Perspectives

Henk Kloppers and Elbé Kloppers

14.1 Introduction

One of the biggest challenges faced when conducting research on the topic of CSR is to provide a definition of this contested notion. Despite the abundance of definitions, it is generally accepted that there is no consensus on a single universally accepted definition of CSR (Carroll 1979; Horrigan 2010; Okoye 2009; WBCSD 2002, 1991).[1] Van Marrewijk (2003) notes that there is a proliferation of terms and that the diversity and overlap in terminology, definitions and conceptual models, poses obstacles to academic debate and research. More than 35 years ago, Sethi (1975) remarked: "the phrase corporate social responsibility has been used in so many different contexts that it has lost all meaning", while Banerjee (2001) notes that CSR is "too broad in its scope to be relevant to organizations".

This uncertainty is exacerbated by the fact that it is argued that CSR is a context-dependent concept that may mean different things to different people (Wan-Jan 2006; Blowfield and Frynas 2005).[2] The uncertainty was aptly described by Votaw (1972) almost 40 years ago when he wrote:

> [C]orporate social responsibility means something, but not always the same thing to everybody. To some it conveys the idea of legal responsibility or liability; to others, it means socially responsible behavior in the ethical sense; to still others, the meaning transmitted is that of "responsible for" in a causal mode; many simply equate it with a charitable contribution; some take it to mean socially conscious; many of those who embrace it most fervently see it as a mere synonym for legitimacy in the context of

[1]To illustrate the lack of consensus regarding a definition of CSR, it must be noted that a period of 30 years went by between the remarks of Carroll and Okoye.

[2]A further major challenge in defining CSR is the need for an agreed normative basis which underpins CSR practice (Okoye 2009; Palazzo and Scherer 2007).

H. Kloppers (✉) · E. Kloppers
North-West University (Potchefstroom Campus), Potchefstroom, South Africa
e-mail: Henk.Kloppers@nwu.ac.za

K. T. Çalıyurt and R. Said (eds.), *Sustainability and Social Responsibility of Accountability Reporting Systems*, Accounting, Finance, Sustainability, Governance & Fraud: Theory and Application, https://doi.org/10.1007/978-981-10-3212-7_14

> belonging or being proper or valid; few see a sort of fiduciary duty imposing higher standards of behavior on businessmen than on citizens at large.

Votaw is echoed by Kitchen (2003) when he notes:

> CSR is a confusing thing. One moment is seems to mean the engagement of non-governmental organisations (NGOs), the next it is all about charitable donations, and five minutes later it seems to mean the ethical treatment of employees. One minute the NGOs are calling the shots, the next the accountants are in the act selling "reputation assurance".

Given the many and often confusing definitions that exist, this contribution will attempt to provide an exposé of various definitions of CSR and a conceptual analysis of both international and South African definitions in order to identify the basic principles of CSR definitions internationally and specifically in South Africa. The international and South African principles will then be compared to identify the similarities and differences between them.

Dahlsrud (2008) identified the following five dimensions of CSR definitions: (a) the environmental dimension, which refers to the natural environment; (b) the social dimension, referring to the relationship between business and society; (c) the economic dimension, referring to financial aspects of CSR; (d) the stakeholder dimension, which refers to stakeholders and the stakeholder approach and (e) the voluntariness dimension, referring to actions not prescribed by law and in most instances based on ethical considerations. These dimensions will be used to analyse some of the most eminent CSR definitions.

The first section of this article focuses on selected international definitions as proposed by individual scholars as well as international institutions. The second section will focus on an African perspective of CSR before it will analyse specific definitions of CSR as accepted in South Africa. In conclusion, some basic principles of international as well as South African definitions of CSR will be identified and compared.

14.2 International Definitions

The topic of CSR has been under discussion for approximately six decades and during this period various scholars and institutions have attempted to provide an acceptable definition of what is today commonly referred to as corporate social responsibility (Carroll 1999).[3] The following section will examine a few of the definitions provided by leading authors and institutions on the subject in order to identify the basic principles thereof. The definitions will be discussed chronologically to illustrate how perspectives have changed over time in keeping with perspectives regarding the role of business in society.

---

[3]For an excellent exposition of the evolution of the definition of CSR, see Carroll (1999) and Crane (2008).

14.2.1 Bowen—1953

In 1953 Bowen, who is referred to as the "Father of Corporate Social Responsibility" (Carroll 1999; Windsor 2001), wrote *Social responsibilities of the businessman*, a work which laid the foundation for the study of corporate social responsibility as an academic field of scholarship. In this seminal work, he formulates two rather inconspicuous questions: "What responsibilities to society may businessmen reasonably be expected to assume?" and "To what extent do the interests of business in the long run merge with the interests of society?" (Bowen 1953). Although Bowen does not define CSR, he notes that the responsibility of business refers to:

> the obligations of businessmen to pursue those policies, to make those decisions, or to follow those lines of action which are desirable in terms of the objectives and values of our society.[4]

This statement supports the notion that businesses have to consider various dimensions when conducting business, which are not limited to the economic dimension. Bowen's early view acknowledges the fact that businesses operate *in* society and as a result businesses need also become aware of the social consequences of their business operations. This also implies that there cannot be clear-cut definitions of what CSR should entail since it should be contextual and will differ from society to society.

From this definition, one can see that Bowen regarded CSR as more than just obeying the law, but as a way of taking the best interest of society into account, in whatever way necessary.

Another important aspect of Bowen's thoughts is that CSR should be part of the core business of a company, by referring to notion that CSR should be included in the company policies. From this it is clear Bowen did not view CSR as "add-on" philanthropy or charity programmes, but rather as a responsible way to conduct business.

14.2.2 Davis—1960

In 1960, Keith Davis wrote that CSR is a "nebulous idea" and defined the social responsibility of business as:

> businessmen's decisions and actions taken for reasons at least partially beyond the firm's direct economic or technical interest (Davis 1960).

This definition was further expanded when he asserted that a business' social responsibility

[4]For a discussion of Bowen's approach, see Windsor (2001).

> arises from concern for the ethical consequences of one's acts as they might affect the interest of others (Davis 1967).

In Davis' view, a business' social responsibility stems from the fact that a business is regarded as an economic unit with impacts on the community, and as a result of these impacts the business is under an obligation to have regard for the communities affected by its actions—the business affects society beyond the gates of the business (Davis 1967).[5] In terms of this view, a socially responsible business will accept that its actions have an influence on the whole social system and act accordingly. The author recognizes that a business' social responsibility is inextricably linked to the business' social power and as a result of its social power a business needs to accept responsibility for the manner in which it influences its communities (Davis 1960, 1967; Davis and Blomstrom 1966).

The fact that Davis refers to "ethical consequences" again shows that CSR should be contextual and that different companies might have different ideas regarding their ethical obligations to society.

Davis continued working on the subject of CSR, conceded that "the concept of social responsibility is not an easily defined one", and eventually defined CSR as a business'

> consideration of, and response to, issues beyond the narrow economic, technical and legal requirements of the firm (Davis 1973).

According to this definition CSR begins where the law ends ("beyond … legal requirements"). Davis supports the notion that the mere fact that a business acts within the boundaries of the law does not imply that the business is being socially responsible—compliance is expected. Social responsibility is an acceptance of social obligations beyond legal requirements (Davis 1973).

14.2.3 Frederick—1960

William Frederick, one of the foremost authors on the subject of CSR, has been conducting research on the topic for almost half a century. As early as in 1960, he wrote that social responsibility implies that:

> businessmen should oversee the operation of an economic system that fulfils the expectations of the public (Frederick 1960).

It further implies that businesses should evince:

[5]In 1967, Davis noted that a business is responsible to a variety of stakeholders (or claimant groups), rather than being responsible only to shareholders.

> a public posture toward society's economic and human resources and a willingness to see that those resources are utilized for broad social ends and not simply for the narrowly circumscribed interests of private persons and firms (Frederick 1960).[6]

Frederick has noted an evolution in the construction of the successive definitions and distinguished between CSR_1, CSR_2 and CSR_3 where CSR_1 refers to the traditional definitions provided for CSR up to 1970, where the focus was on businesses' obligations to work for social betterment (Frederick 1994).[7] CSR_1 posits that the rights demanded by companies are accompanied by responsibilities such as the responsibility to behave responsibly (Frederick 1987).[8] Companies should be held responsible for their actions and decisions to the extent that these affect society. This approach is aptly described by Waddock (2004) and Scherer and Palazzo (2008)[9] where the author remarked that under the CSR_1 framework:

> companies could and should be held responsible for their actions and decisions as they affected society and ought to live up to a higher set of standards than simple adherence to the law for the good of all, and they ought to contribute to the well-being of society.

CSR_2 represented a new strain of thought regarding the role of business in society and the phrase "corporate social *responsiveness*" came into use more frequently. Regarding the change in the phrase, Frederick (1994) remarks:

> Soon it became evident that the promulgators of the "responsiveness" notion did intend it to be a genuine replacement for the idea of "responsibility" and that it was not simply one of those fashionable changes in phraseology that occasionally takes the scholarly community by storm.

In the evolution of the definition CSR_2 refers to "the capacity of a corporation to respond to social pressures" (Frederick 1994).[10] This definition requires a company to consider its stakeholders and to act in a proactive rather than reactive manner, and reflects a move from a philosophical approach to a managerial approach (Moir 2001; Waddock 2004).

CSR_2 evolved into CSR_3, which is described as "corporate social *rectitude*" (Frederick 1994). CSR_3 is an acknowledgement that management strategies and practices have inherent ethical dimensions and that business ethics occupies a

---

[6]As was the case with Keith Davis (see Sect. 14.2.2), Frederick also noted that social responsibility is linked with social power.

[7]For a brief discussion of the evolution from CSR_1 to CSR_3, see Moir (2001).

[8]The six fundamental precepts of CSR_1 are: power begets responsibility; a voluntary assumption of responsibility is preferable to government intervention and regulation; voluntary social responsibility requires business leaders to acknowledge and accept the legitimate claims, rights and needs of other groups in society; CSR requires a respect for law and the rules of the game that govern marketplace relations; an attitude of "enlightened self-interest" leads socially responsible business firms to take a long-run view of profits; and greater economic, social and political stability will result if all businesses adopt a socially responsible posture (Frederick 1987).

[9]For a discussion of CSR_1 see Waddock (2004).

[10]For a discussion of the definition of CSR_2, the implications of the approach and its shortcomings, see Frederick (1994).

central role in the CSR debate (Waddock 2004). In the context of ethical behaviour, Frederick (1987) notes that rectitude or ethics involve "a pervasive sense of rightness, respect and humanity" where ethics is "at the centre of a company's concerns, its policies and its major decisions".

14.2.4 Carroll—1979

In 1979, Archie Carroll added his voice to the CSR chorus—a voice that still echoes through much CSR literature. Carroll initially attempted to define CSR in terms of the various responsibilities that a business has (Carroll 1999).[11] He identified four basic obligations that a business has towards society—those obligations or responsibilities which are not mutually exclusive are economic, legal, ethical and discretionary responsibilities, which in total represent a business' social responsibilities (Carroll 1979).[12] Based on the identification of these four responsibilities, Carroll (1979) stated that the social responsibility of business

> encompasses the economic, legal, ethical and discretionary expectations that society has of organizations at any given point in time.

This definition, based on the four areas of social responsibility, was further elaborated on in 1983 when Carroll noted that:

> CSR involves the conduct of a business so that it is economically profitable, law abiding, ethical and socially supportive. To be socially supportive then means that profitability and obedience to the law are foremost conditions to discussing the firm's ethics and the extent to which it supports the society in which it exists with contributions of money, time and talent. Thus, CSR is composed of four parts: economic, legal, ethical and voluntary or philanthropic (Carroll 1999).[13]

---

[11]For a summation of Carroll's definitions of CSR, see Carroll (1999).

[12]Carroll remarked that the economic responsibility of a business represents the fundamental social responsibility of a business—a business has the responsibility to make profit (Carroll 1979). This economic responsibility results from the fact that society has "sanctioned" business by allowing it to operate as part of the fulfilment of the social contract that exists between business and society. Society expects businesses to conduct their business within the boundaries of the law—this according to Carroll (1979) represents the legal responsibilities of business. In terms of this approach, ethical responsibilities refer to those expectations that society has of business that exceed legal responsibilities. In the final instance, the discretionary responsibilities of business are those voluntary initiatives that can best be described as philanthropic giving—or what some refer to as "pat-a-poor-person" (Thomas and Nowak 2006).

[13]Carroll as quoted in Carroll (1999). Note that in terms of this definition the discretionary responsibilities have been reframed as voluntary or philanthropic responsibilities. The four areas of responsibility were later depicted as pyramidic in structure, with the economic responsibility forming the basis of the pyramid and philanthropic responsibilities forming the top of the pyramid. See Carroll (1991). For a discussion of Carroll's pyramid of responsibilities, see Kloppers (2012).

Extrapolating from this four-domain definition, Schwartz and Carroll (2003) proposed an alternative approach to defining social responsibility where the four-domain approach was replaced with a three-domain approach consisting of economic, legal and ethical domains.[14]

14.2.5 Jones—1980

Thomas Jones (1980) defines CSR as

> the notion that corporations have an obligation to constituent groups in society other than stockholders and beyond that prescribed by law or union contract.

This definition supports the notion that CSR initiatives have to be voluntarily adopted. According to this definition, if initiatives result from the coercive forces of law, such initiatives would not be of a voluntary nature and would consequently not be regarded as being true CSR initiatives. This definition further implies that CSR initiatives should go above and beyond what is expected from them by the law, to enhance the best interest of society at large.

The definition further recognizes the fact that businesses have a responsibility that stretches beyond responsibility towards owners or shareholders to include a variety of stakeholders that can be affected by the business.

14.2.6 World Business Council for Sustainable Development (WBCSD)—1999

The WBCSD is a global association of companies dealing exclusively with the issue of business and sustainable development and provides a base from which companies can explore sustainable development WBCSD (n.d.). The Council is viewed as a "catalyst for change towards sustainable development" that recognizes the important contribution that CSR can make in affecting social change (WBCSD 1991). Resulting from this recognition, the WBCSD (1991)[15] defines CSR as

[14]For a discussion of the Schwartz and Carroll model, see Kloppers (2012).

[15]In 2000, the WBCSD defined CSR as "the commitment of business to contribute to sustainable economic development, working with employees, their families, the local community and society at large to improve their quality of life" (WBCSD 2002). It is noteworthy that the definition provided in 2000 does not refer to the commitment of business as being a "continuing" one, nor does it refer to the fact that businesses are required to "behave ethically". Following on Dahlsrud's classification of dimensions (see Dahlsrud 2008), the definition provided by the WBCSD in 2000 does not include the voluntariness dimension, possibly indicating a move away from the notion that CSR is always based on voluntary actions.

> the continuing commitment by business to behave ethically and contribute to economic development while improving the quality of life of the workforce and their families as well as of the local community and society at large.

This definition illustrates the fact that CSR has a social dimension through the acceptance that business stands in a relationship with local communities and society at large. The WBCSD's definition of CSR acknowledges the fact that CSR has the potential to become an important driver for social progress as a result of the fact that the business sector forms part of society. The interdependency that exists between the business sector and society implies that businesses have an important role to play in improving the quality of life of the stakeholders involved in the businesses (Kotler and Lee 2005).

The WBCSD (1991) views CSR, together with corporate financial responsibility and corporate environmental responsibility, as the pillars for a business' overall responsibility.[16] The Council also supports the idea that a sound CSR strategy will be beneficial to business if the strategy is based on sound business principles. This definition again stresses the notion that CSR initiatives have the ability to make meaningful contributions to the development and transformation of society.

The WBCSD's definition displays certain similarities with the definition of the World Bank. Both of these definitions regard CSR as the *commitment of business* aimed at *contributing to economic development* with the "beneficiaries" of these actions being the *workforce* (*employees*); *their families; local communities and society at large*. This business commitment should lead to an improvement of the quality of life of the "beneficiaries".

14.2.7 McWilliams and Siegel—2001

McWilliams and Siegel (2001) define CSR as

> actions that appear to further some social good, beyond the interests of the firm and that which is required by law.[17]

These authors support the notion that CSR represents those actions that promote the social good beyond legal requirements. It thus assumes that CSR should actively strive to contribute to development and social change by taking action that goes above and beyond of what is expected from them by law. In following this definition, a business that enforces prescribed occupational safety standards will not be regarded as being socially responsible since the business is merely complying with the law. If a business provides extensive first-aid training to its employees

---

[16]From this source, it appears as if the Council equates corporate responsibility (with its three pillars) with sustainable development.

[17]Also see (Siegel and Vitialiano 2007) who remark that CSR occurs when companies "engage in activity that appears to advance a social agenda beyond that which is required by law".

beyond that which is required by law, the business will be regarded as being socially responsible.

14.2.8 European Commission—2001

The European Commission (EC 2001, 2006) the executive body of the European Union, defined CSR in 2001 as:

A concept whereby companies integrate social and environmental concerns in their business operations and in their interaction with their stakeholders on a voluntary basis.[18]

In terms of this definition CSR is essentially a notion whereby businesses decide on a voluntary basis to contribute to a better society and a cleaner environment (EC 2001).

The Commission supports the idea that CSR concerns businesses going beyond (over and above) the minimum legal and other requirements determined by society at large in order to address societal needs, and that it is fundamentally a *voluntary* business initiative (EC 2001).[19] In terms of this definition CSR should form part of and be integrated into the normal business strategy and become part of a business' day-to-day operations.

However, the global economic crisis and the resulting social consequences have damaged the relationship of trust between business and its stakeholders to such an extent that the Commission deemed in necessary in 2011 to reconsider its definition of CSR and provide a new agenda for action. In terms of the updated definition, CSR is simply defined as "the responsibility of enterprises for their impacts on society", a responsibility based on respect for the law, integrated into business operations and aimed at maximizing shared value for stakeholders while limiting the negative impacts of the business' activities (EC 2011). The new definition no longer contains any reference to the notion that CSR starts where the law ends—no reference is made to "going beyond the minimum legal requirements". In fact, it is recognized that public authorities should, through a mixture of voluntary policy measures and complementary regulation, play a supporting role.

The EC's definition pales in comparison with the elaborate definition provided by the ISO, and the usefulness of this definition is questionable. Although it might be argued that the new definition has all of the critical elements, it does not provide an indication of to whom the responsibility is owed nor does it make any reference to the centrality of sustainable development.

[18]This definition encompasses all of the dimensions identified by Dahlsrud (2008). It refers to the environmental, social, economic, stakeholder and voluntariness dimensions.

[19]The Commission is of the view that the voluntary approach is preferable to a comprehensive legal framework and regards any additional obligations and administrative requirements as counterproductive (EC 2006), although it agrees that CSR practices are not a substitute for public policy.

14.2.9 Lantos—2001

Geoffrey Lantos (2001) regards a business as an economic enterprise and inherently a social institution. The social nature of a business is evident from the variety of social consequences that stems from business operations. Lantos (2001) accordingly defines CSR as:

> The obligation stemming from the implicit "social contract" between business and society for firms to be responsive to society's long-run needs and wants, optimizing the positive effects and minimizing the negative effects of its actions on society.

This definition supports the notion that an implicit social contract exists between business and society, similar to the social contract that exists between society and government. A business' societal obligations are founded in this contract in terms of which a business has to accept that in return for being granted a licence to operate by society, it has to become responsive to societal needs and assume responsibility for the social consequences of its business operations (Lantos 2001).[20] The notion of "optimizing positive effects" is an indication that through CSR, business should strive to contribute to social change and development of a variety of stakeholders and society at large.

Lantos (2001) also proposed the idea of strategic CSR where the business itself benefits from its CSR initiatives too. His argument is that business can "do well by doing good" in society, since doing good should enhance the business' image and reputation.

14.2.10 World Bank—2003

The World Bank (2003),[21] a leading international financial institution which provides financial and technical support to developing countries for capital programmes, defines CSR as:

> The commitment of business to contribute to sustainable economic development, working with employees, their families, the local community and society at large to improve their quality of life, in ways that are both good for business and good for development.

---

[20]Lantos (2001) proposed a framework in which he initially identified two different types of CSR —altruistic CSR and strategic CSR (he later added ethical CSR as a third type of CSR (Lantos 2003b) also refer to Lantos (2003a). In terms of altruistic CSR, the motive for the initiative is not an economic one. The business does not expect to receive any benefit from the initiative. A strategic CSR initiative is motivated by the expectation that the initiative would be to the benefit not only of the intended beneficiary but also of the business.

[21]In line with Dahlsrud's CSR dimensions (see Dahlsrud 2008), it appears that the World Bank's definition does not explicitly include the environmental dimension, nor is any reference made to voluntariness.

This definition encompasses a number of extremely important concepts when working with CSR. In the first instance, the definition recognizes that businesses have a social responsibility to contribute to sustainable economic development, thus acknowledging the fact that the primary focus of businesses should be to contribute to the economy and economic growth without negatively impacting on future generations. The second and equally important responsibility of businesses is to ensure, in conjunction with a variety of stakeholders and through its economic responsibility, that the quality of life of those affected by the business' activities is substantially improved. Although this definition has a very distinctive developmental approach, the definition still accepts that CSR initiatives should also be beneficial to the business itself, thus acknowledging the notion of strategic CSR.

14.2.11 Blowfield and Frynas—2005

In an attempt to provide an inclusive definition of CSR, Blowfield and Frynas (2005) propose that CSR be used as an umbrella term which recognizes

(a) that companies have a responsibility for their impact on society and the natural environment, sometimes beyond legal compliance and the liability of individuals;
(b) that companies have a responsibility for the behaviour of others with whom they do business (e.g. within supply chains); and
(c) that business needs to manage its relationship with wider society, whether for reasons of commercial viability or to add to society.

In this definition, the idea of the triple-bottom line is also emphasized, since it refers to business' responsibility towards society and the environment, as well as the economic benefit of the business itself. It furthermore indicates what CSR initiatives can go above and beyond the law if necessary, but does not insist that it should be the case in all situations.

A new idea brought forward in this definition is the notion that a business should not only be responsible for how it conducts its own business, but also take responsibility for others with whom they are doing business. This shows how comprehensive CSR should be, and how it should be integrated in all aspects of business, including choices of who to conduct business with. Finally, Blowfield and Frynas emphasize the relationship between business and society, and by implication also the interdependency of the two entities.

14.2.12 International Organization for Standardization (ISO)—2010

The ISO, the world's largest developer and publisher of international standards ISO (n.d.), defines social responsibility in its *Guidance on Social Responsibility* ISO (2010) as the

> responsibility of an organization for the impacts of its decisions and activities on society and the environment, through transparent and ethical behaviour that contributes to sustainable development, health and the welfare of society; takes into account the expectations of stakeholders; is in compliance with applicable law and consistent with international norms of behaviour; and is integrated throughout the organization and practised in its relationships.[22]

Included in this definition are concepts such as organization, impacts, environment, ethical behaviour, sustainable development, stakeholders and international norms of behaviour. For the purposes of the ISO's definition, "organization" refers to

> … an entity or group of people and facilities with an arrangement of responsibilities, authorities and relationships and identifiable objectives (ISO 2010).[23]

Based on the inclusion of these concepts, this definition represents one of the most comprehensive currently available. It acknowledges the fact that an organization's activities could change society, the economy or the environment in both a positive or negative manner and that an organization should consider these possible impacts. In the context of this acknowledgement businesses have a social responsibility to contribute to the well-being of their stakeholders. The definition supports the notion that social responsibility is found within compliance with applicable legislation and international standards. Note that this definition does not refer to CSR as actions that "voluntarily go beyond the law", as is the case with some of the definitions to be discussed in this section.

In line with the definitions of CSR provided by the World Bank and the WBCSD, the ISO's definition is based on the notion of sustainable development, where the behaviour of an organization contributes to sustainable development.[24]

---

[22]Activities in this regard also refer to products, services and processes. Although this is one of the most complete definitions of CSR, if the definition is measured against Dahlsrud's dimensions (see Dahlsrud 2008) it is evident that the dimension of voluntariness is absent. However, this is not necessarily a shortcoming and it is argued that a definition of CSR should make reference to the fact that CSR activities should in the first instance be in compliance with applicable law and consistent with international norms of behaviour.

[23]Excluded from this definition are governments acting in their sovereign role as legislators or judicial authorities. The definition of the ISO is a clear indication that the ISO accepts that entities other than businesses such as non-profit organizations also have a social responsibility towards their employees, their families and society at large.

[24]ISO (2010) notes that: "Sustainable development is about integrating the goals of a high quality of life, health and prosperity with social justice and maintaining the earth's capacity to support life

Whereas the World Bank and the WBCSD's definitions refer to employees (the workforce), their families, local communities and society at large, the definition of the ISO provides an umbrella term to describe these groups as "stakeholders".[25] The definition further supports the more inclusive (as opposed to the more limited shareholder-centred approach)[26] stakeholder approach to CSR[27] and recognizes that the expectations of stakeholders should be considered in business decisions and activities and that CSR should not simply be bolted onto the existing business management, but should be integrated into management policies and decisions (Grayson and Hodges 2004).

Importantly, the definition also refers to behaviour which is consistent with international norms of behaviour, which are defined as:

> [E]xpectations of socially responsible organizational behaviour derived from customary international law, generally accepted principles of international law, or intergovernmental agreements that are universally or nearly universally recognized (ISO 2010).

This definition is especially pertinent for the discussion of international instruments that address CSR and could be considered relevant for businesses operating in South Africa.

14.2.13 Basic Principles of International CSR

From the discussion of the abovementioned definitions, the basic principles of CSR can be identified as:

- Based on the interdependent relationship and existing social contract between business and society, business has an ethical responsibility towards society which implies that the business should keep society's best interest in mind (Bowen, Davis, Frederick, Carroll, Jones, WBCSD, McWilliams and Siegel, EU, Lantos, WB, Blowfield and Frynas, ISO).
- Business should consider more than just economic aspects into account when making business decisions. Economic, social and environmental implications (triple-bottom line) should be taken into account (Bowen, Davis, Carroll, WBCSD, McWilliams and Siegel, EU, Blowfield and Frynas, ISO).
- CSR should play an active role in addressing social needs and should contribute to sustainable development (Frederick, WBCSD, McWilliams and Siegel, EU, Lantos, WB, ISO).

---

in all its diversity. These social, economic and environmental goals are interdependent and mutually reinforcing. Sustainable development can be treated as a way of expressing the broader expectations of society as a whole". For a discussion of CSR and sustainability, see Porter (2008).

[25]A stakeholder is defined as an "individual or group that has an interest in any decision or activity of an organization" (ISO 2010).

[26]For a discussion of the shareholder-supremacy approach, see Kloppers (2012).

[27]For a discussion of the stakeholder approach, see Kloppers (2012).

- CSR should form part of a company's core business and reflect how the company conducts business, rather than taking the form of add-on charity programmes (Bowen, EU, Blowfield and Frynas, ISO).
- Business should consider the needs, welfare and expectations of a wide variety of stakeholders, not just its stockholders or investors (Davis, Frederick, Carroll, Jones, WBCSD, EU, Lantos, WB, ISO).
- CSR is contextual and may/should differ from society to society (Bowen, Davis).
- CSR should benefit both business and society where the business can profit from doing good and operating responsibly in society (Lantos, Carroll, WB, WBCSD, Blowfield and Frynas).

From this summary, one can conclude that it is widely accepted that business has an ethical responsibility towards society and should take more than its own economic interest in account when making business decisions. Furthermore, CSR should be part of how a business operates and should be incorporated in its core business, rather than taking the form of "add-on" charity programmes. When planning and implementing CSR, businesses should take the needs, expectations and welfare of a variety of stakeholders into account, trying to balance different goals. Furthermore it is now accepted that business should, through CSR, contribute to sustainable development and that CSR initiatives can and should benefit both society at large as well as the company itself.

The two points where the discussed definitions differ are on the idea of voluntary vs compulsory CSR and whether CSR initiatives should go beyond the law, or just comply with the law.

The viewpoints of the different definitions can be summarized as follows:

- CSR should go beyond the legal requirements imposed upon business to be regarded as being socially responsible (Davis, Frederick, Jones, Carroll, McWilliams and Siegel, EU).
- CSR should be taken up voluntarily (Carroll, Jones, EU).

Other authors and organizations differ from the mentioned statements and conclude that:

- Businesses' CSR initiatives should comply with the law and responsible corporate behaviour that falls under the law should be considered as CSR (Carroll, EU, ISO).

It seems as if the idea of voluntary CSR is emphasized in older definitions, but not repeated in newer definitions. Thus, this article suggests that CSR should not be entirely voluntary, especially in developing countries where the need for corporate input is extremely high. The approach proposed by the King III report on corporate governance in South Africa, where business is provided with guidelines and they should "apply or explain" is proposed for CSR as well. This way, one can ensure that business fulfils its social responsibility, but leave room for individual interpretation and application thereof.

Secondly, some definitions indicate that CSR should comply with the law, while others suggest that it should go beyond the law to be considered as CSR. The authors support the idea of Blowfield and Frynas (2005) who argue that "companies have a responsibility for their impact on society and the natural environment, *sometimes* beyond legal compliance". Thus, CSR should always comply with the law and can go beyond when necessary and applicable to do so in the relevant context. The authors do not insist that CSR initiatives should go beyond the law, but rather that it should reflect how business takes responsibility for its actions and contributes to development.

In the next section, an overview of African perspectives on CSR will briefly be discussed, before CSR as defined in South Africa will be explored.

14.3 African Perspectives

14.3.1 The African Union

Unlike the European Union's Commission,[28] the AU has not formulated or endorsed a definition of CSR. It would appear that the subject of CSR has not received much attention from the AU. The issue of CSR was addressed at the first EU-Africa Business Forum where it was proposed that the EU and Africa should work together to create an African business network to promote CSR (EC 2007).

14.3.2 The New Partnership for Africa's Development (NEPAD)

The NEPAD, a programme of the African Union, was established to address the most pressing issues on the African content, which include escalating poverty and underdevelopment. Poverty alleviation and sustainable growth and development were identified as some of the partnership's objectives (Mullerat and Brennan 2011; NEPAD 2010). CSR can be viewed as one of the possible solutions to some of Africa's biggest challenges. Unfortunately NEPAD has to date not provided a definition of CSR, but in its *Business Declaration on Corporate Social Responsibility* (NEPAD 2007) the signatories of the *Declaratio*n recognized the fact that businesses have a profound impact on their constituencies and as a result have an obligation to act in a socially responsible manner. The *Declaration* stresses the fact that CSR initiatives are indispensable in the drive to empower historically disadvantaged persons. Signatories of the *Declaration* further agree that the

[28]See Sect. 14.2.8 for a discussion of the EC's definition.

maintenance of positive stakeholder relationships is a key component of CSR and that businesses are faced with the challenge of balancing financial performance with stakeholder interests (NEPAD 2007).

14.3.3 African Institute of Corporate Citizenship (AICC)

The AICC (2004) provides a wide definition of CSR as:

> The extent to which companies consider and manage their social, environmental and economic impacts and contributions to society as well as the extent to which they do this through stakeholder engagement and reporting on performance.[29]

This definition notes the fact that businesses do not operate in a vacuum and that their decisions and activities have social, environmental and economic impacts on society, which impacts have to be properly managed through a process of stakeholder engagement. The reference to stakeholder engagement as opposed to shareholder engagement is a reflection of the acceptance that businesses should consider and to some extent include stakeholders other than shareholders in the formulation of policies, for example. The definition also supports the prominent role of reporting on CSR performance. Businesses need to demonstrate to their stakeholders that they are acting socially responsibly.

14.4 South African Perspectives

Whereas the international scene is rich with the literature on the subject of CSR, it would appear that surprisingly few institutions or researchers have ventured into the CSR realm in the national context. Even fewer have attempted to provide a definition for CSR.

Given South Africa's unique history and its numerous socio-economic challenges, it is not strange that any attempt to define CSR in the South African context is influenced by this history.[30] The current national landscape places a strong emphasis on Corporate Social Investment as opposed to Corporate Social Responsibility (AICC 2004; Fig 2005; Hamman 2003). According to Fig (2005) South African business

> generally eschews the notion of "corporate social responsibility", despite the wide use of the term among practitioners and in the literature. Instead, it favours concepts of "corporate

[29]This definition includes all of the dimensions identified by Dahlsrud (2008) except the voluntariness dimension.

[30]This position is in line with Horrigan's remark that "definitions of CSR can also be jurisdiction-orientated" (Horrigan 2010).

> social investment" and "corporate citizenship": concepts that ask no questions about legacy, memory, history, justice or moral and ethical responsibilities.

The reference to investment rather than responsibility is indicative of the fact that the South African private sector expects a return on their CSR initiatives and, if properly managed, that the costs associated with the initiatives will be recovered over time through the positive CSR spin-offs. The expected return includes enhanced reputation, an improved bottom line or greater brand recognition.[31] The term CSI is preferred to the notion of responsibility. It might be argued that responsibility is inextricably linked to the notion that the private sector is being held accountable for historical injustices. CSI denotes a more neutral meaning as opposed to CSR and represents an attempt to negate the concept of accountability for historical injustices (Fig 2007).[32] By referring to social investment as opposed to social responsibilities, the private sector is attempting to move away from the stigma attached to business as a result of the apartheid regime. According to Fig (2005)

> "[r]esponsibility" would imply taking action to acknowledge, recognize and offer redress for apartheid-era violations of human rights.

Sections of the private sector reject the notion that the business sector should accept responsibility for historical injustices, and accordingly regard CSR as an acceptance of the obligation to redress these injustices. Any attempt to define CSR within the South African context should reflect the historical realities that were associated with the apartheid era.[33]

For the purposes of this research, the internationally accepted term "corporate social *responsibility*" will be used to refer to business' responsibility towards its stakeholders, while "corporate social *investment*" will be viewed as the manifestation of CSR through CSR initiatives.

The following sections will reflect on the limited variety of national definitions provided for CSR.

14.4.1 King II Report on Corporate Governance

Eight years after the release of the *King Report on corporate governance 1994*, *King II* was published, representing the second edition of the trilogy of King reports promoting corporate governance. *King II* reviewed and expanded the corporate governance measures contained in *King I* and succeeded in linking the concept of

---

[31]See Kloppers (2012) for a discussion of the benefits of CSR.

[32]It is undeniable that in many instances big business has been implicated in and supportive of the legacy of apartheid and consequently these businesses are to some extent being held "responsible" (AICC 2004).

[33]This issue will not be addressed in this section.

CSR and good governance. The King Report on corporate governance for South Africa identifies social responsibility as one of the seven characteristics of good governance (IoD 2002; SAGA 2002).[34] Although the Report does not define CSR, it is noted that a socially responsible business will be aware of and responsive to social issues.

14.4.2 King Report on Governance for South Africa—2009

The third *King Report on Governance* (IoDSA 2009) does not explicitly define CSR although it does provide a glossary of terms which are relevant in the area of corporate governance. Since the preceding *King Report*[35] identified CSR as one of the characteristics of good corporate governance, it was not unexpected that the third report also referred to CSR. The third report notes that CSR is an essential and critical component of the broader concept of corporate citizenship, thus linking CSR not only to corporate governance but also to corporate citizenship (IoDSA 2009). However, it is noteworthy that the third report endorses the ISO's definition as provided in the *Guidance on Social Responsibility*.[36]

Given the confusion between the use of the terms CSR and CSI, the third report distinguishes between these two concepts. The third report notes that CSI[37] is a manifestation of CSR and that:

> [i]n the narrow sense it refers to donations and other kinds of financial assistance (made for an altruistic purpose), and in the broader sense, includes other kinds of contributions beyond just financial assistance (IoDSA 2009).

It should be noted that this definition identifies altruistic donations (which are donations that are purely philanthropic and not strategically linked to the business' core business) as social investments in the narrow sense which might be viewed as contrary to the investment approach, where a return is expected on investments. Purely philanthropic donations are normally gratuitous disposals with no direct returns required or expected.

It is of great importance for the understanding of CSR in South Africa in general, and the analysis thereof in this paper, to note that both *King III* (the leading guideline for business in South Africa regarding corporate governance) as well as the *South African Bureau of Standards* (SABS*)* accepted the definition of CSR provided by the ISO in 2010. The entire ISO 26000 standard was accepted by the South African SABS as a national standard (SANS 26000:2010), and as a consequence the standard has been made applicable to South African businesses—a

---

[34]Other characteristics include transparency, independence, accountability and fairness.

[35]See Sect. 14.4.2.

[36]For a discussion of the ISO's definition, see Sect. 14.2.12.

[37]Also referred to as responsible investment (IoDSA 2009).

move which should assist South African businesses in their CSR efforts. It should be noted that the standard is not a certifiable standard and is only to be regarded as a guidance.

14.4.3 Legislative Definitions

It would seem that the reluctance to the use of the term corporate social responsibility has not been limited to the private sector. The legislator, in the *Notice of the draft 2nd phase of the codes of good practice on broad-based black economic empowerment* (South Africa 2005),[38] also steers clear of referring to corporate social responsibility; instead the *Draft Notice* provides a definition of corporate social investment. In terms of this *Draft Notice* (South Africa 2005), CSI is defined as:

> an enterprise's contributions to society and community that are extraneous to its regular business activities.

This definition implies that contributions made as part of normal business practices are not regarded as CSR contributions. In order to be recognized, contributions must be extraneous to regular business activities and must go beyond normal business activities. It would thus appear as if this definition excludes contributions made by employers in terms of labour legislation, for example.

According to the *Draft Notice* (South Africa 2005), CSI initiatives include but are not limited to development programmes, health programmes, education, training, environmental programmes and programmes that support arts and culture.

The final *Codes of good practice on black economic empowerment* (South Africa 2007a) makes no reference to CSI or CSR. The *Codes* prefer to refer to social investment initiatives as socio-economic development (SED) contributions, which is a collective term for approved SED initiatives.[39] The authors speculate that the move by the legislator away from terms such as CSR or CSI could be an attempt by the legislator to introduce constitutional language to the CSR environment. The reference to socio-economic development is in line with the language used in the Bill of Rights in the *Constitution*. Included in the Bill of Rights are various rights which are described as socio-economic rights. However, it should be noted that the authors do not argue that CSR is a socio-economic right, but merely that some

[38]The BEE legislation and related regulations and Codes of Practice are discussed in more detail in Kloppers (2012).

[39]The authors speculate that the move by the legislator away from terms such as CSR or CSI could be an attempt by the legislator to introduce constitutional language to the CSR environment. The reference to socio-economic development is in line with the language used in the Bill of Rights in the *Constitution*. Included in the Bill of Rights are various rights which are described as socio-economic rights. However, it should be noted that the authors do not argue that CSR is a socio-economic right, but merely that some socio-economic rights might be realized through CSR.

socio-economic rights might be realized through CSR. Approved SED contributions are defined as

> monetary or non-monetary contributions carried out for the benefit of any projects approved for this purpose by an organ of state or sectors.[40]

The *Code* (South Africa 2007a) continues further to define SED contributions as

> monetary or non-monetary contributions actually initiated and implemented in favour of beneficiaries … with the specific objective of facilitating sustainable access to the economy for those beneficiaries.

In the context of this article, SED contributions as defined in the BEE framework are not only considered to be corporate social investments, but they also fall within the wider ambit of corporate social responsibility.

The uncertainty regarding CSI or SED is further perpetuated by the sector charters drafted in terms of Section 12 of the Broad-based Black Economic Empowerment Act 53 of 2003. The *Financial Sector Charter on Black Economic Empowerment* (South Africa 2007b),[41] which was gazetted on the same day as the *Codes of good practice on black economic empowerment*, reverts back to CSI as opposed to SED. This sector charter defines CSI as

> projects aimed primarily at black groups, communities and individuals that have a strong *developmental approach* and *contribute towards transformation*[42] (emphasis added).

In line with the focus of BEE on empowering black persons,[43] this definition singles out historically disadvantaged South Africans as its primary beneficiaries. The requirement that CSR projects must have a nuanced *developmental approach* and *contribute towards transformation* is unique and illustrates how the country's historical background has given rise to a country-specific definition where the focus is on development and transformation. The definition provides support for the argument that CSR initiatives should be aimed at development and that these initiatives should make an actual difference in the lives of its beneficiaries without creating a culture of dependency.

The definitions provided in this section are further evidence that CSR, even within the South African context, is a contested concept with not only various definitions but also with various confusing terms used to denote essentially the same idea.

---

[40] Schedule 1 (South Africa 2007a) (Schedule 1 of the Notice contains a list of definitions used in the *Code*). "Approved SED contributions" refers to projects focusing on environmental issues or projects targeting infrastructure development, enterprise creation or reconstruction in underdeveloped areas or areas identified by the national integrated sustainable rural development or urban renewal programmes. For a discussion of SED contributions, see Kloppers (2012).

[41] For a review of the key provisions of the Financial Sector Charter, see Moyo and Rohan (2006).

[42] The paragraph continues to provide a list of possible CSI initiatives. The contents of this list exhibits many similarities with the *Draft Code* (South Africa 2005) and makes no reference to SED, SED contributions or SED programmes.

[43] For a discussion of this term, see Kloppers (2012).

The following basic principles of CSR in South Africa are in agreement with international principles:

- Business should take more than just economic considerations into account when making decisions—social and environmental implications should also be considered (AICC, King II, King III, SANS 26000:2010).
- Business has an ethical responsibility towards society and should contribute to society (AICC, King II, legislation).
- CSR should play an active role in addressing social needs and should contribute to sustainable development (King III, SANS 26000:2010, legislation).
- CSR should form part of a company's core business and reflect how the company conducts business, rather than taking the form of add-on charity programmes.
- Business should consider the needs, welfare and expectations of a wide variety of stakeholders, not just its stockholders or investors (AICC, King II, King III, SANS 26000:2010).
- CSR should benefit both business and society where the business can profit from doing good and operating responsibly in society (SA Business).

The following principles of CSR seem unique to South Africa, according to the analysed definitions:

- CSR is an important characteristic of good corporate governance and CSR initiatives should be undertaken in order to be regarded a good corporate citizen (King II, King III).
- CSR initiatives should primarily be to the benefit of previously disadvantaged communities or individuals/ black people (legislation).
- CSR initiatives should be extraneous to regular business activities (legislation).
- Business should contribute to transformation through CSR initiatives (legislation).

14.5 Conclusion

Any attempt to define CSR should in the first instance recognize that the definition can differ from society to society and can be influenced by factors such as culture and belief. This variability contributes to the inability to formulate a single universally accepted definition. The South African position serves as an excellent example. In the discussion of the national definitions of CSR, it became evident that local businesses are not totally comfortable with the use of the term CSR owing to their negative perception of the notion of "responsibility". It became clear that local businesses preferred the term corporate social *investment,* although a good case can be made out for the opinion that CSR and CSI do not have the same meaning and that one is a consequence of the other. It also became clear that the legislator is not comfortable with the use of the term CSR and has preferred terms such as CSI or SED. This is partially as a result of South Africa's history and is reflected in references to "contributions towards transformation" or "historically disadvantaged South Africans", which are uniquely South African.

However, regardless of a particular history or culture, it is impossible, even within the context of a particular country, to define CSR to such an extent that it would be applicable in each instance. As a result CSR should rather be used as an umbrella term to indicate that businesses have a responsibility towards the societies within which they operate and that this responsibility needs to be managed.

From the definitions discussed in this article, it has become evident that no two definitions are the same in all respects, although similarities can be identified. The aim of the discussions was not to provide a new (or yet another) definition for CSR but rather to identify possible elements of a common definition.

Firstly, it appears that both international and South African definitions of CSR agree that business has an ethical responsibility towards society, and that society's best interest should be kept in mind when business decisions are being made. Business should contribute to society by taking an active role in contributing to sustainable development. The needs, expectations and welfare of a variety of stakeholders, other than shareholders, should be considered at all times. Business should focus on the triple-bottom line and take economic, social and environmental implications into account, when making decisions and drafting policies.

CSR should furthermore form part of a company's core business and reflect how the company conducts business, rather than taking the form of add-on charity programmes. It is also accepted that business itself can benefit from CSR initiatives, when their responsible behaviour is rewarded through a positive reputation and good relationships with stakeholders. CSR is at its most strategic when it is economically profitable and when it contributes to sustainable economic development.

There is also some consensus on the fact that CSR requires, in the first instance, compliance with the law, but also calls for business to voluntarily go beyond the requirements of the law when necessary in specific contexts.

Finally, an attempt to define CSR should make reference to the fact that CSR is not something that is bolted onto existing business practices, but is rather an approach integrated throughout all levels of the business and practised in all its relationships with its stakeholders. This approach reinforces the need for stakeholder engagement, where stakeholders are included in business decisions and practices which might have an impact on them.

In South Africa, however, CSR activities are regarded as extraneous to regular business activities—businesses should be seen as "doing something more" and responding to specific needs. These extraneous activities should have clearly identified and specific objectives. In the South African context these objectives should focus on contributing to development, contributing to transformation and primarily benefitting previously disadvantaged (black) South Africans. Secondly the concept of CSR is closely linked with corporate governance and is viewed as something business should do in order to be a good corporate citizen.

From this discussion, one can conclude that although there are a number of widely accepted principles of CSR, it should be defined and conceptualized to be relevant to specific country's unique history and development issues.

References

African Institute of Corporate Citizenship (AICC) (2004) Corporate social responsibility (CSR) in South Africa: implications for a potential standards organisation (ISO) management standard

Banerjee S (2001) Corporate citizenship and indigenous—exploring a new dynamic of organisational-stakeholder relationships. J Corp Citizensh 1:39–42

Blowfield M, Frynas G (2005) Setting new agendas: critical perspectives on Corporate Social Responsibility in the developing world. Int Aff 81:499–502

Bowen H (1953) Social responsibilities of the businessman

Carroll A (1979) A three-dimensional conceptual model of corporate performance. Acad Manag Rev 4:497

Carroll A (1991) The pyramid of corporate social responsibility: toward the moral management of organizational stakeholders. Bus Horiz 5(34):5–29

Carroll A (1999) Corporate social responsibility—evolution of a definitional construct. Bus Soc 38:268–295

Crane A (2008) The Oxford handbook of corporate social responsibility, pp 19–46

Dahlsrud A (2008) How is defined: an analysis of 37 definitions. Corp Soc Responsib Environ Manag 14:1–4

Davis K (1960) Can business afford to ignore social responsibilities? Calif Manag Rev 70–73

Davis K (1967) Understanding the puzzle. Bus Horiz 10:45–47

Davis K (1973) The case for and against business assumption of social responsibilities. Acad Manag Rev 16:312

Davis K, Blomstrom R (1966) Business and its environment

European Commission (2007) European Commission's response to the private sector's follow-up recommendations of the first EU-AFRICA business forum. http://www.africa-union.org. Accessed 1 Nov 2011

European Commission (EC) (2001) Green paper—promoting a European framework for (COM (2001) 366)

European Commission (EC) (2006) Implementing the partnership for growth and jobs: making Europe a pole of excellence on corporate social responsibility (COM (2006) 136)

European Commission (EC) (2011) A renewed EU strategy for corporate social responsibility (COM (2011) 681)

Fig D (2005) Manufacturing amnesia: corporate social responsibility in South Africa. Int Aff 81:599

Fig D (2007) Staking their claims—corporate social and environmental responsibility in South Africa

Frederick W (1960) The growing concern over business responsibility. Calif Manag Rev 2:60

Frederick W (1987) Theories of corporate social performance. In: Sethi S, Falbe M (eds) Business and society, pp 144–145

Frederick W (1994) From CSR_1 to CSR_2—the maturing of business-and-society thought. Bus Soc 33:150–154

Grayson D, Hodges A (2004) Corporate social opportunity! 7 steps to make work for your business

Hamman R (2003) Mining companies' role in development: the 'why' and 'how' of from a business perspective. Dev Sout Afr 20:237–238

Horrigan B (2010) Corporate social responsibility in the 21st century: debates, models and practices across government, law and business
Institute of Directors (IoD) (2002) King report on corporate governance for South Africa
Institute of Directors in South Africa (IoDSA) (2009) King report on Governance for South Africa
International Organisation for Standardisation (ISO) (2010) Guidance on social responsibility
International Organisation for Standardisation (ISO) (n.d.) About ISO. http://www.iso.org/iso/about.html. Accessed 2 July 2013
Jones T (1980) Corporate social responsibility revisited, redefined. Calif Manag Rev 22:59
Kitchen T (2003) A brand explanation. J Brand Manag 10:312
Kloppers HJ (2012) Improving land reform through CSR: a legal framework analysis. LLD thesis. North West University
Kotler P, Lee N (2005) Corporate social responsibility: doing the most good for your company and your cause
Lantos G (2001) The boundaries of strategic corporate social responsibility. J Consum Mark 18:595–600
Lantos G (2003a) Corporate socialism unethically masquerades as "CSR"—the difference between being ethical, altruistic and strategic in business. Strat Dir 19:31–35
Lantos G (2003b) The ethicality of altruistic corporate social responsibility. J Consum Mark 19:205–230
McWilliams A, Siegel D (2001) Corporate social responsibility: a theory of the firm perspective. Acad Manag Rev 26:117
Moir L (2001) What do we mean by corporate social responsibility? Corp Gov 1:16–18
Moyo T, Rohan S (2006) Corporate citizenship in the context of the financial services sector: what lessons from the financial sector charter? Dev South Afr 23:289–303
Mullerat R, Brennan D (2011) Corporate social responsibility: the corporate governance of the 21st century
New Partnership for Africa's Development (NEPAD) (2007) Business declaration on corporate social responsibility
New Partnership for Africa's Development (NEPAD) (2010) About. http://www.nepad.org/about. Accessed 3 Nov 2011. http://www.ahi.co.za/current/NEPADBusinessDeclaraton.pdf. Accessed 1 Nov 2011
Okoye A (2009) Theorising as an essentially contested concept: is a definition necessary? J Bus Ethics 89:613–627
Palazzo G, Scherer A (2007) Towards a political conception of corporate responsibility: business and society as seen from a Habermasian perspective. Acad Manag Rev 32:1096
Porter T (2008) Managerial applications of Corporate Social Responsibility and systems thinking for achieving sustainability outcomes. Syst Res Behav Sci 25:398–400
Scherer A, Palazzo G (2008) Handbook of research on global corporate citizenship
Schwartz M, Carroll A (2003) A three domain approach. Bus Ethics Q 13:503–530
Sethi P (1975) Dimensions of corporate social performance: an analytical framework. Calif Manag Rev 17:58
Siegel D, Vitialiano D (2007) An empirical analysis of the strategic use of corporate social responsibility. J Econ Manag Strat 16:773
South Africa (2005) Notice of the draft 2nd phase of the codes of good practice on broad-based black economic empowerment (General notice 2036) Gov Gaz 28351, 20 Dec
South Africa (2007a) Codes of good practice on black economic empowerment (General notice 112). Gov Gaz 29617, 9 Feb
South Africa (2007b) Financial sector charter on black economic empowerment (General notice 110). Gov Gaz 29610, 9 Feb
South African Grantmakers' Association (SAGA) (2002) The king report 2002: implications for corporate social investment in South Africa
Thomas G, Nowak M (2006) Corporate social responsibility: a definition
Van Marrewijk M (2003) Concepts and definitions of and corporate: between agency and communication. J Bus Ethics 44:95–96

Votaw D (1972) Genius became rare: a comment on the doctrine of part 1. Calif Manag Rev 15:25

Waddock S (2004) Parallel universes: companies, academics and the progress of corporate citizenship. Bus Soc Rev 5(109):14–16

Wan-Jan W (2006) Defining. J Public Aff 6:176–182

Windsor D (2001) The future of corporate social responsibility. Int J Organ Anal 9:225–230

World Bank (2003) Public policy for social responsibility. https://www.info.worldbank.org/etools/docs/library/57434/publicpolicy_econference.pdf. Accessed 2 July 2013

World Business Council for Development (WBCSD) (1991) Meeting changing expectations. http://www.wbcsd.org/about.aspx. Accessed 2 July 2013

World Business Council for Development (WBCSD) (2002) The WBCSD's journey

World Business Council for Development (WBCSD) (n.d.) About the WBCSD

Author Biographies

Prof. Henk Kloppers is an Associate Professor at the Faculty of Law of the North-West University (NWU), Potchefstroom campus, South Africa. He holds a LLD from the NWU and his current research focuses on issues related to CSR. He further holds the B.Com. (Law), LLB and LLM degrees. He is the programme leader in the LLM in Estate planning. He teaches tax law and insurance law at undergraduate level and financial planning law in the LLM in Estate planning. He has presented nationally and internationally and has publications in local and international accredited journals. Kloppers acts as supervisor for LLM and LLD candidates in the field of Law (especially mercantile law).

Dr. Elbé Kloppers has been a lecturer at the School of Communication Studies at the NWU for more than ten years and is currently teaching modules in research methodology, communication for social change and public speaking. Her research focuses include corporate social responsibility communication (CSR communication), communication for social change and strategic communication management. Her Ph.D. thesis explored CSR communication in the South African agricultural sector. Kloppers acts as supervisor for M.A. and Ph.D. candidates in the fields of communication for social change and CSR communication. She has published eight peer-reviewed articles/chapters in books and has read twelve research presentations at academic conferences focusing on HIV/AIDS and CSR communication. Kloppers earned her BBc degree in Business communication at the then PU for CHE before obtaining her M.A. and Ph.D. in communication at the North-West University Potchefstroom Campus.

Chapter 15
Exploring Issues and Challenges of Green Financing in Malaysia: Perspectives of Financial Institutions

Azlan Amran, Mehran Nejati, Say Keat Ooi and Faizah Darus

15.1 Introduction

Green financing is a vital but broad concept, involving a wide range of sustainability issues related to financial institutions. Globally, human life, land, and infrastructure have already been impacted by an increasing frequency and severity of extreme weather events. Pressure is growing for building long-term resilience. Progressively, many countries have begun working towards their own initiatives towards green growth development. For instance, China is increasing its renewable power generation in wind capacity and investment in low carbon transport. India has positioned itself to expand solar power generation and reduce its fossil fuel subsidies. Brazil has already reduced its deforestation rate by 70% from 2004 levels and comes to rely primarily on hydropower. Morocco plans to double its energy capacity and increase its renewable energy generation, representing 42% of all power generation.

Whereas developed countries such as Germany, Spain, Italy, and the UK have taken ambitious measures to boost renewable investment and comprehensive energy efficiency measures, including the reduction of building and vehicle emissions (Climate Works Foundation 2010).

A. Amran (✉) · S. K. Ooi
Graduate School of Business,
Universiti Sains Malaysia, Gelugor, Penang, Malaysia
e-mail: azlan_amran@usm.my

S. K. Ooi
e-mail: ooisaykeat@usm.my

M. Nejati
School of Business and Law, Edith Cowan University, Joondalup, Australia
e-mail: m.nejati@ecu.edu.au

F. Darus
Accounting Research Institute & Faculty of Accountancy,
Universiti Teknologi MARA, 42300, Shah Alam, Selangor, Malaysia

K. T. Çalıyurt and R. Said (eds.), *Sustainability and Social Responsibility of Accountability Reporting Systems*, Accounting, Finance, Sustainability, Governance & Fraud: Theory and Application, https://doi.org/10.1007/978-981-10-3212-7_15

Green growth refers to the balance of green economic growth for sustainable development, representing an economic growth pattern with the new driving power of "green". Finding new eco-friendly growth opportunities and the principle of green growth requires continuously improving manufacturing capacities, reducing the environmental pollution by utilizing green technology and knowledge, and expanding the energy and resources (Noh 2010). Green technology is one of the viable solutions adopted by a number of countries to simultaneously address energy and environmental issues (DSD 2011).

New technologies bear a certain amount of uncertainty, thus creating a barrier for its development. Recently, many green technology projects have been implemented with financial assistance, as the uncertainty results in high financing costs for research, development, and deployment. This in turn artificially raises the price of green technology options, delaying their full integration into the green technology marketplace. Typically, the initial cost for green technology equipment is substantially higher than the standard alternative and the payback period or economic return may be unacceptable. Therefore, green technology projects generally face difficulty in obtaining financing and bank loan approval due to the high risks involved as well as the lack of technical knowledge of the part of financiers (Mustapa et al. 2010).

Conceptually, a bank is a type of financial institution. Within the financial industry, banks play a vital role in supporting businesses and projects with various financing activities. Banks act as financial intermediary among various components in the society. The major task of a bank is to accept deposits and deliver surplus capital to people with shortages, through financial products and services such as investment, lending, advising, saving, settlement, and trust of real estate business (Economy Watch 2010).

Globally, financial services are moving towards sustainability. Sustainable finance usually addresses environmental, social, and governance impacts of financial services. Many leading financial institutions have begun to direct their resources and lending decisions towards curbing environmental degradation (DOE 2010). Sustainable finance is about engaging with environmental, social, and financial opportunities and risks in a systematic way while complying with regulation and voluntary standards as well as observing good practices in ethics and governance (Gerster 2011).

Despite government's effort in GTFS establishment, according to Malaysia SME (2010), many green SME entrepreneurs are still struggling to obtain loans from banks. Referring to EUMCCI (2012), the loan rejection rate is high, fifteen GTFS applicants had faced loan rejected by 14 local banks and 6 foreign-based banks. Hence, there is a relatively wide gap between the green SME entrepreneurs and those successfully financed with GTFS. To advance understanding about GTFS and its challenges, this research intends to explore the current state and issues regarding GTFS from the perspective of Malaysian financial institutions. Furthermore, this research will also identify motivations, challenges, and barriers of GTFS in Malaysia from the perspective of Malaysian financial institutions.

15.2 Green Technology in Malaysia

Green technology has been adopted worldwide to save the environment. Consequently, in acknowledging the issues of climate change and energy security, Malaysia has also taken steps to promote green technology as part of the solution. It is expected that the promotion of green technology would facilitate the achievement of Malaysia's Copenhagen commitment to voluntary reduce up to 40% in terms of emissions intensity of gross domestic product (GDP) by 2020 compared to 2005 levels. Additionally, green technology has been highlighted as one of the emerging drivers of economic growth for our country to achieve high-income status while addressing the pressing issue of the sustainability as stated in the New Economic Model (NEM) (Economic Planning Unit 2010). Green technology is a driver which may accelerate the national economy and sustainable development (Ismail 2010). It allows the nation to progress and at the same time minimizes the negative environmental impacts. According to KeTTHA (2011), the term green technology refers to the development and application of products, equipment, and systems used to conserve the natural environment and resources, which minimizes and reduces the negative impact of human activities. Criteria for green technology include the following:

1. Minimizing the degradation of the environment
2. Zero or low GHG emission levels
3. Being safe for use and promoting healthy and improved environment for all life
4. Conserving the use of energy and natural resources
5. Promoting the use of renewable resources.

Though green technology development in Malaysia is still in its infancy (DSD 2011), Malaysia is looking at green technology as the potential area of growth. Green technology has been highlighted as one of the emerging drivers of economic growth for Malaysia to achieve high-income status while addressing the pressing issue of the sustainability as stated in the New Economic Model (Economic Planning Unit 2010). Indeed, green technology deployed judiciously will deliver the double impact of accelerating Malaysia's economic growth while addressing pressing environmental issues. In fact, green technology has broad applications across different sectors, such as in energy production, manufacturing, services, and transport (Razak 2009).

As the environmental and climate change awareness has grown, the Malaysian government has begun to earmark green technology as a new driver for economic growth in a sustainable manner. The establishment of the Ministry of Energy, Green Technology and Water reflects Malaysia's seriousness in driving the clean and green as the way towards creating an economy that is based on sustainable development (DSD 2011).

In order to promote sustainable development and green technology, Malaysia has initiated many incentives, for instance, during the 2010 Budget Speech, Dato' Seri Najib Tun Abdul Razak, the Prime Minister of Malaysia, announced the establishment of Green Technology Financing Scheme (GTFS) amounting to RM1.5 billion as an effort to improve the supply and utilization of green technology. This financing scheme is aimed to assist financial institutions in facilitating companies to pursue business in green technology (Ahmad et al. 2011), as access to finance is frequently cited as one of the key requirements for addressing climate change.

15.3 Method

This study applied a qualitative approach focus due to its shared construction of meaning with participants. The study method offers a flexibility in design, method, and process, which allows subjects to communicate their experiences without having them transformed by the researcher so as to alter their meaning in any significant manner (Bassett 2010). Data obtained from a focus group discussion and open-ended surveys constituted the qualitative data sources for this study. These methods were chosen to allow hearing the individual voices of experts, bankers, and representatives of Malaysian financial institutions, and to bring them together to share their opinions and thoughts regarding green technology financing in the focus group. Focus groups involve "the elucidation of subjective meaning, experience, beliefs, and attitudes, either through one-on-one interviews or small, facilitator-led, group discussion" (Whitley and Crawford 2005).

The focus group discussion consisted of bankers and other representatives from Malaysian financial institutions. The focus group discussion began with the establishment of norms for communication, as outlined by the session moderator. Then, the key themes to be discussed were determined. The focus group discussions were carried out in this project to offer a comprehensive view of the green technology financing and provide in-depth insights about the challenges, motivations, and benefits of green technology financing from the perspective of Malaysian financial institutions. More specifically, narrative analysis was used in this research, which aimed to "understand a particular case or several cases by looking closely at

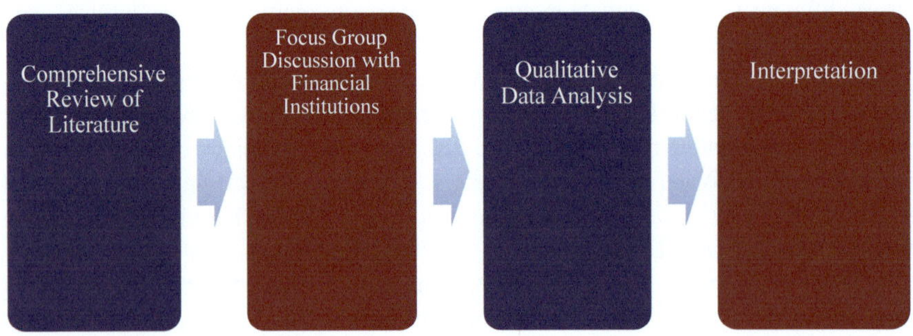

Fig. 15.1 Research methodology applied in the project

the details of each" (Rubin and Babbie 2005, p. 389). Fig. 15.1 depicts the flow of the research methodology applied in this project.

To complement the data collected for the core questions raised in the focus group discussion, an open-ended survey was designed in two sections and distributed among the participants in the focus group meeting. The first section covered questions regarding issues and challenges of green technology financing, while the second section addressed specific questions regarding initiatives, motivations, and perceived benefits of green technology financing. The participants of the round-table discussion were asked to complete the questionnaire after the focus group discussion session.

15.4 Findings

15.4.1 Initiatives

Banks play a vital role in supporting businesses and projects with various financing activities. As a result of this financing process, banks indirectly influence the society and environment through businesses and projects that they support. While green technology financing scheme allows the Malaysian banks to engage in sustainable financing through addressing the environmental, social, and governance impacts of their finances, most of the investigated banks have not undertaken any specific initiatives regarding the green technology financing. They tend to treat the applications for GTFS similar to any other loan applications.

Moreover, a number of the foreign banks also revealed that they had received limited applications under GTFS. Additionally, the representative from one of the banks argued that they promoted the scheme to their customers and did their part in terms of raising awareness regarding the scheme. However, they did not have any takers until that time. Overall, the summary of the findings on the existing initiatives of the banks on GTFS revealed that only 35% of them have established dedicated marketing team to market this special financing package under GTFS, and 17% of the banks have not undertaken any specific initiative for promoting green technology financing. Moreover, 12% of the banks have engaged consultants to obtain their expert opinion and advice on the technical knowledge required for evaluation of GTFS applications.

15.4.2 Challenges

It was found that the banks have gone through a lot of painful process in case of requesting for a claim.

As argued by many of the bankers, it is not easy to obtain a 60% guarantee in case something goes wrong with a loan. Thus, banks are very careful in financing these projects to avoid the lengthy and painful process of requesting for the guarantee. Another major challenge is "total exposure". Based on the current guidelines, most of the current applicants for GTFS are linked to GLCs and other larger companies, which might negatively influence the level of financing provided to these SMEs due to the aggregate exposure guidelines. This limits the amount of the financing that can be provided to the applicant due to its indirect relation to a bigger player which formerly has been financed by the bank.

Moreover, in some specific projects such as solar power panels, the sponsors need to order some parts well in advance in order to obtain the LC, whereas the certification and financing project is also a time-consuming process. At the end of the day, the loan application might even be rejected. Hence, there appears to be a mismatch in this regard. Additionally, in many cases, the investment required for the project is beyond the limit allowed by the GTFS guidelines; hence, in case the project is approved by the bank, the extra amount of financing should be covered by the bank without any guaranteed support for the excess amount of financing. Thus, it creates more risks for the banks.

Another challenge is that according to the bankers, there has not yet been any success story about the projects financed. Even for projects still under construction, the banks face problems regarding delays. Hence, even the leading banks in financing green technology projects now prefer to take a "wait and see" approach to minimize their risks. The key reason is that after financing the project banks' major concerns start and they have to make sure that the project does not encounter any technical delays or failures. Lack of any screening criteria or critical success factors makes evaluating the applications under green technology financing even more difficult for the banks.

Another challenge for the banks is the issue of human capital as the banks lack enough staffs familiar with the technical aspects of green technology projects, and thus, the banks should refer to external consultants for that matter. Despite a lack of technical knowledge concerning green technology projects, banks do not just reject the proposals outright. They will seek necessary expertise for evaluation of the projects. Nonetheless, according to the banks, referring to external consultants does not necessarily provide the banks with reliable information. In some cases, the actual experience of the banks has been different from the projected analysis of the consultants and this has caused difficulties for the banks. Some banks have agreed that there is a need for the banks to have their own experts in various aspects of green technology to assist them in evaluating GTFS applications.

15.4.3 Motivations

The key drivers for GTFS by Malaysian banks have been found to be related to secure financing packages, guarantees and support by the government, feasibility of the project falling within the financing criteria by the bank, interest subsidies obtained, and supporting government and the sustainability agenda. More specifically, the results of our analysis have revealed that the most significant motivation for GTFS, as perceived by banks, is the government guarantee. However, only 25% of the banks adhere to that. Moreover, 15% of the banks consider a feasible and viable project as the key incentive for GTFS, while only 9% of them find a bankable project to be financed as the pivotal driver for GTFS.

Most of the banks investigated appear to be profit-oriented. Other than the interest rate charged by the banks, they are mostly concerned about the viability of the proposed projects and are willing to finance the application if it is feasible and viable. Additionally, the 60% guarantee offered by the government seems to attract some of the banks. However, further discussion we conducted with the bankers revealed that they would be more willing to engage in green technology projects if a higher guarantee were to be provided by the government (Fig. 15.2).

15.4.4 Barriers

Most bankers consider the applicants as the source of barriers for green technology financing and they consider external environment to be the least impeding factor. More specifically, 49% of them perceive the applicant as the key source of impediments to green technology financing. Our findings have shown that the bankers perceive the issues related to both financial institutions and government to play equally important roles as barriers to green technology financing. Interestingly, the banks find the external environment to have the least role in impeding green technology financing.

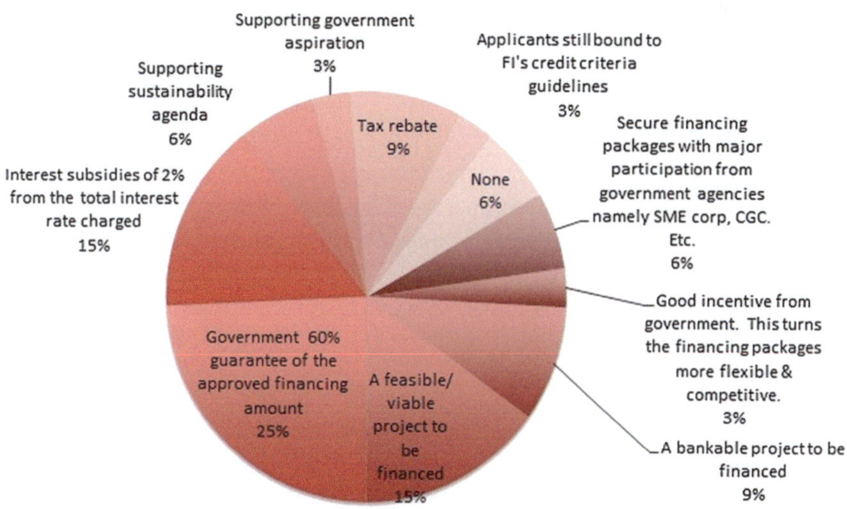

Fig. 15.2 Motivations for GTFS (Percentage)

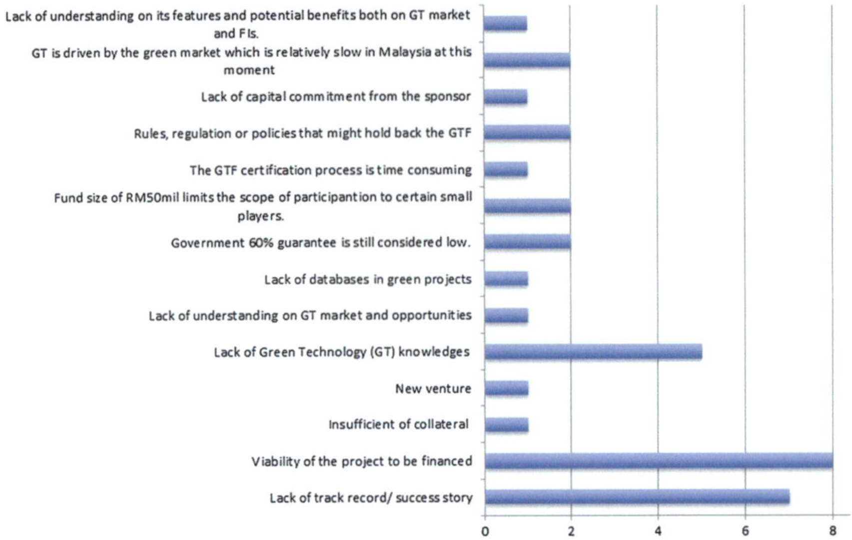

Fig. 15.3 Major barriers for GTFS

More specifically, we found that the top three major barriers to the success of green technology financing from the perspective of bankers include viability of the project to be financed, lack of track record/success study, and lack of knowledge of green technology. This indicates that in financing green technology projects, banks are mostly concerned about the viability of the project. Moreover, the lack of any success story of the similar projects in the past, coupled with the insufficient knowledge of the banks towards green technology financing, further discourages banks from financing these projects (Fig. 15.3).

15.5 Concluding Remarks

Despite targeting SMEs, green technology financing schemes appear to be more attractive to big players and larger companies have been interested to apply for GTFS in the past. The inclusion of large players in the scheme, coupled with the higher amount of investment required for some areas of green technology, requires greater funding capital, which is beyond the current limit supported by the government.

In the current study, a majority of representatives from the banking sector found green technology financing as a risky initiative for their corporation with little or no success story in the past to refer to. Hence, they mainly considered GTFS as a cost to their organizations. Assuming that these opinions by the bank representatives are a reflection of the organizations perceptions towards green technology financing, the high risks involved in the GTFS are the main restraining force for banks to demonstrate a tendency towards this financing scheme.

Since the major driving force for banks to finance any project was found to be monetary returns, according to force field analysis, banks will proactively involve in green technology financing when the driving forces far outweigh the restraining forces. Under current conditions, it appears that the negative forces (risks of financing green technologies and lack of any database for key success factors for green technology) are much higher than the potential benefits obtained from such activity (Fig. 15.4). Hence, banks do not become proactively involved in such a financing scheme and will entertain any application for GTFS similar to other loan applications without giving any priority to GTFS applications despite being a government initiative.

While the government intends to promote the development of green technologies through engaging small and medium-sized enterprises in this green initiative, the banks mainly consider GTFS as a new type of loan application involving huge risk for the banks, coupled with unreliable profit potential due to the immature market for green products. To create a market for these products, the bankers suggested encouraging customers, suppliers, and industry to use green products. This is where government may come into play to raise awareness and promote the usage/ consumption of green products, eventually enhancing the viability of green technology projects and increasing the likelihood of obtaining financing from the banks.

Based on the existing challenges in the efficient implementation of green technology financing scheme and inputs by the representatives from the banks and financial institutions, coupled with a comprehensive review of the literature and existing documents on GTFS, a number of suggestions for enhancing the scheme in future are provided in the following:

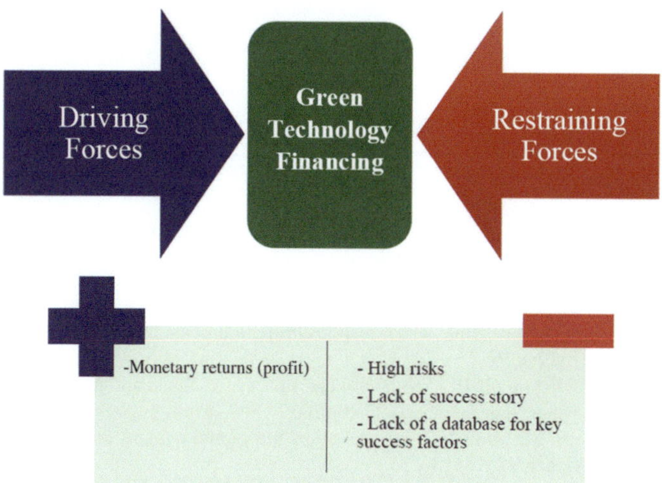

Fig. 15.4 Force field analysis for GTFS by financial institutions

- Making the certification process more efficient by ensuring the bank representatives in the evaluation meeting provide valuable guidance to applicants on how to consider and ensure their business viability.
- Increasing the fund size for GTFS projects and providing a more attractive guarantee or support by the government to encourage the engagement of more banks in green technology financing schemes.
- Formulating the key screening criteria and success factors to help banks assess GTFS applications.
- Training bankers on how to evaluate GTFS applications and addressing the issue of human capital for banks.
- Creating market readiness by encouraging customers, suppliers, and industry to use green products.

Banks are not only the recipient, but also the purveyors of socially responsible investments (Montgomery and Ramus 2003). Thus, they should look at GTFS as an opportunity to fulfil their responsibility towards community through financing and investing in responsible and green projects. Numerous authors have claimed that social and environmental issues may lead to opportunities to develop new financial products or to avoid hidden financial risks from related players. Additionally, it has been found that financial markets may play a key role in achieving the goals of sustainable development in both developed and developing countries (Dasgupta et al. 2001; Labatt et al. 2002; Lanoie et al. 1998).

Implementing corporate sustainability is a complex process requiring continuous internal embedding, human interactions, and understanding of the nature of sustainability (Basu and Palazzo 2008; Pfeffer 2010). As earlier studies have indicated the positive role of internal change agents in catalyzing role in sense-making processes to implement sustainability (Van der Heijden et al. 2010), it is essential to raise awareness in bank managers to proactively support green technology financing schemes in line with the banks efforts to implement corporate sustainability initiatives.

References

Ahmad MM, Ali RM, Inayat A, Yusupa S (2011) Potential development of hydrogen production from biomass in Malaysia: a brief perspective. Int J 2(1):45–50

Bassett R (2010) Time to catch up… qualitative research in child and adolescent psychiatry. J Can Acad Child Adolesc Psychiatry 19(1):2

Basu K, Palazzo G (2008) Corporate social responsibility: a process model of sensemaking. Acad Manag Rev 33(1):122–136

Climate Works Foundation (2010) From climate finance to financing green growth. Project Catalyst briefing paper. San Francisco, California

Dasgupta S, Laplante B, Mamingi N (2001) Pollution and capital markets in developing countries. J Environ Econ Manag 42(3):310–335

DOE (2010) Quarterly DOE update on environment, development and sustainability: IMPAK, issue 3. Department of Environment, Malaysia

DSD (2011) Occupational structure. Green Technology Industry: Department of Skill Development, Ministry of Human Resources, Malaysia
Economic Planning Unit (2010) 10th Malaysia plan, 2011–2015. Economic planning unit. Prime Minister's Department, Putrajaya
Economy Watch (2010) Banking industry. http://www.economywatch.com/banking. Accessed 10 July 2013
EUMCCI (2012) EUMCCI trade issues and recommendations 2012. EU-Malaysia Chamber of Commerce and Industry, Kuala Lumpur
Gerster R (2011) Striking a balance ahead of Rio+20 in 2012. Sustainable finance: achievements, challenges, outlook. Gerster Consulting, Switzerland
Ismail AZ (2010) Development of national green technology. Ministry of energy, Green technology and water, Malaysia
KeTTHA (2011) Green technology financing scheme. http://www.kettha.gov.my/en/content/green-technology-financing-scheme-gtfs. Accessed 10 July 2013
Labatt S, White RR (2002) Environmental finance: a guide to environmental risk assessment and financial products. Wiley
Lanoie P, Laplante B, Roy M (1998) Can capital markets create incentives for pollution control? Ecol Econ 26(1):31–41
Malaysia SME (2010) Where is the green money? Accessed 10 July 2013, from http://www.malaysiasme.com.my
Montgomery DB, Ramus CA (2003) Corporate social responsibility reputation effects on MBA job choice. A Research Note: Stanford Graduate School of Business, Stanford, CA
Mustapa SI, Leong YP, Hashim AH (2010) Issues and challenges of renewable energy development: a malaysian experience paper presented at the PEA-AIT. In: International conference on energy and sustainable development: issues and strategies (ESD 2010). Chiang Mai, Thailand
Razak N (2009) Launch of green technology policy speech, 24 July 2009. Retrieved 22 July 2013, from http://www.mylns.com.my/newsroom.php?id=2
Noh HJ (2010) Strategic approaches to develop green finance. Korea Capital Market Institute
Pfeffer J (2010) Building sustainable organizations: the human factor. Acad Manag Perspect 24(1):34–45
Rubin A, Babbie E (2005) Research methods for social work, 5th ed. Brooks/Cole-Thompson Learning, Belmont, CA
Van der Heijden A, Driessen PP, Cramer JM (2010) Making sense of corporate social responsibility: exploring organizational processes and strategies. J Clean Prod 18(18): 1787–1796
Whitley R, Crawford M (2005) Qualitative research in psychiatry. Can J Psychiat 50(2):108–114

Author Biographies

Azlan Amran started his career as a lecturer at the School of Management, Universiti Sains Malaysia in 2006. He is now a Professor at the Graduate School of Business in the same University. Prior to joining USM, he worked as an accountant for several years. He has published a significant number of articles in the area of CSR in both local and international journals. He is currently supervising Ph.D., MBA, and Masters candidates in CSR. At present, he holds the position of Dean at the Graduate School of Business. In terms of practical experience, he has been involved in several training and consultancy projects in Accounting-related issues and Corporate Social Reporting. He is currently holding several grants to support his research on CSR-related issues. He is also a member of the editorial board for several international journals. At the national level, he is a Technical Committee member for ISO 26000.

Mehran Nejati is a Senior Lecturer and the MBA Director in the School of Business and Law at the Edith Cowan University, Australia. He was a Visiting Scholar at Flinders Business School, Australia in 2015. He holds a Ph.D. in Management and is a Certified Six Sigma Green Belt by American Society for Quality. His main areas of research interest includes marketing, social responsibility, sustainability and ethics. He has published over 30 papers in peer-reviewed journals, indexed by Scopus and ISI, and ranked by ABDC.

Say Keat Ooi is a Lecturer at the Graduate School of Business (GSB), Universiti Sains Malaysia (USM). Previously he worked as manager in few pharmaceutical companies. His research area is in corporate social and environmental reporting, corporate social responsibility, and issues in corporate sustainability. He has published several papers in local and international journals.

Faizah Darus is a Professor of Accounting at the Faculty of Accountancy, Universiti Teknologi MARA (UiTM), Malaysia and a fellow of the Accounting Research Institute (ARI). She is currently the Head of the UiTM-ACCA Asia-Pacific Centre for Sustainability (APCeS), a collaborative research centre between UiTM and ACCA. She lectures at the Faculty of Accountancy and has taught various subjects at the post-graduate and under-graduate levels in the areas of Financial Reporting, Strategic Management and Company Secretarial Practice. She is also currently supervising Ph.D., Master by Research and Master by Coursework students in the area of financial reporting and corporate social responsibility (CSR). Professor Dr Faizah Darus obtained her Ph.D. in Accounting from Adelaide University, Australia, has an MBA from University of Arkansas, USA, a professional qualification from the Institute of Chartered Secretaries and Administrators (ICSA) UK and a bachelor degree in Accounting from Indiana University, Bloomington USA. Her primary research interest is in corporate reporting and her research projects cover areas of mandatory and voluntary disclosures in corporate reports, corporate social responsibility disclosures including from an Islamic perspective and in the area of corporate governance. She is a regular speaker at national and international conferences and has been invited to become a key-note speaker and conference panellist. She is the co-author of a book entitled Financial Accounting and Reporting in Malaysia. She is also the author and co-author of various chapters in books and has published numerous articles in international journals in the areas of financial reporting and CSR. She is currently an editorial board member for the journal Issues in Social and Environmental Accounting Journal (ISEA), issued by the Indonesia Centre for Social and Environmental Accounting Research and Development and a member of the ACCA shortlisting judges for the ACCA Malaysia Sustainability Reporting Awards (MasRA).

Chapter 16
The Issues that Accountants Need to Pay Attention to in Corporate Social Responsibility Projects

Ayşe Pamukçu and Ayça Akarçay Öğüz

16.1 Introduction

The developments experienced in the world removed the competition limits of the businesses with globalization and improvement of information technologies, and caused the businesses to consider the subjects contributing the development of the society rather than focusing solely on economic matters. Particularly, business does not focus only on production, sales, and profit dimensions in determination of their targets but they also became aware of the social and common dimensions.

Accounting is a science recording, classifying the financial transactions of businesses and taking the results obtained to the interest groups through financial statements. With this feature, accounting is considered as a language of a business insuring understanding of the business and classified as "language of business" in the literature (Dinç and Kaya 2006). One of the functions of accounting classified as the language of the business is to provide information to the interested parties. Accounting professional is to perform such presentation properly, objectively, and fairly. Such obligation expected from accounting function and the accounting professional may only be performed only with adoption of social responsibility concept. However, the rational decisions to be made by the applicable parties making the right judgments may insure the business to continue its operations to the best interests of the society and long life of the business. Also, such social responsibility principle laying at the foundation of accounting is available in all small or large businesses. Therefore, supporter and auditor of the social responsibility of the businesses in corporate sense is accounting function (Ateş and Senal 2012).

A. Pamukçu (✉) · A. A. Öğüz
Marmara University, Istanbul, Turkey
e-mail: apamukcu@marmara.edu.tr

A. A. Öğüz
e-mail: aakarcay@marmara.edu.tr

K. T. Çalıyurt and R. Said (eds.), *Sustainability and Social Responsibility of Accountability Reporting Systems*, Accounting, Finance, Sustainability, Governance & Fraud: Theory and Application, https://doi.org/10.1007/978-981-10-3212-7_16

16.2 Corporate Social Responsibility Concept

16.2.1 Definition of Corporate Social Responsibility Concept

Establishment of conscious consumer and investor, increase of environmental sensitivity, increase and forming of international standards with globalization, and insufficiency of the regulatory entities increased the expectations of the businesses of information age. This directed the businesses to change (Kelgökmen 2010). This change caused the necessity of consideration of environment, society, and communication with which businesses have communication rather than focusing on only economic results in performance of the operations of the business (Ersöz 2007). Although it is seen by us as an old concept as a result of such developments, it caused focusing on corporate social responsibility concept.

As the definitions related to social responsibility concept are reviewed, we see very different definitions made by the international entities, commissions, and academicians. Some of them are the following:

- The World Business Council for Sustainable Development defines social responsibility as liability to work in collaboration with the employees, families of the employees, and regional managements in order to establish a sustainable economic growth. Starting from this definition, it is seen that the only purpose of the businesses is not profit; rather, it includes social events increasing the welfare of each section with which it works together and is related (Jamali and Mirshak 2007).
- According to a definition made by the European Commission, corporate social responsibility is a concept that businesses may integrate the social and environmental issues with organizational operations and the interactions made with the social stakeholders on voluntarily basis (Commission of the European Communities 2007). Having social responsibility is not only performance of official expectations but investing in human capital, environment, and relations with shareholders, by going further from voluntarily.
- In terms of Turkey, CSR definition is included as per the Corporate Management Principles as defined by Capital Market Board as one of the international entities. In the report, it is requested to explain the information about the operations related to the environment, location, and public in general (Göcenoğlu and Girgin 2005). Corporate governance principles are defined with which businesses as quoted with Borsa Istanbul are required to comply and a reporting is requested for the shareholders and interest holders other than the operating reports of the businesses for compliance with such principles. In the Accounting System General Application Communiqué, social responsibility concept is emphasized. "Liability of accounting in performance of the function is defined and scope, meaning, lace and purpose of accounting are mentioned. Social responsibility concept means observance of the interests of the entire society not only certain

individuals and groups in issuance and presentation of the financial statement and execution of the accounting applications, and accounting organization, and accordingly acting truly, objectively and honestly in information production" (Accounting System Application general Communiqué Line No 1).

- In broader terms, corporate social responsibility is a concept with some meaning but not having the same meaning for everyone (Votav 1972). In another definition, corporate social responsibility is defined as the role of contributing better society and cleaner environment voluntarily for the organizations rather than the economic operations solely (Carroll 1999).
- Corporate social responsibility is ethical and responsible act of any organization to all stakeholders within and outside an organization, and may be defined as making decisions therefore and application (Aktan and Börü 2007).
- Social responsibility concept means that a company has social role in any area it operates. Pursuant to the scope of this concept, the subjects such as protection of the natural environment, provision of quality and trusted products, respecting the fundamental right and freedoms of the employees, provision of accurate and proper information related to operations, education, health, and art events to increase the welfare of the society may be considered as examples (Kaya 2005).
- In another definition, it is defined as undertaking that the company will minimize the harmful effect on the society or maximize the long-term benefits by eliminating such effect.
- In another definition, additions were made, and the social responsibility is defined as measurement of types of environmental, economic, and social effects of various acts against the social stakeholders, and realization of the transactions to mitigate the negative effects occurred and to contribute development of the society and business above all (Chandler 2003).

When the definitions related to corporate social responsibility concept are reviewed, it is seen that it has different meanings for different groups, sectors, and stakeholders. The subject agreed upon by all is that businesses assume greater role beyond making employment and welfare in global economy. The aim of the businesses is not only to provide the shareholders with profit, employees with salary, and consumers with products and service, but also to protect the social and environmental problems and values (Ersöz 2007: 17). Voluntariness of the businesses in addition to bearing obligations, their honesty, and being responsible against the stakeholders are the common points of the definitions (Balı and Cinel 2011).

16.2.2 Historical Development of Social Responsibility Concept

Where the historical development of corporate social responsibility concept is reviewed, the industry revolution is considered as a start and economic crash in 1929 is considered as one of the most important turning points. The reason therefore is that size of businesses conducting commercial operations prior to the industry revolution was too small operated by the owner only. The responsibility understanding of these small businesses was embodied pursuant to the beliefs, values, and ethical views prescribed by their religions (Alparslan and Aygün 2013).

The developments such as industry revolution, increase in capital accumulation, development of production policies, and transition to serial production caused the businesses to play effective role in social, political, economic, and legal area (Turkey KSS Association Bulletin). The businesses worked to increase production and profits continuously and used the resources without any care acting solution oriented solely in realization thereof, broke the natural balance and environmental pollution. Not only the losses were caused, but also human right violations occurred by disregarding the employees (Alparslan and Aygün 2013).

The economic crisis in 1929 taught that maximization of the profits of the businesses solely does not bring welfare and improvement of society. Social and cultural changes were occurred in all industrialized societies including the USA above all (Ataman 2001). In this new order, for prevention of the heavy damages from the businesses to the environment and society, the laws were made regulating environment, human rights, and commercial subjects, and businesses started to act in compliance with the idea that such subjects are as important as profit and efficiency, acting in compliance with such laws (Alparslan and Aygün 2013).

The labor rights experienced in the 1960s and 1970s, consumer rights protection acts, product boycotts, and environmentalist movements were the indications that the society's expectations from businesses were changed. However, in such years, they tended not to agree their harmful effects on the environment (Emhan 2007). From 1980s, businesses showed more sensitivity against the environmental problems and acted to perform their financial obligations in addition to some voluntarily activities (Aktan and Börü 2007). In 2000, the corporate social responsibility was institutionalized and most notable large-sized companies undersigned Global Principles Contract. In global social responsibility area, businesses were established to provide the businesses with advisory services in social responsibility operations (Ayhan 2009).

16.2.3 Corporate Social Responsibility Approaches

There are two different economic approaches related to corporate social responsibility understanding. One of them is the classical approach setting forth that the sole objective of the businesses is to make profit. And the second one is modern approach claiming that the objective of the businesses is to make profit in addition to protection and development of the welfare of the society (Yılmaz Sert 2012).

16.2.3.1 Classical Approach

The fundamental of the classical approach was established with the invisible hand concept mentioned by Adam Smith and further improved by Milton Friedman to give it the final form. He considers the extra social expenditures as unnecessary since they will be useful for the welfare of the entire society as a result of the efforts to increase the earnings and decrease the losses of the individuals, producers, or consumers (Yılmaz Sert 2012). According to the famous economist Friedman, the liability of the businesses is solely against their shareholders; it is explained as "businesses have sole and only liability, and it is to conduct operations to increase profitability by using the economic resources as long as they are included in the rules of a game based on open and free competition without any fraud and manipulation" (Aktan and Börü 2007). It alleges that businesses do not have any social responsibility but the individuals do, and only social responsibility of a business to make profit (Polat 2009).

16.2.3.2 Modern Approach

Modern approach is occurred from the defects of classical approach considering the business as liable solely against its shareholders and considered as separate from its surrounding. At the foundation of the modern approach, environment exists. According to this opinion, no corporation "shall leave any poisonous wastes to any ground or surface water resource; rather, it shall produce in peace with the ecologic structure, made all elements in the internal and external environment aware for social responsibility aspect, improve education/training opportunities internally and externally, and act responsibly for all problems of the employees (Çelik 2007).

Modern approach is considered as that the priority social responsibility of the businesses is maximization of the profits, as mentioned in the classical approach. Modern approach goes one further step ahead and includes the activities such as conducting performance measurements for businesses and controlling the business operations in addition to protection and development of the social welfare occurred at the development phases of social responsibility (Top and Öner 2008).

16.2.3.3 Corporate Social Responsibility Reporting

While businesses provide with information to their stakeholders, they attempt to define the financial reports by including non-financial indicators and name such reports as "social report," "sustainability report," or "social responsibility report." With these reports, economic, social, and environmental performances are revealed.

As a result of the developments occurred, although the government and competent authorities encouraged businesses for voluntary reporting, they have been recently substituted with legal obligation. It is an indicator that the number of reports will increase every day.

16.3 Liabilities of Accounting in Social Responsibility Projects

Social responsibility concept of accounting as per the Accounting System General Application Communiqué specifies the liability of accounting in performance of its function and indicates the scope, meaning, place, and purpose of accounting. Social responsibility concept means observance of the interests of the entire society not only certain individuals and groups in issuance and presentation of the financial statement and execution of the accounting applications, and accounting organization, and accordingly acting truly, objectively and honestly in information production.

Accounting practices should be conducted with social responsibility consciousness as per the public disclosure principle. As the accounting performs social responsibility duty, it performs more extensive liability than the legal liability, assuming the duty of acting as an instrument needed for reaching the objectives of social framework. Although accounting produces and reports financial information related to businesses, it establishes effects interested to all sections of the society for its financial consequences. The base relied by accounting in performance of such duty fully is the fundamental guiding corporate liability understanding.

It is obvious that businesses perform social liabilities as per the corporate governance principles. The social responsibility concept of accounting and the corporate governance principles serve for the same purpose. In this sense, American Institute of Certified Public Accountants (AICPA) draws the framework of the social responsibilities with the professional behavior principles and rules (e.g., acting independent and objective, observing public benefits, performance of professional liabilities fairly, working pretentiously as per the resources during the production process of accounting information, keeping the customer information) (http://www.turmob.org.tr).

Since the practitioner of all transactions in accounting in the work flow from issuance of the documents through reporting is accountant, the social responsibility of accounting is also the social responsibility of the accounting simultaneously.

16.3.1 Contribution of the Accountant to the Economic Liabilities of the Business

Businesses establish the cornerstones of country economy, and they also have functions such as performance of the activities such as profitability, growth, and service to the society as the fundamental purposes. Increase of financial performances of the businesses shall be effective on increase of their social performance as well in time. And this will insure businesses to perform their corporate social liabilities more effectively (Güneş and Otlu 2002).

Accounting is the key assistant of the managers in execution and auditing of the operations of the business. The information received from accounting and the information developed through analysis of the accounting information underlie the business decisions. Reality of the decisions to be made by the businesses depends on refection of factual situation by the accounting data. The specialization of the parties utilizing the accounting due to differences in accounting applications (e.g., private sector, government, university, professionals and others) on the standards on which accounting practices must rely. Acceptance of the laws regulating the accounting profession in the world and the need of the groups using the accounting information for standardization in information became obvious. Accounting standards define how the accounts should be illustrated and insure preparation of the company reports at certain standards for international borders, cultures, and different times. The fundamental approach in standardization and international harmonization applications is obtainment of economic reality.

16.3.2 Contribution of the Accountant to the Legal Obligations of Business

Accounting provides with the largest contribution to the management information system of the business about the application of the provisions of the tax, debt, trade, negotiable papers, social security, and environment, etc., laws in all areas from establishment of a business till its liquidation or termination. Financial accounting as a branch of accounting provide the data from unique resources and offer it to the applicable parties in a form to show economic and financial structure of the business tax accounting prepares returns/declarations, forms, statements, approval reports on tax etc. subjects under the applicable laws and offers such to the applicable units and managements. Tax is transfer of resource from private sector to public sector. Accounting is the function of business insuring production of tax figures properly, and accountants are professionals assuming significant duties in collection of taxes. The consciousness of the business that payment of taxes would be to the best interests of the public and even to the best interests of the business is a requirement of social responsibility concept of the business. Accounting and accountant have significant role in payment of the taxes of the business and applicable individuals related to the business properly. Assistance by the accounting and accountant for payment of the taxes fully and their routing businesses to payment of taxes properly are obligatory for the best interests of the national economy and the society.

In listing the duties of the accountant in ethical rules issued by International Federation of Accountants (IFAC) and translated into Turkish by TÜRMOB (Union of Chambers of Turkish Independent Accountants Financial Advisors and Sworn Financial Advisors), his behaviors related to legal regulations are explained. According to such, in preparation of the balance sheet and income statements of a business and in determination of financial profit, it should be noted that accounting system and accountant of a business are obligated to consider the tax benefits provided to the business and protect or take advantage of such benefits as they are obligated to comply with the provisions of the tax laws on prevention of decrease in the taxes (http://www.turmob.org.tr).

16.3.3 Contribution of Accountant to the Ethical Responsibilities of Business

Ethic is seen as a feature required to be observed in each individual living in the society. In the analysis of the ethic, it is seen that the characteristics of the individual come from with his gene by hereditary, his growth type, education, and society in which he lives have significant roles have significant roles in formation of the ethical properties of an individual (Yıldırım and Çukacı 2002).

Ethic is the entire moral, principle and values related to which is wrong and which is right in the behaviors of an individual or a group (Yıldırım and Çukacı 2002). In comparison with these two concepts, it is seen that ethic is more extensive expression covering the term "moral." Accounting as one of the business functions is an instrument playing critical role of trust-based communication between the business and the applicable parties. The information produced as a result of accounting studies reflects the economical and financial structure of the business. Therefore, accounting practitioners is to have and be well aware of high ethical standards in their relations with the applicable parties in production of the information and should be liable to protect such standards (Yıldırım and Tek 2004). According to the directives accepted in the European Union, consolidated financial statements are required to reflect assets, liabilities, financial situations of all partners subject to consolidation and their profits and losses truly, properly, and fairly (Yılmaz 2001).

With the Independent Accounting, Independent Accountant Financial Advisory and Sworn Financial Advisory Law No 3568 issued in the Official Gazette number 21094 dd. 13.06.1989 in Turkey and the regulation on Working methods of the Independent Accountants, Financial Advisors and Sworn Financial Advisors issued in the Official Gazette No 20391 dd. 03.01.1990 reveal the general standards of accounting profession in written. By the headings (Büyükbalkan 1998).

- Professional Title and Competency Principle;
- Professional Education and Information;
- Integrity, Reliability, and Objectiveness;
- Keeping Secrets;
- Liability;
- Independence;
- Avoiding Act of Unfair Competition.

16.3.4 Situation of Professional Ethic in the USA

When it is checked the principles for the professional conducting the same operations in the United States in which the social honor of accounting profession is grown, and professional laws and principles are adopted fully;

(a) American Institute of Certified Public Accountants (AICPA) Professional Conduct Code Principles (Yıldırım and Çukacı 2002: 17)

- Liabilities: Operations should not be broken for the benefit or against any of the parties knowing that professionals working independently are at arms' length to all of individuals, colleagues, and public.
- Public interests: Public interests are observed as a result of the operations, and occurrence of the adverse situations to the general economy should be prevented.
- Honesty is to five the idea of that the right of all responsible parties would not be changed for any reason whatsoever, to the responsible parties, and to provide required trust to them.
- Objectiveness and independence: Although work is conducted in consideration of some remuneration, the professional is to act objectively in its operations considering that he would be independent during the work process.
- Prudent working: He conducts the activities responsibly in a manner not to cause any burden to any of the parties, having the technical information pursuant to the consciousness from the professional ethic.
- Scope and nature of the service provided: Choosing the nature and scope of the work considering the professional conduct in preferring the services to be provided by the professionals, other than those indicated under the laws.

(b) AICPA Professional Conduct Law Rules (Yıldırım and Çukacı 2002)

- Independence: The professional is to conduct by considering that his works are not conducted exclusively for one of the parties or the government.
- Integrity and objectiveness: In performance of the accounting activities, the effects of any of the groups or individuals should not be assumed without involvement in any conflict of interests, so that the financial structure of the business will be reflected as is.
- Compliance with general standards: Certain plan should be observed by showing the required professional sensitivity, reached to professional competence as per the existing laws.
- Compliance with standards: It should be acted as per the standards agreed by the professional association, in performance of the activities by the professional.
- Accounting principles and compliance therewith: Professionals should act in accordance with the generally Accepted Accounting Concepts and Principles in performance of the accounting operations.
- Confidentiality of the customer information: Economical or accounting information occurred as a result of the operations of the customer for whom the work

is conducted should not be disclosed to any individual or entity outside the business; rather such information should be kept as confidential.

- Conditional fee: The fee should be agreed at the beginning of the works after determination of the nature of the works to be conducted, not at the end of the works (provided such would be within the upper and lower limits set).
- Act not complying with professional honor: The professionals should avoid any act which may not be complied with professional honor considering their reputation and honor of the profession in the future, along with the general reputation of their colleagues as responsible individuals.
- Prohibition of advertisement: No customer is to be obtained by giving exaggerated or misleading information or by using anything as pressure on such customer.
- Commission and advisory fees: The professional should not act as an intermediary in return of some consideration, for provision of any goods or product or service excluding his own areas of operation.
- Professional title and execution method: In order that the powers granted under the applicable laws would be used, no other title is to be used other than the professional title.

16.3.5 Contribution of the Accountant to the Voluntary Liabilities of the Business

New understanding and approaches in management, improvements in data processing technology, growth of businesses, decision-making process brought new dimensions to collection accumulation and processing transactions of information required for performance of planning and control functions. Today, the information requirement of the business management is not limited to the information obtained from the traditional accounting data, and quite different information is needed for the business operations. Although accounting information system does not provide all of them, they are able to provide significant part thereof (Haftacı and Soylu 2008).

Groups outside the corporation not satisfied with the traditional reports or disclosures, in parallel to the rapidly improving natural environment consciousness, require reports from businesses including environment subjects. Businesses provide regular information as to the environmental activities conducted by them, and they indicate the financial information as well (Yarbaşı 1998). Accounting system has significant obligations in settlement of the environmental problems. As per the social responsibility principle as one of the fundamental concepts of the accounting, the accounting and the accountant are obligated to contribute the settlement of the environmental problems. It is required for the business to perform significant activities on prevention of environmental pollution and protection of the environment. Using the healthy data and information as the foundation of the operations is the most important element insuring success of the operation. In this process, accounting produces significant data and information. It may be stated easily that there are operations to be conducted on accounting area relayed to environmental protection due to the social responsibility of accounting and its other duties brought by the current developments (Haftacı and Soylu 2008).

16.4 Conclusion

Corporate social responsibility is a necessary concept insuring the business to contribute better society and cleaner environment voluntarily for the organizations rather than the economic operations solely. Corporate social responsibility is a scene on which the business operates in a manner meeting the ethical, legal, commercial, and public expectations of the society. Corporate social responsibility shall mean the relation of the entity with all stakeholders. Such stakeholders are consumers, employees, public, owners/investors, government, suppliers, and competitors. It is understood explicitly that a business is not liable to only its shareholders but all other individuals. Social responsibility of the businesses may be classified as economic responsibilities, legal responsibilities, ethical responsibilities, and voluntary responsibilities.

Accounting applications are required to be conducted with social responsibility consciousness in line with the public disclosure principle. As the accounting performs social responsibility duty, it performs more extensive liability than the legal liability, assuming the duty of acting as an instrument needed for reaching the objectives of social framework. Although accounting produces and reports financial information related to businesses, it establishes effects interested to all sections of the society for its financial consequences. The base relied by accounting in performance of such duty fully is the fundamental guiding corporate liability understanding.

Today, due to increasing competition between the businesses, differentiation of a business from the others is embodied with the dealing of the business with corporate social responsibility concept. The benchmark of success in measuring the operating results of a business is not solely profit; rather, its activities in corporate social responsibility are also considered as important.

Accounting as one of the fundamental functions of a business should consider the corporate social responsibility understanding as the base, and the accounting practitioners should adopt such consciousness. In performance of such obligation, the accountant should provide with contribution to the economic, legal, ethical, and voluntary responsibilities of the business.

References

1 Sıra No.lu Muhasebe Sistemi Uygulama Genel Tebiği Resmi Gazete No. 21447 (Accounting System Application general Communiqué Line No 1)

Aktan CC, Börü D (2007) Kurumsal Sosyal Sorumluluk. In: Aktan CC (ed) *Kurumsal Sosyal Sorumluluk*. İktisadi Girişim ve İş Ahlakı Derneği Yayınları, İstanbul, pp 11–36

Alparslan A, Aygün M (2013) Kurumsal Sosyal Sorumluluk ve Firma Performansı. Süleyman Demirel Üniversitesi İİBF Dergisi 18(1):435–448

Ataman G (2001) İşletme Yönetimi: Temel Kavramlar & Yeni Yaklaşımlar. Türkmen Kitabevi, İstanbul

Ateş BA, Senal S (2012) Kurumsal Sosyal Sorumluluk Kapsamında Muhasebenin Sosyal Sorumluluğu: Süleyman Demirel Üniversitesi'nde Bir Araştırma. Çukurova Üniversitesi İİBF Dergisi 16(1):71–85

Ayhan B (2009) Siyasal İktisat ve Kurumsal Sosyal Sorumluluk. Yönetim Araştırmaları Dergisi 9 (2):173–187

Balı S, Cinel MO (2011) Bir Rekabet Aracı Olarak Kurumsal Sosyal Sorumluluk. ODTÜ Sosyal Bilimler Enstitüsü Sosyal Bilimler Araştırmaları Dergisi 2(4):45–60

Büyükbalkan U (1998) Serbest Muhasebecilik, Serbest Muhasebeci Mali Müşavirlik ve Yeminli Mali Müşavirlik Mevzuatı, TÜRMOB Yayınları, Yayın No: 46, Ankara, 88

Carroll AB (1999) Corporate social responsibility evolution of a definitional construct. Bus Soc 38 (3):268–295

Çelik A (2007) Şirketlerin Sosyal Sorumlulukları.Kurumsal sosyal sorumluluk. İşletmeler ve Sosyal Sorumluluk. In: Aktan CC (ed) Kurumsal Sosyal Sorumluluk. İktisadi Girişim ve İş Ahlakı Derneği Yayınları, İstanbul, pp 61–84

Chandler G (2003) The evolution of business and human rights debate. In: Rory S (ed) Business and human rights. Greenleaf Publishing, London

Commission of the European Communities (2007) European Parliament Resolution of 13 March on Corporate Social Responsibility. Retrieved from www.europarl.europa.eu/sides. Accessed on 4th Mar 2016

Dinç E, Kaya U (2006) Muhasebe Meslek Mensuplarının "Meslek Ahlak Kuralları" Açısından Hizmet Satın Alanlar Tarafından Algılanma Biçimi Üzerine Bir Araştırma. Muhasebe ve Denetime Bakış Dergisi (MUFAD) 5(17):139–151

Emhan A (2007) Başarılı İşletmelerin Sosyal Sorumluluk Kavramına Bakış Açısı. Elektronik Sosyal Bilimler Dergisi 6(22):247–258. Accessed on http://www.esosder.org. On 5th Apr 2016

Ersöz HY (2007) Türkiye'de Kurumsal Sosyal Sorumluluk Anlayışının Gelişiminde Meslek ve Sivil Toplum Kuruluşlarının Faaliyetleri, Rol ve Önemleri. İstanbul Ticaret OdasıYayınları, İstanbul, Yayın No. 2007-36

Göcenoğlu C, Girgin ZK (2005) Kurumsal Yönetişimin Türkiye'deki Kurumsal Sosyal Sorumluluk Uygulamalarına Etkileri. IV. Orta Anadolu İşletmecilik Kongresi, TOBB Ekonomi Teknoloji Üniversitesi, 13–14 Mayıs 2005, Ankara, 72–79

Güneş R, Otlu F (2002) Muhasebe Uygulayıcılarının Sosyal Sorumluluk Anlayışı Üzerine Bir Araştırma, Türkiye XXI. Muhasebe Eğitimi Sempozyumu, Bodrum-Muğla, 3

Haftacı V, Soylu K (2008). Çevresel Bilgilerin Muhasebesi ve Raporlanması, Kocaeli Üniversitesi Sosyal Bilimler Enstitüsü Dergisi, Sayı 15, 94

Jamali D, Mirshak R (2007) Corporate social responsibility (CSR): theory and practice in a developing country context. J Business Ethics 72:243–262

Kaya S (2005, Temmuz) İşletmelerde Sosyal Sorumluluk ve SA 8000 (Social Accountability) Standardı. İzmir Ticaret Odası Bülteni, 15–20. http://www.izto.org.tr/portals. Accessed on 29 July 2016

Kelgökmen D (2010) İşletmelerin Kurumsal Sosyal Sorumluluk Düzeylerinin Belirlenmesine Yönelik Bir Literatür Taraması. Ege Akademik Bakış 10(1):303–318

Polat KE (2009) Üniversite Öğrencilerinin Sosyal Sorumluluk Algılamaları: Biga İİBF Birinci Ve Dördüncü Sınıf Öğrencileri Üzerinde Yapılan Bir Araştırma. VI. Uluslararası Sivil Toplum Kuruluşları Kongresi Bildiriler Kitabı 147–155

Top S, Öner A (2008) İşletme Perspektifinden Sosyal Sorumluluk Teorisinin İncelenmesi. ZKÜ Sosyal Bilimler Dergisi 4(7):97–110

Türkiye KSS Derneği Bülteni (Ağustos 2008) Turkish Association of Corporate Social Responsibility (August 2008). Retrieved from http://kssd.org/wp-content/uploads/2013/04/2008_Agustos.pdf. Accessed on 15th June 2016

Votav D (1972) Genius became rare: a comment on the doctrine of social responsibility. California Manag Rev 15(2):25–31

Yarbaşı E (1998) Çevre-İşletme-Maliyet İlişkilerinin Mali Durum Tablolarına Yansıtılması. Yayınlanmamış Doktora Tezi, Marmara Üniversitesi Sosyal Bilimler Enstitüsü, İstanbul

Yıldırım O, Çukacı YC (2002) Muhasebe Sürecinde Kamuyu Aydınlatma Açısından Muhasebe Meslek Elemanının Davranışlarının Etik Boyutu ve İzmir İlinde Bir Uygulama, Türkiye XXI. Muhasebe Eğitimi Sempozyumu, Bodrum-Muğla, 6–18

Yıldırım O, Tek N (2004) Finansal Muhasebe, Birleşik Matbaacılık, İzmir, 16–20

Yılmaz F (2001) Avrupa Birliğinde Muhasebe Uygulamalarında Gelişmeler. XX Türkiye Muhasebe Eğitimi Sempozyumu, Antalya, p 199

Yılmaz Sert N (2012) Türkiye'de Özel Sektörün Kurumsal Sosyal Sorumluluk Anlayışına İlişkin Yarar Algısı: Kurumsal Sosyal Sorumluluk Faaliyetlerinin Duyurulmasında Web Sitelerinin Kullanılması. Online Acad J Informat Technol 3(9):31–50

Author Biographies

Ayşe Pamukçu She is currently a faculty member in the Faculty of Business Administration at Marmara University. She received her B.A. in Business Administration, M.A. in Accounting and Finance, and Ph.D. in Accounting and Finance from Marmara University. She teaches courses on financial, corporate, tax accounting at both the under graduate and graduate levels. Her research interests include tax, audit, international financial accounting standards, firm valuation, auditing and fraud.

Ayça Akarçay Öğüz She is associated professor in Marmara University She has received her B.A. in Economics, M.A. in Accounting and Finance, and Ph.D. in Accounting and Finance from Marmara University. She is currently a faculty member in the Faculty of Business Administration at Marmara University. She teaches courses on financial, corporate, bank and public accounting at both the undergraduate and graduate levels. Her research interests include international financial accounting standards, sustainability reporting, auditing and fraud. She is an active member of the Institute of Internal Auditing - Turkey and the Supervisory Board of Nihad Sayar Education Foundation.

Chapter 17
Sustainability in Personnel Performance Auditing: Case from Turkey

Mehmet Ali Hatikler and Kıymet Tunca Çalıyurt

17.1 Introduction

Transformation, having started within public management systems, has also been the triggering factor to many reforms in our country. The new understanding targeted establishment of a more efficient, more productive, and accountable type of public management directed to adaptation of the existing structure and functioning to contemporary conditions. In this context, the new understanding, aiming efficiency, effectiveness, productivity and economy brought new applications along with itself. By adopting good governance principles through Public Financial Management and Control Law No. 5018 (Law), Turkey started the transition process to corporate governance which is the contemporaneous approach in public management in year 2006. By enactment of the aforementioned law, corporate governance concepts like responsibility, transparency, accountability, and equity to start with and new terms like internal audit and internal control joined public sphere. The projection of performance audit has become another newness. With a holistic and comprehensive approach, performance-based working principles in all areas, from strategic planning to budgeting and from usage of resources to personnel regime, are brought, and the measurement of the performance became the basis.

Within this modern and contemporary public management understanding, the aforementioned law is considered to become one of the most important factors impacting personnel's success and productivity; thus, public servants' performance started becoming a systematic research area. Performance evaluation as a

M. A. Hatikler
Ministry of Justice, Ankara, Turkey

K. T. Çalıyurt (✉)
Faculty of Business Administration and Economics,
Trakya University, Edirne, Turkey
e-mail: kiymetcaliyurt@trakya.edu.tr

K. T. Çalıyurt and R. Said (eds.), *Sustainability and Social Responsibility of Accountability Reporting Systems*, Accounting, Finance, Sustainability, Governance & Fraud: Theory and Application, https://doi.org/10.1007/978-981-10-3212-7_17

managerial tool is used to distinguish between successful and unsuccessful personnel, to determine training needs of the personnel, and to increase work performance. The main objective of performance management is providing quality service by improving the organization's productivity, efficiency, and frugality, as expected by the new public management understanding. By finding the opportunity to give feedback, this system aims at the improvement of performance and enhancement of the personnel, by having established a process of performance measurement based on fair and standard criteria and through an efficient communication mechanism. However, there is not any performance management system within Turkish public personnel regime. This system aims to improve the personnel and his performance by reviewing his success with fair and standardized criteria, giving feedback to individuals by creating an effective communications process and having the chance of observing and reviewing the behavior, knowledge, and skill of the personnel. However, there does not exist a performance management system that is in effect with the civil servant regime in Turkey. Furthermore, only a limited number of studies can be reached in the national literature. For this reason, the purpose of this study is determined to be theoretically reviewing the performance management and audit system in Turkey and doing case analysis by measuring the perception of personnel who are working in a rural organization which is attached to public administration.

17.2 Public Financial Management and Control Law No. 5018 within the Frame of Good Governance Applications

17.2.1 Good Governance: Conceptual Research

The critical success factor for the public sector can be defined as the rate of its ability to achieve its objectives (Bolton 2003: 21). In this sense, alongside global changes, the first condition for a public sector to be deemed successful appears to be the application of good management. For this reason, in this section of the study the definition of good management is established and the term is clarified.

Good management, governance, or corporate governance can be defined as a combination of structures and processes that are applied with the purpose of reporting, directing, managing, and observing the activities of the institution which is aimed at reaching the goals of the institution. Governance which reflects a comprehensive style of management appears as a concept that includes the interaction between government–private and non-governmental, within–outside of the government, national–international organizations, and actors. Thus, the classical management understanding which is identified with the government gave its place to governance that emphasizes participation and which organizes the interactional ties between social, executive, and political actors (Topcu 2013).

The new understanding of management advocates to reduce and narrow the public management and the public field of activity starting from the ones that are economical, and secondly, in these fields that are reduced, to manage the public activities according to management techniques and the market system of the private sector. Strategies such as privatization, decentralization, delegation, outsourcing, and public–private sector collaborations that improve the corporate performance and reduce the productivity and performance crisis of the public are emphasized. Toward the end of the 90s, in the report that the World Bank has prepared, two base strategies were determined to provide effectiveness of the activities that are undertaken by the government: The first one is to limit the role of the government to improve the effectiveness and effective use of resources; the second one is to reinforce the capacity of the government. Because of this reason, the need to restructure in a way that will increase the performance of the public personnel was underlined.

In this context, approaches such as providing effectiveness by reinforcing the capacity using the way of institutional change, defining boundaries and rules that the government itself will obey, providing a competitive environment within and without government institutions, and increasing the participation of the voters came into prominence. Furthermore, a structure should be formed contrary to the traditional approach where the social services are provided by institutions which distance themselves from market discipline and the price mechanism and the financial discipline is provided by the various processes during budgeting by central controls. According to this, while giving financial objectives about presenting goods and services of a certain quality to these institutions, the authority of the superintendants of these institutions should be reinforced with flexible management in order to reach those financial goals.

It can be expressed in the business sector that the understanding of *new public management* is taking place, rather than being budget and input oriented, focusing on the results and from the bureaucratic processes to active management, from control to expansion of authority, from monopoly to competition, from standardized services that are offered to individuals to services that shape accordingly the necessity, and from being organization oriented to being service oriented. In this context, the main objectives of the new public management are to ensure productivity, to make the political management system work better, and to make significant changes in the system by being focused on the process, having limited control, having administrative autonomy, more clarity, delegation, and contracting. The main priority to reach these goals is given to the management of people, resources, and programs rather than the management of activities, procedures, and adjustments. In this sense, it mentions the need for each institution to create its own culture to counter the existence of traditional centralized controls that effect the management of financial capacity of the institutions negatively. The differences between traditional and new public management are gathered in the six titles below (Guy and Wright 1996: 630–638).

- The thought of public management being self-sufficient is replaced by the codependency and completion of the public and the private sector.
- Methods such as simple organizations, authorizing the lower ranks, teamwork, and total quality management replace the hierarchical/bureaucratic organization method.
- Monotony and centralism are replaced by decentralization, differentiation, and flexibility.
- The model that required bureaucrats to be absolutely partial to and separate from politicians left its place to the interaction of the politician and the bureaucrat.
- Human resources management and wage policies that value individual performance, success, or failures replace the classical personnel regime that bases itself on the position of the civil servant.
- Upward responsibility is deemed inadequate, and citizen satisfaction and performance supervision are in effect.

Finland's Department of Finance almost talks about GPRA when explaining the reform plan of their government: "…effective, correctly proportioned and high quality policy management is for the benefit of all of us. Such an understanding of services will increase the trust of the citizens towards the state because it will increase the decision making capacity. In this respect the state being active has emerged as an obligation in today's globalization environment. In this context, Finland has to provide the vital competitive power" (Kanerva 1994). It is seen that in the USA, there has been progress about audit toward the 1990s. Those years were the period where multinational corporations increased in number, big companies improved, and taxation became more important. In this period where corporate investors and professional managers became more proficient, the understanding of sustainable competition was also seen in the context of auditing.

The increasing importance of corporate management principles has widened the shareholder group in commercial companies' portfolio in terms of accountability and took a shape that consists of shareholders, stockholders, investors, fund providers, customers, suppliers, public organizations, and the general public. The liability of accountability has also increased with the widening of the scope of social responsibilities. Furthermore, information technologies improved, and trust toward statistical applications increased. The risk-centered approach has taken a step forward in independent audit; research has been done about customers and the strong and weak points of the company and the sector; analytical observations have been made to determine the risk of audit; the dependability of the internal control system has been tested. In USA, public institutions are subject to the rules of Government Performance and Results Act (GPRA, 1993). The Office of Management and Budget reviews the budget request of institutions depending on their performance.

17.3 Good Governance in Turkey

The new public management suggests the state to be shrunk and public management to operate in this shrunk area in an effective manner. In this context, the new public management understanding emphasizes on the similarities between the private and public sector, rather than the differences and defends the values, methods, and techniques that are successfully used in the private sector to be transferred to the public sector. In this direction, in public institutions and organizations transitions to applications such as being customer centered, total quality management, strategical management, and performance management are made.

As shown briefly above, the public management system in our country is in a process of reconstruction. Within the scope of restructuring of public management in Turkey, Public Financial Management and Control Law No. 5018, Metropolitan Municipalities Law No. 5216, and Municipal Law No. 5272 are passed and enacted. However, Fundamental Principles of Public Management and Restructuring of Public Management Law No. 5227 has not been passed.

While localization, governance, privatization, and marketization as basic concepts of the conversion of Turkish public management come to the forefront, the concepts of business administration, like market, customer, human resources, performance, and strategy, are imbedded into public management discipline and organization (Karci 2008).

17.4 Modern Approach in Public Administration

Since the end of 1970s with the erosion of the traditional understanding of state, other values and principles that possess this understanding have been criticized and questioned. The welfare state which is built upon a new understanding about the role of the state on social and economical fields with the coming of this period created an environment in which the private sector is taken as a role model and the state restructured and shrunk as a result of public spending getting out of control and becoming unsustainable because of economical crisis (Balci and Kirilmaz 2015). The criticisms which focus on the public sector, the changes in economy and politics theories, the increasing importance of individuals and civil society, and finally the improvements in public sector management, with the added effect of financial crisis, emerged a significant paradigm shift in the field of public management in the beginning of the 1980s. This change refers to the structure of the state, its field of activity, society, individuals and market relations, service methods, the role of personnel and their status, in short a comprehensive and radical restructuring process in the relations of public sector with its environment, rather than a simple reform or a partial transformation in management style (Eryilmaz 2010).

States that are organized according to the centralized system in the competitive environment that is caused by globalization face numerous problems when they perform their public services. The basis of the need to change which appeared in the entirety of our public management system is to use public resources effectively, efficiently, and economically in accordance with the strategical objectives and goals, as well as providing flexibility, accountability, and transparency in activities.

17.5 Public Financial Management and Control Law

The legislation about public management has become dated and complicated. This situation causes public services progress slowly because of correspondences, some services being carried out by multiple institutions or organizations with different applications or some services become unattended. This also affects auditing in a negative way, effectivity disappears in auditing due to lack of legislature and efficiency, and quality cannot be established because of the confusion between units (Gülhan 2003: 121).

In light of the recent developments in the globe, the understanding of management changes and public management continuously renews itself. Turkish public management lags behind the changes that happened in the 1990s in the world. The bulky bureaucratic structure and management mentality which fell behind global developments can be pointed as the culprit of the economical problems and the inability to find solutions to many social issues in this period. Many problems not being able to be resolved with the current structure clearly indicate that it is high time to restructure public management. Actually, this sort of restructuring has become an obligation rather than a necessity. Restructuring in public management, first of all, is mandatory in acquiring and increasing the trust of society toward the state. On the other hand, succeeding in this sort of restructuring will ensure that the public resources are used more efficiently and effectively. Besides, the success of the fight against corruption hugely depends on such a restructuring (Bilgin 2004a: 35).

In this direction, in order to prosper the level of country's welfare, establishing a public management, which will run more efficiently and productively, has been stated as baseline policy, and activities to restructure the public sector have been started. For this purpose, in order to restructure the public management and control system to international practices and European Union, Public Financial Management and Control Law No. 5018 has been drafted, passed, and, on December 19, 2003, published in the Official Gazette No. 25326. This law has been enacted from the year 2006 on.

With the new financial structure established under Public Financial Management and Control Law No. 5018, the functions to be executed and responsibilities of public administration units have increased. There has been a passage to a new understanding, where financial management and control are to be executed under

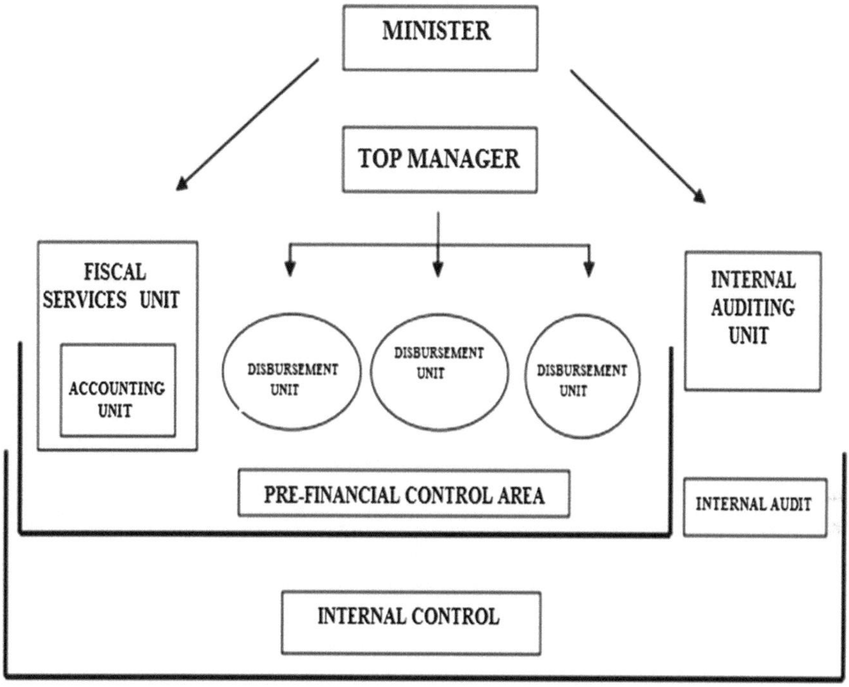

Fig. 17.1 Public financial management and control structure

the management responsibility of administrative units. It is projected that each public administration unit's budget will have a political supervisor and administrative supervisor. With the help of financial services department, which is to be established under public administrative unit, the execution of financial administration and control is aimed to be under the responsibility of administration. Under this law, prefinancial control duties, which are done by Ministry of Finance and Turkish Court of Accounts, have been delivered to administrative units. The structure set forth under this law is shown in Fig. 17.1.

The purpose of Law No. 5018 is defined in the law's text as "The purpose of this law is to regulate structure and functioning of the public financial management, preparation and implementation of the public budgets, accounting and reporting of all financial transactions, and financial control in line with the politics and objectives covered in the development plans and programs, in order to ensure accountability, transparency and the effective, economic and efficient collection and utilization of public resources." The Law No. 5018 brought innovations to our country's public financial management system like preparation of strategic plans, transition to performance-based budgeting based upon strategic planning, accountability and financial transparency, multi-annual budgeting coherent to medium term—three year spending programs, establishment of internal control and internal audit systems, and transition to accrual basis accounting system.

Furthermore, new applications such as separating political, administrative, and financial responsibilities, widening the scope of Chamber of Accounts, transferring the prepurchase control duty to institution management, liquidating circulating capital corporations and funds, gathering all income and outcomes of administrations in their budgets were brought into life.

The statement "Acquisition and usage of public resources in an effective, economical and productive way" in the first article of the law which paves the way for performance applications in Turkish public administration proves the obligation of performance evaluation and audit. Likewise, the 5th article of the law of the decree (g) "In ensuring production of goods and services of public administrations and meeting their needs, it is required to make cost-effectiveness or cost-benefit or other necessary economic and social analyses in accordance with the principles of economic or social efficiency" hands the duty of exercising performance analyses to public organizations.

The 9th article of the law directly regulates the matters of strategical planning and budgeting based on performance. In this article, it is stated that the public organizations will prepare their budgets in line with the mission, vision, and strategical purpose and goals in their strategical plans, and the Department of Finance is made the authority in determining matters about performance-based budgeting.

17.6 Personnel Performance Management and Audit in Government

Auditing in general can be defined as establishing standards in order for the results of an action to be in line with the plans as much as possible, comparing the gathered results to these standards and defining correcting precautions wherever these actions separate from the plan (Sanal 2002: 5).

17.6.1 Auditing Within the Scope of Public Financial Management and Control Law No. 5018

17.6.1.1 Independent External Audit

Independent audit is defined as a systematic process that impartially and neutrally gathers tangible evidence in order to determine the fidelity of both financial and non-financial actions in organizations to the predetermined standards and to report the results to the authorities, and interprets the gathered evidence (Rittenberg et al. 2010: 7). Independent audit not only examines the financial structure of the institution, but also helps determining if the actions are conducted according to regulations. Alongside these, it finds out the negative impact of personnel including management upon institution activities. During independent audit, the internal control systems and accounting process of institutions are examined and the hindrances and lacking aspects are determined. The auditor as a result of independent audit reports the deficient aspects of the institution and applications that are incorrect and not appropriate if present, to the executives and top management of the corporation. Thus, independent audit, looking the corporation from the third perspective while objectively fulfilling its function of determining deficiencies and correcting wrongdoings, also aids in the education of executives and personnel (Kaval 2005: 5). Independent audit also has positive effects on the activity, effectiveness, and productivity of personnel alongside their honest work. The information that there will be an independent audit will lessen the mistakes and losses that personnel make in activities and prevent assets being embezzled. In a similar manner, the event of independent audit has a restrictive effect on company owners and executives. Controlling the accuracy and reliability of information in the financial charts can prevent executives from committing fraud.

17.6.1.2 Regulatory Audit

In the general sense, regularity audit is a type of static audit on operations after they are concluded (Özer 1992: 31–32). Regularity audit which is a traditional approach gives information about financial status and regularity toward rules by using only financial information. Regularity audit uses conventional occupational rules and audit techniques. Regularity audit focuses on operations and reports about mistakes, deficiencies, forgery, and corruption and if expenses are made by the book. Regularity audit does not evaluate if the public administration satisfies the expectations of the receiving mass or the quality of their services. It does not give suggestions to public administrations about elevating their economy, activity, and effectivity (Candan 2007: 73).

17.6.1.3 Performance Audit

In a management style which depends on improvement and change, the role of measurement and evaluation is significant. In institutions that aim for constant improvement, determining plans and goals toward improvement, determining areas that require improvement by spotting potential problems beforehand, and conducting operations toward improvement are possible by the opportunities that the measurement and assessment system provide. The phrase "which cannot be measured cannot be managed" signifies the importance of measurements. The apparent purpose of performance audits is improving management by control and adapting it to changing conditions. There is a direct relation between performance audit and performance improvement. With regular feedback as a result of measurements, the management status can be reviewed and directed toward reaching a better level

(Kubali 1999). Performance audit is different to the financial or regularity audits in its process. Traditional financial audit is carried out regularly; on the other hand, performance audit is a unique work which is done when it is required. In performance audit, there are not specified rules as there are other types of audit. The performance criteria can change with each audit. An institution can be taken as a subject as a whole as well as an operation or programs that consist of multiple operations. Following steps can be taken in performance audit.

- Establishing the criteria that will be used in the audit,
- Creation of the criteria,
- Defining the measurements and quality of the data to be used, and the validity of its ability of representation,
- The level of activity realizing previously set objectives or not,
- Reviewing the difference between the measured levels of activities and criteria in a relation of cause and effect,
- Formulating the result of performance audit (calculating the improvement as a result of the audit, such as cost savings) and activity improvement suggestions.

Performance audit reviews the economy, effectiveness, and efficiency of resource use, using non-financial information as much as financial information. Performance audit, while emphasizing the existence of any fault, deficiency, or forgery, also gives reports about the general performance of an organization, a program of a project. Performance audit reviews if the public administrations satisfy the expectations of the masses they serve, the quality of the services and gives advices (Candan 2007: 73). While conducting a performance audit, the auditor begins a duty where he has to write and apply plans and make reports. The main duty of the performance auditor, without forgetting that he should be an advisor that observes the truths and analyses in order to reach objective findings and give reasonable suggestions, is the report that he writes on his duty.

While thinking about if the performance measurement will be done or how it will be done, the answer to the question with which purpose the performance measurements will be used in public institutions should be thought as well. Because performance measurement requires a considerable amount of expenditure and effort, steps such as developing suitable performance standards, processing this information, analyzing and placing the gathered information inside the prepared standards, preparing measurement reports and sending them to their respective locations, and reading and interpreting these reports all have their cost. Even though computer software and hardware can be used for the steps of processing information, analysis, placing in suitable standards and producing information, additional costs such as advisors for the software and hardware, education and licensing rights are required. It should be made sure while setting up goals for both institutions and individuals related to human resources that these goals are quantifiable. This process contradicts with the traditional public management understanding where the good of the public is dominant. However, avoiding placing quantifiable goals because the services in question are public services and are for the good of the public will affect performance measurements negatively, so it is needed to define performance goals in principle as quantifiable as they can be. The principle of quantifiable performance standards is bringing quantifiable performance standards in line with quantifiable performance goals. Thus, the managements' position of performance related to their goals can be determined. Bringing quantifiable performance standards is as hard as defining performance goals. However, it is possible to succeed in revealing the performance in every step for an administration which acts according to the principle of quantifiable performance goals (Halis and Tekinkuş 2003: 171).

17.6.1.4 Internal Audit

Internal audit which depends on process improvement, adds value to business operations, acts as an advisor alongside education is an approach that provides reasonable assurance (Topcu 2013: 7). Internal audit is an independent type of audit which is established within the business in order to examine all operational activities and reviewing them. The definition of internal audit in the 63rd article of Law no. 5018 is given as "The independent, objective assurance and advising activity which is done by reviewing if the resources are managed in accordance with the principles of economy, effectiveness and productivity in order to add value to the work of public administration and improve them."

Internal audit reviews the effectiveness, efficiency, and productivity of corporate governance, risk management, and internal control processes which are the three main activities of a business by measuring the compatibility of these activities with laws, corporate policies, and procedures and to business plans and programs (Topcu 2013: 7). The relation between these four functions is shown in Fig. 17.2.

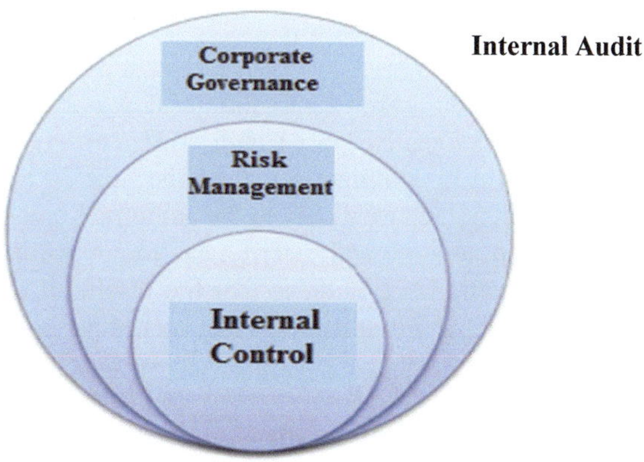

Fig. 17.2 Internal audit

17.6.1.5 Financial Audit

Financial audit is the investigation of the institutions' financial charts about their compliance to the regulations and generally accepted accounting principles. The main purpose of financial audit is to determine the compliance of the financial charts with regulations and generally accepted accounting principles. When institutions prepare their financial charts, they need to focus on accuracy and honesty. The term accuracy is in short the research of compliance to requirement as to form of the element (Bozkurt 1999: 27). On the other hand, honesty is the existence of the element that has been confirmed to be accurate in real life. These concepts can be explained in the example below; the cash being shown in the balance sheet in 100 Cash Account shows that it is accurate, but the fact that it is accurate does not mean that the cash is actually in the register. The cash actually being in the register shows that the operation is honest. With financial audit, the auditors uncover the fraudulent or false statements of the businesses in their financial reports and ensure the security of financial charts (Akgül 2000: 8). It is possible to list the qualities that financial chart audit entails as shown below (Bozkurt 1999: 28).

- To ensure the security of business' financial charts,
- Making sure that the auditor who controls the financial charts is not tied to the business or any other group,
- Making sure that its purpose is to uncover incorrect statements in the financial charts,
- Making sure that the auditor presents a comprehensive and integrative view about the financial charts, not go over mistakes one by one,
- That the auditor justifies his opinions about the security of the financial charts,
- That the audit does not provide 100% insurance to the financial charts.

17.6.1.6 Compliance Audit

Compliance audit is the examination of how much the personnel comply with rules and policies defined by law (Türedi 2007: 26). Predetermined rules are the criteria of comparison in compliance audit (Gücenme 2004: 2). Since the results of compliance audit are reported only to the authorities and officers, it can be conducted by both internal auditors and external auditors when it is needed. The most defining quality of compliance audit is that the results of the audit are not shared to the public, but to the administration that makes it.

17.6.1.7 Performance Audit

Performance audit is the examination of the operations of an institution in order to determine if the resources are managed with the principles of productivity, effectiveness, and economy and if the requirements of financial responsibility are met in a reasonable fashion (Atakan 1997: 4).

Performance audit is the comparison of previously set objectives with the current situation in order to determine if the operations of the institution are productive, effective, and sparing. Based on the performance audit definitions, how effective the institutions' operations are, if the resources used during this operation process are acquired according to principle of economy, and if the resources, that are acquired according to the principle of economy, are used in a productive fashion are all subjects that performance audit investigates. While conducting performance audit, non-financial operations as well as financial operation can be made subject of audit. The audit is not the purpose, but a tool that aims to make the organization operate in a more productive fashion and help it toward its goals. Auditing is a systematic, planned, purposeful, and continuous process and is carried out by individuals and institutions which are qualified experts. Modern auditing is conducted while taking into account risky and important fields according to strategical priorities and is perceived as an operation with a system that is connected to annual programs (Polat 2003: 74). Auditing is reviewing of results that occurred in line with economical activities and events by objectively analyzing and measuring them with predetermined goals, criteria, and standards. Auditing consists of steps such as performance control and report and takes corrective measures.

Performance audit results may not be trustworthy because measurement of the data in the public is difficult. Furthermore, the political behavior of administrators in public sector and their concern for their future status affect the administrative decisions they make (Halis and Tekinkuş 2003: 169). Performance audit, taking into account the principles of productivity, effectivity, and economy, does not show how operations are done, but how well they are carried out. The audit holds institutions responsible for their levels of performance and helps the respective units in reaching a better level of success. Thus, the public services can possess the desired qualities. In the presentation of public services, increasing the performance of public personnel has importance in carrying out the best service possible and establishing productivity.

Conducting audits that are continuous strengthen the accountability of the organization as a sign of timely and effective resource usage with proper programs. Accountability can be confirmed by reviewing written records, with clear, open, and regular reports, and analyzing performance standards with the help of transparent business processes. Even though accountability is necessary and important for performance audit, it is not enough by itself. Alongside measuring the output that is acquired as a result of conducted operations, converting these outputs to results and managing them, correctly analyzing the output information, and using it in improving the services of the institution, in other words the learning process is more important. As a result, it is possible to list the purpose of performance audit as listed below (Öztürk 2006: 158).

- Providing measurement of success or failure about the application of a project or a program,
- Determining success or failure,
- Making suggestions toward the future,
- Assisting the responsibility of performance accountability,
- Improving performance,
- Providing performance information,
- Adjustment and use of resources in a productive manner,
- Improving public administration.

17.6.1.8 Internal Control

The system that enables controls to be approached in a disciplined and systematic integrity is the internal control system. The internal control system provides putting the current and investment expenditures under discipline and enables the workers to embrace the company and conduct more productive labor by granting them some opportunities, thus helping the resources to be used more efficiently and productively (Hasanefendioğlu 2004: 84). The first step toward standardizing internal control methods and procedure has been taken with the Public Financial Management and Control Law No. 5018. The Public Financial Management and Control Law establishes the internal control system in public fiscal system. The fifth section of the aforementioned law is reserved for the internal control system. While the starting point of the internal control system is financial concerns, it also encompasses non-financial operations. The existence of the internal control system serves to increase the accuracy and reliability levels of the financial charts and to minimize possible mistakes and risks (Bakir 2002: 49). The control problem comes into play especially when the businesses expand and operations become complex. Because growth, alongside compliance with regulations, brings with it some weaknesses while requiring tight coordination between departments (Akişik 2005: 90).

An active and effective internal control is an essential part of taking correct and timely decisions in order for governance to emerge in an institution because there are benefits to an effectively working internal control system. For example, it provides more opportunities for the management to attune itself to the global and changing technological and economical environment, to provide and keep a sustainable competitive advantage, and most important of all to keep the business alive (Ratcliffe and Landes 2009: 2).

Internal control is defined by COSO (2011: 2) as a process designed to reach the goals of the security of financial reporting, the effectivity, and activity of the operations and to provide compliance with regulations, all of which are affected by everyone from the top management to lower level personnel. IIA considers the internal control system as an inseparable part of business management and defines it as an insurance in providing the effectivity, activity, and productivity of the operations, applying the budget in the current year, ensuring the reliability of all reports, especially financial ones, and providing compliance with positive law and regulations. INTOSAI defines internal control as a system designed to provide reasonable assurance in minimizing risks in the subject of reaching institutional goals which is affected by every employee of a business, including the top management (Professional Accountants in Business Committee 2011: 10). In this context, it is possible to summarize the common points gathered from the definitions above, as below.

- Providing correct information to the management and both internal and external shareholders,
- Protecting assets against loss, fraud, theft and damage,
- Providing compliance to regulations,
- Ensuring the activity and effectivity of operations.

The internal control system which has a dynamic and open to improvement structure is established in order to protect institutional assets, provide active, effective, and productive use of those assets, comply with institution goals and regulations, gather regular and reliable information about business operations, and prevent corruption and irregularity (Topcu 2013: 7–8). Among the internal control systems, the COSO Internal Control Model has been widely accepted and has become a global standard. The components of COSO's internal control system are shown in Fig. 17.3 (Kaval 2005: 125).

- Control environment,
- Risk assessment,
- Control activities,
- Information and communication,
- Monitoring.

The control environment is the basis of other internal control elements. To talk about an active, effective, and reliable internal control system, there needs to be an acceptable control environment. The control environment establishes organizational discipline and structure (Erdoğan 2001). The components of control environment in

Fig. 17.3 COSO model components

the scope of the COSO model are defined as honesty and moral values, management philosophy and work style, commitment to competence, organizational structure, authority and responsibility, human resources management policies and applications (COSO 1994). The prerequisite to risk assessment is the creation of institutional goals related to each other in the scale of the institution. Risk assessment in actuality is establishing an institutional principle in risk management and developing controls by determining the risks in this sense (Reding et al. 2009: 6–11). In this context, risk assessment is a process which consists of the three steps below (Moeller 2009: 39).

- The prediction of the significance of the risk,
- Evaluating the possibility and the frequency of the risk to occur,
- How the risk will be managed and which actions will be considered in assessment.

Control activities, following the determination of risks, are activities done to prevent, acquiesce, or avoid the risks. At this step, proper processes are defined in order to reduce risks with proper control methods (Topcu 2013: 11). Control activities consist of the application of institutional policies and procedures defined against risks that can possibly prevent reaching the institutional objectives (Gönen 2009: 199).

The information and communication component which is one of the main elements of the internal control system is an integral and supplemental part to all other components of the COSO model. The accounting process which is an information system in the case of financial reporting is designed to produce the most correct and reliable information. The dynamic structure of the internal control system enables the organization to consistently adjust to possible risks spotted for the organization and changes that happen depending on environmental factors. The adjustment of the internal control system to the changing environment, objectives, resources, and risks seems possible only with constant monitoring. Monitoring, in general, is the process of reviewing the effectivity and performance of a system (Doyrangöl 2002: 36).

17.7 Civil Servant Performance Management

The performance management system plays a significant role for an institution to determine its strategies by providing reliable and valid information on topics such as planning human resources activities, establishing, reviewing standards, giving feedback and detection of educational improvement, and providing effective communication. The performance management system is an institutional system which considers the term performance assessment as a dynamic process rather than a static one, which aims to plan, review, and improve the performance of personnel and which approaches the subject from a wider angle. The performance management system has a big role and immense importance in strategical planning, wage and salary administration, career development system, determining education needs, and layoff decisions in institutions. These decisions being taken in a healthy manner depend on the system working efficiently. For this reason, in this section of the study, performance, performance management, performance assessment for public personnel regime are approached with a conceptual study.

17.7.1 Conception of Performance

The dictionary definition of the concept of performance which originates in the French word "performance" is "success, accomplishment." Its meaning in public management is defined as "accomplishment, success and reaching objectives". Performance is the realization of goals that have a meaning for individuals step-by-step with daily programs. In other words, performance is the demonstration of behavior which is appropriate for predetermined standards as required by a duty and the degree of reaching expected goals (Canman 1993: 7).

Performance, according to another definition, is the execution level of an assignment according to defined conditions or the behavior pattern of personnel. In other terms, it can be defined as "the level of conducting business of an individual." Performance is the defining of where an individual, group, or institution which performs a work can reach toward the set goals as quantitative (quantity) or qualitative (quality). The main factors that affect performance which emerges as a concept which defines what has been gained as a result of purposeful and planned activity as quantitative or qualitative are objectives. What makes the objectives so important is whether they be organizational or personal, success is not possible without them, in other words personnel performance and performance in the scope of the organization not meaning anything.

Individual performance in a business can be defined as an individual conducting an operation which is suitable to his defined traits and skills within reasonable limits. In this sense, to talk about employee performance in a business, first an individual has to be facing a defined operation, this operation has to be suitable to the traits and abilities of the individual, and there needs to be a standard which indicates the level of success for that operation. Reaching that standard means the success of the individual, while falling short of the standard means failure. Performance management is an understanding of management toward the application of planning and auditing functions of an administration in wider boundaries while taking into consideration the improvements within the concept of performance. Performance management is defined as a system where executives convey their feedback in a helpful and constructive manner, where the plans of improvement are supported with creative ideas (Öztürk 2006: 39).

The executive directing his team to disclosed and shared objectives, motivating them, informing and sharing responsibility directly affects work quality and productivity. The responsibility of the executive and the team also includes the actions of executing mutual decisions, how and by whom the operation will be conducted, and observing the process. Performance management is a tool of receiving better results from the organization, the teams, and the individuals by understanding and managing performance within goals, objectives, and standards that are agreed upon. In this sense, performance management consists of a systematic approach to human management by using objective measurement, feedback, and recognition toward motivating people to realize their potential.

Performance management practices in organizations debuts as a system applied by managers who, instead of daily evaluations have a long-term view about developments. Performance management provides support in planning, monitoring, review, and assessment steps, which are integrated with business processes. Following the comparison of realized practices to planned ones, it encourages systematic learning activities. The secret of performance management is establishing structures where ordinary people make extraordinary contributions. Performance management has to aim progressing individual's potential and competences, while trying to meet performance expectations. Managing performance is ensuring the realization of work-directed expectations. Managing performance is managing expectations. From this angle, performance management resembles vision. Hereby, there is a desired and an expected result, and we set our potentials to strike the result. The result is tried to be obtained by effectively managing the gap between current situation and desired result.

Performance management serves as a key to conversion, which supports both individual and team success. Performance management system has a huge and important role in organizations for planning, wage–salary management, career development system, determination of training needs, and in taking decisions regarding cancelation of labor contracts. Taking these decisions in a healthy way depends on efficient functioning of the system. With the help of performance management system, managers are enabled to do planning and control functions more effectively, employ the relations and communication with their employees function more favorably; and as they became familiar to their subordinates, delegate their authority more easily, develop their managing abilities, and construct the conditions where they comfortably exercise these abilities.

The employees, on the other hand, are enabled to find out what is expected from themselves and how their performance has been assessed, get familiar to their strengths and weaknesses to be developed, and conceive their responsibilities in a better way, and with the help of the positive feedback, they received about their performance, and they improve their job satisfaction and self-confidence feelings. Positive progresses from perspectives of employees and managers increase the effectiveness and profitability of the organization, enhance quality of the services, help determining employees' advancement potential, and, as a result of this training needs and training budget, are ascertained in a more easily and accurate way.

17.8 Purposes of Performance Management in Public

The most generalized purpose of the performance management system is to create a culture where the personnel, for both individuals and as a team, can provide constant improvement to their knowledge and skill. Measurement of individual performance with fair and standardized criteria, giving feedback to the personnel and increasing the organizational activity by improving individual performance and achieving mutual improvement and success are the leading intentions of the performance management system. Performance management focuses on "self management." Improvement is encouraged by helping and guiding people. The people in the organization need the executives and the organization in this topic. The necessity of education becomes apparent in the context of gaining skills that are required to reach the goals set by performance management. During this process, employees receive feedback, their performance is reviewed, and they receive counseling services.

The main objective of performance management, besides evaluating the success of an individual, is to aid institutional improvement by way of increasing self-improvement by giving thought to subjects such as how an individual's contribution to the institution can be improved positively or how reaching the desired potential will be realized. The performance management system has a set of goals to enable organizations to work more efficiently. These goals can be gathered in three main groups: administrative goals, improvement goals, and research goals. The goals of performance management which are gathered in three main groups can be listed in more detail as below (Barutçugil 2004: 127).

- Converting institution objectives to individual objectives,
- Providing transition to a phase in which the positions in the institution are objective and structured assessment criteria are mutually known beforehand,
- Informing personnel about their performance status, their successful aspects, and their aspects that need to be improved,
- Clarifying the connection between performance and reward,
- Fair, equal, and timely assessment of the personnel according to predetermined criteria,
- Carrying out an effective communications process between the subordinates and the superiors (evaluative and evaluated) in order for the individual to compare his actual success status with his expected performance results,
- The organization, executives, superiors, and subordinates to be in collaboration with order to improve the performance,
- Defining the strong and weak aspects of the organization,
- Motivating the personnel through feedback,
- Providing the necessary information to the administration about the topics of career planning and education,
- The conversion of organizational targets to clearly defined individual targets,
- Defining the necessary performance criteria in order for the objectives to be realized,

- Assessing the personnel in a fair and timely manner according to the determined criteria,
- Comparing and assessing the expected performance results of the personnel with the actual success,
- Creating an effective environment of communication and understanding between the executive and the personnel,
- Executive and personnel making mutual effort to improve performance,
- Recognizing the success of the personnel and rewarding it,
- Defining the strong and weak aspects of both the organization and the personnel,
- Endorsement of employees through feedback and strengthening their motivation,
- Providing necessary information to the management for training development and career planning.

17.9 Public Performance Management Process

Public performance management can be defined as activities and processes to provide work performance in goods and services production, where duties and responsibilities have been taken in accordance with the organization's success in public management (Bilgin 2004b: 20). Public performance management is reflection of features like locality in services and empowerment of regionalism, governance, total quality management, public enterprises and globalization, which aroused following the critics brought to traditional public management understanding and practices. It was apparently seen that instead of realizing the main objective of public organizations and institutions, taking care of cost elements, reaching targets of productivity, effectiveness, and performance, public organizations tend to grow unnecessarily and exceedingly emphasize rules, forgetting that the rules are means only. Therefore, with the help of public performance management, it is required to produce appropriate amount and quality of public goods and services, by doing the right duty at the right time with the right people (Bilgin 2008: 60).

Managing performance gains importance as it does in private sector. The proliferation of taxpayers' awareness about how and on what the money they pay is spent brings up the performance management to agenda. With the help of performance indicators utilized in performance management, the progress between current and previous performance levels can be monitored, the trend the public service has been following over the years can be caught, organizations can be compared to each other, and the best practices may prevail (Balci 2015: 5).

Performance management, attempting to lead the organization to desired direction, is a management process assuming duties like collection of information about present and future statuses of the organization, comparing them, and starting new and due activities, and arrangements to enable continuous progress in performance (Akal 1992). Performance management system is a process of emplacing a common understanding of organizational objectives to be reached and performance to be produced by people working in this direction and the management, appraisal, pricing and/or rewarding, and improvement of employees in a way to raise the level of their contribution to combined efforts (Barutçugil 2002: 125).

As a management tool, the relationship of performance management with main functions of management is giving support to administration in preparation of objectives, strategies, policies, and tactical plans accurately; monitoring the conformity of practice to plans, in other words measuring the performance; and establishing a sequential system to pass the information collected to management and employees not in a punitive, but in an encouraging way. At this point, it will be helpful to emphasize that performance management is not a result oriented, but a continuous process.

Management processes and performance management stages are structures completing each other. Objectives agreed upon, knowledge, skills and competences, performance progressing, and personal development plans compose the basis for performance management process. This process is a structure, where actual results are compared to objectives agreed upon, and participation and long-term plans are monitored in continuity. Performance management is setting forth the procedures and criteria which will form the basis for individual and team performance evaluation during the process realized according to a specific plan.

Within this scope, performance management system consists of a three-stage system. The starting point of performance management is determination of strategies and forward objectives in order to bring competitive power to business. At the second stage, it is required to measure and assess the current performance level of the organization and to assure the conformity of management systems and processes to strategies. Performance development-oriented planning process follows this stage. Along with planning, studies to improve measurement systems start, and for this purpose, it is worked on what to measure for which reason, and data collection and analyses techniques, thus a decision is taken at the end. The third stage of performance management is determining the precautions to develop performance, preparing tactics related to these and put them in progress.

17.9.1 Personnel Performance Auditing Pursuant to Public Financial Management and Control Law No. 5018

Public Financial Management and Control Law No. 5018 assigns public administrations with duties; (art. 8) public administrations shall prepare their budgets on performance basis; (art. 8) put forth the accountability of those, who are assigned duties and vested with authorities for the acquisition and utilization of public resources of all kind; (art. 9) public administrations shall prepare strategic plans in a cooperative manner in order to form missions and visions for future within the framework of development plans, programs, relevant legislation, and basic principles adopted; to determine strategic goals and measurable objectives; to measure their performances according to predetermined indicators; and to monitor and evaluate this overall process. This law also gives the duty (art. 11) top managers are responsible for preparation and implementation of the strategic plans and budgets of their administration in conformity with the development plan, annual programs as well as with the strategic plan and performance objectives and service requirements of the administration, and assigns the duty (art. 68) Court of Accounts is to make external audit of performance at public organizations and institutions.

17.10 Research

17.10.1 Civil Servant Performance Management System Perception: Provincial Organization Sample

17.10.1.1 Performance Evaluation

Performance evaluation, for which several terms like "success evaluation," "merit rating," "employee calibration," "personnel assessment," "productivity assessment," "reference," and "enrollment" are used in literature in shortest definition, is the assessment process of employee's success at work, against job specifications (Mathis and Jackson 1988: 299; Geylan 1991: 90; Can et al. 1998: 173). Performance evaluation is an assessment study done on specific periods to determine whether an employee shows the desired behavior at work or not. Performance evaluation is gaining popularity as a practice reflecting the approach of human resources department and managers establishing relations with employees, not in groups but on individual basis. An efficient performance evaluation assists in taking proper action about high motivation, accumulation of information, on-time, exact, and accurate decision taking, and handing training needs and employee development, properly. Performance evaluation takes into consideration individual differences and to measure the performance accurately combines subjective and objective tools.

17.10.1.2 Research Objective and Scope

The main objective of the study is the determination of perception of personnel employed at a provincial unit of a public organization about performance assessment. The research is conducted on 50 employees via a questionnaire prepared, and findings are reviewed statistically.

17.10.1.3 Research Objective

Basically, the only objective of the research is to set forth the perception of public servants, related to performance evaluation. On the other hand, contributing to government personnel regime lacking performance evaluation would be regarded as an objective as well.

17.10.1.4 Importance of Research

For the time being, there is not any performance evaluation in public sector; this increases the importance of the study. Besides, the research being on a provincial unit at only one organization increments to the importance of the study. Within this frame, it is expected that the study will contribute to performance management system.

17.10.1.5 Research Model and Questions

- Research Model
- With the questionnaire, public servants' perception level for each of items listed under 21 questions is searched. Therefore, there is no research model; analyses are made on the basis of scale factors, instead.
- Research Questions

Questions and hypotheses built based upon conceptual framework explained in previous sections are to be listed as follows.

Research questions:

(a) What is the demographic structure of the respondents?
(b) Is it possible to implement a reliable measurement tool related to performance assessment?
(c) What are the perceptions of public servants about performance evaluation?

17.10.1.6 Limitations of Research

Findings gathered at the end of the research may differ depending on the sample; therefore, findings of the research are limited with the sample data collected from. For this reason, the model needs to be tested for several samples. The research has a cross-sectional design. Since the variables are apt to changes through time factor, the findings of the research are limited to the time period the questionnaire is conducted. The scale utilized in the research is composed of evaluation items simultaneously directed to individuals, and within this scope, it is reviewing the perception of individuals. This is why, the existence of Hawthorne effect and common method variance is to be taken into consideration while evaluating the findings.

17.10.1.7 Population and Sample

The population of this research is 50 employees at a provincial unit of a public organization. The sample is made up of respondents randomly chosen to present the population. Data collected from 250 personnel through questionnaire method are used in the research. Questionnaires printed on paper have been used in order to collect data from respondents. Out of 250 questionnaires sent, 227 returned; thus, return rate became 90.80%. As a result of preanalysis inspections on lost data and basic variables, nine uncompleted questionnaire forms, and data of 15 persons, whose marks were condensed on lower or upper values, were excluded, and thus, the analyses continued with remaining a sample of 203 responds.

17.10.1.8 Descriptive Statistics

- Age-related information of respondents is given in Table 17.1. Employees' ages of the public organization, where the research has been conducted, ranges between 23 and 56, the average is 36.78, and standard deviation is 8.78.
- Considering the gender, 40 of respondents are males, namely 80%, and 10 of them are females, which makes 20%.

Table 17.1 Frequency distribution of respondents according to their job positions

	Frequency	Percentage	Valid percentage	Cumulative percentage
Civil servant	20	40.0	40.0	40.0
Unit supervisor	4	8.0	8.0	48.0
Social worker	1	2.0	2.0	50.0
Preacher	1	2.0	2.0	52.0
Psychologist	5	10.0	10.0	62.0
Teacher	3	6.0	6.0	68.0
Accounting official	3	6.0	6.0	74.0
Food engineer	1	2.0	2.0	76.0
Submanager	9	18.0	18.0	94.0
Manager	3	6.0	6.0	100.0
Total	50	100.0	100.0	

Table 17.2 Frequency distribution of respondents according to their education levels

	Frequency	Percentage	Valid percentage	Cumulative percentage
Lyceum	3	6.0	6.0	6.0
Vocational school	8	16.0	16.0	22.0
Undergraduate	37	74.0	74.0	96.0
Master's degree	2	4.0	4.0	100.0
Total	50	100.0	100.0	

Table 17.3 Frequency distribution of respondents according to tenure at the organization

	Frequency	Percentage	Valid percentage	Cumulative percentage
less than 1 year	2	4.0	4.0	4.0
1–3 years	15	30.0	30.0	34.0
3–5 years	6	12.0	12.0	46.0
5–7 years	1	2.0	2.0	48.0
7–14 years	11	22.0	22.0	70.0
15–20 years	4	8.0	8.0	78.0
More than 20 years	11	22.0	22.0	100.0
Total	50	100.0	100.0	

- When respondents' job positions are analyzed, there are 12 managers and submanagers, namely 24%, and the rest are mainly civil servants. There are 20 public servants, making up 40% of respondents.
- As shown in Table 17.2 the education levels of respondents, 74%, namely 37 persons, have undergraduate degree. There are eight persons having a vocational school diploma, which makes up 18%, and three of the respondents have lyceum diploma, namely six percent. Last, there are two master's degree owners, which make up four percent.
- As shown in Table 17.3 the tenure of respondent at the organization, 23 persons, which make up 46%, have tenure shorter than five years at the organization. Those who have tenure between five years and 20 are 16 persons, namely 32%. Last, there are 11 respondents, who have tenure over 20 years; this makes up 22%.

17.10.2 Measurement Tool of the Research

Questionnaire method has been used in this research. The questionnaire form used is placed at appendices. The questionnaire consists of two sections. The first section is composed of explanation and questions related to demographic information of respondents. The second section encompasses performance measurement scale. Five-scale Likert has been utilized as scale on a continuum starting from "1-Absolutely Disagree" and ending with "5-Absolutely Agree." Reliability of the sample has been tested with Cronbach's alpha, and confidence coefficient is found as 0.89.

According to Özdamar (1999: 522), Cronbach's alpha coefficient between 0.00 and 0.40 shows that the questionnaire is not reliable, it being between 0.40 and 0.60 means that it has a low reliability, and if it is between 0.60 and 0.80, the questionnaire is quite reliable. A coefficient between 0.80 and 1.00 shows that it is highly reliable. Under these circumstances, it is assessed that the scale is highly reliable.

17.11 Conclusion and Recommendations

Following the world economic depression arousing in 1970s and in the aftermath, there had been fundamental changes in management under the influence of liberal movement. From this date on, many developed countries particularly USA, New Zealand, Australia entered a huge wave of change. Globalization phenomenon, technological conversions, disengagement from traditional management horizon and the increase in the expectations of the managed masses from the services rendered and factors alike caused to adaptation of a fresh understanding of public administration, transparency, accountability, and efficiency, strategic planning, performance management and auditing kinds of notions to come to the forefront within the new globe order.

Conversion having started in public management systems became the triggering factor in many reforms in the previous years in our country. The new management understanding targeted a more efficient, more productive, and accountable public management directed to adapt to current circumstances. By adopting good governance principles through Public Financial Management and Control Law No. 5018, Turkey started the transition process to corporate governance which is the contemporaneous approach in public management in year 2006.

By enactment of the aforementioned law, corporate governance concepts like responsibility, transparency, accountability, and equity to start with and new terms like internal audit and internal control joined public sphere. The projection of performance audit has become another newness. With a holistic and comprehensive approach, performance-based working principles in all areas, from strategic planning to budgeting and from usage of resources to personnel regime, are brought, and the measurement of the performance became the basis.

Performance management as one of these new notions and techniques is a management style, aiming the continuous improvement of performance of all employees of all organizations, uniting them in common goals, and in order to catch these goals prescribing an execution in coordination with planning, measuring, leading, controlling duties and other management functions as a management style. Performance auditing is the assessment of the organization's exercises to observe whether sources are managed according to principles of productivity, efficiency, and prudence and the requirements of fiscal responsibility are met or not.

The management of performance in public sector gains importance gradually as it is in the private sector. The proliferation of taxpayers' awareness about how and on what the money they pay is spent brings up the performance management to agenda. With the help of performance indicators utilized in performance management, the progress between current and previous performance levels can be monitored, the trend the public service has been following over the years can be caught, organizations can be compared to each other, and the best practices may prevail.

In our country, thoughts about performance application in public management being topical issue often started especially in the second half of the 1990s (Şentürk 2004: 121). Moreover, there is an increase in the number of studies attracting the attention recently about performance management applications in public administration organizations.

Public performance reaching the desired level seems to be achievable with the help of qualified personnel regime. It is apparent that managing the abilities at hand and potential employees to be hired, there is a need for performance management system. However, there is no observation of any performance assessment methodology applied, yet. However, performance management system is a requisite for the current public management.

Additionally, saying that public audit understanding reached the capacity to perform, performance auditing seems to be impossible. Specifically, there is neither a personnel regime with a contemporary personnel management understanding, nor is it possible to mention about the existence of a system capable of auditing this. Within this outlook, in order to measure the perception about performance management in public management, a questionnaire is designed and research is conducted among personnel working at a provincial organization of a public administration.

General review of findings collected via questionnaire brings out that performance management which is not implemented officially is not supported by supervisors either and is not being associated with human resources exercises like carrier management, training and improvement, job appraisal, and that a style of management appropriate to corporate governance principles has not been adopted.

When findings collected via questionnaire are reviewed in detail:

- While 32% of respondents are unfamiliar to strategic planning concepts, 68% say these concepts are pronounced to them. While 44% of respondents are unfamiliar to strategic planning targets, 56% say these targets are pronounced to them.

- The rate of respondents considering criteria and standards are not in accordance with plans and targets is 62%. Job description forms are unfamiliar to 40% of the respondents. Respondents at a rate of 74% state that their opinions are not asked at the time of criterion and standard setting.
- Those believing that their performance has not been evaluated make up 62% of the respondents. The rate of respondents stating that not the work done, but the personnel is evaluated is 48%. Respondents at a rate of 64% state that objective criteria are not used.
- Respondents at 60% say that activities are organized to improve performance of personnel. Those believing that not the personnel's success at job, but their relations with the superiors are assessed during performance evaluation make up 68%. Respondents at 56% state that complaints and suggestions are ignored within the organization.
- Those believing that the level of their knowledge and abilities are satisfactory to do the job are 88% of the respondents. However, 52% of them state that they do not find enough resource and support to do the work, and 66% say they do not find enough means to improve skills. Respondents at an 88% rate state that personnel with high levels of performance are not rewarded, and 76% believes promotions within the organization are not based on capability and performance. The respondents also indicate at 90% that performance evaluation does not affect determination of salaries.
- At a 66%, respondents declare performance evaluation system does not promote personal development. Those believing that employees are not treated equally and fair make up 70% of the respondents. According to 76% of the respondents, supervisors neither support performance evaluation system, nor exhibit this with their behaviors. However, 82% of the respondents think that performance evaluation system will positively contribute to the organization.

Some points among findings reached with the conduction of the questionnaire are to be stated as follows. Though the mission and vision of the organization are known, recognition level of plans and objectives is not satisfactory. It is observed that targets as a part of strategic plans are not popularized to the individual level. There are a considerable number of respondents believing that job descriptions are not clear.

Personnel are not encouraged to be involved in performance criteria determination. Performance evaluation is subjective and not based on the work done. More than half of respondents conceive that objective criteria are not used in performance evaluation. Participation level to activities organized for personnel development is at low levels. Bilateral relations are believed to affect performance evaluation. There are doubts whether complaints and suggestions within the organization are taken into consideration or not. The personnel deem they are meeting the requirements of the work.

It is stated that resources needed to do the job are not procured. It is declared that enough means to improve personnel's skills are not offered. There is a lack of rewarding within performance management system, and it is also observed that performance management system is not associated with carrier management. Performance management does not impact salaries. Most of the respondents think that they are not fairly treated. It is believed that managers do not support performance management system. However, it is thought that performance evaluation system will have positive contributions to the organization.

Therefore, making policies that will establish coordination among public organizations and fulfill needs should be the basis. The issues among problems which may arise during the execution of performance audit would be as follows.

- Even though there is no impeding provision, not delegating the authority and duty to audit units to make performance audit,
- Internal control mechanism of organizations and institutions is far from meeting the performance audit standards and requirements,
- It is hard to determine standards to be used in performance auditing,
- The program budgeting system, which is being used in our day and has properties to support performance audit, is not implemented thoroughly,
- Performance management concept necessary to actualize performance auditing has not yet been established at public organizations and institutions,
- Again at public organizations and institutions, modern information systems have not been installed; rather, there are management structures inducing bureaucracy, and decision performers, instead of decision makers, are encumbered with responsibility,
- Conceiving auditing mostly as statutory and procedural auditing and conducting it as such, performance auditing did not find enough space in literature; thus, time allocated for auditing is consumed for statutory and procedural auditing,
- For the sake of efficiency of performance auditing, there is need for relations, different than traditional audits to be established with the employees of the organizations and institutions being audited, on transparency basis, instead of pecking order form,
- The belief that performance auditing deduces about the accuracy/falsity of political decisions even though it is not among objectives of performance auditing,
- The need for the transparency of execution and announcement of the opinions at the end of performance audit,
- The lack of experienced audit personnel to realize performance auditing,
- Inefficiency of technical and social resources to be provided to auditors who are to make the performance audit,
- Performance audits yield results in the scope of future-driven suggestions and warnings, instead of revealing corruption, bribery, and illegal acts driving the public interest,
- Audit units lack high capacity archives, where data required for an efficient performance audit are collected and evaluated.

Appendix: Questionnaire

See Table 17.4.

Table 17.4 Questionnaire on personal opinion about the working environment

Please mark according to your level of agreeing		Absolutely disagree	Disagree	Uncertain	Agree	Totally agree
1	Vision and mission of the organization are plainly stated and announced to the personnel	1	2	3	4	5
2	Information related to organizations' plans and objectives are announced to the personnel	1	2	3	4	5
3	Performance criteria and standards are prepared according to plans and objectives set beforehand	1	2	3	4	5
4	Job descriptions are done explicitly and announced to the personnel	1	2	3	4	5
5	The view of personnel has been asked at the time of corporate standard setting and determination of performance criteria	1	2	3	4	5
6	Performance of personnel is being assessed	1	2	3	4	5
7	Performance assessment evaluates the work done, not the personnel	1	2	3	4	5
8	Objective criteria are used in performance assessment	1	2	3	4	5
9	Trainings, seminars, and foreign mission type of events are organized for the development of the personnel	1	2	3	4	5

(continued)

Table 17.4 (continued)

Please mark according to your level of agreeing		Absolutely disagree	Disagree	Uncertain	Agree	Totally agree
10	Instead of personnel's success at work, his/her relations with supervisors determine the result of the assessment, mostly	1	2	3	4	5
11	Complaints and suggestions are taken into consideration within the organization	1	2	3	4	5
12	I have the required knowledge and capability level to do my job	1	2	3	4	5
13	I find enough resources and support to do my job	1	2	3	4	5
14	There are satisfactory facilities to improve my abilities	1	2	3	4	5
15	Personnel with high levels of performance are rewarded	1	2	3	4	5
16	Promotions within the organization are bases on capabilities and performance	1	2	3	4	5
17	Performance assessment impacts salaries	1	2	3	4	5
18	Performance evaluation system inspires individual development	1	2	3	4	5
19	All employees are treated fair and equal	1	2	3	4	5
20	I think that managers support the performance evaluation system and they reflect it with their behaviors	1	2	3	4	5
21	I believe that performance evaluation system will positively contribute to the organization	1	2	3	4	5

Dear Respondent,

This questionnaire is prepared for a post-graduate project conducted at Trakya University. The aim of this questionnaire is to determine the perceptions about performance assessment. The questionnaire has two pages and there are two different sections to be answered. The answers given are going to be used solely for research. There are no correct/wrong answers of any expressions in the questionnaire; the important thing is your opinion about any specified topic. Therefore, in order to make healthy assessment, you are required to fill all items. Since the findings are to be processed according to statistical rules, you are not asked to put any ID information. Thank you very much for your sincere and valuable opinions.

Prepared by:
Mehmet Ali HATIKLER
Trakya University
Social Sciences Institute
Administrative Sciences Department
Accounting and Auditing Distance Education
Non-thesis Master Program Student

Advisor:
PROF. DR. Kıymet Tunca ÇALIYURT
Trakya University
Social Sciences Institute

1. Age : ....

2. Gender : ☐ Male ☐ Female

3. Job Position : ....

4. Your Tenure at This Organization:

☐ less than 1 year

☐ 1-3 years ☐ 3-5 years ☐ 5-7 years

☐ 7-14 years ☐ 15-20 years ☐ 20 years and more

5. Your Education:

☐ Literate ☐ Elementary/Secondary/Grade school ☐ Lyceum

☐ Vocational High School ☐ Vocational School ☐ Undergraduate

☐ Master Degree ☐ Doctoral

References

Akal Z (1992) İşletmelerde Performans Ölçüm ve Denetimi Çok Yönlü Performans Göstergeleri, MPM Yayinlari, No: 473, Ankara
Akgül BA (2000) Türk Denetim Kurumlari. Türkmen Kitabevi, Istanbul
Akişik O (2005) İç Kontrol Sistemi ve Bağimsiz Denet im İçindeki Yeri. Muhasebe ve Denetime Bakiş 14:89–102
Atakan N, Çoşkun A, Sonuvar SM (1997) Performans Denetimi; Pakistan Sayiştay'i Uygulamasi, T.C. Sayiştay Başkanliği Yayinlari 135. Kuruluş Yildönümü Yayinlari, Ankara
Bakir M (2002) Denetim. Akademi Yayinevi, Rize
Balci A (2015) Kamu Yönetiminde Çağdaş Yaklaşimlar ve Kamu Hizmet Sunumuna Etkileri. http://www.sobiadacademy.net/sobem/e-kamuyonetim/kamuda-kalite/balci.pdf, 05/09/2015
Balci A, Kirilmaz H (2015) Yeni Kamu Yönetimi Anlayişinin Türk Sağlik Sektörüne Yansimalari. http://www.performans.saglik.gov.tr/content/files/performansyazilari/ykytssy.pdf, 01/09/2015
Barutçugil I (2002) Performans Yönetimi. Birinci Baski. Kariyer Yayincilik, Istanbul
Barutçugil I (2004) Stratejik İnsan Kaynaklari Yönetimi. Birinci Baski. Kariyer Yayincilik, Istanbul
Bilgin KU (2004a) Kamu Performans Yönetimi, Memur Hak ve Yükümlülüklerinin Performansa Etkisi. TODAIE, Ankara
Bilgin KU (2004b) Kamu Performans Yönetimi. TODAIE Yayin No: 323, Ankara
Bilgin KU (2008) Kamu Performans Yönetimi: Vali ve Kaymakamlar Performans Ölçümü Araştirmasi. Amme İdaresi Dergisi, Cilt 41 sayi 2, Haziran
Bolton M (2003) Public sector performance measurement: delivering greater accountability. Work Study 52(1):20–24
Bozkurt N (1999) Muhasebe Denetimi (2. Baski). Alfa Basim Yayim, Istanbul
Can H, Akgün HA, Kavuncubaşi S (1998) Kamu ve Özel Kesimde Personel Yönetimi. Üçüncü Baski. Siyasal Kitabevi, Ankara
Candan E (2007) Türk Bütçe Sisteminde Performans Denetimi. Ankara
Canman AD (1993) Personelin Değerlendirilmesinde Çağdaş Yaklaşimlar ve Türkiye'de Kamu Personelinin Değerlendirilmesi. TODAIE Yayinlari, No: 252, Ankara
COSO (1994) Internal control—integrated framework, two-volume Edition. American Institute of Certified Public Accountants, New Jersey. http://www.snai.edu/cn/service/library/book/0-framework-final.pdf (Accessed on: 18 Sept 2015)
COSO (2011) Internal control—integrated framework. http://www.ic.coso.org/download.aspx (Accessed on: 19 Sept 2015)
Doyrangöl N (2002) İşletme Çevresindeki Olumsuz Gelişmeler Karşisinda İç Denetimin Yeri ve Önemi. Mali Çözüm Dergisi 60:33–42
Erdoğan M (2001) Denetim. Eskişehir
Eryilmaz B (2010) Kamu Yönetiminde reform: Statüko ve Değişim. http://www.pdrforum.net/index.php?topic=1597.0, 01/06/2010
Geylan R (1991) Personel Yönetimi. Anadolu Üniversitesi Matbaasi, Eskişehir
Gönen S (2009) İç Kontrol Sisteminin Unsurlarindan Kontrol Ortaminin İncelenmesine Yönelik Bir Araştirma. Muhasebe ve Bilim Dünyasi Dergisi 11(1):189–217
Gücenme Ü (2004) Muhasebe Denetim. Aktüel, Bursa
Gülhan M (2003) Türk Kamu Yönetiminde Yeniden Yapilanma Çalişmalari ve Denetim Sistemi, Sorunlari ve Çözüm Önerileri. Unpublished Master Thesis, Abant İzzet Baysal Üniversitesi, Bolu
Halis M, Tekinkuş M (2003) Kamuda Performans Yönetimi. Kamu Yönetiminde Çağdaş Yaklaşimlar; Sorunlar, Tartişmalar, Çözüm Önerileri, Modeller, Dünya ve Türkiye Yansimalari, Ankara
Hasanefendioğlu D (2004) Kurumsal Yönetim. Vergi Dünyasi 275:79–84
Kanerva I (1994) government decision-in-principle on reforms in central and regional Government. Ministry of Finance, Helsinki

Karci ŞM (2008) Yeni Kamu İşletmeciliği Yaklaşiminin Temel Değerleri Üzerine Bir İnceleme. Akdeniz İ.İ.B.F. Dergisi, Sayi 16
Kaval H (2005) Muhasebe Denetimi: Uluslararasi Finansal Raporlama Standartlari Uygulama Örnekleriyle, 2nd edn. Gazi Kitabevi, Ankara
Kubali D (1999) Performans Denetimi. Amme İdaresi Dergisi Cilt 32, Sayi: 1, pp. 31–62
Mathis RL, Jakson JH (1988) Personel/human resource management, 6th edn. West Publishing Company, USA
Moeller R (2009) Brink's modern internal auditing: a common body of knowledge, 7th edn. Wiley, United States of America
Özdamar K (1999) Paket Programlar ile İstatistiksel Veri Analizi. Eskişehir, Kaan Kitabevi
Özer H (1992) Performans Denetimi. Sayiştay Dergisi, Sayi 7, 30–41
Öztürk Ü (2006) Organizasyonlarda Performans Yönetimi. Sistem Yayincilik, Istanbul
Peters BG, Wright V (1996) Public policy and administration, old and new. In: Goodin RE, Klingemann H-D (eds) The new handbook of political science, pp 630–638
Polat N (2003) Saydamlik, Hesap Verme Sorumluluğu ve Denetimin Etkinliği, SD 49:65–80
Professional Accountants in Business Committee (2011) Global survey on risk management and internal control results, analysis, and proposed next steps. Information Paper
Ratcliffe TA, Landes CE (2009) understanding internal control and internal control services. American Institute of Certified Public Accountants, New York
Reding KF, Sobel PJ, Anderson UL et al (2009) Internal auditing: assurance & consulting services (second edition). The Institute of Internal Auditors Research Foundation
Rittenberg LE, Johnstone KM, Gramling AA (2010) Auditing a business risk approach, 7th edn. Nelson Education Ltd, Canada
Sanal R (2002) Türkiye'de Yönetsel Denetim ve Devlet Denetleme Kurulu, Ankara
Şentürk H (2004) Belediyelerde Performans Yönetimi. İlke Yayincilik, Istanbul
Topcu MK (2013) Kamuda İç Kontrol Sisteminin COSO Modeli Bağlaminda Taşrada Uygulanabilirliği: İhalelerde Uygulanmasina Yönelik İki Vaka Analizi. Sayiştay Dergisi 91:6–31
Türedi H (2007) Denetim. Celepler Matbaacilik, Trabzon

Author Biographies

Mehmet Ali Hatikler holds Business Administration Master from Trakya University and works in Ministry of Justice.

Prof. Dr. Kıymet Tunca Çalıyurt CPA, CFE, graduated from the Faculty of Business Administration at Marmara University, Istanbul, Turkey. Her master's and Ph.D. degrees are in Accounting and Finance Program from the Social Graduate School, Marmara University. She has worked as auditor in Horwath Auditing Company, manager in McDonalds, and finance staff in Singapore Airlines. After vast experience in private sector, she has started to work in academia. She is holding CFE and CPE titles. Her research interests are in accounting, auditing, fraud, social responsibility, corporate governance, finance, and business ethics, with a special interest in aviation management and women rights in business. She is the Founder of the International Group on Governance, Fraud, Ethics and Social Responsibility (IGonGFE&SR) and the President of the National-International-Students' Conference Series on Governance, Fraud, Ethics and Social Responsibility (IConGFE&SR). In 2009, she also founded the International Women and Business Group, which organizes a global, annual conference. she has published papers, chapters, and books both nationally and internationally on fraud, social responsibility, ethics in accounting/finance/aviation disciplines and NGOs in Springer and Taylor Francis Routledge, and some titles are Emerging Fraud (with Sam Idowu); Corporate Governance: An International Perspective (with

Sam Idowu); Women and Sustainability in Business: A Global Perspective, Sustainability and Management: An International Perspective (with Ulku Yuksel); Globalization and Social Responsibility (with David Crowther). She is regular speaker at International Economic Crime Symposium in Jesus College, Cambridge University. She is Member in Editorial Board of Social Responsibility Journal, Journal of Financial Crime, International Journal of Law and Management.

Chapter 18
Auditor Stress: Literature Review and Classification

Iffet Kesimli, Serol Karalar and Özgür Tasdemir

18.1 Introduction

External auditors have important roles in moving the economy on solid foundations. "An external auditor performs an audit, in accordance with specific laws or rules, of the financial statements of a company, government entity, other legal entity, or organization, and is independent of the entity being audited. Users of these entities' financial information, such as investors, government agencies, and the general public, rely on the external auditor to present an unbiased and independent audit report."[1]

The most important role in the progress of the external auditing industry is to look for safe investment ports of the companies' interest groups. It is a search for a neutral expert to audit the financial statements prepared by the companies. Although external auditors have the training and experience to carry out audits of very large companies, the management corruption, financial crises, and strict working conditions of auditors after the 1980s created stress for auditors.

The training, internship, and post-examination continuing education required to become an external auditor will increase the professional qualification of the external auditor and at the same time ensure that the country's economy is reliable and sustainable. For this reason, external audit practice is spreading all over the

[1]External auditor, https://en.wikipedia.org/wiki/External_auditor, Accessed on March 15, 2017.

I. Kesimli (✉)
Kırklareli University, Kırklareli, Turkey
e-mail: ifkesimli@gmail.com

S. Karalar · Ö. Tasdemir
Trakya University, Edirne, Turkey
e-mail: serolkaralar@trakya.edu.tr

Ö. Tasdemir
e-mail: ozgurtasdemir@trakya.edu.tr

K. T. Çalıyurt and R. Said (eds.), *Sustainability and Social Responsibility of Accountability Reporting Systems*, Accounting, Finance, Sustainability, Governance & Fraud: Theory and Application, https://doi.org/10.1007/978-981-10-3212-7_18

world. Nevertheless, competition in the market, customer retention habits, and external auditors who violate fair competition rules have proved that it is not important to set rules only in the external audit sector. All of these create stress for external auditors who want to work ethically.

External auditing is prepared in a much wider perspective than national standards and very differently from tax-oriented financial statements. In this context, external auditing has to implement international accounting and valuation standards as well as international auditing standards in terms of accountability.

External auditing firms are obliged to undertake and constantly monitor certain stresses in order to improve quality. Institutions that regulate external auditing in Turkey and in the world[2,3] disclose quality control standards for raising the working standards of external auditors, guaranteeing the accuracy of auditor reports to the public and related organizations after company audit, and strengthening ethical behavior in audit firms. For example, quality control standards for audit firms are described in detail in USA.[4] In Turkey, the quality standards to be complied with by auditing firms and auditors are published by the Public Oversight—Accounting and Auditing Standards Authority.[5] In order for the auditor to be able to implement the quality standards in a healthier way, the external auditor should be considered in conjunction with "ISA 200, Overall Objective of the Independent Auditor, and the Conduct of an Audit in Accordance with International Standards on Auditing."

The Sarbanes Oxley Act[6], enacted in 2002 following Enron and other similar management scandals, has brought significant sanctions and challenges to external auditors and audit firms. With this law, the codes of ethics that external audit firms must comply with have been expanded, and the conditions of competition have been improved. For example, it will not be possible for the audit firms and the audit team to audit the same company for more than five years. It will also be impossible for the audit firm to conduct business with the audited company other than audit of the financial statements and specific tax reports. The introduction of stringent measures, both in terms of ethical codes and quality standards, has put the auditors and supervisors of the audit companies under stress. In this context, we will focus primarily on the quality standards that the auditor should comply with and then examine how each quality standard is reflected to the audit firms and auditors as stress. Subsequently, auditor stress and international literature content will be classified in terms of research methodology.

---

[2]Turkish Public Oversight—Accounting and Auditing Standards Authority, http://www.kgk.gov.tr/Home/.

[3]American Public Company Accounting Oversight Board https://pcaobus.org/.

[4]Quality Control, https://pcaobus.org/standards.

[5]Independent Auditing of Financial Tables and Limited Independent Audits and Other Assurance Audits and Independent Auditing Conducting Related Services and Quality Control for Independent Auditors http://www.kgk.gov.tr/DynamicContentDetail/5166/Kalite-Kontrol-Standartlar%C4%B1, Accessed on January 15, 2017.

[6]Sarbanes Oxley Act of 2002 https://www.sec.gov/about/laws/soa2002.pdf, Accessed on March 5, 2017.

18.2 Quality and Standardization in Auditing

The quality rules are rules the external auditing firms in the USA, where most audit corruption is experienced, must comply with. The "system of quality control for a CPA firm's accounting and auditing practice" provided the most important contribution to the legislation and the literature in the independent audit. These rules are as follows:

"This section provides that a CPA firm shall have a system of quality control for its accounting and auditing practice and describes elements of quality control and other matters essential to the effective design, implementation, and maintenance of the system."

The American Institution of Certified Public Accountants (AICPAs), Principles of Professional Conduct, provide, among other things, that "members should practice in firms that have in place internal quality control procedures to ensure that services are competently delivered and adequately supervised. Because of the public interest in the services provided by and the reliance placed on the objectivity and integrity of CPAs, this section provides that a CPA firm shall have a system of quality control for its accounting and auditing practice."

Auditing firms have to establish a quality control system. This system will standardize the audit firm's business procedures and increase audit quality. In this context, the following rules should be cared for while establishing the system of quality control in the USA.

"A firm has a responsibility to ensure that its personnel comply with the professional standards applicable to its accounting and auditing practice. A system of quality control is broadly defined as a process to provide the firm with reasonable assurance that its personnel comply with applicable professional standards and the firm's standards of quality. The policies and procedures designed to implement the system in one segment of a firm's practice may be the same as, different from, or interrelated with the policies and procedures designed for another segment, but the purpose of the system is the same for all segments of a firm's practice."

"A firm's system of quality control encompasses the firm's organizational structure and the policies adopted and procedures established to provide the firm with reasonable assurance of complying with professional standards. The nature, extent, and formality of a firm's quality control policies and procedures should be appropriately comprehensive and suitably designed in relation to the firm's size, the number of its offices, the degree of authority allowed its personnel and its offices, the knowledge and experience of its personnel, the nature and complexity of the firm's practice, and appropriate cost-benefit considerations."

"Any system of quality control has inherent limitations that can reduce its effectiveness. Variance in an individual's performance and understanding of (a) professional requirements or (b) the firm's quality control policies and procedures affects the degree of compliance with a firm's prescribed quality control policies and procedures and, therefore, the effectiveness of the system."

"The system of quality control should provide the firm with reasonable assurance that the segments of the firm's engagements performed by its foreign offices or by its domestic or foreign affiliates or correspondents are performed in accordance with professional standards in the United States when such standards are applicable."[7]

Established in Turkey after establishing and implementing a new quality system in external audit firms in USA, Public Oversight—Accounting and Auditing Standards Authority (POA) has begun to challenge companies and demand that audit firms establish their own quality standards. Within this scope, quality control standards were established by Public Oversight Authority (POA).

18.3 Stress Factors for Audit Firms

The search for quality in the audit sector brings stress with it. Different studies have examined work stress in different ways. Beehr and Newman (1978) have defined stress as a situation that would compel someone to deviate from normal functioning. This is due to psychological and/or physiological changes in the person, such that the person is forced to deviate from normal functioning.[8] Qureshi et al. (2012) argued that perceived work overload leads to increased stress.[9] In the original table, which is created by Kesimli (2015, 212),[10] audit quality elements in terms of auditing firm, auditor, customer, and law regulator are examined. In Table 18.1, the "auditor's stress elements" column is added by the authors.

The main source of the literature survey is Web of Science; 98 relevant articles published in the prestigious journals of Web of Science have been identified. American Accounting Association publications are used as secondary resource. From this source, 20 academic studies related to the subject were taken. The limitations of the survey is the usage of the above-mentioned Web resources; therefore, non-indexed research is ignored. The two sources used for the literature search were scanned for the keywords "auditor" and "stress", thus, the articles were identified. In only 22 of the articles obtained, the subject we sought to investigate had been studied. Though words "auditor" and "stress" are found in remaining articles, the articles are not directly related to the subject, and these words are only in referred articles of the papers read. All articles are listed in the "References section and Table 18.3". Along with other criteria, all of these studies are classified according to their research questions and methods.

---

[7]QC Sect. 20 System of Quality Control for a CPA Firm's Accounting and Auditing Practice, https://pcaobus.org/Standards/QC/Pages/QC20.aspx, Accessed on January 3, 2017.

[8]Beehr and Newman (1978).

[9]Qureshi et al. (2012).

[10]Kesimli (2015).

Table 18.1 Quality elements and stress elements of external audit

	Element	Explanation	Stress element/s
Auditor	Independence		The most stressful element is independence because of the abuses the auditors are involved in. The requirement to constantly check whether the auditor's case matches the element of independence is a stress element
	Legal compliance	Scale, examinations (if any), warnings, penalties	Due to the rapid change of laws, difficulties in adaptation lead to stress
	Compliance with auditing standards	Scale, examinations (if any), warnings, penalties	Inadequate training on frequently updated auditing standards and the lack of case analysis make the auditor to find it more difficult in practice
	Average experience of audit professionals		Inspection in the sector where the auditor is not experienced causes stress
	Number of audited companies		A surplus of customers is the cause of stress
	Knowledge and experience about client and industry		
	Rotation		Every five years, change of client causes the auditor to feel under stress
	Declaration/opinion repeats		The fact that the auditor's time is limited will further increase his/her stress
	Professional skepticism		The professional skepticism, which is important for the profession, increases stress level
	Over self-confidence		The sense of superiority causes the auditor not to follow the current rules

In these studies, four issues were considered in terms of the year of the article, the aim of the article, the methodology, and the stress items mentioned in the article, and the classification was made under these four headings. The examined 29 studies are listed in Table 18.2 according to the year they are published.

Table 18.2 Literature on auditor stress examined according to: Year, aim, methodology, and stress items mentioned in the article

Year	Author/s	Title of the paper	Aim of the paper	Methodology	Stress element/s mentioned in the article
2016	Bills, K., Swanquist, Q., & Whited, R.	Growing Pains: Audit Quality and Office Growth	Authors investigated how local office growth affects audit quality	A sample of 17,062 firm-year observations between 2005 and 2010 were examined. A mathematical model was established, and descriptive statistics were given. Pearson (Spearman) correlation coefficient and robustness tests were performed	Significant recent growth will temporarily stress office resources and time constrains
2016	Breger, David, & Edmonds, Mark	The Impact of Audit Room Noise on Audit Quality: A Theoretical Inquiry	The effects of noise on performance of auditors is examined and provides auditors with solutions to potential noise problems	The methodology is reviewing the literature involving individual task performance in social settings	Noise
2016	Eutsler, J., Nickell, E., & Robb, S.	Fraud Risk Awareness and the Likelihood of Audit Enforcement Action	Authors wanted to examine the counterfactual reasoning theory, where experimental research suggests that a documented awareness of fraud risk actually increases the likelihood of litigation against the auditor following a fraud	Review Auditing and Accounting Enforcement Releases (AAERs) issued by the Securities and Exchange Commission (SEC) for alleged financial reporting frauds between 1995 and 2012. The first data set consists of 789 unique companies with at least one set of financial statements declared forged. The authors had given descriptive statistics and established a probit regression model	They wanted to understand how specific audit actions, such as opinion modification, affect auditor liability following harmful events (e.g., fraud, bankruptcy) is an important part of safeguarding the audit reporting process and improving audit quality

(continued)

Table 18.2 (continued)

Year	Author/s	Title of the paper	Aim of the paper	Methodology	Stress element/s mentioned in the article
2016	Gimbar, C., Hansen, B., & Ozlanski, M.	The Effects of Critical Audit Matter Paragraphs and Accounting Standard Precision on Auditor Liability	Our results highlight the similarities between the effects of imprecise accounting standards and CAMs on negligence assessments. These results provide insight for regulators and the auditing profession about the potential consequences of the proposed regulatory changes	Responses from 234 students enrolled in introductory accounting courses at a large U.S. public university were analyzed by logistic regression and mediation analysis. In addition, Demographic data were given and Shapiro-Wilk W-test and Fisher's exact tests were applied to data. Prior research suggests that judgments of students are not significantly different from those of individuals who report for jury duty, both in general and specifically in an audit litigation setting	Under precise standards, unrelated CAMs lead jurors to question the quality of the audit and the auditor's intent to take the necessary actions to prevent an accounting misstatement (CAM: Critical Audit Matter). Auditor litigation
2016	Smith, S., Tayler, W., & Prawitt, D.	The Effect of Information Choice on Auditors' Judgments and Confidence	To examine whether litigation risk and auditor experience influence auditors' susceptibility to the information choice effect, which has potential implications for audit effectiveness and efficiency	Experimental methodology by creating a setting that manipulates whether there is a choice to acquire information, while holding constant other aspects of the setting (including information source). An online audit case study was completed by 136 auditor participants. Statistical analysis was done	Information small in quantity. Time pressure. Uncertainty

(continued)

Table 18.2 (continued)

Year	Author/s	Title of the paper	Aim of the paper	Methodology	Stress element/s mentioned in the article
2016	Umans, T., Broberg, P., Schmidt, M., Nilsson, S., & Olsson, E.	Feeling well by being together: Study of Swedish auditors	The paper aims to explore organizational culture as an antecedent of auditors' well-being, which is assumed to have important consequences or the quality of auditors' work	This study is based on a survey of 207 Swedish auditors. Using established and validated instruments measuring aspects of organizational culture and personal well-being, the study employed correlations and multiple regression analysis in testing the relationship between the two	Job satisfaction, life balance and life satisfaction. Overflow of work task, complex tasks, time pressure
2015	Shafaghat, A., Keyvanfar, A., Ferwati, M., & Alizadeh, T.	Enhancing staff's satisfaction with comfort toward productivity by sustainable Open Plan Office Design	It is aimed to determine the features of Open Plan Office Design (OPOD) and its sub-features into positive and negative categories which affect staff's satisfaction with comfort that simultaneously impact their performance and productivity at open-plan office buildings	Authors identified all relevant literatures. Cause–effect analysis, Content analysis, pre and final Weight-value analysis were performed	Physical and psychological stress, occupational stress

(continued)

Table 18.2 (continued)

Year	Author/s	Title of the paper	Aim of the paper	Methodology	Stress element/s mentioned in the article
2012	Bhattacharjee, S., Moreno, K., & Riley, T.	The Interplay of Interpersonal Affect and Source Reliability on Auditors' Inventory Judgments	The goal of the current study is to examine when the irrelevant personality-based source characteristic, and interpersonal effects impact auditors' sensitivity to the relevant source characteristic, client competence, to influence persuasion	Conducted an experiment in which 174 auditorsresponded to an inventory obsolescence task where interpersonal effects toward the client (positive, negative, and neutral) and client competence (higher and lower competence) were manipulated	Interpersonal interactions with audit clients
2012	Koch, Christopher, Weber, Martin, Wüstemann, Jens.	Can Auditors be Independent? Experimental Evidence on the Effects of Client Type	The objective is to find out whether type of auditors' client affects auditors' behavior contingent on the degree of the perceived threats to independence or not	In an experiment, it is tested whether the type of client affects auditors' independence. Two of the International Big Four audit companies have agreed to support the experiments. A training program was applied to Auditors at the audit firm. The number of samples was 72. Descriptive statistics were given and used a structural-equation-based path analysis and logistic regression analyses were applied to data	Auditors' client retention incentives and accountability pressure

(continued)

Table 18.2 (continued)

Year	Author/s	Title of the paper	Aim of the paper	Methodology	Stress element/s mentioned in the article
2012	López, D. M., & Peters, G. F.	The effect of workload compression on audit quality	The aim is to investigate whether workload pressures, as proxied by the audit busy season (i.e., December fiscal year-end date) and auditor workload compression (i.e., relative concentration of companies with the same fiscal year-end date in an auditor's client portfolio), affect audit quality. It was also investigated whether the factors typically associated with individual auditors influence the performance of collective audit engagement	A sample of 8,384 firm-year observations during the period 2006–2009 was used. Logistic Regression of Going-Concern Tests, Logistic Regression of Earnings Benchmark Tests, Alternative Earnings Management Tests, Ordinary Least-Squares Regression of Abnormal Accruals, Correlation Table, and Abnormal Accrual Tests were applied	Workload pressures, time budget constraints
2012	Stefaniak, C., Houston, R., & Cornell, R.	The Effects of Employer and Client Identification on Internal and External Auditors' Evaluations of Internal Control Deficiencies	By using post-SOX experimental data to compare the levels and effects of employer (client) identification on the control evaluations of internal (external) auditors	Analysis of responses from 40 internal auditors and 48 external auditors who completed an online experiment. Seven-point Likert-type scale was used. One-Sample t-tests, independent t-tests and regression analysis were performed	None

(continued)

Table 18.2 (continued)

Year	Author/s	Title of the paper	Aim of the paper	Methodology	Stress element/s mentioned in the article
2011	Ameer, R., Isa, R., & Bin Abdullah, A.	A Survey on the Usage of Derivatives and Their Effect on Cost of Equity Capital	The research is about the usage of derivatives and their impact on the listed companies' cost of equity (COE) capital in Malaysia	**Stage 1.** For the investigation of the usage of derivatives, the main data requirement was information about the usage (or nonusage) of derivative instruments. In first stage of data collection, a survey questionnaire was adapted from Bodnar et al. [1998] and Maliin et al. [2001]	Factors causing pressure and impairing auditor independence, pressure to retain the client, and to conform, pressure enforced by management owing to their power to hire and fire auditors at will
				Stage 2. For testing the hypothesis of the derivatives impact on COE capital, secondary data on derivatives usage were obtained from the 2007-2008 annual reports of the companies. Responses were analyzed by factor analysis	
2011	Kelly, T., Margheim, L., & Pattison, D.	Survey On The Differential Effects Of Time Deadline Pressure Versus Time Budget Pressure On Auditor Behavior	This study examines the differential effects of time deadline pressure vs time budget pressure by surveying both senior and staff auditors	Seven point Likert type scale is used in surveys. Surveys targeted senior and staff auditors in public accounting firms. Descriptive statistics are used, paired comparison t-test is applied	Time deadline pressure, time budget pressure

(continued)

Table 18.2 (continued)

Year	Author/s	Title of the paper	Aim of the paper	Methodology	Stress element/s mentioned in the article
2007	Leanne C. Gundry, Gregory A. Liyanarachchi	Time budget pressure, auditors' personality type, and the incidence of reduced audit quality practices	This paper aims to extend the literature on reduced audit quality practices (RAQPs) by examining the relationship between time budget pressure, auditors' personality types, and the incidence of two RAQPs – premature sign-off of an audit step (PSO) and accepting a weak client explanation (WCE)	The aim of this paper is to collect data. A research instrument was developed and administered to audit practitioners in New Zealand using postal and web link methods. The research instrument included several hypothetical audit scenarios and Blumenthal's Type A Self-Rating Inventory Scale (TASRI)	Time budget pressure
2006	Larson, Linda Lee, Murff, Elizabeth J. Tipton	An Analysis of Job Stress Outcomes Among Bank Internal Auditors	The aim of this paper is to find out how many and varied responsibilities cause job stress for a bank's internal auditors, which then may result in job dissatisfaction or job burnout	Data for this study came from a sample of 180 bank internal auditors gathered as part of a prior study of internal auditors conducted by the first author. Data for the initial study were obtained by mailing a survey instrument to a nationwide random sample of 1,500 internal auditors who were members of the American Institute of Certified Public Accountants (AICPA). The research instrument consisted of items from previously validated	The most significant individual stressors are time pressure, quantitative overload and career progress

(continued)

Table 18.2 (continued)

Year	Author/s	Title of the paper	Aim of the paper	Methodology	Stress element/s mentioned in the article
				questionnaires, followed by a set of demographic questions. Work-related stressors are measured using the Ivancevich and Matteson Stress Diagnostic Survey (SDS). This scale measures 15 types of job stressors: eight individual job stress variables (role conflict, role ambiguity, quantitative overload, qualitative overload, time pressure, responsibility for others, career progress and job scope) and seven organizational variables (politics, human resource development, rewards, participation, underutilization, supervisory style and organization structure). Job burnout is measured by using Quinn and Shepard Self-Esteem Scale. Factor analysis was used and established a logistic regression model	

(continued)

Table 18.2 (continued)

Year	Author/s	Title of the paper	Aim of the paper	Methodology	Stress element/s mentioned in the article
2006	Pennington, Robin R. Kelton, Andrea S. DeVries, Delwyn D.	The Effects of Qualitative Overload on Technology Acceptance	The purpose of this study is to examine the effect of this stressor on intention to use technology	A study was conducted at a large southeastern university in which graduate accounting students (43 Master of Accountancy (MAcc) students) were required to complete class assignments using ACL1. This application is used by many future employers of these students and was appropriate for the audit task simulations conducted during the class. Use of the ACL software was also a relevant setting for examining qualitative overload, perceived ease of use, and intention in an audit context. Chi-squared test, Mediation test, and factor analysis were applied to data	Role ambiguity, qualitative overload stress, job-related factors (stressors), Occupational stress

(continued)

Table 18.2 (continued)

Year	Author/s	Title of the paper	Aim of the paper	Methodology	Stress element/s mentioned in the article
2004	Ahson, U., & Asokan, A.	Dimensions of pressures faced by auditors and its impact on auditors' independence: A comparative study of the USA and Australia	The objective was, first, to increase understanding of the underlying dimensions of pressures faced by these auditors; and second, to examine any similarities between two countries, similar in culture, but significantly different in such respects as the legal environment	Responses to case studies sent to auditors in the USA and Australia were analyzed via factor analysis	Factors causing pressure and impairing auditor independence
2004	Larson, L. L., Meier, H. H., Poznanski, P. J., & Tipton Murff, E. J.	Concepts and Consequences of Internal Auditor Job Stress	This paper presents the results of a large national survey designed to examine how potential sources of job stress affect job dissatisfaction and job burnout among internal auditors	The survey gathered data concerning job burnout, job dissatisfaction, and various facets of job stress. Fifteen job stress scores, a job burnout score, and a job dissatisfaction score were then calculated for each respondent. The stress variables were next consolidated into two primary factors that were then used in two regression models. The environmental factor was positively related to both increased job burnout and job	Environmental stress and workload stress. Quantitative overload, qualitative overload, time pressure, and responsibility for others. The survey gathered data concerning job burnout, job dissatisfaction, and various facets of job stress

(continued)

Table 18.2 (continued)

Year	Author/s	Title of the paper	Aim of the paper	Methodology	Stress element/s mentioned in the article
				dissatisfaction. In contrast, the workload stress factor was positively related to an increase in job burnout and yet negatively related to job dissatisfaction. In addition, the regression models indicated that being male and being married each reduced job burnout. Furthermore, these models also indicated that being a parent and being a career auditor each decreased job dissatisfaction	
2004	Larson, Linda Lee	Internal auditors and job stress	The author wanted to collect data on work stress for a large national sample of US internal auditors	Ivancevich and Matteson Stress Diagnostic Survey is used to gather data concerning job stress for a large national sample of internal auditors in the USA	Organizational job stressors, including rewards, participation, politics, and career development, were serious sources of job stress for the internal auditors in this study

(continued)

Table 18.2 (continued)

Year	Author/s	Title of the paper	Aim of the paper	Methodology	Stress element/s mentioned in the article
2002	Clarkson, P., Emby, C., & Watt, V.	Debiasing the outcome effect: The role of instructions in an audit litigation setting	Authors investigated the results of an experiment in an applied auditing setting that tests the efficacy of two different sets of instructions as potential mitigators of the biasing effect of outcome knowledge	A total of 122 graduate students enrolled in an electronic commerce program at a major university participated in the survey. Likert type scale was used for the evaluation of the auditor's judgment quality. Variance analysis and Tukey's HSD test were applied to data	None
2001	Bierstaker, J. L., & Wright, A.	The effects of fee pressure and partner pressure on audit planning decisions	Authors investigated the impact of an explicit suggestion from a partner to improve efficiency on auditors' program planning decisions in the presence or absence of a reduction in audit fees	Eighty-three auditors with an average of 25.4 months of experience (standard deviation of 8 .8 months) participated in the study. Auditors with between 2 and 3 years of experience were sought because they are normally the individuals assigned to perform audit program planning (Houston, 1999). To control for potential confounding effects as a result of differences in audit approach, all participants	Fee pressure, partner pressure and also in today's competitive audit environment, auditors face significant pressure to reduce costs

(continued)

Table 18.2 (continued)

Year	Author/s	Title of the paper	Aim of the paper	Methodology	Stress element/s mentioned in the article
				came from a single Big 5 firm and were obtained under controlled conditions during staff training sessions. One of the researchers was present at each of the training sessions. A one-way ANOVA and chi-square tests were performed. A regression model was established	
2001	Fisher, Richard T.	Role Stress, the Type A Behavior Pattern, and External Auditor Job Satisfaction and Performance	The paper examines the relationship between elements of role stress and two important external auditor job outcome variables	Data is collected by a survey questionnaire to auditors in two of the B6 public accounting firms in New Zealand	Time pressure, role stress (role conflict and role ambiguity)
2000	Braun, R. L.	The effect of time pressure on auditor attention to qualitative aspects of misstatements indicative of potential fraudulent financial reporting	Authors investigated the effect of time budget pressure, a contextual feature of the audit environment, on auditor attention regarding the task of detecting potential fraudulent financial reporting	The method employed to test the hypothesis was an experiment in which participants were presented with materials detailing the objectives for the audit of inventory for a hypothetical audit client	Time pressure

(continued)

Table 18.2 (continued)

Year	Author/s	Title of the paper	Aim of the paper	Methodology	Stress element/s mentioned in the article
2000	Carcello, J., Hermanson, D., & Huss, H.	Going-concern opinions: The effects of partner compensation plans and client size	The authors examine, in an archival setting, the association of partner compensation plans and client size with auditors' propensity to issue going-concern audit opinions to stressed clients	The authors used descriptive statistics and established a logistic regression model to test the hypothesis. Opinion =f(Compensation Plan, Plan*Size, CR, PCHCR. RLP, CFTL, TLTA, Client Size, Default Status, Audit Structure, Time Period)	Stressed clients, client-imposed pressures
1996	Otley, D. T., & Pierce, B. J.	Auditor time budget pressure: consequences and antecedents	The study sets out to examine whether the inverted U-shaped relationship between budget tightness and dysfunctional behavior (suggested by the industrial psychology literature and empirically supported by a previous study of auditors in a USA setting) exists in a different setting	By prior agreement with senior management, a survey questionnaire was sent to all audit seniors in three Big Six firms in Ireland. Owing to the sensitive nature of the data, questionnaires were anonymous and participants were given a guarantee of confidentiality regarding their responses. Respondents were requested to mail completed questionnaires directly to the researcher using postage-paid envelopes, and a follow-up letter was sent to all subjects two weeks after the initial request. From a total of 356	Time budget pressure

(continued)

Table 18.2 (continued)

Year	Author/s	Title of the paper	Aim of the paper	Methodology	Stress element/s mentioned in the article
				questionnaires distributed, 260 usable responses were received, representing a response rate of 73 per cent. Demographics and descriptive statistics were given. One way ANOVA, Tukey analysis and t-test were applied to data and regression model was established	
1995	Choo, F.	Auditors' Judgment Performance Under Stress: A Test of the Predicted Relationship by Three Theoretical Models	This study aims comparing three competing theories of stress and judgment performance, namely, working memory capacity theory (Eysenck, 1979), cue utilization theory (Easterbrook, 1959), and coping behavior theory (Folkman, 1984). These were compared for their efficacy in explaining the form of stress-induced performance changes in auditors' judgment	Five-phase field research that included the development of an Audit Mental Stress Scale and the usage of a complex audit judgment case. The second study reinforced the findings with a laboratory experiment. Forty-eight auditors were randomly assigned to four groups of 12 subjects each and the four groups assigned to one of four time pressure conditions. ANOVA, U-curve, F statistics test	Time pressure, task related mental stress, overall job related stress

(continued)

Table 18.2 (continued)

Year	Author/s	Title of the paper	Aim of the paper	Methodology	Stress element/s mentioned in the article
1992	PONEMON, L. A.	Auditor underreporting of time and moral reasoning: An experimental lab study	This paper introduces the theory of moral reasoning as a valid determinant of the underreporting of audit time	An experimental study exploring three determinants of underreporting for a sample of 88 staff-level auditors (subjects) from a national public accounting firm was conducted. All subjects were newly hired, were from three different offices, and were attending a one-week training program located in a northeastern city. Data were collected for each auditor during a classroom training exercise under the direct supervision of the researcher. The experiment utilized a between subjects lab design and required the examination of a bank reconciliation and the completion of a cash work paper. Subjects were randomly assigned to one of three classes (groups). All participants completed the audit task, biographical	Time budget pressure, work-related pressure, explicit peer pressure, the auditor's personally held beliefs and ethical values, client fee arrangements, the auditor's perceptions of performance appraisals, firm size, the auditor's position level within the firm

(continued)

Table 18.2 (continued)

Year	Author/s	Title of the paper	Aim of the paper	Methodology	Stress element/s mentioned in the article
				information sheet, the Defining Issues Test, and a debriefing questionnaire in less than two hours. Defining issues test, one-tailed t-test, the Spearman test, Wilcoxon signed rank test, Kolmogorov-Smirnov test, two way ANOVA, and Chi-square test were used	
1990	Haskins, Mark E., Baglioni, Jr., A. J. Cooper, Cary L.	An investigation of the sources, moderators, and psychological symptoms of stress among audit seniors	The paper aims to identify major sources of stress for audit seniors	Survey responses from 168 audit seniors attending two identical training seminars conducted by one of the Big Eight firms in the United States were analyzed hierarchical factor analysis, path analysis and multiple regression	Job Stressors (time pressures and deadlines, work overload, tasks outside competence, making mistakes, working long hours, work interfering with family/private life, taking work home, feeling undervalued, inadequate leisure time)
1990	Rebele, James E. Michaels, Ronald E.	Independent auditors' role stress: Antecedent, outcome, and moderating variables	The authors aim to examine antecedents to and consequences of role stress (role conflict and ambiguity) experienced by independent auditors	Data for the study were collected from offices of 4 large international accounting firms via questionnaires. Descriptive statistics were given, Path analysis, Moderated Multiple regression were performed	Role stress (role conflict and ambiguity), job-related tension

18.4 The Findings

In the external auditing profession; legislation in bulk quantities and frequently changing, complicated and wide theoretical knowledge required, and the need of using the most accurate and recent standards create heavy pressure on auditors. The number of scientific researches examining auditor stress is not parallel to this fact. One of the main causes of this situation stems from the avoidance of audit firms to contribute to academic research; the other one the psychologists' approach to stress studies, where they are interested in the issue regarding the society as a whole, thus resulting in low numbers of auditor stress studies. This points to the need of interdisciplinary research in this area.

In the light of international audit quality standards, auditor stress elements, and literature survey the following findings were observed:

- There are not many studies in the literature that directly examine auditor stress.
- The *time pressure* is studied as the auditor stress factor, in approximately half of the studies.
- The *role stress* is searched as the auditor stress factor, in approximately 20 percent of the studies.
- Not specific but any of the job-related stress factors are investigated as the auditor stress factor in approximately 33 percent of the studies.
- In addition to time pressure and role stress, *overflow* of work tasks, *complex* work tasks, outcome *uncertainty*, stressed *clients*, and client-imposed *pressures* are stress factors encountered in researches.
- In almost all of the studies, data were collected through questionnaire method and/or face-to-face interview method.
- In general, questionnaires were filled by the auditors.
- Almost all of the studies applied statistical analysis techniques.
- Almost each research utilized a different statistical analysis method. Some of these are chi-square test, t-test, Anova, Turkey's HSD test, factor analysis, principal component analysis, regression analysis and path analysis.
- The percentage of the examined studies that are directly related to "auditor stress" is 68, while the remaining 32 percent of the studies are not directly related to *auditor stress* (Table 18.3).
- It is observed that, "auditor stress" had since long been a research topic in different countries not small in number.

Table 18.3 Papers Examined: "auditor" and "stress" missing in the main text

Anderson, U., Koonce, L., & Marchant, G. (1994). The Effects of Source-Competence Information and its Timing on Auditors Performance of Analytical Procedures. *Auditing-A Journal of Practice & Theory, 13*(1), 137–148
Asare, S. (1992). The Auditors Going-Concern Decision—Interaction of Task Variables and the Sequential Processing of Evidence. *Accounting Review, 67*(2), 379–393

(continued)

Table 18.3 (continued)

Autore, D., Billingsley, R., & Schneller, M. (2009). Information uncertainty and auditor reputation. *Journal of Banking & Finance, 33*(2), 183–192. https://doi.org/10.1016/j.jbankfin.2008.07.011
Barbadillo, E., Aguilar, N., & Pena, N. (2009). The End of Mandatory Rotation of Audit. Firms and Audit Quality. *Revista De Economia Aplicada, 17*(49), 105–134
Basioudis, I., Papakonstantinou, E., & Geiger, M. (2008). Audit Fees, Non-audit Fees and Auditor Going-concern Reporting Decisions in the United Kingdom. *Abacus-a Journal of Accounting Finance and Business Studies, 44*(3), 284–309. https://doi.org/10.1111/j.1467-6281.2008.00263.x
Bauer, T. (2015). The Effects of Client Identity Strength and Professional Identity Salience on Auditor Judgments. *Accounting Review, 90*(1), 95–114. https://doi.org/10.2308/accr-50863
Bennett, M. (2014). Confronting Cognitive "Anchoring Effect" and "Blind Spot" Biases in Federal Sentencing: A Modest Solution for Reforming a Fundamental Flaw. *Journal of Criminal Law & Criminology, 104*(3), 489–534
Bhattacharjee, S., Maletta, M., & Moreno, K. (2007). The Cascading of Contrast Effects on Auditors' Judgments in Multiple Client Audit Environments. *Accounting Review, 82*(5), 1097–1117. https://doi.org/10.2308/accr.2007.82.5.1097
Bhattacharjee, S., & Moreno, K. (2017). The Role of Informal Controls and a Bargaining Opponent's Emotions on Transfer Pricing Judgments. *Contemporary Accounting Research, 34*(1), 427–454. https://doi.org/10.1111/1911-3846.12230
Bigus, J. (2016). Optimism and auditor liability. *Accounting and Business Research, 46*(6), 577–600. https://doi.org/10.1080/00014788.2015.1133275
Bowlin, K., Hobson, J., & Piercey, M. (2015). The Effects of Auditor Rotation, Professional Skepticism, and Interactions with Managers on Audit Quality. *Accounting Review, 90*(4), 1363–1393. https://doi.org/10.2308/accr-51032
Brody, R., & Kaplan, S. (1996). Escalation of Commitment Among Internal Auditors. *Auditing-a Journal of Practice & Theory, 15*(1), 1–15
Brown, P., Beekes, W., & Verhoeven, P. (2011). Corporate Governance, Accounting and Finance: A Review. *Accounting and Finance, 51*(1), 96–172. https://doi.org/10.1111/j.1467-629X.2010.00385.x
Brown-Liburd, H., Issa, H., & Lombardi, D. (2015). Behavioral Implications of Big Data's Impact on Audit Judgment and Decision Making and Future Research Directions. *Accounting Horizons, 29*(2), 451–468. https://doi.org/10.2308/acch-51023
Camus, J. (1996). Auditory Orienting of Attention in Dichotic Listening—Comparison of a Verbal Cue and a Lateralized Tone Cue. *Annee Psychologique, 96*(1), 31–52
Carey, P., Geiger, M., & O'Connell, B. (2008). Costs Associated with Going-concern-modified Audit Opinions: An Analysis of the Australian Audit Market. *Abacus-a Journal of Accounting Finance and Business Studies, 44*(1), 61–81. https://doi.org/10.1111/j.1467-6281.2007.00249.x
Carpenter, T. (2007). Audit Team Brainstorming, Fraud Risk Identification, and Fraud Risk Assessment: Implications of SAS No. 99. *Accounting Review, 82*(5), 1119–1140. https://doi.org/10.2308/accr.2007.82.5.1119
Carpenter, T., Reimers, J., & Fretwell, P. (2011). Internal Auditors' Fraud Judgments: The Benefits of Brainstorming in Groups. *Auditing-a Journal of Practice & Theory, 30*(3), 211–224. https://doi.org/10.2308/ajpt-10054
Choo, F. (1986). Job Stress, Job-Performance, and Auditor Personality-Characteristics. *Auditing-a Journal of Practice & Theory, 5*(2), 17–34
Christ, M. (1993). Evidence on the Nature of Audit Planning Problem Representations—An Examination of Auditor Free Recalls. *Accounting Review, 68*(2), 304–322

(continued)

Table 18.3 (continued)

Chung, J., Cullinan, C., Frank, M., Long, J., Mueller-Phillips, J., & O'Reilly, D. (2013). The Auditor's Approach to Subsequent Events: Insights from the Academic Literature. *Auditing-a Journal of Practice & Theory, 32*, 167–207. https://doi.org/10.2308/ajpt-50328
Cianci, A., & Bierstaker, J. (2009). The Impact of Positive and Negative Mood on the Hypothesis Generation and Ethical Judgments of Auditors. *Auditing-a Journal of Practice & Theory, 28*(2), 119–144. https://doi.org/10.2308/aud.2009.28.2.119
Clor-Proell, S., & Nelson, M. (2007). Accounting Standards, Implementation Guidance, and Example-based Reasoning. *Journal of Accounting Research, 45*(4), 699–730. https://doi.org/10.1111/j.1475-679X.2007.00248.x|https://doi.org/10.1111/J.1475-679x.2007.00248.X
Cluskey, G., & Vaux, A. (1997). Is Seasonal Stress a Career Choice of Professional Accountants? *Journal of Employment Counseling, 34*(1), 7–19
De Beelde, I. (2002). Creating a Profession 'Out of Nothing'? The Case of the Belgian Auditing Profession. *Accounting Organizations and Society, 27*(4–5), 447–470. https://doi.org/10.1016/S0361-3682(01)00045-9
Driessen, E., van der Vleuten, C., Schuwirth, L., van Tartwijk, J., & Vermunt, J. (2005). The Use of Qualitative Research Criteria for Portfolio Assessment As an Alternative to Reliability Evaluation: A Case Study. *Medical Education, 39*(2), 214–220. https://doi.org/10.1111/j.1365-2929.2004.02059.x
Fanning, K., & Piercey, M. (2014). Internal Auditors' Use of Interpersonal Likability, Arguments, and Accounting Information in a Corporate Governance Setting. *Accounting Organizations and Society, 39*(8), 575–589. https://doi.org/10.1016/j.aos.2014.07.002
Fargher, N., & Jiang, L. (2008). Changes in the Audit Environment and Auditors' Propensity to Issue Going-Concern Opinions. *Auditing-a Journal of Practice & Theory, 27*(2), 55–77. https://doi.org/10.2308/aud.2008.27.2.55
Fennema, M., & Perkins, J. (2008). Mental Budgeting Versus Marginal Decision Making: Training, Experience and Justification Effects on Decisions Involving Sunk Costs. *Journal of Behavioral Decision Making, 21*(3), 225–239. https://doi.org/10.1002/bdm.585
Frost, C. (1994). Uncertainty-Modified Audit Reports and Future Earnings. *Auditing-a Journal of Practice & Theory, 13*(1), 22–35
Ganguly, A., Herbold, J., & Peecher, M. (2007). Assurer Reputation for Competence in a Multiservice Context. *Contemporary Accounting Research, 24*(1), 133–170. https://doi.org/10.1506/Y224-5Q33-G6R2-817M
Geiger, M., & Raghunandan, K. (2001). Bankruptcies, Audit Reports, and the Reform Act. *Auditing-a Journal of Practice & Theory, 20*(1), 187–195. https://doi.org/10.2308/aud.2001.20.1.187
Geiger, M., Raghunandan, K., & Rama, D. (2005). Recent Changes in the Association Between Bankruptcies and Prior Audit Opinions. *Auditing-a Journal of Practice & Theory, 24*(1), 21–35. https://doi.org/10.2308/aud.2005.24.1.21
Geiger, M., Raghunandan, K., & Riccardi, W. (2014). The Global Financial Crisis: US Bankruptcies and Going-Concern Audit Opinions. *Accounting Horizons, 28*(1), 59–75. https://doi.org/10.2308/acch-50659
Geiger, M., & Rama, D. (2003). Audit Fees, Nonaudit Fees, and Auditor Reporting on Stressed Companies. *Auditing-a Journal of Practice & Theory, 22*(2), 53–69. https://doi.org/10.2308/aud.2003.22.2.53
Gibbins, M., & Jamal, K. (1993). Problem-Centered Research and Knowledge-Based Theory in The Professional Accounting Setting. *Accounting Organizations and Society, 18*(5), 451–466. https://doi.org/10.1016/0361-3682(93)90041-4

(continued)

Table 18.3 (continued)

Grenier, J., Pomeroy, B., & Stern, M. (2015). The Effects of Accounting Standard Precision, Auditor Task Expertise, and Judgment Frameworks on Audit Firm Litigation Exposure. *Contemporary Accounting Research, 32*(1), 336–357. https://doi.org/10.1111/1911-3846.12092
Hatfield, R., & Mullis, C. (2015). Negotiations Between Auditors and Their Clients Regarding Adjustments to the Financial Statements. *Business Horizons, 58*(2), 203–208. https://doi.org/10.1016/j.bushor.2014.11.008
Hess, M., & Broughton, E. (2014). Fostering an Ethical Organization from the Bottom Up and the Outside In. *Business Horizons, 57*(4), 541–549. https://doi.org/10.1016/j.bushor.2014.02.004
Hill, C., Thompson, B., & Williams, E. (1997). A Guide to Conducting Consensual Qualitative Research. *Counseling Psychologist, 25*(4), 517–572. https://doi.org/10.1177/0011000097254001
Hirshleifer, D., & Teoh, S. (2009). The Psychological Attraction Approach to Accounting and Disclosure Policy. *Contemporary Accounting Research, 26*(4), 1067–1090. https://doi.org/10.1506/car.26.4.3
Horvath, F., McCloughan, J., Weatherman, D., & Slowik, S. (2013). The Accuracy of Auditors' and Layered Voice Analysis (LVA) Operators' Judgments of Truth and Deception During Police Questioning. *Journal of Forensic Sciences, 58*(2), 385–392. https://doi.org/10.1111/1556-4029.12066
Hurtt, R. (2010). Development of a Scale to Measure Professional Skepticism. *Auditing-a Journal of Practice & Theory, 29*(1), 149–171. https://doi.org/10.2308/aud.2010.29.1.149
Hvozdarova, J. (2002). Development, Current State and Trends in Balance Sheet Consolidation. *Ekonomicky Casopis, 50*(2), 317–330
Kadous, K., & Mercer, M. (2012). Can Reporting Norms Create a Safe Harbor? Jury Verdicts Against Auditors Under Precise and Imprecise Accounting Standards. *Accounting Review, 87*(2), 565–587. https://doi.org/10.2308/accr-10203
Kaplan, S., & Williams, D. (2013). Do Going Concern Audit Reports Protect Auditors from Litigation? A Simultaneous Equations Approach. *Accounting Review, 88*(1), 199–232. https://doi.org/10.2308/accr-50279
Kida, T., Moreno, K., & Smith, J. (2010). Investment Decision Making: Do Experienced Decision Makers Fall Prey to the Paradox of Choice? *Journal of Behavioral Finance, 11*(1), 21–30. https://doi.org/10.1080/15427561003590001
Kleinman, G., & Palmon, D. (2009). Procedural Instrumentality and Audit Group Judgment: An Exploration of the Impact of Cognitive Fallibility and Ability Differences. *Group Decision and Negotiation, 18*(2), 147–168. https://doi.org/10.1007/s10726-008-9116-z
Knechel, W., & Leiby, J. (2016). If You Want My Advice: Status Motives and Audit Consultations About Accounting Estimates. *Journal of Accounting Research, 54*(5), 1331–1363. https://doi.org/10.1111/1475-679X.12150
Knechel, W., & Vanstraelen, A. (2007). The Relationship Between Auditor Tenure and Audit Quality Implied by Going Concern Opinions. *Auditing-a Journal of Practice & Theory, 26*(1), 113–131. https://doi.org/10.2308/aud.2007.26.1.113
Koonce, L., Seybert, N., & Smith, J. (2011). Causal Reasoning in Financial Reporting and Voluntary Disclosure. *Accounting Organizations and Society, 36*(4–5), 209–225. https://doi.org/10.1016/j.aos.2011.03.006
Leung, P., & Trotman, K. (2005). The Effects of Feedback Type on Auditor Judgment Performance for Configural and Non-configural Tasks. *Accounting Organizations and Society, 30*(6), 537–553. https://doi.org/10.1016/j.aos.2004.11.003
Low, K., & Tan, H. (2011). Does Time Constraint Lead to Poorer Audit Performance? Effects of Forewarning of Impending Time Constraints and Instructions. *Auditing-a Journal of Practice & Theory, 30*(4), 173–190. https://doi.org/10.2308/ajpt-10180

(continued)

Table 18.3 (continued)

Luippold, B., & Kida, T. (2012). The Impact of Initial Information Ambiguity on the Accuracy of Analytical Review Judgments. *Auditing-a Journal of Practice & Theory, 31*(2), 113–129. https://doi.org/10.2308/ajpt-10259
Mckeown, J., Mutchler, J., & Hopwood, W. (1991). Towards an Explanation of Auditor Failure to Modify the Audit Opinions of Bankrupt Companies. *Auditing-a Journal of Practice & Theory, 10*, 1–13
Messier, W., & Quilliam, W. (1992). The Effect of Accountability on Judgment—Development of Hypotheses for Auditing. *Auditing-a Journal of Practice & Theory, 11*, 123–138
Moore, D., Tanlu, L., & Bazerman, M. (2010). Conflict of Interest and the Intrusion of Bias. *Judgment and Decision Making, 5*(1), 37–53
Moorthy, M., Seetharaman, A., Mohamed, Z., Gopalan, M., & San, L. (2011). The Impact of Information Technology on Internal Auditing. *African Journal of Business Management, 5*(9), 3523–3539
Moreno, K., Bhattacharjee, S., & Brandon, D. (2007). The Effectiveness of Alternative Training Techniques on Analytical Procedures Performance. *Contemporary Accounting Research, 24*(3), 983–1014. https://doi.org/10.1506/car.24.3.11
Moynahan, G. (1999). Ernst Cassirer, Theoretical Biology, and the Clever Hans Phenomenon. *Science in Context, 12*(4), 549–574
Murphy, P., & Dacin, M. (2011). Psychological Pathways to Fraud: Understanding and Preventing Fraud in Organizations. *Journal of Business Ethics, 101*(4), 601–618. https://doi.org/10.1007/s10551-011-0741-0
Nelson, M. (1993). The Effects of Error Frequency and Accounting Knowledge on Error Diagnosis in Analytical Review. *Accounting Review, 68*(4), 804–824
Nolder, C., & Riley, T. (2014). Effects of Differences in National Culture on Auditors' Judgments and Decisions: A Literature Review of Cross-Cultural Auditing Studies from a Judgment and Decision Making Perspective. *Auditing-a Journal of Practice & Theory, 33*(2), 141–164. https://doi.org/10.2308/ajpt-50657
Nouri, H., & Parker, R. (2013). Career Growth Opportunities and Employee Turnover Intentions in Public Accounting Firms. *British Accounting Review, 45*(2), 138–148. https://doi.org/10.1016/j.bar.2013.03.002
O'Reilly, D., Leitch, R., & Tuttle, B. (2006). An Experimental Test of the Interaction of the Insurance and Information-signaling Hypotheses in Auditing. *Contemporary Accounting Research, 23*(1), 267–289. https://doi.org/10.1506/2607-8PDH-WKCV-R3RD
Painter, R. (2000). Lawyers' Rules, Auditors' Rules and the Psychology of Concealment. *Minnesota Law Review, 84*(5–6), 1399–1437
Parkerson, G., Michener, J., Yarnall, K., & Hammond, W. (1997). Duke Case-Mix System (DUMIX) for Ambulatory Health Care. *Journal of Clinical Epidemiology, 50*(12), 1385–1394. https://doi.org/10.1016/S0895-4356(97)00217-5
Patterson-Kane, J., & Rich, T. (2014). Achilles Tendon Injuries in Elite Athletes: Lessons in Pathophysiology from Their Equine Counterparts. *Ilar Journal, 55*(1), 86–99. https://doi.org/10.1093/ilar/ilu004
Peecher, M., Solomon, I., & Trotman, K. (2013). An Accountability Framework for Financial Statement Auditors and Related Research Questions. *Accounting Organizations and Society, 38*(8), 596–620. https://doi.org/10.1016/j.aos.2013.07.002
Pei, B., & Davis, F. (1989). The Impact of Organizational-Structure on Internal Auditor Organizational-Professional Conflict and Role Stress—An Exploration of Linkages. *Auditing-a Journal of Practice & Theory, 8*(2), 101–115

(continued)

Table 18.3 (continued)

Pomeroy, B. (2010). Audit Committee Member Investigation of Significant Accounting Decisions. *Auditing-a Journal of Practice & Theory, 29*(1), 173–205. https://doi.org/10.2308/aud.2010.29.1.173
Raghunandan, K., & Rama, D. (1995). Audit Reports for Companies In Financial Distress—Before and After SAS-No-59. *Auditing-a Journal of Practice & Theory, 14*(1), 50–63
Raghunandan, K., & Rama, D. (1999). Auditor Resignations and the Market for Audit Services. *Auditing-a Journal of Practice & Theory, 18*(1), 124–134. https://doi.org/10.2308/aud.1999.18.1.124
Raman, K., & Wilson, E. (1994). Governmental Audit Procurement Practices and Seasoned Bond Prices. *Accounting Review, 69*(4), 517–538
Ratzinger-Sakel, N. (2013). Auditor Fees and Auditor Independence-Evidence from Going Concern Reporting Decisions in Germany. *Auditing-a Journal of Practice & Theory, 32*(4), 129–168. https://doi.org/10.2308/ajpt-50532
Ricchiute, D. (2010). Evidence Complexity and Information Search in the Decision to Restate Prior-Period Financial Statements. *Journal of Accounting Research, 48*(3), 687–724. https://doi.org/10.1111/j.1475-679X.2010.00366.x
Ruiz-Barbadillo, E., Gomez-Aguilar, N., & Carrera, N. (2009). Does Mandatory Audit Firm Rotation Enhance Auditor Independence? Evidence from Spain. *Auditing-a Journal of Practice & Theory, 28*(1), 113–135. https://doi.org/10.2308/aud.2009.28.1.113
Shanteau, J., Weiss, D., Thomas, R., & Pounds, J. (2002). Performance-based assessment of expertise: How to decide if someone is an expert or not. *European Journal of Operational Research, 136*(2), 253–263. https://doi.org/10.1016/S0377-2217(01)00113-8
Trompeter, G., Carpenter, T., Desai, N., Jones, K., & Riley, R. (2013). A Synthesis of Fraud-Related Research. *Auditing-a Journal of Practice & Theory, 32*, 287–321. https://doi.org/10.2308/ajpt-50360
Viator, R. (2001). The Association of Formal and Informal Public Accounting Mentoring with Role Stress and Related Job Outcomes. *Accounting Organizations and Society, 26*(1), 73–93. https://doi.org/10.1016/S0361-3682(00)00002-7
Wainberg, J., Kida, T., Piercey, M., & Smith, J. (2013). The Impact of Anecdotal Data in Regulatory Audit Firm Inspection Reports. *Accounting Organizations and Society, 38*(8), 621–636. https://doi.org/10.1016/j.aos.2013.10.005
Warming-Rasmussen, B., & Windsor, C. (2003). Danish Evidence of Auditors' Level of Moral Reasoning and Predisposition to Provide Fair Judgments. *Journal of Business Ethics, 47*(2), 77–87. https://doi.org/10.1023/A:1026044615768
Wlodarczyk, D., & Jaskowski, P. (2002). Influence of Sleep Deprivation and Auditor Intensity on Reaction Time and Response Force. *Perceptual and Motor Skills, 94*(3), 1101–1112

References

Ahson U, Asokan A (2004) Dimensions of pressures faced by auditors and its impact on auditors' independence: a comparative study of the USA and Australia. Manag Audit J 19(1):99–116

Ameer R, Isa R, Bin Abdullah A (2011) A survey on the usage of derivatives and their effect on cost of equity capital. J Deriv 19(1):56–71

Beehr TA, Newman JE (1978) Job stress, employee health and organizational effectiveness: a facet analysis, model and literature review. Pers Psychol 31(4):665–699

Bhattacharjee S, Moreno K, Riley T (2012) The interplay of interpersonal affect and source reliability on auditors' inventory judgments. Contemp Acc Res 29(4):1087–1108. https://doi.org/10.1111/j.1911-3846.2011.01139.x

Bills K, Swanquist Q, Whited R (2016) Growing pains: audit quality and office growth. Contemp Acc Res 33(1):288–313. https://doi.org/10.1111/1911-3846.12122

Bierstaker JL, Wright A (2001). The effects of fee pressure and partner pressure on audit planning decisions. Advances in accounting, incorporating advances in international accounting. pp 1825-1846.https://doi.org/10.1016/S0882-6110(01)18004-1, 29.02.2016

Braun RL (2000) The effect of time pressure on auditor attention to qualitative aspects of misstatements indicative of potential fraudulent financial reporting. Acc Org Soc 25(3) 243–259; ISSN 0361-3682, http://dx.doi.org/10.1016/S0361-3682(99)00044-6.(http://www.sciencedirect.com/science/article/pii/S0361368299000446) (April)

Breger D, Edmonds M (2016). The impact of audit room noise on audit quality: a theoretical inquiry. J Theor Acc Res Spring 2016, 11(2):78–93

Carcello J, Hermanson D, Huss H (2000) Going-concern opinions: the effects of partner compensation plans and client size. Auditing-a J Pract Theory 19(1):67–77. https://doi.org/10.2308/aud.2000.19.1.67

Choo F (1995) Auditors' judgment performance under stress: a test of the predicted relationship by three theoretical models. J Acc Audit Finance 10(3):611–641 (Summer)

Clarkson P, Emby C, Watt V (2002) Debiasing the outcome effect: the role of instructions in an audit litigation setting. Auditing-a J Pract Theory 21(2):7–20. https://doi.org/10.2308/aud.2002.21.2.7

Eutsler J, Nickell E, Robb S (2016) Fraud risk awareness and the likelihood of audit enforcement action. Acc Horizons 30(3):379–392. https://doi.org/10.2308/acch-51490

Fisher RT (2001) Role stress, the type a behavior pattern, and external auditor job satisfaction and performance. Behav Res Acc 13(p143):28p

Gimbar C, Hansen B, Ozlanski M (2016) The effects of critical audit matter paragraphs and accounting standard precision on auditor liability. Acc Rev 91(6):1629–1646. https://doi.org/10.2308/accr-51382

Gundry LC, Liyanarachchi GA (2007) Time budget pressure, auditors' personality type, and the incidence of reduced audit quality practices. Pacific Acc Rev 19(2):125–152

Haskins ME, Baglioni AJ Jr, Cooper CL (1990) An investigation of the sources, moderators, and psychological symptoms of stress among audit seniors. Contemp Acc Res. Part 1, 6(2), 361–385 (Spring)

Kelly T, Margheim L, Pattison D (2011) Survey on the differential effects of time deadline pressure versus time budget pressure on auditor behavior. J Appl Bus Res (JABR) 15(4): 117–128. http://dx.doi.org/10.19030/jabr.v15i4.5666

Kesimli I (2015) Assessment of Turkish Auditing firms from the perspective of International Quality Control Standard, Trakya University Social Graduate Schools, Unpublished PhD Thesis, Edirne

Koch C, Weber M, Wüstemann J (2012) Can auditors be independent? Experimental evidence on the effects of client type. Eur Acc Rev 21(4):797–823. https://doi.org/10.1080/09638180.2011.629416

Larson LL (2004) Internal auditors and job stress. Manag Audit J 19(9):1119–1130. http://dx.doi.org/10.1108/02686900410562768

Larson LL, Murff EJT (2006) An analysis of job stress outcomes among bank internal auditors. Bank Acc Finance 19(4):39–43. 5 p (Jun 2006)

Larson LL, Meier HH, Poznanski PJ, Tipton Murff EJ (2004) Concepts and consequences of internal auditor job stress. J Acc Finance Res 12(6):35–46

López DM, Peters GF (2012) The effect of workload compression on audit quality. Auditing 31(4):139–165. https://doi.org/10.2308/ajpt-10305

Otley DT, Pierce BJ (1996) Auditor time budget pressure: consequences and antecedents. Acc Audit Acc J 9(1):31–58

Pennington RR, Kelton AS, DeVries DD (2006) The effects of qualitative overload on technology acceptance. J Inf Syst 20(2):25–36, 12 p (Fall)

Ponemon LA (1992) Auditor underreporting of time and moral reasoning: An experimental lab study. Contemp Acc Res 9(1):171–189

Qureshi I, Jamil RA, Iftikhar M, Arif S, Lodhi S, Naseem I, Zaman K (2012) Job stress, workload, environment and employees turnover intention: Destiny or choice. Archives of Sciences, 65(8):230–241. Retrieved from http://ssrn.com/abstract=2152930. Access 5 Jan 2017

Rebele James E, Michaels Ronald E (1990) Independent auditors' role stress: antecedent, outcome, and moderating variables. Behav Res Acc 2:p124

Shafaghat A, Keyvanfar A, Ferwati M, Alizadeh T (2015) Enhancing staff's satisfaction with comfort toward productivity by sustainable Open Plan Office Design. Sustain Cities Soc 19:151–164. https://doi.org/10.1016/j.scs.2015.08.001

Smith S, Tayler W, Prawitt D (2016) The effect of information choice on auditors' judgments and confidence. Acc Horizons 30(3):393–408. https://doi.org/10.2308/acch-51493

Stefaniak C, Houston R, Cornell R (2012) The effects of employer and client identification on internal and external auditors' evaluations of internal control deficiencies. Auditing-a J Pract Theory 31(1):39–56. https://doi.org/10.2308/ajpt-10179

Umans T, Broberg P, Schmidt M, Nilsson S, Olsson E (2016) Feeling well by being together: study of Swedish auditors. Work-a J Prev Assess Rehabil 54(1):79–86. https://doi.org/10.3233/WOR-162270

Wittlin M (2016) Hindsight Evidence. Columbia Law Rev 116(5):1323–1394

Author Biographies

Iffet Kesimli She got her B.A. from Business Administration. Within the "10 Young Executive Candidates" program of Türkiye Tütüncüler Bankası (Turkish Tobacco Producers' Bank) and Irving Trust Bank, which were partners at the time, she got training at all departments of the Bank in Izmir and assigned as assistant manager and became the Assistant to the CEO Dr. Antonio Puja. Following the break of the partnership of two banks, she worked as Assistant Personnel Manager until leaving the bank, which moved the headquarters to Istanbul; and started working at Raks Holding as Assistant Manager of Budgeting and Planning Department. Following the radical management changes at the company, she decided to work as freelancer and assisted budgeting processes of BMC OMPAŞ A.Ş., Rapak Ambalaj etc. until becoming the partner and manager of Bilda Bilgisayar Sistemleri Ltd. Şti., a software company. Ownership of a trading company and trade life followed. After two decades of private sector experience, she started lecturing at vocational schools. In the meantime she got her MBA from Business Administration at Trakya University and enrolled with PhD program at the same university, which is completed successfully in 2015. She is affiliated to Kırklareli University, Lüleburgaz Vocational School as Head of Accounting and Taxation Program; lectures at Tourism Faculty and Lüleburgaz Vocational School. She speaks German and English.

Serol Karalar Serol is research assistant in Department of Business Administration in Faculty of Economics and Business Sciences. He received his Ph.D. on Business Administration from Trakya University.

Özgür Tasdemir He has completed his Ph.D. in 2015 in Anatolian University, Institute of Science and Technology, Mathematics Department. He is also currently continuing his doctorate in Department of Business Administration at Trakya University. He has been working as an lecturer in Trakya University, Department of Business Administration since 2012. He continues to academic research in specific topics in numerical methods and mathematics.

Chapter 19
Sustainable Competitive Advantage in Green Supply Chain Management

Onur Çetin and Mohamed Knouch

19.1 The Emergence of Sustainable Competitive Advantage

In the last years, the theory of Sustainable competitive advantage (SCA) has developed as one of the most promising theoretical frameworks in the field of management, especially in strategic management. Therefore, the subject of sustainable competitive advantage is of great importance in the studies of management scientists. Alderson pointed out that the main aspect of the competition is the rapid adaptation of suppliers to meet changes in customer demands. Alderson returned in 1965 and explained that competition is based on having distinct resources to competitors (Foon and Nair 2010). The notion of SCA emerged in the year 1984, when Day proposed strategies to sustain competitive advantage (CA), while the first appearance of the word SCA is in the research of Harvard Business School professor Michael Porter in 1985 on the strategies through which the organization can gain SCA. These strategies are the low-cost strategy and excellence strategy (Pirayesh and Forouzandeh 2016). Most of the research focused on explaining the sustainable competitive advantage of the search for "excellence" (Porter 1985).

From the beginning of 1990, the concept of resource-based view (RBV) and intangible resources became very important in the research on sources of SCA. These notions were later analyzed by the scientists (Barney 1991) to provide a detailed definition and assessment of their use as a source of SCA and subsequently focused on intangible resources as sources of SCA, such as brand, marketing orientation, organizational learning, creativity, customer value, marketing

O. Çetin (✉) · M. Knouch
Trakya University, Edirne, Turkey
e-mail: onurcetin@trakya.edu.tr

M. Knouch
e-mail: mohamedknouch@gmail.com

K. T. Çalıyurt and R. Said (eds.), *Sustainability and Social Responsibility of Accountability Reporting Systems*, Accounting, Finance, Sustainability, Governance & Fraud: Theory and Application, https://doi.org/10.1007/978-981-10-3212-7_19

relationships knowledge workers as a source of CA and sustainable (Foon and Nair 2010).

In this century, there is a change in managerial thought, to the creation of new terms for instance knowledge management, organizational learning, technology and innovation, management information systems, globalization. But this has not diminished the importance of SCA as one of the most important topics in strategic management according to (Foon and Nair 2010). Buffett Warren (2001) posed the question: "What is the most essential thing to consider when assessing an institution?" Most of the responses were the competitive advantage of the institution. In the new millennium, the emphasis on building an initial sustainable competitive advantage for the enterprise is being pursued by senior management, and its source no longer relies on intangible resources like reputation or brand, but on broader dimensions of business relationships. Hoffman (2000) has summed up the development of the notions of SCA until 1999, which were born in the year 1965. From the summary, the progress of sustainable competitive advantage contributed by those researchers could be classified into two main notions:

- Differential and cost advantage concepts—noted on by an earlier group of researchers from 1960 to early 1980s;
- Resource-based notion—noted on by a latter group of scholars from mid 1980s.

The first part focused on enhancing the importance of skills and intangible resources as a source of SCA. Originally, there were no clear differences between the two groups; both sections and concepts are interrelated.

According to Kotze (2000), the new model of competitiveness in this century is based on time, value and interaction, flexibility, knowledge and intellectual capital, speed and creativity, as well as organizational culture as a combination that ensures sustainable competitive advantage. Organizational learning is vital in ensuring sustainable competitive advantage. Flam holtz and Wei pointed out that organizational infrastructure (resource management, operating systems, management systems) and organizational culture are the source of SCA; Kotelnikov (2004) has divided the competitive advantage into three sections: first: the basic competitive advantage, which can be considered as a reminder to the institution to enter the international competition; second: the apparent competitive advantage, which allows the institution to take part of the market or ensure its presence in the market; third: the SCA, which allows the institution to improve and strengthen its competitive position in the market.

The historical development of the notion of SCA can be traced to Table 19.1.

Table 19.1 Historical evolution of the concept SCA, this table prepared based on the table of Foon and Nair (2010)

Author and date	Main contribution
Alderson (1965)	Introduction to the three principles of excellence: technological, legal, and geographic, and three strategies to achieve the advantage of excellence: retail strategy, selective strategy, and excellence strategy
Hall (1980)	Successful firms achieve the lowest cost through excellence over competitors in the market
Henderson (1983)	The discussion on competitive advantage affirms that a firm can adapt itself more and more quickly to gain an advantage over competitors
Porter (1985)	Introduction to the value chain concept as a way for analyzing sources of CA
Coyne (1986)	Determine the conditions that must be met to achieve SCA. Explain the concept of capacity gaps
Ghemawat (1986)	Debates the advantages that tend to be sustainable: size in market, achievement of excellence in access to resources and/or buyers, restrictions on competitors and options available
Day and Wensley (1988)	Possible sources of advantage are high skills and superior resources; in evaluating ways to gain SCA both competitors, buyers and perspectives must be considered
Dierickx and Cool (1989)	Sustainability of a firm's advantage is not to replace assets or tradition
Hamel and Prahalad (1989)	The firm should not be searching for a SCA, but instead how to create CA to gain global leadership
Hamel and Prahalad (1990)	SCA comes from the inherent competences of the firm. The firm should support competences and skills and allocate all resources to achieve adaptation quickly to gain advantage of the opportunities offered in environmental changes
Barney (1991)	Four resources are sources of SCA: value, scarcity, impossibility of imitation, and irreplaceability
Conner (1991)	For the firm to gain above average results, it is necessary to provide a featured product from the view of customers and achieve difference and low cost compared to competitors
Peteraf (1993)	Debates the conditions that must be met to gain SCA, superior resources, competition, pre-competition limits, and mobility of resources
Bharadwaj et al. (1993)	Evaluates the SCA in the context of marketing services; the SCA exists only if it is recognized by buyers
Hall (1993)	Determines intangible resources that allow firms to gain the ability to create relevant differences that result in a SCA
Day and Nedungadi (1994)	The firm uses strategy and feedback to make the environment conducive to SCA
Hunt and Morgan (1995)	In the new classical theory and the theory of comparative advantage of the firm, a relative advantage in resources can become a CA in the market

(continued)

Table 19.1 (continued)

Author and date	Main contribution
Oliver (1997)	Model for a consistent homogeneity between capital, resources, and firm capital to gain SCA
Thompson and Coe (1997)	Proposes a value pricing approach that can be used to gain a CA, which yields a price that reduces the risk that customers will not see a value equivalent to at least those provided by the reference product
Srivastava et al. (1998)	Market assets are defined in two basic types: relational and intellectual. They are intangible, and through these, assets can gain SCA
Hoffman (2000)	Discussion about the notion of SCA and other notions in strategy like market orientation, customer value, relationship marketing, and networks
Burden and Proctor (2000)	Studies how to represent the needs of buyers within the framework of providing training in the firm, to satisfy the needs of buyers on time, every time, and is the way to gain and sustain CA; training is the tool that firms should use to gained it
Sardiandlees (2001)	The positive culture in firm can make a CA
Coates and McDermott (2002)	Sources of competences, skills, and technology, which are an important source of CA
Adams and Lamont (2003)	Organizational innovation and the effectiveness of KM systems like a determinant of innovation practices, as a way to achieve SCA
Sharkie (2003)	Gaining SCA is a vital management function and very important requirement that arises because of the importance given to creating knowledge inside the firm and creating an environment to enable the firm to exploit and develop better resources than its competitors
Weerawardena and Cass (2003)	Entrepreneurship is an important factor in gaining a SCA for a firm, and although a market-focused learning ability leads to higher degrees of innovation, marketing ability enables in a SCA
Kotelnikov (2004)	Suggests a model for synergies of distinct capabilities and replication capabilities as sources of SCA
Khandekar and Sharma (2005)	Contributed to the existing theory on the importance of the strategy of human capital to organizational performance and SCA. The results of the study revealed that HR capabilities are positively associated with organizational performance. Moreover, a strong relationship between human resources has been found to give a sustainable competitive advantage
Javalgi and Radulovich (2005)	Internet companies can achieve sustainable competitive advantage by developing interactive Internet capabilities, increasing interactive customer relationship capabilities, increasing marketing effectiveness, increasing customer share and retention, boosting revenues, and enabling Internet companies to build sustainable competitive advantage through trust in the issuer, trust in exchange intermediaries, loyalty

19.2 The Concept of Sustainable Competitive Advantage

The concept of sustainable competitive advantage is presented in various formats such as continuous competitive advantage, all of which bear the same meaning. It should also be noted that the notion of SCA is based mainly on the concept of CA. The views of writers and researchers have varied in defining the concept of sustainability; Porter (1985) explained this when he used the term long-term profitability to refer to the concept of sustainability (Mouin 2010, 6), The review of management literature shows that the basic concept of competitive advantage is that of Chamberlin and Selzmick (2005) which linked advantage by power. There was an evolution in this concept when Chandler and Hofer described competitive advantage as the unique status developed by the organization, and Porter and Day developed the next generation of conceptualization of competitive advantage (Samlali 2005).

Fahey (1998) believes that competitive advantage is anything that distinguishes the enterprise or its products from its competitors or the products of its competitors, from the point of view of its buyers or end users. Kay defines competitive advantage as a kind of feature that gives preference to positive excellence and progress to competitors in a particular market or industry and to understand the meaning of SCA; sustainability in competitive advantage is not meant to be sustainable or sustained in a fixed period of time or does it mean sustainability or continuity to an indefinite date. But it is related to the possibility and frequency of this feature, because the objective of the institution is not only to have a competitive advantage, but also to maintain it (Foon and Nair 2010).

Richard Hall believes that the organization can achieve a sustainable competitive advantage when it consistently produces or delivers products or services that meet the basic purchasing standards of most customers in the target market (Hall 1993).

Based on previous definitions, we can define sustainable competitive advantage as: the superior performance achieved by the enterprise through the exploitation of various resources, especially intangible, in a manner that is difficult to imitate by competitors, with the requirement of repeating this feature or excellence.

19.2.1 The Sources of SCA

The researchers presented different explanations for the sources of SCA, as follows (Hua 2011):

According to Porter (2000), the source of SCA depends mainly on the status of the institution in its surroundings, especially its industry and its ability to defend itself against competitive forces or influence them in their favor. Porter said in 2010 that what he called “excellence in implementation” everywhere and in all will be the basis for building sustainable competitive advantage (Abdul et al. 2015).

Davidson has identified eight sources of SCA: products with high characteristics; unique competences such as high knowledge of business and clients; focus on creative and difficult to compete markets; legal advantage, due to patents and copyright; excellent customer knowledge, markets, science, or technology; low-cost operations; effective communications; and finally offensive positions, competitive rigidity, and determination to win.

According to Barney, an organization can build a sustainable competitive advantage using resources characterized by: scarcity, incompetence, and exceptional competences (Jamaliah et al. 2016).

According to the RBV, Hamel and Brahallad (1994) see an institution as a source of excellence for sustainable competitiveness, through its ability to develop outstanding competences that allow it to outperform its competitors.

According to Tilson (2000) in the new millennium, the emphasis on building an initial sustainable competitive advantage for the enterprise is being pursued by senior management, and its source is no longer dependent on intangible resources such as brand or reputation, but on broader dimensions of business relationships.

Bharadwaj (1993) believes that the organization is a source of SCA, by reaching special ways to achieve excellence in its products and services compared to competitors, making this distinction visible to customers in the target market. According to Bharadwaj (1993), this distinction is achieved by focusing on a market based on innovation, flexibility in responding to changes in the market, and changes in international conditions.

Based on the above, we can conclude that there are three main sources of sustainable competitive advantage (Moursi 1999):

Efficiency: Efficiency is the optimum utilization of available resources and is measured by the amount of inputs used to produce specific outputs, as the organization is a tool for converting inputs into outputs. The higher the efficiency of the organization, the lesser the inputs required to produce certain outputs. The organization has lower costs if it has higher productivity efficiency with its competitors, allowing it to build a sustainable competitive advantage.

Quality: As a result of the speed changes and successive developments, the interest of organizations has increased to meet the desires of consumers and to satisfy them, as the price is no longer the engine of consumer behavior, but quality is the first interest and the value sought by the organizations that want to stay in competition to offer high-quality products.

Knowledge: Ikujiro Nonaka and Ryoko Toyama believe that knowledge is a source that contains all the conditions that qualify as the basis for building sustainable competitive advantage. Intellectual assets are an essential foundation for the continued activity of the organization in a competitive environment based on information and knowledge. The interest of those organizations based on measurable intellectual assets has increased, as knowledge is a prerequisite in their investment policy. The measurement of the true value of knowledge has become necessary for organizations with special transactions, patents of invention, distinctive trademarks, etc. Successful organizations invest in what they know, transferring that knowledge through their organizational channels for use in the production of goods and services or in the development of structures, functions, and processes.

The sustainable competitive advantage does not exist if the firm does not efforts to replicate that advantage has ceased. And for a firm's resource to provide sustained competitive advantage, the firm must use resources that characterized by (Aradhana and Anuradha 2005):

- Must add positive value to the firm;
- Must be unique or rare among a firm's current and potential competitors;
- Must be imperfectly imitable;
- The resource cannot be substituted.

19.2.2 The Characteristics of Conditions of Sustainable Competitive Advantage

According to Coyne and Barney, there are a set of conditions that must be met to convey any advantage that is a sustainable competitive advantage (Sundar et al. 2003):

- Must be of value;
- Must be rare and relatively unreachable to competitors;
- Must not be partially replaceable or replaceable;
- There should be no strategic alternatives to these resources or skills.

Among the conditions to be provided as well (Coyne 1986):

- Customers should note that there is a consistent difference in important attributes between the product or the service compared to the product or service provided by competitors;
- This difference must be a direct result of the capacity gap between the producer and his competitors;
- Finally, both the difference in the important qualities and the gap in capacities must be repeated or repeatable.

19.2.3 The Criteria for Judging the Quality of SCA

The quality of SCA is determined by three main factors (Moursi 1999):

Source of advantage: There are three sources of SCA if the organization is to have a high-quality advantage, relying on the resources already mentioned: efficiency, quality, and knowledge.

There are many sources of advantage owned by the organization: The adoption of only one advantage leads to easy simulations or overcome by competitors, while it is difficult to imitate the sustainable competitive advantage with multiple sources.

The degree of continuous improvement and innovation: the organization must seek to create new and faster features before competitors mimic its current advantage and create new competitive advantages from a high level.

19.2.4 The Motives to Develop Sustainable Competitive Advantage

The organization, through its Sustainable competitive advantage, can achieve many advantages, so that it is a source of strength for the organization in achieving a high performance and creating value for it, so that without the ability to create value, there is no need for the organization to stay in the market on the organization's good performance by maximizing profits and ensuring high levels of operational efficiency. This will indirectly help the organization to implement strategies to improve its efficiency and competitiveness (Jamaliah et al. 2016), The development of the organization for its sustainable competitive advantage, and its modernization and sustainability, guarantees the organization's survival and profitability. The development of this feature requires a long-term, comprehensive and dynamic vision in mobilizing all resources necessary to achieve the objectives under current challenges. The most important reasons or motivations that lead the organization to develop its sustainable competitive advantage can be summarized in the following points (Moursi 1999).

The Emergence of New Technology

Technological change can create new opportunities in many areas, such as computer product design and Internet marketing, and this leads the organization to introduce new technology at the latest stage of its sustainable competitive advantage, to reduce cost or enhance product differentiation (Moursi 1999).

The Change or Emergence of New Consumer Needs

The organization must be aware of the changes that may occur in consumers' preferences. If the consumer is not interested in the products provided by the organization, the organization must constantly be informed on the changes in the wishes of consumers and adjust their products accordingly. This is the new orientation in marketing, starting from the market through the study and knowledge of the needs of consumers and what they want and do not want to be in the product or service of the organization (Moursi 1999).

Change of Input Costs

A sustainable competitive advantage is often affected by a significant change in input costs when the value of the input increases. In this case, the organization seeks to find another advantage to reduce costs and then achieve excellence again (Moursi 1999).

Change in Government Restrictions

New legislations especially about environmental protection may result with new requirements regarding product specifications or market entry conditions (Moursi 1999). This may lead to a change in competitive environment of that region.

19.2.5 Defense Strategies to Protect SCA

Organizations in the competitive market are often subject to challenges and attacks by competitors. Offensive moves in the market can be caused by new entrants in the industry or by existing organizations seeking to improve their market conditions. The primary purpose of defense strategies is to reduce the risk of attack, to mitigate the impact of any attacks that may occur, as well as to influence competitors to direct their efforts to other competitors. Although defensive strategies do not enhance the competitive advantage of the organization, they help strengthen the competitive situation, the protection of its valuable resources and capabilities from tradition, and to support any sustainable competitive advantage it has. There are two main approaches to defense strategies (Arther et al. 2006):

– *Strategy to Close the Market to Competitors*

The most common guidance used to defend the current situation of the organization includes procedures that prevent the challenger from starting any competitive attack, and there are many obstacles that can be put in the way of competitors who appear (Porter 1982).

– *The Strategy of Referring to The Possibility of Revenge and Violent Retaliation*

The other approach to defense strategies requires sufficient explanation for united competitors that if they attack, there is likely to be strong retaliation or violent retaliation. The goal is to discourage competitors who are united to the attack at all by strengthening the likelihood that the competitive battle will cost more or at least divert their attention to less comprehensive options on the threat, and it is possible to communicate the message to the challenger through (Arther et al. 2006),

- Declaring the commitment of the organization to maintain its current market share in public, clearly and indisputable;
- Publicizing plans to use adequate energy to meet needs, as well as announcing the expected growth in industry for all;

- Advertising a new branding scheme or new mission models in the hope of urging competitors to postpone their market moves;
- Declaring the organization's commitment to the policy of matching the conditions, prices, and equivalents of other competitors;
- A strong backlash from time to time on the movements of weak competitors to enhance the image of the company as a strong defender of its position and position in the market.

19.3 Supply Chain Management and Logistics

Activities regarding materials flow and storage were not regarded as a business function until 1970s. The term physical distribution was used for a group of interrelated activities such as storage, packing, materials handling, and transportation. In 1970s, the role and power of manufacturers' decreased, whereas the role and power of retailers increased. This rising power of retailers is derived from their influence on distribution channel. After understanding the importance of physical flows, companies focused on the upstream activities which include huge flows from suppliers. Supplier management and materials management functions are integrated with physical distribution and a new concept named supply chain management (SCM) occurred (Rushton et al. 2000: 8–9). In 1990s, SCM is regarded as a new business model all over the world. SCM is defined as a network *consisting of firms collaborating to leverage strategic positioning and to improve operating efficiency*. The drivers behind this new business model can be summarized as developments in information technology, increasing importance of supply function, globalization, the need for collaboration, and integrative management (Bowersox et al. 2002: 4–7).

SCM and logistics are different concepts. Logistics is consisting of supply, materials management, and distribution activities (Rushton et al. 2000). Logistics activities perform moving and positioning the inventories in the supply chain (Bowersox et al. 2002). In other terms, logistics is flow of tangible and intangible sources in the supply chain (Frazelle 2002: 5). It can be said that logistics activities include forward flows, reverse flows and positioning of materials, money, and information. Logistics and SCM concepts are similar but do not exactly have the same meaning. Some activities of SCM are not associated with logistics. New product development is a good example for this (Cooper et al. 1997: 1–2). Besides this, SCM is a whole of companies collaborating and includes strategic decisions rather than series of operations. Logistics includes more operational decisions (Rushton et al. 2000: 8–9).

19.3.1 Competitive Advantage in Supply Chain

Supply chain members collaborate to achieve customer satisfaction and gain competitive advantage. CA can be obtained through competitive products and services delivered by the supply chain. Companies have to determine which dimensions are important for competitiveness in SCM to deliver competitive products and services. As mentioned before, one insight for gaining CA was the strategy based on differentiation or low cost. These two concepts are analyzed with different dimensions, and these dimensions can be classified in different ways. In general it can be said that, cost, differentiation, and responsiveness are the dimensions of CA. Low overhead, inventory management, and effective capacity use make up cost dimension, design innovation, after sales service and experience, broad product line composes differentiation dimension, and lastly, responsiveness dimension includes reliability, flexibility, and quickness (Heizer et al. 2017: 37).

In another classification, there are four dimensions: cost, quality, time, and flexibility. Cost is defined as cost operations; quality dimension consists of top quality and consistent quality; time consists of delivery speed, on-time delivery, and new product development speed, and flexibility, which consists customization, variety volume flexibility (Krajewski et al. 2014: 4). Li et al. (2006) described CA with price/cost, quality, delivery, dependability, product innovation, and time to market. Chang (2011) measured competitive advantage using six items: quality, R&D activities, managerial capability, profitability, corporate image, and uniqueness of competitive advantage. Molina et al. (2004) determined 14 criteria for competitiveness from market share to firms reputation. It should be noted that there may be more classifications, but generally, the instruments used in competition are summarized as cost, quality, differentiation or flexibility, time or responsiveness, and innovation. The answer of the question which instrument or dimension is prior to others is based on competitive strategy of the company.

19.3.2 Supply Chain Sustainability

Sustainability is one of the important issues in SCM in the last decade. Companies have to fulfill multiple purposes in order to survive in the new environment, and sustainability is one of the main purposes. They have to improve productivity while producing environmentally-safe sustainable products by developing sustainable processes. Sustainability is not about only the environment or green activities. Actually, sustainability *refers to meeting the needs of the present without compromising the ability of future generations to meet their needs.* Sustainability considers product as an instrument that effects the future life of the people during its lifetime and disposal. Besides this, society has some common assets such as air, sol, sea, forests, and icebergs. In order to satisfy customers but especially to improve profitability, companies may devastate these common assets. Sustainability suggests considering these issues which will affect the future life significantly. As a result of this, sustainable decisions in SCM deals with more variables and multiple purposes (Heizer et al. 2017: 18–19).

Organizational sustainability consists of three parts: natural environment, society, and economic performance. Besides these transparency, culture, strategy, and risk management are other characteristics of sustainability. Sustainability is a vital concept not only in operations management but also in supply chain management. Sustainable Supply Chain Management (SSCM) can be defined as (Carter and Rogers 2008: 368):

> strategic, transparent integration and achievement of an organization's social, environmental, and economic goals in the systemic coordination of key interorganizational business processes for improving the long-term economic performance of the individual company and its supply chains.

From a responsibility viewpoint, supply chain sustainability consists of three parts: financial responsibility, environmental responsibility, and social responsibility. Financial responsibility mainly focuses on financial needs of shareholders, employees, customers, and any other partners in the supply chain. Environmental responsibility is about focusing the ecological needs and protecting the environment in each process of the supply chain. Caterpillar's recycling of two million pieces annually using reverse logistics may be a good example of environmental responsibility. Lastly, social responsibility cares about the needs of the society. DHLs aids to the people affected by natural disasters may be an example of social responsibility (Krajewski et al. 2013: 462–464). The sustainability in the SCA is based on the unique resources; While the sustainability in the SSCM is based on the adoption of the environmental issues in operation of the firm.

19.3.3 Environmental Management Practices and Green Supply Chain Management

Environmentally Management Practices (EMPs) are the practices accomplished under the aim of protecting the environment and reducing the pollution (Christman 2000). As a system, EMPs consolidate environmental process in order to monitor and improve environmental performance (Sroufe et al. 2002). When it comes to supply chain, it can be said that EMPs aim to develop a greener supply chain. The concept of green supply chain management (GSCM) has different definitions according to the literature. GSCM can be defined as considering environmental factors in SCM. From a reverse logistics viewpoint, GSCM includes recycling and remanufacturing (Zhu and Sarkis 2004). Reuse of materials, reduction of wastes, recycling, and reverse logistics are the main parts of sustainable environmental purchasing in GSCM (Zsidisin and Siferd 2001). Cooperation in new green product development, green process development, using green technologies, using pollution preventive technology, reducing waste in energy usage are activities of green partnership in GSCM. For example, cooperation of IKEA with its catalog suppliers about using environmentally-friendly green inks is a good example of green partnership with suppliers (Vachon and Klassen 2006).

19.3.4 Sustainable Supply Management

Procurement and purchasing activities are a vital part of SCM (Sarkis and Talluri 2002). The importance of decisions regarding these activities has been gaining importance in last decades. Instead of manufacturing the most of the product themselves, manufacturers chosen to supply 60–80% of the parts of a product from suppliers. The amount of materials and semi-finished products purchased by manufacturers has been increasing since 1980s. This caused an enormous flow of raw materials and semi-finished goods flow from suppliers to manufacturers (Benton 2010). However, this is not the only reason for increasing important of purchasing activities. It is understood that purchasing activities can effect environmental performance of the company as the environmental effects such as pollution can be directly related to purchasing (Handfield et al. 2002). In order to be greener, environmental effects of materials purchased materials can be analyzed and alternatives should be searched (Zsidisin and Hendrick 1998). Eventually, procurement and purchasing activities are widened in range and are integrated with other sourcing activities to constitute supply function.

Ageron et al. (2012) developed a model for sustainable supply management (SSM) (Fig. 19.1). In this model, all of seven parts are linked with suppliers. One of the reasons for companies to implement SSM is to monitor, evaluate, and encourage the sustainable activities of current and potential suppliers. Right performance criteria including sustainability should be integrated to supplier selection and evaluation system. Some of the barriers against sustainability may be the capabilities, culture, and financial statement of the suppliers (Ageron et al. 2012).

19.3.5 Sustainable Supplier Selection and Evaluation

In supply management decisions, one of the most important subjects is supplier selection and evaluation. As a result of this, the research on SSM generally focused on environmental supplier selection and evaluation. Green criteria have become an important aspect while evaluating suppliers in last decades. Noci (1997) developed a method for evaluation of suppliers according to environmental criteria. Zsidin and Siferd (2001) analyzed the environmental purchasing concept and mentioned the relationship between environmental purchasing and transaction cost analysis. Humphreys et al. (2003) developed a decision support system for supplier selection and evaluation by inserting the environmental criteria into the decision mechanism. Tuzkaya et al. (2009) developed a multi-criteria decision making (MCDM) method

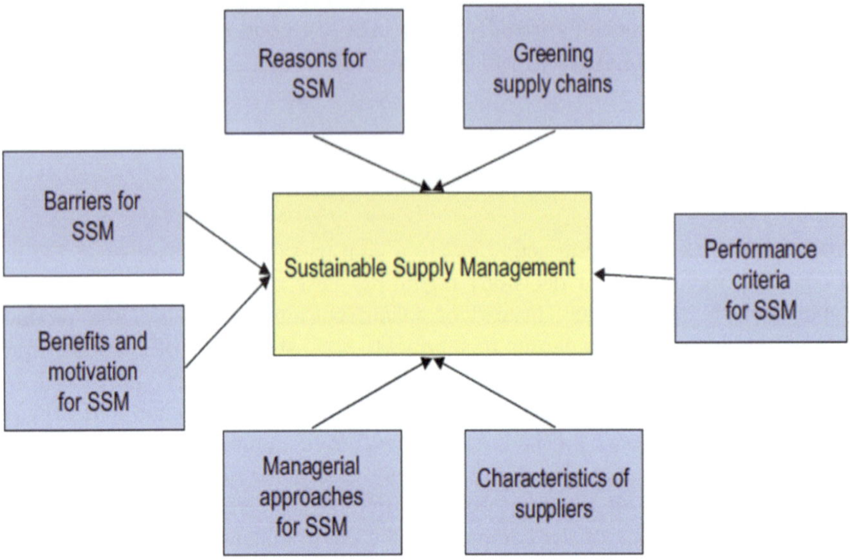

Fig. 19.1 Sustainable supply management model. *Source* Ageron et al. (2012)

to assess green performance of suppliers. Ageron et al. (2012) developed a theoretical model and analyzed it empirically. Kannan et al. (2014) developed a model for selecting green suppliers based on GSCM practices. Sarahye and Marendi (2017) analyzed the role of green procurement on performance. They reported a strong relationship between supplier evaluation and performance.

19.4 Green Supply Chain Management and Sustainable Competitive Advantage

The relationship between SCM practices and performance is analyzed from different aspects. For example, from a manufacturing viewpoint, Lewis (2000) analyzed the relationship between lean production and SCA. Supplier-related practices constitute one third of the lean practices. SCA provided by lean production is affected by market context. From a supplier relationship aspect, Cannon and Homburg (2001) reported that SCM practices impact on CA and strategic supplier relationships as part of SCM has a share on this relationship. Supplier relationships are crucial as they contribute to SCA. Liao et al. (2010) reported an indirect relationship between SCM practices and performance.

Manufacturing practices, SSM, EMP, reverse logistics, and other GSCM practices are examples of green practices in SCM. Geng et al. (2017) analyzed the relationship between the GSCM practices and performance by using the systematic literature review. In this meta-analysis, they examined 50 articles published between 1996 and 2015, and identified a positive relationship between GSCM practices and four kinds of performance; economic, environmental, operational, and social performance.

The relationship between GSCM practices SCA can be analyzed from different perspectives as well. However, research regarding SSM and SCA is limited (Hollos et al. 2012). The literature on green supply chain management and its relation with sustainable competitive advantage is analyzed; however, logistical activities such as recycling, reverse logistics, cannibalization are distinguished from GSCM activities. The findings according to the review are as follows:

- Zhu and Sarkis (2004) researched GSCM practices and performance relationship among Chinese manufacturers. They used quality management and Just In Time as moderators. GSCM practices comprised of four parts: internal practices, external practices, investment recovery, and eco-design. According to the results, it is found that GSCM practices effect environmental performance and economic performance. In a similar study, Zhu et al. (2007) aimed to see the situation of the green supply chain management practices in the automobile industry in China. As a result of this study, they detect that the green supply chain management practices in the automobile industry in China are still emerging. According to the results, green purchasing has a significant effect on environmental performance, however, no significant effect on economic performance and operational performance. Zhu and Sarkis (2007) analyzed the mediating effect of institutional pressures in GSCM practices performance relationship. According to the results, institutional pressures moderate the relationship between GSCM and environmental an economic performance.
- Rao and Holt (2005) studied the relationship between green inbound function, green outbound function, competitiveness, and economic performance where green inbound function is mainly consist of green purchasing activities. Significant relationship is found between the green supply chain and outcomes which are defined as competitiveness and economic performance.
- Hervani et al. (2005) provided new insights into GSCM performance measurement system.
- Melissa and Lenita (2007) aimed to exploring the competitive advantage by using the sustainable supply chain, and they found that the sustainable supply chain can be very strong source for the competitive advantage in the firm.
- Chien and Shih (2007) analyzed the relationships between environmental regulations, external stakeholders, GSCM practices and performance outcomes; environmental performance and financial performance. GSCM practices are divided into two categories: green procurement and green manufacturing. It is reported that GSCM practices have significant effect on two performance outcomes.
- Zhu et al. (2008), they investigate the firm-level correlates of emergent green supply chain management practices in China, and they searched the relation between the organizational learning and management support; with the extent of

adaptation of the GSCM practices in some firms, they find positive relation between the both notions and the adaptation of GSCM practices.

- Reuter et al. (2010) proposed that sustainable global supplier management competences constitute a base for competitive advantage. Companies applying sustainable supply activities earlier than competitors can improve competitive advantage. Nyaga and Whipple (2011) studied the importance of relationship quality and its impact on supply chain operational and strategic performance using both buyer and supplier samples. Large and Thomsen (2011) analyzed the drivers of GSCM performance and reported that the degree of green supplier assessment has an impact on environmental performance.
- Zhu et al. (2012) analyzed the mediating effects of internal and external GSCM practices where external GSCM practices consist of green purchasing, customer cooperation, and environmental concern. It is reported that internal GSCM practices mediate the relationships between external GSCM practices and environmental performance, and external GSCM practices mediate the relationships between internal GSCM practices and economic performance.
- Sandberg and Abrahamsson (2011) studied the effect of logistics capabilities on competitive advantage in a case study. They found that not only logistics capabilities itself but a combination of logistics capabilities and in-house developed IT systems that can be a foundation for sustainable competitive advantage. This can be obtained through five dynamic capabilities, and one of them is supply chain relationships.
- Hollos et al. (2012) analyzed the effect of sustainable supplier cooperation on social and environmental practices and reported that sustainable supplier cooperation improves green and social practices. However, practices with suppliers do not have a direct effect on operational performance, and they support sustainability of the firm.
- Samarrokhi et al. (2014) analyzed the effect of several operations strategies on sustainable competitive advantage. They also analyzed the moderating effect of sustainable sources on the relationship between operations strategies and sustainable competitive advantage.
- Masoumik et al. (2014) researched how the firm can achieve competitive advantage by using the strategic green supply chain management where green purchasing and green supplier management are a part of GSCM.
- Hsu et al. (2017), the authors tested the influence of the sustainable supply chain initiatives on the reverse logistics, and they search on the impact of the eco-reputation and eco-innovation orientations on the sustainable supply chain; they find that the firms that implement SSC initiative can achieve positive reverse logistics outcome.
- Kirchoff et al. (2015), searched the effects of the strategic organizational orientations on the GSCM and the firm performance; in the empirical research, they find that the strategic organizational orientations have positive effect on the GSCM and the firm performance.
- Khaksar et al. (2016) analyzed the relationship between green supplier, green innovation, environmental performance, and competitive advantage; the results

were interesting. It is reported that green suppliers have significant positive relationships with environmental performance and significant negative relationship with competitive advantage.

- Alshura and Awawdeh (2016) analyzed the effect of green supply chain practices on green performance and reported that green supplier selection and green purchasing had significant effect on green performance.
- Chavez et al. (2016), the researchers explored the impacts of customer-centric GSCM on operation performance and customer satisfaction; they find that there are positive impacts to customer pressure on the implementation of customer-centric green supply chain management, and he improved the operational performance.
- Gold et al. (2010) explored how can a firm gain competitive advantage through SSCM. They reported that the firm by adding the environmental and social practices to the SCM will change the SCM to SSCM which will lead to achieve CA.
- Lim et al. (2017), in their research paper, they studied the knowledge management in sustainable supply chain management and their effect on performance; they found that the operation of knowledge management (knowledge creation, sharing knowledge, knowledge storage, and others operation related to knowledge) helps the firms to gain sustainable supply chain management to improve the performance.
- Genovese et al. (2017), they searched the green and sustainable supply chain management and the transition toward a circular economy; the paper asserts that if the firm work to integrate the principals of circular economy in the SSCM can achieve competitive advantage from on environmental point view.

As it can be seen above, research generally demonstrates a positive relationship between GSCM and performance outcomes. However, the research analyzing the relationship between GSCM practices and SCA are limited.

19.5 Discussion

The subject of SCA is of great importance in the studies of management scientists as it is one of the most attracting era in management. After exploring the literature review on sustainable competitive advantage and its evolution, it can be concluded that it is very important for any firm to achieve it.

One approach to achieving the sustainable competitive advantage is low-cost strategy. In this strategy, firm offers low-cost products produced by low-cost operations and transactions. This can be realized by reducing the waste with a good planning throughout the whole supply chain (Alan et al. 2000). The other approach to gaining the SCA is the differentiation; this approach means that the firm can gain the sustainable competitive advantage if it can differentiate itself from the other competitors in the sector. Differentiation is closely linked with GSCM activities as imitation of GSCM activities by competitors is not easy (Mentzer and Williams 2001).

It can be concluded that SCA is not independent of SCM. It is argued that GSCM which is defined as considering environmental factors in SCM is also associated with SCA. GSCM practices can be analyzed from different points of view. Green supplier management or SSM, EMPs, internal practices, external practices, supplier-buyer relationships, green criteria for performance or supplier selection, and reverse logistics activities are analyzed in GSCM. It is questioned that if these practices are linked with SCA and other performance output. It can be concluded that some direct and some indirect relationships are seen in literature review. It can be said that GSCM practices expressed as green inbound function, green outbound function, green supplier selection, green purchasing have effect on performance output expressed as economic performance, environmental performance, operational performance however there is limited reserach on the effect of GSCM practices on SCA.

References

Ageron B, Gunasekaran A, Spalanzani A (2012) Sustainable supply management: an empirical study. Int J Prod Econ 140(1):168–182

Abdul AAJ et al (2015) Intellectual capital: the pathway towards sustainable competitive advantage. Int J Econ Comm Manage III(8)

Alderson W (1965) Dynamic marketing behavior: a functionalist theory of marketing. Irwin, Homewood, IL

Alshura MSK, Awawdeh HZY (2016) Green supply chain practices as determinants of achieving green performance of extractive industries in Jordan

Aradhana K, Anuradha S (2005) Managing human resource capabilities for sustainable competitive advantage: an empirical analysis from Indian global organizations. Emerald Group Publishing Limited 47(8/9):628–639

Arthur AT, Strickland AG (2006) Strategic management: concepts and practical situations. Lebanon Library with McGrawhill, Edn 1, pp 204–205

Benton WC (2010) Purchasing and supply chain management, 2nd Edn, McGraw-Hill Irwin, USA

Bharadwaj SG, Varadarajan PR, Fahy J (1993) Sustainable competitive advantage in service industries: a conceptual model and research propositions. J Mark USA 57:83–99

Bowersox DJ, Closs D, Cooper BM (2002) Supply chain logistics management. Mc Graw Hill/ Irwin, New York

Cannon JP, Homburg C (2001) Buyer-supplier relationships and customer firm costs. J Market 65 (1):29–43

Carter CR, Rogers DS (2008) A framework of sustainable supply chain management: moving toward new theory. Inter J Phys Distrib Logistics Manage 38(5):360–387

Chang CH (2011) The influence of corporate environmental ethics on competitive advantage: the mediation role of green innovation. J Bus Ethics 104(3):361–370

Chien MK, Shih LH (2007) An empirical study of the implementation of green supply chain management practices in the electrical and electronic industry and their relation to organizational performances. Int J Environ Sci Technol (IJEST) 4(3):383

Christman P (2000) Effects of best practices of environmental management on cost advantage: the role of complementery assets. Academt Manage J 43(4):580–663

Cooper MC, Lambert DM, Pagh JD (1997) Supply chain management: more than a new name for logistics. Int J Logistics Manage 8(1):1–14
Coyne KP (1986) The anatomy of sustainable competitive advantage. Ihe Mckinsey Quarterly, USA
Foon LS, Nair PB (2010) Revisiting the concept of sustainable competitive advantage: perceptions of managers in Malaysian MNCs. Int J Bus Account 1(1):63–78
Frazelle EH (2002) Supply chain strategy. McGraw-Hill, ABD
Geng R, Mansouri SA, Aktas E (2017) The relationship between green supply chain management and performance: A meta-analysis of empirical evidences in Asian emerging economies. Int J Prod Econ 183:245–258
Genovese A, Acquaye AA, Figueroa A, Koh SL (2017) Sustainable supply chain management and the transition towards a circular economy: evidence and some applications. Omega 66:344–357
Gold S, Seuring S, Beske P (2010) Sustainable supply chain management and inter-organizational resources: a literature review. Corporate Social Responsibility and Environmental Management:n/a-n/a
Hall R (1993) A framework linking intangible resources and capabilities to sustainable competitive advantage. Strategic Manage J 1
Handfield R, Walton SV, Sroufe R, Melnyk SA (2002) Applying environmental criteria to supplier assessment: a study in the application of the analytical hierarchy process. Eur J Oper Res 141(1):70–87
Heizer J, Render B, Munson C (2017) Operations management. Pearson
Hervani AA, Helms M, Sarkis J (2005) Performance measurement for green supply chain management. Benchmarking Inter J 12(4)
Hoffman NP (2000) An examination of the sustainable competitive advantage concept: past, present, and future. Academy of marketing science review (Online) 2000(4). Available: http://www.amsreview.org/articles/hoffman04-2000.pdf
Hollos D, Blome C, Foerstl K (2012) Does sustainable supplier co-operation affect performance? Examining implications for the triple bottom line. Int J Prod Res 50(11):2968–2986
Hsu C-C, Tan K-C, Zailani SHM (2017) Strategic orientations, sustainable supply chain initiatives, and reverse logistics empirical evidence from an emerging market. Int J Oper Prod Manage 36(1):2016
Hua LT (2011) Sustainable competitive advantage for market leadership amongst the private higher education institutes in Malaysia. J Global Manage 2(2)
Humphreys PK, Wong YK, Chan FTS (2003) Integrating environmental criteria into the supplier selection process. J Mater Process Technol 138(1):349–356
Jamaliah S et al (2016) Entrepreneurial orientation for sustainable competitive advantage and risk management: evidence from government-linked companies in Malaysia, Int J Appl Business Econ Res 14(10)
Kannan D, de Sousa Jabbour ABL, Jabbour CJC (2014) Selecting green suppliers based on GSCM practices: using fuzzy TOPSIS applied to a Brazilian electronics company. Eur J Oper Res 233 (2):432–447
Khaksar E, Abbasnejad T, Esmaeili A, Tamošaitienė J (2016) The effect of green supply chain management practices on environmental performance and competitive advantage: a case study of the cement industry. Technol Econ Develop Econ 22(2):293–308
Kirchoff JF, Tate WL, Mollenkopf DA (2015) The impact of strategic organizational orientations on green supply chain management and firm performance. Int J Phys Distrib Logistics Manage 46(3):2016
Kotelnikov V (2004) Sustainable competitive advantage, how to survive against your competition over a long period of time (Online). Available: http://www.1000ventures.com/business_guide/crosscuttings/sca_main.html
Kotze J (2002) Sustainable competitive advantage in the 21st Century. Accountancy, Feb, 11–16
Krajewski LJ, Ritzmann LP, Malhotra MK (2013) Oper Manage. Pearson, England
Lai KH, Wu SJ, Wong CW (2013) Did reverse logistics practices hit the triple bottom line of Chinese manufacturers? Int J Prod Econ 146(1):106–117

Large RO, Thomsen CG (2011) Drivers of green supply management performance: evidence from Germany. J Purchas Supply Manage 17(3):176–184
Lewis MA (2000) Lean production and sustainable competitive advantage. Int J Oper Prod Manage 20(8):959–978
Li S, Ragu-Nathan B, Ragu-Nathan TS, Rao SS (2006) The impact of supply chain management practices on competitive advantage and organizational performance. Omega 34(2):107–124
Liao Y, Hong P, Rao SS (2010) Supply management, supply flexibility and performance outcomes: an empirical investigation of manufacturing firms. J Supply Chain Manage 46(3): 6–22
Masoumik SM, Abdul-Rashid SH, Udoncy Olugu E (2014) Gaining competitive advantage through strategic green supply chain management: from a literature review towards a conceptual model. Int J Supply Chain Manage 3(3)
Mentzer JT, Williams LR (2001) The role of logistics leverage in marketing strategy. J Mark Chann 8(3–4):29–47
Molina MA, del Pino IB, Rodríguez AC (2004) Industry, management capabilities and firms' competitiveness: an empirical contribution. Manage Decis Econ 25(5):265–281
Moursi NK (1999) Strategic management: composition and implementation of strategies, Dar Al Ma'aref, Egypt
Noci G (1997) Designing 'green'vendor rating systems for the assessment of a supplier's environmental performance. Eur J Purchas Supply Manage 3(2):103–114
Nyaga GN, Whipple JM (2011) Relationship quality and performance outcomes: achieving a sustainable competitive advantage. J Business Logistics 32(4):345–360
Pirayesh R, Forouzandeh R (2016) The effective deployment of brand through sustainable competitive advantage and corporate image. J Adm Manag, Edu Train (JAMET) 12(4)
Porter ME (1985) Competitive advantage: creating and sustaining superior performance. Free Press, New York
Porter M (1999) l'Avantage Concurrentiel: comment devancer ses concurrents et maintenir son avance, traduit France
Rao P, Holt D (2005) Do green supply chains lead to competitiveness and economic performance? Int J Oper Prod Manage 25(9):898–916
Rushton A, Oxley J, Croucher P (2000) Handbook of logistics and distribution management. Kogan Page Limited, London
Samarrokhi A, Jenab K, Arumugam VC, Weinsier PD (2014) Analysis of the effects of operations strategies on sustainable competitive advantage in manufacturing systems. Int J Ind Syst Eng 19(1):34–49
Sandberg E, Abrahamsson M (2011) Logistics capabilities for sustainable competitive advantage. Int J Logistics Res Appl 14(1):61–75
Samlali Y (2005) The impact of strategic management of human resources and competency development on the competitive advantage of the firm (entrance to quality and knowledge), Ph.D. thesis, University of Algeria, Faculty of Economic Sciences and Management Sciences
Sroufe R, Narasimhan R, Montabon F, Wang X (2002) Environmental management practices: a framework. Greener Manage Int 40:23–45
Tuzkaya G, Ozgen A, Ozgen D, Tuzkaya UR (2009) Environmental performance evaluation of suppliers: a hybrid fuzzy multi-criteria decision approach. Int J Environ Sci Technol 6(3): 477–490
Vachon S, Klassen RD (2006) Green project partnership in the supply chain: the case of the package printing industry. J Clean Prod 14(6):661–671
Zhu Q, Sarkis J (2004) Relationships between operational practices and performance among early adopters of green supply chain management practices in Chinese manufacturing enterprises. J Oper Manage 22(3):265–289
Zhu Q, Sarkis J, Lai KH (2007) Green supply chain management: pressures, practices and performance within the Chinese automobile industry. J Clean Prod 15(11):1041–1052
Zhu Q, Sarkis J, Lai KH (2012) Examining the effects of green supply chain management practices and their mediations on performance improvements. Int J Prod Res 50(5):1377–1394

Zsidisin GA, Hendrick TE (1998) Purchasing's involvement in environmental issues: a multi-country perspective. Ind Manage Data Syst 98(7):313–320

Zsidisin GA, Siferd SP (2001) Environmental purchasing: a framework for theory development. Eur J Purchas Supply Manage 7(1):61–73

Author Biographies

Onur Çetin He has bachelor's degree of Industrial Engineering in 2002, masters degree of Business Administration in 2006. His master thesis was about agile manufacturing. He had Ph.D. of production management in 2013. His Ph.D. thesis was about Vehicle Routing Problem in Fuel Distribution. He has a one year job experience as industrial engineer at Akkanat Holding, four years experience as research assistant at Trakya University, and six years experience as research assistant at Istanbul University. He is assistant professor in Trakya University since 2015.

Mohamed Knouch He has bachelors degree of management in 2008, masters degree of Management and Sustainable development in 2012. His master thesis was about knowledge management and its role to achieve sustainable competitive advantage. He has a one year job experience as Chief Investigator for competition and economic investigations. at Ministry of trade in Algeria from 2011 to 2012. He was worked as lecturer at Setif University in Algeria during 2011–2014. He is student in Ph.D. program on business administration of Trakya University since 2014.

Author Index

K. T. Çalıyurt and R. Said (eds.), *Sustainability and Social Responsibility of Accountability Reporting Systems*, Accounting, Finance, Sustainability, Governance & Fraud: Theory and Application, https://doi.org/10.1007/978-981-10-3212-7

Subject Index

K. T. Çalıyurt and R. Said (eds.), *Sustainability and Social Responsibility of Accountability Reporting Systems*, Accounting, Finance, Sustainability, Governance & Fraud: Theory and Application, https://doi.org/10.1007/978-981-10-3212-7

FSC
www.fsc.org
MIX
Papier aus verantwortungsvollen Quellen
Paper from responsible sources
FSC® C105338

If you have any concerns about our products,
you can contact us on
ProductSafety@springernature.com

In case Publisher is established outside the EU,
the EU authorized representative is:
Springer Nature Customer Service Center GmbH
Europaplatz 3, 69115 Heidelberg, Germany

Printed by Libri Plureos GmbH
in Hamburg, Germany